Modern and Contemporary Poetry and Poetics

Series Editor
David Herd
University of Kent
Canterbury, UK

Founded by Rachel Blau DuPlessis and continued by David Herd, Modern and Contemporary Poetry and Poetics promotes and pursues topics in the burgeoning field of 20th and 21st century poetics. Critical and scholarly work on poetry and poetics of interest to the series includes: social location in its relationships to subjectivity, to the construction of authorship, to oeuvres, and to careers; poetic reception and dissemination (groups, movements, formations, institutions); the intersection of poetry and theory; questions about language, poetic authority, and the goals of writing; claims in poetics, impacts of social life, and the dynamics of the poetic career as these are staged and debated by poets and inside poems. Since its inception, the series has been distinguished by its tilt toward experimental work – intellectually, politically, aesthetically. It has consistently published work on Anglophone poetry in the broadest sense and has featured critical work studying literatures of the UK, of the US, of Canada, and Australia, as well as eclectic mixes of work from other social and poetic communities. As poetry and poetics form a crucial response to contemporary social and political conditions, under David Herd's editorship the series will continue to broaden understanding of the field and its significance.

More information about this series at
http://www.palgrave.com/gp/series/14799

Miriam Nichols

A Literary Biography of Robin Blaser

Mechanic of Splendor

Miriam Nichols
University of the Fraser Valley
Abbotsford, BC, Canada

Modern and Contemporary Poetry and Poetics
ISBN 978-3-030-18326-4   ISBN 978-3-030-18327-1   (eBook)
https://doi.org/10.1007/978-3-030-18327-1

This Palgrave Macmillan imprint is published by the registered company Springer Nature Switzerland AG
The registered company address is: Gewerbestrasse 11, 6330 Cham, Switzerland

For the poets

FOREWORD

In her introduction to *A Literary Biography of Robin Blaser: Mechanic of Splendor*, Miriam Nichols sets the poem and its thinking at the center of the poet's life: "Nothing mattered more to him than poetry and his life story is inextricable from its working out of a poetic practice." To read this book and therefore to follow Robin Blaser's story is to find out, in its unfolding, what that sentence means.

Nichols's telling of Blaser's story works on numerous levels. Through her account of the phases of Blaser's life—from his Idaho childhood, through his education at Berkeley, to Boston, his journeys through Europe, San Francisco, and Vancouver—we witness the gradual emergence of the person in all his generosity and cares. Blaser taught Nichols and she became his friend, and as we read her account of his life we come to know him in his brilliance and his insecurities. As that human story emerges, and as the contingencies that form a personality take shape before us we also become intimate with the loyalties and tensions that inform a poet's life. Blaser's writing found its way at a time and in the company of major poets, poets for whom the poem was a way of changing and reimagining social life: Robert Duncan, Jack Spicer, Charles Olson, Denise Levertov, Steve Jonas, John Wieners, John Ashbery, and Adrienne Rich. As Nichols traces these friendships and intersections, both as they inspired Blaser and caused him pain, what we are given is a whole new history of the New American Poetry, told with feeling and from the vantage point of one of its most subtly expansive practitioners.

At the same time, however, and throughout, what Nichols unfolds is a life in which nothing matters more than the poem. This does not mean, for one moment, that people didn't matter to Blaser, and the book is a story, among other things, of Blaser's commitments to those he loved and with whom he was friends. Nor does the centrality of the poem to Blaser mean that his life was driven by poetic ambition, whether for prizes or for critical recognition, though both prizes and recognition came. What Nichols's statement means, and what the book shows, is that for Blaser poetry was, above all, a way of being in the world, a way of comprehending its conditions and bringing its possibilities into view. Always as he read—whether in poetry, philosophy, the history of art, mythology—and as he talked and taught and traveled and looked, Blaser's preoccupation, as Nichols shows, was the shaping of the poetic utterance, of a language whose objective was to make a public world present.

Impeccably calibrated as it is, and underwritten by rare scholarly authority, what Nichols's story shows us is how, in the midst of everything and out of all the influences, Blaser's poems emerged, those great exploratory series that make up *The Holy Forest*: *Cups, The Park, The Faerie Queene, The Moth Poem, Les Chimères, Pell Mell, Exody*, and *Image-Nations*. This story of the way these poems took shape will matter to anybody who reads Blaser and his contemporaries, since what it details is the working out of a crucial postwar poetic stance. Detailed as it is, however, and crucial as it will prove to understandings of postwar North American poetry, Nichols's book reaches well beyond the readership already versed and invested in this period of literary history. What she shows, in the precision of her narrative, is the way a poet and poetry can form, the way a language capable of reaching out to things takes shape through dialogue and events. What we have here, in other words, is the biography of a creative practice, from which anybody interested in the possibilities of language as a medium of knowledge and public intervention will learn.

In her introduction, Nichols gives the reader permission to make of her biography what they will. "Readers," as she says, "should skip around." And of course they should and will. I can only add that, as a reader, I was more obedient to the text's trajectory than this suggests, and so rather than skipping I read from beginning to end. What I experienced, as I did, was a deeply moving account of the way a poet came to terms with the world. Blaser wrote some of the most beautifully enabling poetry of the second half of the century, open in its syntax to the reality of happenings and events. What he gives us is a world and what Miriam Nichols shows us is the way that world was made. What we have here, in other words, is a life in which poetry matters.

University of Kent   David Herd
Canterbury, UK

ACKNOWLEDGMENTS

I have many people to thank for this book. Blaser gave me permission to access his unpublished archives and made me his literary executor along with his widow David Farwell, smoothing the way. David has been cooperative in every way, opening up his home to my searches, giving interviews, organizing archival materials, and answering endless questions. My lead research assistant, Jennifer Colbourne, worked in the Simon Fraser University Special Collections and Rare Books room for three years, cataloguing and annotating the Blaser fonds in date order. Her superb record has been the foundational document of this biography. Students who joined her in this work were Matthew Loewen and Niki Robinson. Mark Toews contributed to the project handsomely by digitizing "The Astonishment Tapes" and Katrina Janzen worked on checking the transcript against the audio. I could not have undertaken this project without the hard work of these patient, brilliant students, and the financial support of the Social Sciences and Research Council of Canada which enabled me to hire them. I also thank the University of the Fraser Valley for course releases and funding, and the very helpful staff in Special Collections at Simon Fraser who have assisted my research over the many years this project has been in process.

To the many friends and scholars who have contributed substantially to this biography, I couldn't have done it without you. Stan Persky has given multiple interviews, reading responses, and much good advice. Kevin Killian read the manuscript and offered essential corrections. Peter and Meredith Quartermain have provided interviews and information as well as much needed moral support. Blaser's nephew, Mark Samac in Boise, Idaho has kindly shared his collection of archival material; he and his partner Faron Dean Woods hosted me handsomely on my 2014 trip to Boise. Michael Seth Stewart made available his manuscript edition of the John Wieners Letters, forthcoming from the University of New Mexico Press. The comments of the anonymous reviewers and of series editor David Herd have made this a better book. David's support has been invaluable in getting this manuscript over the finish line. To everyone who granted an interview and who fact-checked their roles in this book, I owe a deep thank you.

I would like to thank the following persons for permission to quote from unpublished archival materials:

Letter of Helen Adam appears by permission of the Poetry Collection of the University Libraries, University of Buffalo, State University of New York.

Excerpt from "Introduction" by Charles Alexander is printed with permission.

Letters of Don Allen are printed with permission of the Don Allen estate.

Letters of John Ashbery are printed with permission of the estate of John Ashbery. All rights reserved. Used by arrangement with George Borchardt Inc., for the estate.

Letters of Sophia Nichols Auer appear courtesy of Millie Blaser and the Blaser estate.

Unpublished materials held by the Bancroft Library appear courtesy of The Bancroft Library, University of California, Berkeley.

Letters of William [Bill] Brodecky Moore are printed with permission.

Letters of Jess Collins and Robert Duncan are used by permission of the Jess Collins Trust which has long encouraged this project.

All materials from notebooks, photo albums, and correspondence by David Farwell are printed with his permission.

Email by Brian Fawcett to Miriam Nichols appears courtesy of Brian Fawcett.

Letter of Peter Gizzi is printed with his permission.

Poem titled "November 6th, 1982" by John Hulcoop is printed with his permission.

Letter of Steve Jonas appears courtesy of the Jonas estate.

Works by Charles Olson published during his lifetime are held copyright by the Estate of Charles Olson; previously unpublished works are copyright of the University of Connecticut. Used with permission.

Letters of Stan Persky are printed with his permission.

Unpublished materials by Peter Quartermain are printed with his permission.

Unpublished materials from the Contemporary Literature Collection, Special Collections and Rare Books Division. W.A.C. Bennett Library, Simon Fraser University. Burnaby, B.C. appear courtesy of Special Collections.

Excerpt from Interview by Michael Smoler, "Sounding the Air with Robin Blaser," is printed with his permission.

Letters of Jack Spicer appear courtesy of the Spicer estate.

Letter of Warren Tallmen appears courtesy of Karen Tallman for the estate.

Letter of Anne Waldman is printed with her permission.

Letters by John Wieners appear courtesy of the John Wieners estate.

Letters by Patrick Wright are printed with his permission.

Praise for *A Literary Biography of Robin Blaser*

"In the second half of the twentieth century, there was a golden moment for literature called 'The New American Poetry.' A central figure of the San Francisco branch of this national movement was poet Robin Blaser (1925–2009). Blaser thought a poem was an 'action' in language, a 'performance of the real,' and believed that poetry was a mode of knowledge, distinct from narrative, discourse and the languages of science. Now, for the first time, Blaser's long-time editor, Miriam Nichols, tells the story of a poetry-dedicated life, and offers a lucid account of the meaning of Blaser's intellectually charged poetry."

—Stan Persky taught philosophy at *Capilano University in North Vancouver, BC, Canada*. His most recent books are: *Reading the 21st Century* (2011), *Post-Communist Stories* (2014), and *Letter from Berlin* (2017)

"It took Robin Blaser awhile to get started, and he spent his twenties very much in the shadow of two 'great companions,' the poets Robert Duncan and Jack Spicer—but after that, he took off in unique directions, and at times exceeded them. Miriam Nichols, his friend and editor, has taken on a Herculean task with style and grace, and an almost Shakespearean gift for illuminating the souls and ambitions of her principals."

—Kevin Killian, poet, novelist, *Jack Spicer scholar*

"Miriam Nichols is without doubt one of the most insightful interpreters of the New American Poetry, tracking the connections it wove, as she writes in her book *Radical Affections*, between the human being and 'planetary life.' With *A Literary Biography of Robin Blaser*, her nuanced and informative study of the life and work of poet Robin Blaser, our understanding of post-war poetry, and that near-mythical triumvirate Blaser formed with Robert Duncan and Jack Spicer during the San Francisco Renaissance, takes a great leap forward."

—Stephen Collis, *Simon Fraser University, Canada*

"Robin Blaser stands out as one of the central figures in the San Francisco Renaissance, often linked in a trinity that included Jack Spicer and Robert Duncan. Miriam Nichols has given us a brilliant biography of a poet who lived a life of 'astonishments' in poetry where the real—a moth caught in piano strings—yields a new music and ultimately a new knowledge. Drawing on unpublished manuscripts, correspondence and interviews Nichols provides the first biography of this important American and Canadian poet."

—Michael Davidson, *Professor Emeritus of American Literature, University of California, San Diego, USA*, author of *Invalid Modernism: Disability and the Missing Body of the Aesthetic* (2019)

"This highly accessible biography is the first major study of Robin Blaser, a pivotal figure in North American poetry and poetics. Through extensive archival research and engaging close readings, Miriam Nichols tracks Blaser's explorations of surrealism, the sacred, and seriality. She analyses Blaser's navigation of mid-century sexuality and his deep enthusiasm for the visual arts. Carefully guiding the reader through his diverse career, Nichols demonstrates Blaser's role and significance within the Berkeley Renaissance, the Boston hub of New American poetry, the Vancouver poetry scene, and Canadian literature more generally. Given Blaser's shifts between cities, his interdisciplinary reach, and extensive network, this book provides a singularly rich and detailed insight into the distinctions and affiliations that would emerge between east and west coast, America and Canada, and North America and the United Kingdom in twentieth-century poetry."

—Ann Vickery, *Associate Professor of Writing and Literature,*
Deakin University, Australia

"This is a wonderful biography of a wonderful poet, full of the details of a fascinating life and its impact on the unforgettable poetry that grows out of it. A 'New American' poet who found new contexts for the sacred, new resources in linguistic exploration, and a new form in the 'open space' poem, Blaser contributed decisively to the postwar poetry scenes in San Francisco and Boston and went on to become a primary figure in Twentieth-Century Canadian poetry. Nichols is Blaser's ideal biographer, having edited his collected poems, his collected essays, and an extensive biographical interview, *The Astonishment Tapes*."

—Stephen Fredman, author of *Contextual Practice:*
Assemblage and the Erotic in Postwar Poetry and Art (2010)

"Robin Blaser was a central figure not only in the Berkeley Renaissance, but also in much of Canadian poetry since. This much-needed book brilliantly demonstrates the intricate weave of the ways in which the story of the poet's life is inseparable from the multiple social and intellectual dimensions of a larger world. The poet's words reach for what they can never finally grasp, passionately exploring an evolving poetic practice. Essential reading."

—Peter Quartermain, editor of *The Collected Poems and*
Plays of Robert Duncan (2012, 2014)

"Robin Blaser, a central figure in the Berkeley Renaissance along with Robert Duncan and Jack Spicer, moved to Canada in 1966, and through his teaching and writing altered the literary landscape of postmodern Canadian poetry. Miriam Nichols' biography—lucid, affectionate, and illuminated by her scholarly editions of Blaser's writings, raises the standard for contemporary literary biography. Blaser's intellectual, social, and poetic responses to the challenges of post-structuralism and neoliberalism are as vitally important today as they were during their emergence in the late twentieth century."

—Sharon Thesen, *Emeritus Professor of Creative Writing,*
University of British Columbia, Canada

"Critics have long recognized Robin Blaser's importance as an innovative and visionary writer. They have known him as a giant in, first, San Francisco's mid-century counterculture and, later, in Vancouver's literary scene. Until now, though, we have lacked someone to teach us how best to read his verse, how to find solid purchase on a body of work that is simultaneously mystical and rigorously philosophical, at once abstractly cerebral and powerfully sensual. Miriam Nichols proves more than up to the task. She is alert to every aspect of Blaser's craft and in command of the whole of his worldview, and, in a compelling manner, she leads readers through his life, career, and publications, following the through-lines of his developing intuitions and detailing his many poetic triumphs. *A Literary Biography of Robin Blaser* is a major contribution to the study of American and Canadian poetry."

—Brian Reed, *Milliman Endowed Chair in the Humanities, University of Washington, Seattle, USA*

"Robin Blaser is the less-noticed genius of the circle of North American poets that includes Olson, Duncan, and Spicer. His inspired aesthetic and philosophic charms resonate throughout this work. Miriam Nichols writes Blaser's life with loving care, consummate scholarship, and an abiding commitment to illuminate and contextualize Blaser's astonishing poetics."

—Charles Bernstein, author of *Pitch of Poetry* and *Attack of the Difficult Poems* (2016)

CONTENTS

1   **Introductions**   1
    Pause/Reset   2
    Through-Lines   4
    The Order of Things Here   7
    A Guide to the Text   7

2   **Family Matters**   11
    The Homeplace   17
    Growing Up Idaho   20
    Flight   28

3   **Berkeley**   35
    Leaving Normal   35
    The Berkeley Vortex   41
    The Writers' Conference   48
    Graduate School   50

4   **Boston: The Librarian**   57
    The Boston Scene   60
    A Company of Poets   69
    The Boston Poems   74
    The Grand Tour   83

5   **San Francisco: The Artist of the Beautiful**   95
    Poetry Wars   95
    The Handsome Sailor: Stan Persky   103
    The Blanche Jantzen Affair   109
    The Peacock Gallery: Painters and Poets   112
    The Artist of the Beautiful: The First Serial Poems   116
    Les Chimères   124
    Spicer's Death   126

6   **Vancouver in the Sixties: Context as Explanation**   133
      Professor Blaser   138
      Pacific Nation: *Poetry and Politics*   146
      Image-Nations 1-12 and the Stadium of the Mirror   151
      The Collected Books of Jack Spicer *and "The Practice of Outside"*   155
      Personal Affairs   157

7   **Cher Maître**   165
      Trafalgar Street   165
      Canadian Content   169
      The Scholar-Poet   173
      The Turner Tour   182
      Syntax   185
      Retirement   188

8   **Big Poetry**   191
      AIDS   192
      Great Companion: Robert Duncan   198
      The Holy Forest *Tours*   205
      Big Poetry and the Recovery of the Public World   208
      Departures   215

9   **The Irreparable**   221
      Great Companion: Dante Alighiere   226
      The Last Supper   231
      Wanders   238
      Gigs and Parties   240
      The Last Image-Nation   246
      Butterflies of Darkness   250
      Epilogue   255

Archival References   259

References   273

Index   285

ABBREVIATIONS

AT	*The Astonishment Tapes*
"AT"	The Astonishment Tapes, manuscript
Fire	*The Fire: Collected Essays*
HF	*The Holy Forest: Collected Poems*
LJW	Letters of John Wieners, manuscript
LS	*The Last Supper*

LIST OF FIGURES

Fig. 2.1   Grandmother Sophia Nichols Auer with Robin in Orchard, Idaho, c.1927. Photo courtesy of Millie Blaser and the estate   15

Fig. 2.2   Robin with dog, Pepper, and new bike in Twin Falls, Idaho, c.1936–1938. Photo courtesy of Millie Blaser and the estate   21

Fig. 2.3   Robin Blaser in Twin Falls, c.1940–1942. Photo courtesy of Millie Blaser and the estate   26

Fig. 4.1   Menu of the Café Soufflot, Paris, 1959   88

Fig. 5.1   Robin Blaser in San Francisco, 1962. Photo by Helen Adam. Copyright the Poetry Collection of the University Libraries, University at Buffalo, SUNY. Reproduced with permission   103

Fig. 5.2   Stan Persky and Robin Blaser at Stinson Beach, c.1964. Photo by Helen Adam. Copyright the Poetry Collection of the University Libraries, University at Buffalo, SUNY. Reproduced with permission   108

Fig. 5.3   *Triptych*, by Robin Blaser, 1960. Collage, 14 × 24½″. Collection of Anne and Robert J. Bertholf. Reproduced courtesy of the Blaser estate   115

Fig. 5.4   *Cups*, by Robin Blaser, c.1960. Oil on canvas, 20 × 24″. Collection of Alan Franey. Photo by Alan Franey. Reproduced courtesy of Alan Franey and the Blaser estate   116

Fig. 7.1   Blaser in *Criteria* T-Shirt, c. 1976. Photo by Ardele Lister and Bill Jones. Reproduced courtesy of Ardele Lister and the Blaser estate   166

Fig. 7.2   *IKARIA: POEM = ESPACE, EXPLORER I*, 1976–1984. Hand-colored photograph and collage, 48 × 69″ by Christos Dikeakos. Collection of Brian DeBeck and Karen Tallman. Photo by Christos Dikeakos, reproduced courtesy of Christos Dikeakos   177

Fig. 8.1   Left to right: Brian Fawcett, Stan Persky, and Robin Blaser at Persky's home in Vancouver, 1995. Photo by David Farwell, reproduced courtesy of David Farwell   192

Fig. 8.2   Blaser at the opening dinner of the Recovery of the Public World Conference, Vancouver, B.C., 1995. Photo by David Farwell, reproduced courtesy of David Farwell   208

Fig. 8.3   Robin Blaser and David Farwell in hotel room, on vacation in
            Victoria, B.C., 1996. Photo by David Farwell, reproduced courtesy
            of David Farwell   216
Fig. 9.1   Blaser in London, en route to the Tate, 1996. Photo by David
            Farwell, reproduced courtesy of David Farwell   232
Fig. 9.2   Blaser in pink jacket, Bilbao, Spain, 2001. Photo by David Farwell,
            reproduced courtesy of David Farwell   241
Fig. 9.3   Blaser dressed for Order of Canada ceremony, Ottawa, 2005. Photo
            by David Farwell, reproduced courtesy of David Farwell   244

CHAPTER 1

Introductions

Robin Blaser was born in Denver, Colorado, in 1925 and grew up in small town Idaho. In 1944, he moved to Berkeley to attend the University of California where he would meet Jack Spicer and Robert Duncan and join a community of poets and artists whose explorations would come to be called the Berkeley Renaissance. Blaser spent 11 years at Berkeley, leaving in 1955 with an MA and a Master of Library Science (MLS) to accept a position in the Widener Library at Harvard. In Boston, his friends included John Wieners, Steve Jonas, and Ed Marshall; importantly during this period, he also met Charles Olson, Denise Levertov, John Ashbery, and Frank O'Hara. Donald Allen, editor of the landmark *New American Poetry* anthology (1960), was a frequent interlocutor. Blaser did well at Harvard, but he came to dislike the place as did his partner, Jim Felts. In 1960, they returned to San Francisco, but the scene around Spicer and Duncan had changed. By 1965, Blaser had split with Felts and fallen out with Duncan. That same year Spicer died of acute alcoholism. A faculty position in the Department of English at the newly established Simon Fraser University (SFU) in Burnaby, British Columbia, offered a fresh start and Blaser moved to Vancouver in 1966. He would remain at SFU for 20 years and spend the rest of his life living and working in Vancouver with his life partner, David Farwell. Blaser died of a brain tumor in 2009.

I first met Robin in 1978 when I was an undergraduate student in English at Simon Fraser. I took his Arts in Context course on modernism, as well as a Directed Studies on music and literature and an audit on Mallarmé. When I stopped being a student and started writing about his work, we became friends. Both of us came from small towns and conservative, religious families; both of us fled. These were recognitions between us. Blaser mentored me through academia and many years of personal storm. He had a particular way of doing this. I would arrive at his door—no point in calling because most of the time he wouldn't answer the phone—and if he wanted to, he would open it. Very

© The Author(s) 2019
M. Nichols, *A Literary Biography of Robin Blaser*,
Modern and Contemporary Poetry and Poetics,
https://doi.org/10.1007/978-3-030-18327-1_1

often I came full of trouble and he would begin to talk, not letting me get a word in edgewise. He could do this for hours without a real pause, cruising through the ends of sentences as if periods were orange lights at an intersection. It would all be about the books that had just arrived or an art show or news from the poetry world. After an hour or two, he would ask what I had come to talk about. By that time, I had forgotten, my self-concern utterly lost in the worlds of imagination he unfolded for me. Blaser offered entrance to those worlds. This book is my map of that magical territory he offered to students and friends. "'Map is not territory,'" he loved to say.[1]

PAUSE/RESET

When Robin Blaser arrived in Berkeley in 1944 to attend the University of California, he was a 19-year-old gay boy from a place where gay wasn't welcome. He had no concept of contemporary poetry beyond that of Vachel Lindsay, a poet who literally took his poems to the street, but without seriously challenging the formal or philosophical assumption of Anglo-American traditions.[2] At Berkeley, he had his first introduction to the moderns—Ezra Pound, T.S. Eliot, H.D., James Joyce, Federico García Lorca, and Mary Butts among them—through Robert Duncan's off-campus reading circles. What began for Blaser there was a lifelong odyssey through twentieth century poetry, art, and philosophy. In *The Astonishment Tapes*, he says that he went to Berkeley to express his sexuality and join the world (*AT*, 60). He was a young man full of ambition and promise—prize pie as he later referred to his younger self. But the world he had grown up with wasn't there. That world was Catholic (mother), Mormon (father), Anglo-American, and heteronormative. Blaser had already experienced anxiety in adolescence over same-sex attractions (he did not act on these feelings until Berkeley), but the loss of a religiously-based world order and set of values was a deeper shock. James Joyce was the one who represented a real challenge because he had flattened the hierarchal order of Irish Catholicism in *Ulysses* and *Finnegans Wake*, and that hierarchy came pretty close to Blaser's adolescent imagination. As a teenager, he had considered the priesthood.

As Blaser read and developed and changed as a thinker and poet at Berkeley, and as his range of reference and circle of literary acquaintants grew, he began to join a generation of young poets who also had to find their way in a world that had come unglued after two world wars. "The center cannot hold," Yeats had said (Yeats 1962, 99). White male privilege was about to come under review, especially after African Americans and Indigenous peoples had fought for the Allies and women had collected paychecks in factories. Those factories, ramped up for wartime production, soon began to push out consumer goods that changed the way people lived and they would set up the conditions for environmental problems to come: more cars, more plastics, more big oil. Television became widely available and prepared the way for an intensified culture industry that included pushback against the various liberating genies that had escaped the bottle during the war. High-profile international art movements like Dada had already mocked the pretensions to respectability of a middle class that had acquiesced to catastrophe; surrealism had tapped the repressed, psychological and social, and it would turn up in Berkeley through exploratory arts journals like *Circle*. Looking back on the postwar period, Blaser would say that the postmodern was a search for a new relation among things and a corrective to the authoritarian elements in modernism. Pound, of course, was quickly taken as the poster child for the latter: he had advocated for Mussolini during the war and was on trial for treason. Eliot had turned toward the esoteric Anglican tradition in his great wartime poem, *Four Quartets*. Both were major poets and both presented problems as models.

Blaser shared this set of cultural conditions with his generation. However different they were, the New Americans, as they came to be called after Allen's famous anthology, responded to the same problematic: how to imagine "others" in a less fearful and arrogant way; how to reposition humanity as part of nature instead of its master; how to create meaning and value in a world without religious foundations, which is to say without the means to compel belief. In retrospect, the issues of the later twentieth century were already on the horizon when Blaser arrived in Berkeley: civil rights, decolonization, sex and gender parity, and the ecological footprint. What seemed to be required even in 1945 when these issues had not been widely articulated was a pause/reset on the culture. Of those poets closest to Blaser, Robert Duncan would go on to develop his grand collage—not the tale of the tribe as Pound had called his epic poem, *The Cantos*, but the story of the species, opened up to include, at least virtually, all cultural narratives, high and low. Jack Spicer would develop the serial poem, a way of working that took the book, rather than the individual poem, as a unit and positioned the poet as a character in his own narrative, thus limiting his or her authority. The poet, no more than the reader, would know what was coming next. Spicer later claimed a poetry by dictation, where the poet became a transmitter of messages received from the "outside" as he called it, rather than a master of his field—energy transferred to the reader from where the poet got it with minimal interference of the ego, to paraphrase Charles Olson in "Projective Verse" (Olson 1997, 240). A major influence for Blaser, Olson worked through the philosophy of Alfred North Whitehead to articulate an embodied "human universe," fully embedded in planetary life.[3] Common to these poets was the thought that instrumental reason had to be stitched back into a complex fabric of affective relationships. It is worth noting in this context that Bern Porter, a risk-taking publisher of avant garde writing in 1940s Berkeley (Bern Porter Books), and Jess Collins, the visual artist who wound up as Duncan's life partner, switched from science to the arts after working on the Manhattan Project (the making of the first nuclear bomb).

Blaser maintained all his life that poetry was a distinctive discourse among others and that it proposed a mode of knowing as valid as the scientific or philosophical. To follow his thinking, poetry does not fall under the rubrics of subjective/objective or true/false: it is relational thought that has more to do with meaning than knowing, although the poet cannot afford ignorance. The real, as Blaser liked to call it, is what comes out of the interaction between the poet and the world: "To hold an image within the line by sound and heat is to have caught something that passed out there," he says in "The Fire" (*Fire*, 3). The poem is the record of that meeting—the poet's view-from-here. The point is not to convince the reader to accept the poet's perspective but to articulate a common ground where meetings might take place. Or as Olson says, citing Keats, "a man's life ... is an allegory" (Olson 1970, 17). This is the corrective to modernism: the view-from-here is not definitive and certainly never complete, but it can be rigorous and sincere, and may, perhaps, become exemplary. Blaser had a lifelong fascination with Dante that dated from his Idaho boyhood and memories of the Gustave Doré illustrated *Inferno* in the family home, all the way through to his "Dante Alighiere: Great Companion" piece of 1997. Dante had created a world image out of Catholicism; Blaser took as his task the making of an analogous image for the twentieth century, but he did not have the Christian tradition on which to build it. He had, instead, the loosened syntax of *Finnegans Wake*, *The Waste Land*, and the *Cantos*. Without the passionate assurance of a cosmic order, Blaser, like the moderns before him, as well as his generational peers, had to descend to the underworld of culture and history in order to retrieve whatever orders and relationships he could find from the past that might suggest a way to imagine the present. So it turns out that all the cool poets go to hell—but we know that, don't we?

THROUGH-LINES

"Well, a biography used to mean that you'd done something," Blaser once said to me, registering disapproval of one he'd just read. What Blaser did to merit a biography by his own reckoning was to participate in an important postwar venture in poetry. His particular contribution to the New American poetry was a lifelong mediation on the sacred. As Blaser began to work his way through twentieth century philosophy and literature at Berkeley, he lost his naïve faith in Church doctrine, but rather than abandon the sacred, he came to understand it as a descriptor of experience. At issue is what Ralph Waldo Emerson called the me and not-me.[4] Despite the many discourses that undermine the validity of experience—philosophy has done so since Plato—we cannot not perceive ourselves as singular somethings within a larger something that is "not-me." Blaser thought that a refusal to recognize this affective dimension of human life was dangerous. It meant an over-reliance on instrumental reason and a vulnerability to the unacknowledged affections that motivate it—or to cite Karel Kosik, "The unreason of reason, and thus the historical limitation of reason, is in its denial of negativity" (Kosik 1976, 60). The sacred is a limit concept of the not-me, as death is a limit concept of consciousness. At the level of the atoms or the stars, the minims of language, or the statistical parsing of societies, neither exist. Blaser was interested in how to live, rather than the philosophical question of what can be thought with certainty or the scientific quest for empirical validity. In order to explore the experiential realm without giving it undue authority, he placed perceptual experience in relationship to its "unthought" (Foucault's word).[5] This was also a response to *mythopoiesis* as he encountered it through Duncan and Olson. The gods were names for chronic relationships with the world that could no longer be articulated by those names in a secular era. So in his early serials, Blaser unnames the old powers, even as he recognizes their ghostly presence-as-absence in the language.

Another important theme, worked out in Boston through the poem "Hunger of Sound" and carried all the way through to the end of *The Holy Forest*, was the nature of language. Through Spicer, Blaser was aware of the structuralist view of language early on. Spicer had studied linguistics at Berkeley and had read Edward Sapir and Benjamin Lee Whorf. Structuralism denies any kind of organic relationship between words and things, and Blaser accepted this, but he saw language as a human *techne* that was grounded in real historical acts: language was how the human creature reached for the world. At the level of the whole, rather than that of the linguistic unit, language is affective and historical. So, for example, Blaser was interested in etymology, not because earlier usages are more authentic than those of the present, but because he saw the language as a repository of human acts and qualities.[6]

A third contribution to poetics was Blaser's open space poem. In 1964, Stan Persky, Blaser's lover at that time, initiated *Open Space* as a newsletter that circulated among the Spicer–Duncan crowd. The idea was to share new work as news, as it was being written. *Open Space* was a means through which a community of poets and artists could become present to themselves as a community. As Blaser began to incorporate more and more collage work in his writings, his poems and essays took on the quality of a virtual forum of voices, living and dead, engaged in commentary on what was happening in the world. Open space would become Blaser's response to the missing *imago mundi* he had expected to find at Berkeley. As the progressive aspirations of the civil rights era faded into the social inequities and civic impotence of the 1970s and 1980s, the open space poem indexed the absence of a viable public sphere in the real world. As demonstrated in *Syntax*, a serial poem of 1978, the voices in Blaser's poems range from bathroom graffiti to the latest in high art and theory. The twentieth century analogue of Dante's cosmos could not be a hierarchy or even a completed image; it had to be processive and "catholic" small "c"—καθολικός, "general," "universal," or "according to the whole," meaning, in Blaser's context, according to the world at large.

Blaser's capacity to develop these themes that others could not or did not develop represents a unique contribution to postmodern poetics. The sacred, for example, was not a highly visible *topos* among New American poets, even those who embraced *mythopoiesis*, because it was too heavily freighted with dogmas that had lost credibility for secular intellectuals. Similarly, Blaser took a different tact on the language theme than did his peers. The mid-twentieth century was a time when many writers and artists were foregrounding the various ways in which mediating systems shape perceptual experience. Language is foremost of these systems, especially if it is understood broadly to include text and image, but Marshall McLuhan's writings on the media and art critic Clement Greenberg's emphasis on the formal properties of painting focused more narrowly on "the medium [as the] message."[7] Blaser's take on language is both an acknowledgment of the significance of it as a shaper of experience and an effort to hang onto the poet's capacity to imagine the world, rather than negate it as ideologically suspect.

The open space poem is distinctive as well because it explores the meaning of a public world at a time when the term "public" was becoming very hard to define, given the increasing visibility of cultural heterogeneity: whose world? which public? How might a poet enact the *communal* at a time when identities and alliances had become fractured and fractious?

Unlike his first-beloved companions—Duncan, Spicer, and Olson—Blaser lived, wrote, and thought his way through two full generational shifts in Anglo-American poetry, marked in the experimental realm by the New Americans and the Language poets, "Language" being a moniker that stuck to the younger generation. He was keenly interested in the latter, although his particular reading of language and his fascination with the sacred put some distance between their concerns and his. Like them, however, and unlike his New American peers, Blaser read carefully the theory coming out of the U.S. and France during the 1970s and 1980s—Maurice Merleau-Ponty, Roland Barthes, Jacques Lacan, Jacques Derrida, Geoffrey Hartman, Michel Serres, Gilles Deleuze, and on and on, as he liked to say, right up to his fascination with Giorgio Agamben in the 1990s and early 2000s. He treated these philosophers as companions to think with rather than sources, dragging them onto his own poetic turf and reading their work as confirmations of the poetics he was always working out for himself.

Another mark of difference: Blaser made his home in two countries and cultures. He was deeply rooted and invested in classic American literature—Hawthorne, Poe, and Dickinson in particular—but he embraced the poets of his adopted home in Canada, producing selected editions of Louis Dudek and George Bowering, and following with great attention the writings of friends such as Brian Fawcett, Steve McCaffery, Erin Mouré, bp Nichol, and Sharon Thesen, to name just a few. This is to say that Blaser is a liminal figure, balanced between the New American poetry and the Language writers; poetry and philosophy; the U.S. and Canada. He also spent considerable time in the visual art world, addicted as he was to gallery hopping and collecting local art. Blaser's take on twentieth century art and poetry is informed by this liminality. On one hand, he was intimate with the making of a North American postmodernity; on the other, he had enough distance from any one poetry circle or art scene to get some perspective on the polemics sometimes associated with schools or cliques. It is a proposition of this biography that Blaser brings a distinctive perspective to well-known poetry circles.

THE ORDER OF THINGS HERE

In "The Fire," Blaser makes the point, via Edith Cobb and Margaret Mead, that the story of a life is also the story of a world and that such stories are the stuff of poetry (*Fire*, 6). Nothing mattered more to him than poetry and his life story is inextricable from its working out of a poetic practice. Begin with a person and you will find a world; begin with a world, and sooner or later you will end up with a person. This is to say that I do not think a poet's work separable from his or her life, nor do I think the life can be severed from the multiple dimensions in which it is lived. I have tried to weave together three narrative lines in this biography: Blaser's personal story, his social context, and his ventures in poetry. The chapters are roughly chronological, but they are not symmetrical in time period or length. Instead, I have followed the natural phases of Blaser's life and work. Chapter 2 is about the Idaho childhood; Chap. 3 covers the student years at Berkeley; Chap. 4, Blaser's Boston period; Chap. 5, San Francisco; Chap. 6 the transition to Vancouver, and the last three chapters the mature working years. So, for example, Blaser spent his first 18 years in Idaho, the next 11 at Berkeley, and a mere four years in Boston, and yet of these three periods, Boston was the most eventful in terms of his development as a poet and it is therefore longer than the first two chapters. Each chapter is also divided into titled sub-sections that signal the different narrative threads, self-evidently I hope. Readers should feel free to skip around at will.

A GUIDE TO THE TEXT

This biography is based on archival materials housed in the Contemporary Literature Collection at Simon Fraser University; the Bancroft Library, Berkeley; and the Thomas J. Dodd Research Center, University of Connecticut. David Farwell, Blaser's widow, and Mark Samac, Blaser's nephew, have made their private archival collections available and many people have granted interviews. In addition to these sources, I have drawn on my personal experiences with Blaser over 30 years. Not all of the archival materials fall easily into accepted methods of documentation. The following is a guide to references and textual peculiarities that need some explanation.

The Astonishment Tapes: In 1974, Blaser recorded 20 autobiographical audio tapes in Vancouver over ten recording sessions. The project was initiated by University of British Columbia Professor Warren Tallman and attended by a small group of writers. The regulars were Daphne Marlatt, Dwight Gardiner, Martina Kuharic, and Angela Bowering, as well as Tallman himself; George Bowering and Frank Davey came to one session. Because I needed a quotable version of the tapes for the biography, I had them transcribed and then, because I thought them of independent interest, I edited them for publication. The complete transcript was about 840 pages in length—too long for a book. The published version of the tapes (University of Alabama Press, 2015) is about half the length of the transcript. This edited version is cited in the biography as *The Astonishment Tapes* (abbreviated *AT*) and the references are straight forward. However, I have also drawn on unpublished sections of the tapes and cited these as "The Astonishment Tapes" (abbreviated "AT"). In preparing the transcript, I kept the ten sessions as separate files. A citation from session one will look like this: "AT" 1, 20, meaning manuscript copy, session one, page 20. A copy of this manuscript on Universal Serial Bus (USB) has been placed in the Contemporary Literature Collection at Simon Fraser University and the original audio version of the tapes is available on PennSound, an online poetry archive.

The Holy Forest and *Charms*: Between 1964 and 1968, Blaser worked on a series of poems that he then called "The Holy Forest" and these were published in *Caterpillar* 12 (1970) as "The Holy Forest section from THE HOLY FOREST" (24–47). When the first collected edition of *The Holy Forest* was published in 1993, he changed the name of the series to "Charms."

The Letters of John Wieners: At the time of preparing this biography, The Letters is still in manuscript form, generously made available to me by editor Michael Seth Stewart. Stewart has divided the manuscript into two parts and footnoted them extensively. I have cited the Letters as LJW 1 or 2, identifying the letter in question by date and Stewart's footnotes by number. Correspondence between Blaser and Wieners not marked as LJW comes from the Blaser fonds and is documented as such in "Archival References."

Documentation: The archival sources do not easily fall into standard formats. To avoid repetition and streamline the documentation, I have created a separate Archival References list in the back matter of this book. This list is divided into three sections: Correspondence, Miscellaneous, and List of Interviews. In Correspondence, I've used author-date where possible and first phrases to identify undated letters. In Miscellaneous, I have created two subsections, dated and undated, under Blaser's name. In parenthetical documentation in the text, dated references are given in author-date format; undated references I have prefaced with the word "Undated" to refer readers to that section of the Blaser entries in Miscellaneous. I have identified undated items with a word or phrase. For example, a reference to an undated Blaser notebook entry might look like this: Undated, "Problems."

Typography: In quoting handwritten and archival materials, I have reproduced the typography in the original: underlining rather than italics, original capitalizations, and bolding. A peculiarity of Blaser's typography is that the subtitles of the *Image-Nation* series are all in open parentheses, like this: "Image-Nation 1 (the fold."

Notes

1. "Map *is not* territory" comes from Alfred Korzybski's *General Semantics Seminar 1937* (29, original emphasis).
2. Vachel Lindsay was a populist poet and author of "The Chinese Nightingale." Blaser mentions this poem in *The Astonishment Tapes* as a first brush with contemporary poetry (*AT*, 59).
3. Blaser traces Olson's reading of Whitehead's *Process and Reality* in "The Violets" to show that Olson saw in Whitehead "The end of the subject-object thing—Wow" (*Fire*, 218).
4. The "me" and "not-me" come into Emerson's introduction to "Nature" (Emerson 1982, 36).
5. The term "unthought" is from Michel Foucault's *Order of Things* (Foucault 1970, 326). Foucault's description is particularly relevant to Blaser: "The unthought (whatever name we give it) is not lodged in man like a shrivelled-up nature or a stratified history; it is, in relation to man the Other: the Other that is not only a brother but a twin, born not of man, nor in man, but beside him and at the same time, in an identical newness, in an unavoidable duality." Blaser cites the term "unthought" in "Stadium of the Mirror" (*Fire*, 35) and "The Practice of Outside" (*Fire*, 137).
6. I have adapted the phrase "acts and qualities" from the title of Charles Altieri's book, *Act & Quality* and I have benefited from Altieri's discussion in this book of a performance-oriented Wittgensteinian reading of poetic language.
7. "The medium is the message" is a phrase of Communications theorist Marshall McLuhan, first published in his 1964 book, *Understanding Media: The Extensions of Man.*

CHAPTER 2

Family Matters

> that intruder and calamity, way back there, was born in Denver,
> Colorado, in 1925—coverlet arranged by his mother's teachers
> at the Sacred Heart Academy, Sisters Seraphina and Mary
> Madeleva... (*HF*, 382)

Ina Mae McCready, born in Rock Springs, Wyoming and resident at the Sacred Heart Academy in Ogden, Utah was not quite 20 years old when she gave birth to her first son that May 18 in 1925. The father was Robert Augustus Blaser, born in Montpelier, Idaho, age 24. On the birth certificate, Ina Mae declares her occupation as teacher; Robert was a fireman for the railroad. By his own reckoning, Robin Francis Blaser was a "five-months child" (*AT*, 16), conceived out of wedlock in a field outside the Sacred Heart Academy (*AT*, 16).[1]

> My birth certificate shows my mother's address as the Sacred Heart Convent in
> Ogden, Utah. I'm born in Denver, Colorado at a hospital where obviously my
> mother was sent to cover the birth in some sense. Then apparently my father
> agreed to the marriage. (*AT*, 16)

"[T]he resentment," Blaser says, "was intense" (*AT*, 16) and he would grow up under the shadow of it.

With a few crucial exceptions, the Blasers were Mormons and railroad workers. The paternal side of their Idaho story begins with the immigration of the Swiss Fredrick Augustus Blaser and Elizabeth Lerch, Blaser's great grandparents. Both of them worked for the railroad in Switzerland until Fredrick became ill and had to quit. When he had recovered enough to work again, he found employment in a tile factory where he met John Steiger, a Mormon elder, and converted, accepting baptism 23 February 1883 (Cope n.d., 2). Fredrick's conversion inspired him to take his wife Elizabeth and seven children to

© The Author(s) 2019
M. Nichols, *A Literary Biography of Robin Blaser*,
Modern and Contemporary Poetry and Poetics,
https://doi.org/10.1007/978-3-030-18327-1_2

America. The family sold their possessions, cashed out their railroad pensions, and joined a group of Mormon immigrants on the SS Nevada in Liverpool, to arrive in New York, 16 May 1883. From there, they took a train west, landing in Montpelier, Idaho, 2 June 1883.

Augustus Fredrick Blaser (1871–1954), Blaser's grandfather and the inheritor of the family name, was 12 years old when the family immigrated. He had been born in Valderne sur Fontaine Neuchatel, 6 October 1871.[2] In *The Astonishment Tapes*, Blaser speaks of learning a few French songs from his grandfather (17–18). When Gus was 17, he began to work for the Oregon Shortline Railroad Company (Union Pacific) as a laborer. Over his 47-year career with the railroad, he was promoted to the rank of Section Foreman and later Road Master. Gus acquired farm and pasture land outside of Dempsey or Lava Hot Springs as it is now called, but the family moved around within the region as work required, living in Montpelier, Sage, Lava, Richfield, Twin Falls and Kemmerer, Wyoming. Gus's property was sited several miles from Lava at a crossing the railroad named after him: Blaser, Idaho.

In 1898, Gus married Minnie John (1881–1942) from West Portage, Utah. Minnie came from a polygamist Mormon family headed by Charles John, a Welsh immigrant (born in 1848 in South Wales), sheep herder, and leather worker (Cope n.d., 122). Like the Blasers, the Johns had converted to Mormonism in the old country and immigrated to join the Mormon settlements in the U.S. Their story is that of the self-made immigrant. Charles John, however, was arrested for polygamy in 1890 and the family was broken up. By that time, he was a propertied farmer and he divided his sheep and cattle between his three wives. Minnie's mother Elizabeth, also from Wales, remained in Utah for several years and then remarried. The family relocated to Dempsey (Lava), Idaho, in 1893 (Cope n.d., 11) where Minnie met and married Gus at the age of 17. She would bear eleven children, seven of whom survived. One of them was Robin's father, Robert.

Both Gus and Minnie, Blaser's paternal grandparents, were active in the Mormon Church throughout their lives. Gus was ordained a Bishop in the Dempsey Ward and Minnie held various positions in Church-related organizations such as the Young Women's Mutual Improvement Association and the Relief Society (Cope n.d., 22). A Blaser family history compiled by granddaughter Patricia Cope records Minnie's life principles. Honor, integrity, honesty, and loyalty were the desired character traits. Drugs, cards, and gambling were prohibited as was commerce on the sabbath. The family was obliged to keep a year's supply of food, clothing, and fuel on hand and they were to raise a garden. The domestic ethos was hard work, thrift, independence, and home ownership. On the spiritual side, there were the tenets of the Mormon faith and a belief in the development of the inner person (Cope n.d., 105–06).

Robin's father, Robert Blaser would inherit this tradition, if rather less enthusiastically than his parents. Baptized in a Mormon temple as a child, he was not devout, but neither would he tolerate criticism of the Mormons (Mark Samac interview with author, 2 July 2013) and he received a Mormon burial at the end of his life on 7 May 1978. Like his father Gus, Robert began to work for the railroad at an early age, leaving school, Blaser says, with a grade four education ("AT" 2, 20). According to the *Astonishments* narrative, Robert lost the family farm through mismanagement in the first years of his marriage. He then worked for the railroad in small track-side settlements like Wapai and Kimama where the family lived in converted freight cars. He was a cowboy of a man—a my-way-or-the-highway kind of guy as Blaser's nephew, Mark Samac, remembers (Samac interview, 2 July 2013). Needless to say, this caused considerable tension between him and his son. His aggressions, Blaser says, took the form of play. In *Astonishments* he recalls a very early experience of being thrown as a toddler from a bridge into the hot springs at Lava and then dived for (*AT*, 35). Blaser suggests that his father resented him not only because pregnancy forced the marriage but because his mother's family had some pretensions to old American roots (*AT*, 17).

On the maternal side, the Johnson family traced themselves to a Captain John Johnson of England (1590–1659) who had served under Governor John Winthrop in various official positions in the Massachusetts Bay colony. They were also proud of a link to the West family through marriage. The Wests claimed kinship to the painter Benjamin West (1738–1820) (*AT*, 17). Born in Springfield, Pennsylvania, West was an important history painter and a friend of Benjamin Franklin's, whose portrait he painted. The Johnsons and the Wests, then, came from old American settler stock, yet in the more immediate past, they too had the same history of railroad work and Mormonism as did the Blasers.

One of the most vivid of the Johnson ancestors was Aaron Johnson, Blaser's great great grandfather (1806–1877), married to Mary Ann Johnson (1831–1913). Born in Connecticut, Johnson began as a farm worker and then an apprentice gun-maker in Hadam. Originally Methodist, he converted to Mormonism and was baptized on 15 April 1836. Johnson became a personal friend of Joseph Smith's, and followed the prophet westward, homesteading in various places from which he was repeatedly driven for his faith and practice of polygamy. At one point, he had 11 wives, three of whom were teen-aged sisters that he had married together. After losing several farms to hostile communities, Johnson arrived in Springville, Utah, in 1851 where he worked as a farmer and served the Church in a number of important roles, eventually becoming a man of property and influence. Johnson's daughter with Mary Ann was Blaser's great grandmother, Ina Johnson, a stern matriarch in Blaser's childhood memories. In her younger years, she had worked as Brigham Young's private telegrapher.

In great grandmother Ina Johnson, born 21 December 1854 in Springville, Utah, the Johnson family had a rebel. As Blaser remembers, she detested the practice of polygamy.

> Hated Mormons, hated men that had more than one wife. My latest memory of her was her sitting in a rocking chair, where she would do nothing but hum a terrible sound and when the train would stop, the sound of this hhmmm-mmrrrrrr—and you could hear it for miles.... (*AT*, 22)

On one occasion, great grandmother commanded Robin to sing. In *The Park*, one of his early serial poems, Blaser tells the story this way:

> She beat on the floor with her stick
> until I came   she said 'Sing'   Which
> I did   She commented that my voice
> was thin, but that I had enough silliness to
> amount to (hesitation) a poet   Old
> lady whose false breasts were made of
> cambric stuffed with cotton and hung
> around her neck on a ribbon, kept a
> goldfish bowl full of life-savers to
> sweeten the sour breath she was aware of (*HF*, 52)

In *Astonishments*, Blaser also remembers the matriarch tossing him out of the house for playing with the treadle on the sewing machine when he was a toddler (*AT*, 29). He remembers, as well, peeking at her on bath nights, astonished at the fact that she had no breasts and made her own prosthetics (*AT*, 28). The singing incident, however, Blaser would take as a directive rather than a reproof: he was not a singer, but he might be *something* (*AT*, 43).

Ina Johnson must have passed her impatience with Mormonism to her daughter Sophia Nichols Van Aukin McCready—Sophia Nichols Auer, after her second marriage—who chose the Unitarian Church and later rejected formal religion altogether ("AT" 1, 47–48). Here the story touches Blaser very directly. Sophia Nichols, his much beloved grandmother, was his most significant childhood influence, and indirectly his conduit to the Catholicism of his youth. Partly because of her own great imagination and narrative ability, and partly because of the strained relationship between Blaser and his father, Sophia was a refuge from family storms. The photographs show a square-faced, rounded figure—"dumpy," Blaser called her affectionately ("AT" 2, 16), unlike her elegant sister Mae who was stylish and had been to San Francisco for music lessons (*AT*, 29). Sophia Nichols, born 12 May 1876 in Soda Springs, Wyoming, was *homely*, not really in appearance—her youthful photographs show a handsome face—but in her rootedness in family matters (Fig. 2.1).

Deserted by her first husband, Cassius Dewitt McCready, Sophia divorced him in 1909 and was left with a three-year-old daughter and household property in the amount of $150. She placed Ina Mae, Blaser's mother, in the Sacred Heart Academy at the age of six, because she needed to work (*AT*, 40) and feared that McCready might steal her (Samac interview, 2 July 2013). Sophia worked as a telegrapher for the Oregon Short Line, at first in Lava and then in Orchard, Idaho where she remained until her retirement in 1941. By 1924, she had remarried to Simon Auer, a German immigrant and fellow railway worker. Grandpa Auer would be another important childhood influence on Blaser.

Sophia kept her steady employment with the Oregon Short Line through the Depression, providing financial stability for the whole family. Both Ina Johnson, Sophia's mother, and Tina West, her aunt, lived with Sophia and

Fig. 2.1 Grandmother Sophia Nichols Auer with Robin in Orchard, Idaho, c.1927.
Photo courtesy of Millie Blaser and the estate

Simon Auer in a converted freight car in Orchard. Like Sophia, Aunt Tina
(1862–1945) was a longtime employee of the Union Pacific and Oregon Short
Line, but she retired in 1924, 20 years before her death in 1944, and moved in
with Sophia. This would have meant four people in the house. During the
Depression, however, Robert, Ina Mae, and the children wound up in Orchard
as well. By this time, Blaser's siblings, Irvin (who everyone called Gus), and
Hope had come along, in 1927 and 1928, respectively. Robert had been fired
from the railway for subsistence theft—probably coal ("AT" 1, 9)—and it was
up to Sophia to hold the family together. Of his grandmother during this
period, Blaser says: "I know once she had spotted fever, which you get from
wood ticks, and she never stopped. I don't think she could, because we were
all living on that" (*AT*, 23). "That," in a 1936 tax record, was $1750.88 a year,
a decent income for a time when the average American wage was $1713, the
cost of a new house was $3925, and a Studebaker could be had for $665, but
hardly generous for an extended family (*People History*, n.d.).

In addition to financial support, Sophia offered nurturance and homespun advice, but perhaps her most important gift to Blaser was her story telling. Many of Blaser's Idaho stories in *The Park*, "Sophia Nichols," *The Astonishment Tapes*, and the autobiographical poem "Image-Nation 24 ('oh, pshaw,'" center on Sophia's tales. The pockmarks in the desert after a rain became matter for divination. A sudden storm that created a large pond between the house and the commissary occasioned a childhood enactment of the Odyssey. Grandmother had been reading Robin the story, and when the pond formed, she put her grandson in the family washtub and had him row across it to fetch her needments (*AT*, 28–29). Sophia also taught curiosity and regard for the creaturely. The root cellar in Orchard where the family kept their hams and turnips was home to plenty of spiders and bull snakes. The constrictors were welcome because they kept out the deadlier rattlers, their natural enemies. When grandmother descended, she would hold out her arms and the snakes would wrap around them, as if in recognition (*AT*, 21). On another occasion, grandmother rescued a den of baby coyotes from a sagebrush fire after the adults had run off (*AT*, 23). Despite the bites she received for her trouble, she kept the brood until they could fend for themselves.

Sophia's attunement to the creaturely directly contrasted with more common attitudes. Blaser remembers that an Idaho pastime was to catch a rattler and a bull snake, lure them into a closed space with a fruit slug and take bets on which snake would kill the other (*AT*, 21). One of the lessons of his youth, Blaser says, was of the consequences of interfering thoughtlessly with nature's things. Attracted to birds and a lifelong defender of them against marauding felines, he built a cage for sparrows in Orchard. This turned out to be a disaster when the bull snakes climbed the legs of the cage and devoured the trapped birds. Robin responded with a rage, attacking the snakes with an axe until grandmother intervened and taught him that he had, in fact, set up the slaughter (*AT*, 20). This was a lesson Blaser would not forget. In *Astonishments*, he tells the story of flying into a temper, decades later, as a professor at Simon Fraser University. A Blake scholar and candidate for a romantics post challenged Blake's position that everything is holy:

> And though I have a very funny response to snakes, my grandmother never really got me through into the kind of sense of them that she had. And she had this on all levels. It accounts for a recent rage ... when a man came to Simon Fraser wanting to be hired to teach Blake. Now it became very clear to me, shortly after the interview started that he knew nothing about Blake, but the example that he used to show me how much he knew about Blake—Blake had to be insane because "everything that lives is holy" could only be the remark of an insane man, "because," he said, "if a scorpion bites me obviously it's not holy," at which point drunken Robin Blaser threatened to hit him with the wine bottle, disgracing the Department of English at Simon Fraser, etc. I was in such a rage, and I only now realize ... that he was touching a whole range of information that was coming to me out of something else, that wouldn't be conscious to me on a fucking academic occasion... (*AT*, 25)

In comparison to the cutting-edge arts scene that Blaser would enter at Berkeley, his childhood might seem culturally bare to an outsider, but with Sophia's tutelage he learned to look and listen closely, so the Idaho of his youth became a live and informing seedbed of the imagination.

THE HOMEPLACE

Stuffed in Blaser's high school yearbooks are a number of loose-leaf poems that date from childhood. One of them is identified as sixth grade and the undated others seem to belong roughly to the same period. Here is "The Desert," marked up with spelling and punctuation corrections as well as an encouraging "very good." The spelling is original.

> A desert in the spring time
> Is a lovely sight to see;
> The one thing God created
> That humans will let be.
> Its dust and sand are polk marked
> By the newly falen rain
> And its pink and yellow cactus
> Can look up and smile again
> It's silence oft is broken
> By the shrill cry of a hawk
> Or a frightened grayhaired rabbit
> That will scurry off a rock.
> It's clean damp scent of sage brush
> The ant mounds fresh and neat
> And its cool gray rocks invite you
> To climb up and have a seat
> It's sunset there at evening
> And it's moonlight clear and still
> Make the desert God's own chapel
> Where ones soul may roam at will. (Undated, "The Desert")

This poem associates the desert with sensual beauty and comfort ("its cool gray rocks invite you") and it steps away from anthropocentrism in suggesting that this is a place that humanity has "let be," perhaps because people misperceive it as empty or of little interest. The speaker sets himself apart from these others through his appreciation of natural beauty and his ease in the desert. The hawk and rabbit, predator and prey, he accepts equally as elements of nature, and the ants he regards as models of domesticity, "fresh and neat," rather than a household nuisance. To notice as well is that the poem is unpeopled. In *Astonishments*, Blaser says that he felt set apart as a child, not only because he was alienated from his father but also because he perceived himself as out of step with school mates and siblings (*AT*, 37). Describing his grade school experience in Dietrich, Blaser says:

My tendency is always go off to the edge, and the work up at Cold Mountain[3] got the image out of me, the little boy standing there listening with his back, rubbing his shoe and I suddenly realized the whippings I got because my left shoe was always—the polish and leather rubbed off because I was standing over there with one foot on the other ... and then, of course, became rebellious. (*AT*, 37)

"The Desert" imagines an outdoors that is clean, fresh, neat, clear, and still—a place that the speaker compares to a chapel and which he interprets as a place of freedom. Back of this imagined homeplace would have been the experience of living in close quarters with an extended family. Clean, fresh, neat, clear, and still would have been difficult to maintain in a railcar with nine people living in it.

In *Astonishments*, Blaser says he wants a "sacred geography" (*AT*, 95) to come out of the taped sessions—that he is "build[ing] a landscape" of the imagination (*AT*, 94). This landscape is first of all and literally the Idaho desert—the landscape of the serial poems *Cups*, *The Park*, and "Image-Nation 4"—but the *imaginative* geography also includes the water world that Robin had never seen until he moved to Berkeley. From Idaho, he takes the sage and sand, the desert creatures, and the brush fires. Water was present as absence: in Orchard, it came from a water tower, a storage unit for the water that had to be trucked in. Blaser remembers it as a site of magical transformation. The tower leaked and the pond that formed beneath would fill with insects and even frogs (*AT*, 20–21). The wonder of it was where they came from.

Water comes into Blaser's imaginative landscape as well through the Lost River. This is a river that runs from the Rockies and passes underground before resurfacing at a place called Thousand Springs in southern Idaho, where the water gushes from a mountain side (*AT*, 15).[4] In the 1930s, the family acquired a holiday cabin on the Snake River, close to this spot. The hiddenness of the water contrasts with its dramatic visibility on release. Water was also part of Blaser's childhood book world. Charles Kingsley's *The Water-Babies* was another important point on the imaginative map. On the "Tapes," Blaser spends considerable time in retelling Kingsley's story and with evident pleasure ("AT" 6, 18–29). The story is of a little chimney sweep who is abused by the man who exploits his labor. He escapes to a river and, with the help of fairies, is magically transformed into a water-baby, gills, and all. What follows are many underwater adventures. The validation and metamorphosis of an unwanted little lad, and the escape from a hostile adult male, was a story that Blaser could identify with. Much later, the desired water world would become an element of poetics:

Then I also translate the whole job of poetry into the task of knowledge, so that the narration of that task is what I'm trying to get into this story so that I build a landscape, and the landscape that is built is, yes, the desert with the unfinished water landscape that was to match that which not only polarizes the landscape from which I came, but it actually is the unknown landscape. Water becomes the unknown for me. (*AT*, 94)

In addition to books like Kingsley's and the stories of his grandmother, Blaser found imaginative stimulation in the story-telling of Cleo Adams, a 24-year-old railroad laborer he met in Orchard at the age of nine. Adams had a liking for rocks and would take Robin on walks along the railroad tracks to pick up garnets and agates for polishing. Although their relationship never became sexual, Blaser remembers him as a first love:

> ...I'm nine years old and this guy named Cleo Adams who's twenty-four, and I can remember now, my mother carefully checking to see what was going on in this passionate relationship between this little boy who's taken out to hunt jack-rabbits in the evening, following the railroad tracks, and so on and so forth, and this man who made fudge for him and taught him how to polish rocks and how to pick garnets and agates up out of the rocks by the road beds. (*AT*, 18–19)

Cleo told stories about the rocks he found. Agates, he said, had fallen from the moon; garnets were pieces of coyotes' blood (*AT*, 19). Adams's kindness filled a gap left by the distance between Blaser and his father. So in "Image-Nation 4 (old gold," a poem written in the early 1960s, Blaser writes:

> Cleo, nearby, picks up agates and
> moonstones between railway ties,
> works at his wheel to polish and open
>
> well, when the whole place was mud,
> a part of it froze in with the
> sunset, and these shadows were
>
> only curls in the mud, but
> the moonstone   that's a piece
> of the cheese fell out of the moonstream. (*HF*, 92–93)

As this poem attests, another magical place in Blaser's childhood landscape was the Craters of the Moon in Sun Valley, about 90 miles from Twin Falls. These are lava fields, solidified in waves, that preserve a number of small trees to create what locals call Devil's Orchard. The trees died in the volcanic eruption estimated as occurring about 2000 years ago, but the lava holds them upright. An outstanding feature of the Craters is that while the "orchard" preserved in the solidified stone looks dead, the park is actually intensely alive with a wide variety of plant and animal life. It is, as Blaser writes in "Image-Nation 4," "a black garden" (*HF*, 92). The poem links the lava fields to cinders spread out over a field to burn out, as if a fire still burned beneath the crusted stone. Ella Cinders comes into the poem as well, a comic strip character created by Bill Conselman and Charles Plumb. The comic series, distributed by United Feature Syndicate, launched on 1 June 1925 and ran until 1961. The story line follows the adventures of Ella, a stepdaughter of "Ma" Cinders. Like Tom of *The Water-Babies*, Ella is an unwanted child, a Cinderella. She eventually escapes her nasty step family when the judge in a beauty contest selects her photo at random for a trip to Hollywood. Although Ella is never really successful there, she greets her misfortunes with irony and aplomb.

A common thread in this imaginative geography is metamorphosis. The desert comes alive with the scents and sounds of plant and animal life; a puddle from a water tower mysteriously generates skeeters and frogs; a rainstorm provides the occasion for an odyssey; a Lost River flows underground to emerge with magnificent force from the side of a mountain; a maltreated little boy makes his escape as a water-baby; the railroad tracks become a treasure trove of stones and stories; the Craters of the Moon mask a fiery energy; an abused cartoon character quips her way out of the indignities she is made to suffer. The discounted and the hidden blossom in these landscapes as they are storied out of bareness.

Growing Up Idaho

Although the sequence of moves that the Blaser family made after leaving the farm at Blaser, Idaho is not clear, it seems to have been Wapai, Kimama, Dietrich, and then Orchard. By age five, Blaser would have two toddler siblings, Gus and Hope; Harold James—Jimmy—would be born much later in 1936, when Blaser was already half grown. "My first real memory of them is they're very different from me," Blaser says: "The sister is very blond, and the brother, showing even more of the French blood than I do, is very dark-skinned and curly-headed and very dark hair, and big and strong, very tough, and marvelous" (*AT*, 17). In this remark, the childhood memories segue seamlessly into those of the adult. What is clear, however, is Blaser's feeling of apartness, as if he had been an only child.

By the time Blaser was of school age, the family had moved to Dietrich, a somewhat larger settlement than Wapai. Grade one "was the most awful thing" (*AT*, 37), Blaser says, because the school seemed large and the students intimidating. In 1931, six-year-olds in Dietrich were introduced to the three "R's" plus Physical Education, Music, Drawing, and Phonics. Blaser seems to have gone through a steep learning curve. His report card records Cs and Bs for these subjects in the first segment of the school year, but by the second, he was consistently earning As for reading and Bs for Writing, Arithmetic, Language, P.E. and Hygiene, Music, Drawing, and Phonics (Report card, 1932). His school "citizenship record" climbed from Bs to As between the first and second terms as did his "preparation of lessons." He was promoted to second grade on 12 May 1932.

Although Blaser mentions only one year in Dietrich, family records suggest more. In 1933, two years after Blaser had started school, the family bought a piano from the Baldwin company on time. The initial receipt lists Robert Blaser's residence both as Dietrich and Kimama while the final payment in 1936 was made in Orchard. As Mark Samac recalls, the piano was precious to Ina Mae and later it would enable Blaser to take lessons from his Aunt Mae in Twin Falls (Samac interview, 2 July 2013). Somewhere between 1933 and

1936, however, the Depression must have hit the family hard. This is when everyone moved in with Grandmother Sophia in Orchard. Mark Samac, Blaser's nephew, remembers a family story that Robert and Ina Mae slept in an unheated lean-to beside the house, piling on the blankets in winter, because there simply was not enough room for everyone (Samac interview, 2 July 2013). Blaser was moved to a one-room school in Orchard where, he would recall later in *Astonishments*, the teacher didn't seem to be a real one since he remembers learning nothing much except some Protestant songs and "The Star-Spangled Banner" (*AT*, 38).

Out of school, however, there were plenty of lessons. The sparrows and the bull snakes were one such. In another, Blaser talked his mother into helping him round up orphan lambs, left behind by the sheepherders, and for a time he had his own little flock. Hard times, however, meant that some of the lambs were sold and some were butchered for the table. "It was years before I could eat lamb," Blaser says (*AT*, 39). Somehow, the family got through. They ate venison (*AT*, 39), they scavenged for dumped railway ties that might be sold for wood in the towns, and, with the help of Sophia on the purchase of a dilapidated truck, Robert began to carry water to the sheepherders (*AT*, 23–24). In 1936, the family was able to move to a small house at 527 Main Street in Twin Falls (Fig. 2.2).

Fig. 2.2 Robin with dog, Pepper, and new bike in Twin Falls, Idaho, c.1936–1938. Photo courtesy of Millie Blaser and the estate

Sophia was the rock. In a letter to her grandson, 31 July 1936, she replies to three notes from "Bobbie":

> I received your three letters OK and my I was delighted to get them and so happy you like the bike. Always try and make people like you and one can get so much more out of life by making someone else happy.
>
> When school starts I want you to be sure and join the boy scouts. It is such a great help to one and they go on these Hiking trips, and teach one so very many useful things.
>
> School will soon start, and I hope you can all come down and see me before. I would love to come down, but I simply must not leave Grandma alone. Am glad you like the books. Cultivate the habit of reading for books are such wonderful company. (Auer to Blaser)

This is advice that Blaser would take to heart. During his adolescence in Twin Falls, he would learn to master the scared little boy in the corner of the school-room to become something of a social butterfly. In a childhood game that must have dated from somewhere between ages 11 and 12, he was already thinking big. The house on Main Street was situated next to a vacant lot which became a playground for Robin and his friends, notably Bill Halley. The boys dug tunnels in the lot and played at being masters of the world, dividing the globe into kingdoms for themselves. This experience turns up in *The Park*, a serial poem from 1960.

> (Bill took out the atlas and began to divide
> the world between us   General William Halley
> England, the Americas, Russia   he used his
> own name, so I kept mind, but added Duc of
> Orleans because I held France, China and Africa
>
> (We gave the imaginary kingdoms to the late
> comers   Mu, Atlantis, the Arctics
>
> (Then I held power in a vacant lot where I
> built a tunnel dedicated to their sex play. (*HF*, 54–55)

In *Astonishments*, Blaser explains his penchant for France and China, although Africa remains a mystery. Grandfather Gus had told his grandson that he, Augustus, was the lost Dauphin of France, which would have made Robin heir to the French throne. This was doubly a fancy because Augustus's birth records show that he was Swiss rather than French, as Blaser insisted into adulthood. On the "Tapes," made at age 49, Robin says of his grandfather:

> That was the secret between us, that he was the lost Dauphin which meant of course that I was the Prince de Paris or the Duc d'Orléans or something. In child-hood the games we played with maps—we divided the world. ("AT" 2, 21)

...

The few childhood friends would divide the map and I would fight to have France. There were literally fistfights over that. I had to have France because I was the Duc d'Orléans. ("AT" 2, 22)

...

It was so extreme ... my sense of that and the lost Dauphin thing, that I could carry that off in manner. One day in school, in Twin Falls, a girl ... punched me in the back and she said, "I'm sure that you must be a prince or something." And I remember my response was that "I am." ("AT" 2, 23)

The French connection would become lifelong. French became the desired second language and Blaser retained a leaning toward things French for the rest of his life. China, as well, had special significance. As Blaser explains on the "Tapes," his middle name was Francis after Saint Francis Xavier ("AT" 2, 8), and he had grown up on stories of the adventures of the Saint as related by Grandfather Auer. St. Francis (1506–1552) was a Catholic missionary, born in Navarre (now Spain). A co-founder of the Society of Jesus (the Jesuits) with St. Ignatius of Loyola, he traveled to India, Malacca, the Malaku Islands, and Japan. It was his ambition to tour China, but he died of a fever at Shangchuan Island before reaching the mainland. According to grandfather's stories, however, Francis was one of the great emissaries of the faith in China and he had the surprising ability to fly on Persian carpets across the Mediterranean as well ("AT" 2, 9).

The game Blaser describes in *The Park*—dividing the world with playmates—speaks of a vivid sense of potentiality and a will to self-fashion. Later this passion for transformation would enter the poetry. In a poem called "Giant" from *Pell Mell*, the vacant lot returns as "protean shape, the sacred vacant lot" (*HF*, 310). A recurring trope for Blaser, the vacant lot was a place of imagination; much later the concept of an open space would become a signature element in his poetics. For the 12-year-old, however, the vacant lot was also a source of family tension, and perhaps rebellion, as well as a playground. Samac recounts Robert's anger when he drove his truck onto the lot only to have it fall into the tunnels the children had dug (Samac interview, 2 July 2013). From the father's point of view, the tunnels simply created a parking nightmare; from the son's perspective, the vacant lot was a world in the making.

A little School Memories book from 1937 confirms Blaser's early interest in the creative arts. At age 12, his "social activities" included music and drama and his favorite subject was art. Included in this booklet are many parting verses from fellow students at the end of the term in May 1937, suggesting his popularity. Best friend Wayne Jepson's verse catches the general level of humor: "Dear Robin, Yours untill [sic] the dresser falls down stairs and looses [sic] its drawers." Other ditties reveal the social norms of the period that the students had unwittingly absorbed: "When you get married and your wife get [sic] cross / Pick up the broom and say (Im [sic] boss). Yours til Bear Lake has cubs." On the subject of race as well as sex and gender, this autograph book underlines the fact that in 1937, civil rights and the feminist revolution, not to mention Stonewall, were a long way off: "Robin, God made negros / He made them at night / He made them in such a hurry / He forgot to paint them white." Included as well are congratulatory teacher's comments and this from Ina Mae: "Robin, Cultivate self confidence. Learn to say 'No'! It is a great thing to be a man but far greater to be a master—Master of Yourself. Mother."

Although this 1937 Memories book offers a glimpse of a popular, engaged young man, the social landscape in Twin Falls would have made cognitive dissonance out of adolescence for a gay boy with sexual stirrings. In an autobiographical poem called "Curriculum Vitae," Blaser mentions a nervous breakdown at age 13 and a "therapeutic" stint at a sheep farm in Wyoming meant to cure him of such nonsense (HF, 400). The breakdown, he says in this poem, was "actually sexuality edging towards the unknown, but I couldn't tell that to the doctor" (HF, 400). The "therapy" would continue through Blaser's teenage years. At this time, Robert was working as a trucker and Blaser's job was to help load

> hundred-pound sacks of flour
> or tongs in either hand to carry as many bricks as I could
> handle.... (HF, 400)

In *Astonishments*, Robin says that his father would assign him laboring jobs that would stiffen his hands when he had piano recitals scheduled (AT, 44). Other jobs included window washing and seed sorting for the Globe Seed and Feed Warehouse (HF, 400–01).[5] These laboring jobs suggest Robert's view of suitable employments for his adolescent son. Much later, when Robert started his own trucking business, the Trail Blasers, both Gus and Jimmy would become drivers. Robin would leave home. "I was accused of every kind of faggotry before I'd ever heard of a faggot," he remarks on *Astonishments*, "except my father loved to use the term cocksucker and I knew what that meant before I'd ever done it..." (AT, 44). Sophia remained the refuge, although she, too, supported summer employment. In a letter of 15 May 1938, she urges her 13-year-old grandson to stick it out with the new job rather than come to Orchard. "If you came up this summer," she says, "you might lose out, and I would not have that happen for the world, for it is a little pin money and maybe you can get several lawns to mow this summer you know every little [sic] helps" (Auer to Blaser, 15 May 1938) Sophia, however, tempered such advice with kindly indulgence. In a letter home dated 14 August 1940, a 15-year-old Robin tells his mother about a "spree" in Boise with Grannie. This included an overnight stay in a nice hotel, dinner in a restaurant, and two movies, *Tom Brown's School Days* (Dir. Robert Stevenson, 1940) and *Vigil in the Night* (Dir. George Stevens, RKO Pictures, 1940).

In adolescence, Blaser took a sharp turn to Catholicism that would, for the adult poet, morph into a pursuit of the sacred. In the desert there had been no priests or churches, but Twin Falls offered Saint Edward's and Monsignor O'Toole and there was his mother's relationship with the Holy Cross nuns at the Sacred Heart Academy that established a line to the Catholics. On adolescence, Blaser says,

> I had two sides to me: one was that I had to be the leader, the top, the president of everything insofar as I could. There were a few defeats but not too many. On the other, was a very deep religious side. I mean I would kneel on my knees at fourteen, fifteen before the Virgin for hours waiting for her statue to nod—like I had the whole Catholic thing that it was magical. (*AT*, 46)

The piety was noticed and the Monsignor, "a very crotchety, very proud, very difficult and erudite old man" (*AT*, 46), began to mentor the boy who seemed like a good candidate for the priesthood, at least until the social activities interfered. In high school, Blaser joined a fraternity called the Red Knights and became president. Then it was the DeMolays:

> ...I'm out here trying to be president of everything and the DeMolays dig me so I joined the DeMolays. Now, I wound up president of DeMolay. In some weird part of my brain I had so fixed it that I never let myself know that the Catholics burned DeMolay at the stake.... We had long velvet gowns and I wore a crown. By the time I was president each spoke of the crown had a jewel on it. I can't tell you I dug that scene something awful and we acted out the burning of DeMolay. (*AT*, 46–47)

The connection between Blaser's religious passion and the club scene is right here. Both the Church and the youth clubs offered a sense of belonging to something larger, of ritual, of sensual richness, and of social position. These graces were important to the point where the teenager did not let himself see the doctrinal differences between the masonic DeMolays and the Catholics. The story Blaser liked to give of this confusion was Monsignor O'Toole's response to a newspaper picture of him as president of DeMolay. The priest was furious and gave Blaser a full Latin exorcism. "It was the end of DeMolay," Blaser says, "I pulled out immediately. But also it was the end of—Monsignor would have nothing to do with me" (*AT*, 47).

After Sophia's retirement in 1941, the Blasers bought a house at 191 Polk Street in Twin Falls and Sophia and Aunt Tina moved in with the family.[6] Sophia helped with the purchase and Robert bought rugs and furniture. This was the year that Blaser entered high school, taking English, Latin, French, biology, maths, and drama. Over the high school years, he was particularly active in drama. That year, he acted the part of Professor Willard in Thornton Wilder's play, *Our Town*, and the next year, he joined the Thespian Club, playing Randolph in *The Magnificent Obsession* by Lloyd C. Douglas, and Clarence in *A Connecticut Yankee in King Arthur's Court* by Mark Twain. He also began to make friendships that would turn out to be important later on. Frances Schweickhardt, Tom Jones, and Marlin Sweeley were on the *Bruin*, the school newspaper staff that Robin would join later. Sweeley's father was a judge ("AT" 3, 4) and the three friends were several years older than Blaser. Their families were the social elite of Twin Falls and Blaser would soon become an item himself. The society page of the local newspaper announces in a paragraph titled

"Younger Set Entertains" that Dick Brizee and Robin Blaser were hosts to a dance party at the Sibyl Frazier party house, assisted by their mothers. In another society page noticing, Blaser plays Li'l Abner at a Sadie Hawkins Day dance, costumed in a plaid shirt and carrying a jug. He is flanked by two girls, one of whom, Virginia Benson, has him firmly in hand. His fellow Li'l Abner and Red Knight buddy, Jack Jordan, "is having a little more success in evading Rosie" according to the caption, but the really amusing thing about the photograph is that there is nothing of the hillbilly in Blaser's style or demeanor (*Twin Falls Evening Times* 1939, n.p.). He looks more like Fred Astaire in drag than an Appalachian homeboy—one can almost see the suit beneath the plaid shirt. Devastatingly handsome, Blaser charmed his fellow students. "When it comes to a perfect fellow—the kind every girl likes to lean & depend on your [sic] tops! I hope we can have fun together next year," writes an impressed fellow student in the Twin Falls high school yearbook of 1942 (*Coyote* 1942) (Fig. 2.3).

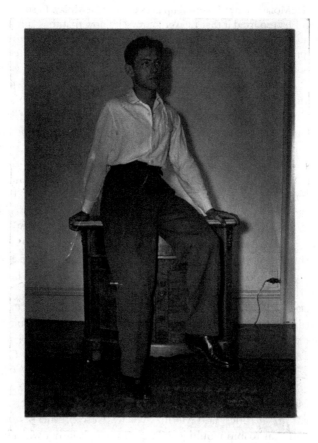

Fig. 2.3 Robin Blaser in Twin Falls, c.1940–1942. Photo courtesy of Millie Blaser and the estate

That year, 1942, the war arrived in Twin Falls, not just through the absence of men but also the presence of POW and relocation camps. President Roosevelt had issued an executive order in February of that year, relocating all persons of Japanese ancestry away from the coast. The Minidoka War Relocation Center, 17 miles from Twin Falls, operated from 1942 to 1945, housing more than 9000 Japanese Americans, mostly from Oregon, Washington, and Alaska. Too young for the draft (it was aimed at 21- to 25-year-olds), Blaser was part of a small group that created cultural liaisons between the Japanese and Twin Falls residents. He also worked in Men's Wear at the Idaho Department Store, hired, he said, to serve those that others would not. These included the Japanese, allowed one day a month out of the Relocation Center to shop, and Blacks from the Bahamas, hired to fill the labor shortage on the farms.

> ...I bent on one knee to measure, with trepidation, the inner leg for the bright green and sharp blue suits they bought on Saturdays after work—I still imagine them—as I found them later in back-country enclaves dancing stunningly to country music with the lonely wives. (*HF*, 402)

The other social outcasts that Blaser would serve were the prostitutes from the Paramount Hotel. The Men's Wear Department curiously carried silk stockings for men to give as gifts. The only people who bought them were the prostitutes.

> ...One of them became
> a close, secret friend, and it was she who gave me my first
> lesson in countering clichés—'Never,' she said, 'tell any-
> one I'm a whore with a heart of gold.' (*HF*, 401)

In Twin Falls, Blaser was very much in the closet, although he remarks in a poem that one of the salesmen at the Department Store commented on his red lips, saying "'You know that always means you're queer'" (*HF*, 401). Despite the clubs and the social successes, however, he had an empathy for the outsider and an interior life that was more intense than Li'l Abner parties.

Blaser's high school poems, several of which were preserved by his mother, suggest both the popular thespian and the rather more introspective and religiously inclined young man who could not yet express his sexuality openly. The first of these is suggested by Blaser's take on Chaucer's Wife of Bath in a poem that begins,

> My what a woman was this wife of Bath.
> Though a wee bit shady was her trodden path. (Undated, "Wife")

Like the Wife, Robin had a gap between his top front teeth and this he carefully preserved through adulthood and many trips to the dentist. The Wife was one of his lifelong personas—sociable, well-dressed, flirtatious, earthy, and ready to sinfully enjoy the social opportunities of religious occasions. Her pilgrimage to

Canterbury, she lets us know, is more to catch a husband than to atone for her naughtiness. When he wanted to show it, Blaser had a social side that was broad and bawdy. After a few drinks, he could also play the cowboy, "dirty and noisy," as he remembered his father (*AT*, 43). The tone of this untitled, undated poem, however, is quite different:

> Find you the path in night, perhaps,
> to walk upon and crowd the brush
> that cut your face.
>
> Throw you the rock you touch upon
> and stoop to drink the discs begun
> in stone on space.
>
> Think on the song a nymph has sung;
>> Christ was born in night
>> And I, to him, have sacrificed
>> An ox with golden horns.
>
>> Christ was born in night
>> And I, to him, have sacrificed
>> Four trees in cruciforms.
>
> then laugh to see the gaseous stars
> fall out of place. (Undated, "Find you the path")

The first image suggests a difficult passage through brush and the inability to see where one is going. In the second stanza, the time and space frame seems to shift from close to far—to "stone in space." The last line, in which the "gaseous stars / fall out of place," reinforces the cosmic perspective and hints of disruption, perhaps the epoch-making birth of Christ or the Christian apocalypse. Is the sacrifice of the ox and trees a giving over of paganism to Christianity? I'm not sure the poem tells us, but it does include elements that look like a Blaser poem, if only in hindsight. There is "the path in the night" that suggests a proceeding without knowledge of the final goal, a premise of the serial poem. There is a hint of the cosmicity that would later displace Catholicism in Blaser's thinking. There is the attraction to myth and ritual, and in the "I have sacrificed" there is also something of the priestly. Countering all this is a certain rage against order when the speaker urges the reader to laugh when the stars fall out of place. I do not know whether Blaser would have so identified these elements as a teenager, but this juvenile poem suggests a certain *weltschmerz* and an attraction to religious feeling that is quite removed from the good-timing Wife of Bath.

FLIGHT

On graduation from high school Blaser received a scholarship for a summer program in journalism at Northwestern University. He had studied English and Journalism with Mercedes Paul at Twin Falls High and had been involved in the high school paper. Journalism may have seemed like the most likely career path for a young man interested in drama and the arts, although Blaser says in *Astonishments* that he never had a deep inclination toward the profession: "I got a scholarship in journalism, which I could never write—I was never able to write a decent descriptive line in my life..." (*AT*, 48). He did, however, have an inclination for getting out of Twin Falls. Robert was not about to make that easy. When it came time to leave for the train to Chicago, he took the car, leaving his son to scramble a ride with friends to the station in Shoshone (*AT*, 48). Robin was off, though, and the letters home over the course of the trip and summer program at Northwestern are full of excitement.

A high point of this trip was a visit to Saint Mary's College at Notre Dame to pay respects to Ina Mae's mentor, Sister Mary Madeleva (born Mary Evaline Wolff).[7] In a letter home on 19 June 1943, from the Hotel LaSalle at South Bend, Indiana, Robin tells his mother that he has dined at Saint Mary's with Sister Madeleva and 40 nuns. In *Astonishments*, he remembers the visit vividly. With money that Sophia had given him for the trip, he had bought two dozen roses for the Sister which she then instructed him to offer to the Virgin because the Holy Cross nuns may not accept gifts. Such austerity, however, did not extend to church property, and Blaser found himself handsomely accommodated. "Notre Dame is a dream world," he writes (Blaser to family, 19 June 1943); remembering it later in *Astonishments*, he says that it was "elegant beyond belief ... with Persian rugs and old paintings and, you know, the whole rich Catholic trip..." (*AT*, 42). At dinner, the Sisters had prepared a separate table for him because their order precluded dining with men (*AT*, 42). Each of the 40, however, asked him a question over dinner about his life and vocation. They were interested, Blaser says, in whether he would join the priesthood. The visit concluded with mass at Notre Dame in the morning and then a return to Chicago for school. "Oh, folks, it's grand!" he writes. "I'm having a hilarious time and I haven't been spending wildly" (Blaser to family, 19 June 1943). Given the roses, the spending bit may not have been true, but the elegance of Saint Mary's struck deeply. This was the kind of world that had drawn Blaser, ironically, into DeMolay with its robes and crowns.

In contrast, Northwestern's journalism program must have seemed rather prosaic. In 1943, the Medill School of Journalism offered two summer sessions for high school graduates and graduate students. The 13th annual program of the Institute ran from 22 June to 17 July 1943. It included a preview of university training in journalism, contact with professionals, lectures and laboratory exercises in news reporting, writing, feature writing, editing, and make-up. Students would write about "plays, dances, beach parties, lectures, major league baseball, and scores of other activities in the Chicago area" (*Northwestern University Bulletin* 1943, 67). They would also take field trips to publishing houses. Thirteen boys and 45 girls were accepted into the program in 1943 (Blaser to family, 22 June 1943). In *Astonishments*, Blaser complains that these students had been lured by scholarships to the campus to be tested rather than taught: "It wasn't really a scholarship at all—we were guinea-pigs, those bastards. ...they tested us for eight hours a day, IQs, I don't know, everything..."

(*AT*, 48–49). The 22 June letter home is a little more measured. Classes started with a four-hour test, Blaser tells the folks. Then on the 5 July, "We have been taking tests of all sorts. They tell me my 'I.Q.' is very high [133 he says in a 10 July letter] and I made the highest score in the Institute on my achievement test" (Blaser to family, 5 July 1943).

Despite the testing, the students were able to make a number of field trips. On 24 June, Blaser sent a postcard from the Museum of Science and Industry. In the 5 July letter, he writes of plans to hear the Chicago Symphony and remarks on a visit to the Lakeside Press that then published *Life*, *Readers Digest*, *Fortune* and *Time*. Another trip on 9 July was to hear speeches by officials from the Office of Price Administration and discussions of AFL-CIO Union officials (American Federation of Labor and Congress of Industrial Organizations). "I didn't agree with everything," he writes primly, "but it was broadening. I reiterate broadening but biased" (Blaser to family, 10 July 1943). There were also visits to the Chicago Art Institute and the Board of Trade. On another occasion, he attended a pacifist meeting whose speaker was being watched by the FBI: "He feels that it is the fault of the older generation that we have a war today. His whole theory is based on kindness. Interesting but too idealistic," he decides (Blaser to family, 25 June 1943).

Lodging in Holgate House with the 13 male students in the program, Blaser quickly began to assume the leadership role he had taken in high school. The boys elected him House Counselor (Blaser to family, 25 June 1943) and he began to excel in his studies. "The competition here is tremendous," he writes, "because everyone is so smart, but thus far I have gotten along rather well. Today I wrote an editorial and they said it was so good and the narrative style so different that I had to read it to everyone—I get a big thrill when something like that happens" (Blaser to family, 7 July 1943). He also comments on the ethnicities of his fellow students. There was a German girl who was a refugee ("She also has a lovely accent" (Blaser to family, 7 July 1943)), dozens of Jewish students, and a girl from China. His roommate was a Polish Jew. There was one other Catholic boy and several girls who attended church with him on Sunday. On *Astonishments*, however, Blaser is rather less upbeat, discussing the discrimination he and another student faced for being fey.

> They pulled me in with six faculty members and I had no homosexual experience.
> I daydreamed but those had never been spoken to anybody. ("AT" 2, 59)

The other gay boy fared somewhat worse. He was expelled for lying. Apparently, he had written home, claiming honors that he had never received, and his proud parents had published these fictional accomplishments in the local newspaper along with a picture of their son. A copy of this landed on the mail table in the fraternity house at Northwestern and the boy was expelled. "I led a protest," Blaser says.

I was called in and asked, "Do you like girls," and all the trick questions and all of this thing and then the attacks start on my poetry. Well in my mind I had no way of separating what it was that was being attacked other than to destroy the poetry and [I] became very sick and returned and was sent to the College in Idaho. ("AT" 2, 60)

This account of things is abridged. Blaser returned after the summer program and enrolled at the College of Idaho that September. The fusion of homophobia and criticism of the poetry, however, would remain a vivid and transformative memory. Blaser claimed an early facility in poetry:

It was Whitmanic, which means that it's a large, long-running line, which I've only recently been able to use again. It's about the sounds of trees, it's extremely—I even picked up on sexuality in Whitman. What I picked up was the nature and the imagery of being inside all the sounds and so on. (*AT*, 49)

Mrs. Arpan read and critiqued the poems. This would have been Eleanore Holferty Arpan, wife of Floyd G. Arpan, the founder of the high school program at Northwestern and Director of foreign journalism at Northwestern's Medill School of Journalism. Eleanore Arpan ("Holly") was a writer too and she taught journalism in the summers at Northwestern. Although she is not listed as faculty for the courses offered in 1943, her husband was, and she must have played the role of mentor to Blaser. Floyd Arpan was known for his friendly support of students. For her comments on the poetry, however, Mrs. Arpan became something of a bugbear to Blaser:

I was then attacked for this [Whitmanesque poetry] by Mrs. Arpan who told me that I should be a priest and not a poet—that my poetry all moved toward the questions why, when, where, and whither and only priests ask such questions. So as a consequence why in the fuck—she didn't put it that way, but she did put it sort of that way—why didn't I stop writing poetry and go become a priest because it was just no place as poetry. (*AT*, 49)

Mrs. Arpan also pointed out some plagiarism: Blaser had used the phrase "simple separate souls" from Whitman ("AT" 2, 62). His response was to burn the work. For the rest of his life, he would point to this incident as the end of his ease in writing. Blaser did not go to Berkeley as a poet despite his subsequent role there in the literary scene. In fact, he was a late bloomer, remarking in "The Fire" essay that he did not begin to assume the role of poet until he was 30 years old (*Fire*, 9). When the poems did begin to come, quotation would morph into method. "I am still that way," he comments on "Astonishments," "I will just take something. I usually underline them [citations] or something" ("AT" 2, 62). Blaser returns to the subject of Mrs. Arpan several times on the *Tapes*, and she turns up in *The Moth Poem* in uncomplimentary terms as the "wife of a sailor" (*HF*, 67). Floyd Arpan had served in the U.S. Navy as a photographer, on leave between 1943 and 1946 (*Harold Times* 1990, n.p.).

Blaser's response to Mrs. Arpan reveals a combination of fragility and defiance. The Northwestern experience would have been Blaser's first encounter with serious academia and it seems possible, at least, that Mrs. Arpan was merely trying to save a young man some time. Not quite all of the poems were destroyed. Blaser includes this one in a letter home:

Blue shadows and greenish hills made up the scene.
A few noticed perhaps and wondered,
What of the protective screens
Made by the rolling soft, white clouds?

The blues and greens slowly faded
And a hellish machine rolled by.
Now the beauty is gone forever,
Changed to a hole and a dirt pile
Under a smoke-filled sky. (Blaser to family, 5 July 1943)

This distinction between nature and industrial development recalls the sentiments of "The Desert": in the earlier poem, nature is protected from interfering people because they do not see the value of it, but here the "protective screens" roll away, nature's colors recede, and the industrial world comes forward. Read by image as an imaginative landscape, the poem is about the destruction of serenity and beauty after the loss of a protective cover—about a fear of exposure. If people can see the landscape, they will destroy it. The Lost River runs underground until it pours out of a mountain side with force and glory. The link between the trauma over Mrs. Arpan, the untitled poem sent to Ina Mae, and the remarks on the tapes seems to be avoidance of emotional exposure and a corresponding search for refuge. If nature provided such a space in Blaser's youth, the life of the mind would become the go-to at university.

At Caldwell, Blaser took a room at 1910 Hazel Street. It was in a basement and shared with a roommate, but right on campus and complete with "rugs on the floor and a fireplace in the sitting room," Blaser writes to the family (19 September 1943). Blaser had enrolled in Sociology, Freshman Orientation, French, Physical Education (calisthenics and obstacle courses), English Composition, and History. He also kept himself busy with the *Trail Coyote*, the college newspaper, the *Trail* yearbook, and regular piano practice in a room secured through the good offices of the Dean of Men. Part-time work at Alexander's, a clothing store, provided the essential pocket money (40 cents an hour) and perhaps an excuse not to go home: the job, he tells his folks, may require that he work through the fall and winter holidays. As if this were not enough busyness, Blaser tutored French and kept up his social life. His campus nickname, he writes, was Frank Sinatra. In the Caldwell letters, there are signs of withdrawal from the family, although not so definitively that Blaser could not accept home baking: "Could you some one of these days bake some cookies or a potatoe [sic] cake and send it to me. We are always hungry just before we go to bed," he writes (Blaser to family, 28 September 1943). There was also the convenience of sending laundry home, facilitated by the family's railroad connections.

In March of 1944, Blaser received a conciliatory visit from his father. Writing to the folks on 21 March, he says that Dad offered him a cigarette for the first time, took him for dinner, and gave him $20. "Tell him thanks again, will you?" (Blaser to family, 19 March 1944). In *Astonishments*, Blaser remembers his father arriving at the door after delivering sacks of flour, covered in the white powder.

> ...he's at the door of this little room and I won't come home from Caldwell which is 140 miles or something like that from Twin Falls. I won't go home and he comes to the door and asks me to have dinner with him. And when I looked at him, I don't know whether I was slightly ashamed—I know he was—because how do you—Christ, your father covered with flour. And so anyway in the evening, there he is in a suit and I'm offered my first cigarettes and so on. (*AT*, 49–50)

It would take the better part of a lifetime to process the relationship with Robert. On the occasion of his father's death in 1978, Blaser wrote a poem called "Tumble-Weed" for

> the flour-man, powdery, at the door
> becomes finally, a sweat-body of spiritual
> enemies... (*HF*, 200)

Syntactically, this is a difficult poem that makes an uneasy effort to "move speech to its violent / marvelous teeth" in memory of a father who had become a spiritual enemy. Robert was everything Robin was not—macho, homophobic, and, of course, Mormon. And yet. Someone cries out at the end, "'father / of wax'" and kisses the still forehead. The syntax of the poem circumvents the identity of that voice, but the emotional intensity of it surely belongs to a sad son, who by this time knew how to take cover in the pyrotechnics of language.

Caldwell ended for Blaser, he says, with a letter from the Dean of Women to his mother:

> ...she gets ahold of my mother, writes her a letter and says: "Don't leave him here, there's nobody here, he's all by himself." And it's true. All I did was A+, the top in Caldwell, Idaho.... Now I get pulled out of Caldwell and get sent to Berkeley because the Dean of Women told my mother I was too bright and I needed some competition.... I not only run into Jack Spicer and Robert Duncan but I get my ... ass in a sling everyplace. (*AT*, 50)

With Sophia's support—$75 a month from her pension—and the encouragement of old high school friends, Schweickhardt, Jones, and Sweeley who were already there, Blaser was off to Berkeley in the fall of 1944. He had wanted to go to Bowdoin College as a boy because Nathaniel Hawthorne had gone there. Then he favored Black Mountain,[8] but as far as Ina Mae and *Time* magazine were concerned, it was communist and that was that. So Berkeley it was.

NOTES

1. The story of his conception as a five-month child was one that Blaser maintained throughout his life. Mormon records, however, cast some doubt on this account of the birth. In a genealogy included among Blaser's personal papers at Simon Fraser, Special Collections (MsA1a Box 22, Folder 1), his parents' marriage date is given as 1923, which would place his birth two years after the marriage. Was the record adjusted for the sake of respectability, or did Blaser make up a story that he then clearly came to believe? His birth certificate was issued from Denver, Colorado, and his mother's place of residence is listed as Ogden, Utah, Sacred Heart Academy. The same document says that the mother was resident in Denver two months before delivery. This record would seem to favor Blaser's story. If the parents were located in Dempsey, Idaho, why record the mother's address as Sacred Heart, and why go all the way to Denver for the birth?

2. Mormon church birth records show that Augustus Blaser was born on 6 October 1871 at Geneva, Neuchatel, Switzerland (MsA1a Box 31, Folder 1, Blaser fonds).

3. Cold Mountain (now called Hollyhock Retreat Centre) was a personal growth institute with centers on Cortes Island (off the coast of British Columbia) and Granville Island in Vancouver. Through his connections with the therapy community in Vancouver after his move there in 1966, Blaser gave Tarot readings on Cortes (see Chaps. 6 and 7).

4. Idaho's Lost River is part of the landscape of *The Park* (*HF*, 49–50).

5. In *Cups* 2, Blaser writes: "The window washer / returns, / stepping out of his shame. / He was not rich" (*HF*, 32).

6. Ina Johnson, Blaser's great grandmother and Sophia's mother died in 1939, before the family moved.

7. Sister Mary Madeleva Wolff mentored Ina Mae, Blaser's mother, when the latter was resident at the Sacred Heart Academy. Then the Sister moved to Saint Mary's at Notre Dame University where she founded the first graduate school of theology for women: Saint Mary's College School of Sacred Theology. A Chaucer scholar, she was also an accomplished poet.

8. Black Mountain College was founded by John A. Rice. It was a small, experimental institution, based on democratic governance and the idea that the study of the arts was essential to education. Black Mountain attracted a stunning array of influential artists, writers, dancers, and musicians over the course of its institutional life (1933–1957), including Charles Olson, a poet who would later become a major influence on Blaser. Olson joined the faculty in 1948 and served as Rector from 1951 to 1956.

CHAPTER 3

Berkeley

LEAVING NORMAL

My astonishment was absolutely complete. He astonished me completely. He wanted to astonish me. One of the first stories that I remember that he told me was that he liked to stand at the corner of Hollywood and Vine—and it wasn't specifically a queer story—but he liked to stop girls and ask them if their cunts tasted like oranges. Now that is a literal quote. And I would just be—when I was in Idaho we never asked what cunts tasted like. (Blaser on Spicer (*AT*, 57))

Blaser remembers his arrival at Berkeley as a sensory and intellectual explosion. He came by bus, dropped off at the bottom of University Avenue, where Frances Schweickhardt and Tom Jones were waiting to take him to the Durant Hotel, "my dear grandmother paying for all this stuff out of her pension," he recalls (*AT*, 53). That first evening, Schweickhardt and Jones took their friend to a performance of Euripides's *Trojan Women* at the Greek Theatre, an amphitheater operated by the University. After the play, they introduced him to Rosario Jiménez, later to become his Greek tutor and the one who would steer the habitués of Robert Duncan's reading circle through Lorca. At her "funny little cottage" (*AT*, 53), Rosario retold Oliver Onion's ghost thriller, "The Beckoning Fair One." Jiménez, it turned out, was a *wiederstudentin* (*AT*, 53), a mature student who simply continued to take courses for intellectual pleasure. She belonged to a current of student life at Berkeley that was not about quick graduation into a career, but about imagination and intellectual discovery.

Blaser quickly joined the social circle of his Twin Falls friends. This included Gene Wahl, a musician, a beauty, and Blaser's first real lover:

Now Big Gene—I get involved with Big Gene,[1] and that's a lousy scene. Big Gene was so beautiful when he walked down the street with me people would stop and comment. I don't think I've ever seen anybody quite like him. But Big

© The Author(s) 2019
M. Nichols, *A Literary Biography of Robin Blaser*,
Modern and Contemporary Poetry and Poetics,
https://doi.org/10.1007/978-3-030-18327-1_3

Gene really didn't know how to manage it and neither did I—like it was a disaster. Three years later he's phoning me up saying, "I know how now," and I'm saying, "It's too late," and it was too late by that time. (*AT*, 54–55)

Wahl wanted to be a composer, but he was a little deaf: "he was always trying to hear this [tuning] fork and we would travel on the F-train to San Francisco hitting his fucking fork and then he would be going 'ahhhhhh' trying to get the right key" (*AT*, 55). Hitting the right note was not so easy for Blaser, either. Although his childhood crush on Cleo Adams had never been acted out physically, Blaser attributed in hindsight his periodic "breakdowns" through adolescence to a developing sexuality. At Berkeley, he was finally free to explore these feelings. "I went to San Francisco because I wanted to find my sexual form," he says on the "Tapes" ("AT" 3, 22). But there was no gay boy's manual for such adventures. The bumbled sexual relation with Gene Wahl was exacerbated by bouts of gonorrhea (*AT*, 55). Again, on the *Tapes*, "…I kept getting clap and that meant to me that there was something wrong. Like I mean I had a very funny sense that somehow the sexuality was diseased, because it just became a disaster, I mean just an utter disaster and I gave up for quite a while" (*AT*, 55).

Meanwhile, Blaser settled into Berkeley life with a room on Channing Way. It had a fireplace, a lemon tree, and a piano (*AT*, 53) and it took $40 of the $75 stipend that Grandmother Sophia sent each month from her pension. This meant stealing food and saving the rest for trips to the opera and items of desire (*AT*, 55). At the university, there were classes in French, German, Music, Zoology, English, and Philosophy. Very quickly, however, Blaser plunged into off-campus activities. In that first academic year, 1944–1945, he knew nothing of the poets Jack Spicer and Robert Duncan who would later become so important. Poetry, in fact, was not Blaser's first focus after the disappointment of Northwestern. Instead, he turned to performance where he had had successes in high school and at Caldwell.

> …I belong to a ballet group and I'm a classical ballet dancer and we put on—you can read reviews of it, it was terrific. We did it to Rachmaninoff's *Isle of the Dead* … it was all modern except for this girl and me who had classical training. So we're the dead with white faces…. I did the makeup and it took hours… (*AT*, 54)

The ballet was acted in a cemetery scheduled for demolition as part of an ongoing effort by the Board of Supervisors in San Francisco to move cemeteries outside the city limits.[2] It was a first "'happening' of landscape dance," Blaser says ("AT" 4, 12). In addition to dance, Blaser took part in an occultist group that held séances in the Greek Theatre (*AT*, 54).

Although Blaser is not exact about the chain of events, he moved to a student co-operative residence ("AT" 4, 13–14), unhappily so: "I couldn't eat in the dining room because there weren't enough chairs for everybody," he says on the "Tapes"; "you had to fight and I didn't know how to do that" ("AT" 4, 14). Blaser credits Gene Wahl for getting him out of the co-op but it was Jim

Felts who offered a real alternative. Sometime between 1944 and the summer of 1945, he met James Martin Felts, with whom he would live until 1964. In his Berkeley stories in *The Astonishment Tapes*, Blaser is curiously silent about Felts, perhaps because Felts did not participate in the poetry scene, but perhaps also from residual reticence about discussing a relationship that was illegal when it began. Berkeley was a haven of permissiveness, comparatively speaking, but in 1945, homosexuality was still a crime punishable by a prison sentence of one to ten years. In 1947, the first sex offender registry was enacted, requiring convicted "perverts" to register as sex offenders (*History of Sodomy Laws*, n.d.). It would take decades to repeal anti-gay laws, and progress would be slow and piecemeal. This kind of hostile climate may suggest why the bohemian underground seemed like a natural and attractive place to be: if you were gay, you lived in the counterculture by default.[3]

Documents which Blaser held show that Jim Felts was a Texan who first entered the University of Texas at Austin in 1940 and later transferred to Berkeley. At Texas, he studied investment math, chemistry, and zoology plus the usual array of token first-year arts courses. He went on to algebra, physics, organic chemistry, zoology, and psychology, later to specialize in biochemistry. What seems to have lasted through the vicissitudes of his relationship with Blaser was an appreciation of gracious living and the benefits of shared finances. In their correspondence over the years, Felts praised Blaser's poetry, but he seems not to have understood it. In a 12 July 1952 letter—after about six years of living with Blaser—he says that he is impressed by a poem Robin has sent but finds the ideas obscure. What can be gleaned from such letters suggests warmth, rather than fiery passion. Blaser could still admire other beauties, as indeed he did when he met fellow Berkeley student and poet Landis Everson. Somewhere between 1945 and 1946, however, the new relationship with Felts occasioned a move to 2520 Ridge Road, which meant better housing with a stable partner.

However slow to recognize gay rights California may have been, Berkeley was alight with countercultural energy in other spheres when Blaser arrived in 1944. Apart from the ballets and séances, there was a literary scene with Kenneth Rexroth, William Everson, Robinson Jeffers (Carmel), and Henry Miller (Big Sur) as presiding spirits. Anarchists, pacifists, artists, and off-the-grid inventors, these writers were bold beyond the politically permissible of their times, particularly in their writings on sexuality and in their anarcho-pacifist resistance to the war. Everson, for example, served at a Civilian Public Service work camp for conscientious objectors during the war, where he founded a fine arts program. Blaser remembers him working as a janitor at the Berkeley library circa 1946 ("AT" 5, 6). Jeffers, famous for his stonemasonry and his preference for non-human nature over humanity, was building Tor House and Hawk Tower on his property in Carmel. Henry Miller did his bit by pushing the boundaries of what it was possible to say publicly about sex. He was not, Blaser recalls, considered suitable for study at the university. Rexroth was the *éminence grise*; he had an established literary reputation, as well as recognition, among conscientious objectors for his pacifist work. With his wife, Marie, he would turn his home into a center for Bay Area pacifists and literary communities with Friday evening soirées (Hamalian 1991, 147). By 1946, he had organized a Libertarian Circle and was holding Wednesday meetings on Steiner Street in San Francisco. The goal was "'to re-found the radical movement after its destruction by the Bolsheviks and to rethink all the basic principles and subject to searching criticism all the ideologists from Marx to Malatesta'" (Hamalian 1991, 149).

Outlets for this energy that Blaser particularly remembers were the important magazines *Circle* and *Horizon*. *Circle* was edited by George Leite, a friend of Henry Miller's, and co-published with Bern Porter. Porter was a renaissance man, an artist-writer-philosopher-scientist-visual artist and avant garde publisher who had turned from his work as a scientist on the Manhattan Project to the arts. Bern Porter Books risked the publication of Henry Miller. Between 1944 and 1948, Leite and Porter also produced *Circle* from 2252 Telegraph Avenue, just off campus. It was an experimental journal of the arts with an antiwar, anarchist, civil libertarian bent and surrealist leanings. The first issue in 1944 included poems by the young Berkeley surrealist Philip Lamantia and Josephine Miles, the first female full professor at Berkeley and soon-to-be mentor of Blaser, Spicer, and Duncan. Lawrence Hart also appeared in this issue and he was the leader of a group of young writers who called themselves Activists. In *Circle* 6, Hart published an essay explaining some of the principles of his group. They were opposed, he says, to the rationalist criticism of Yvor Winters and they championed a poetry of associative pattern and emotional logic—the kind of poetry Hart called *active* (Hart 1945, 6). The point was to control "emotional pattern ... through a surface of sensory images" (Hart 1945, 7). The Activists rebelled against decontextualized rationalism; it had, after all, helped bring the Manhattan Project into the world.

Blaser repeatedly argues on the *Tapes* and in his published essays for a view of modernism that comes from the idea that the world wars finalized a collapse of western traditions deriving from a Greco-Roman, Judeo-Christian lineage. This collapse then meant that basic relationships such as that between the individual and society, the human and non-human had to be reconstructed, and it assumed that such basic relationships *could* be reconstructed. As Duncan's friend psychiatrist Hilde Burton put it, in postwar Berkeley, anything seemed possible (Burton interview, 30 December 2008). In the 1940s, the real action in Berkeley, whatever the shenanigans in cemeteries, was taking place in the working-through of an intellectual position—a view of truth, justice, and history, and of poetry's role in it all. *Circle* was a serious event in this story. In *Circle* 9, Ernst Kaiser published an article titled "The Development from Surrealism," in which he introduces surrealism as a movement that turned toward the "problematik of the human psyche ... what is exploited by psychology as well by art" (Kaiser 1946, 74). Kaiser says that art cannot base itself on a science that is itself still experimental, but it can go back to the sources of psychoanalysis: the human faculties themselves. And the reason for such self-examination is a collapse of tradition. The political breakdown manifest in the two world wars, Kaiser says, is a symptom of a "general breakdown" in western culture.

> In such an era of frustration and collapse, when so many connections have broken down, and not only under aerial bombardment, there is no hope in trying to have an art that is rational and based on solid facts. Solid facts are a luxury that even natural science cannot afford any longer. We are in a world that has lost internal balance, where there is no intellectual or spiritual focus, and hence no possibility for the artist to apply such terms as good or evil.... (Kaiser 1946, 75)

Kaiser asks the question of the purpose of art in this historical context and turns to the investigation of "fundamental complexes" in the psyche, an investigation that surrealism had already launched. "The greater the artist," Kaiser writes, "the more he is able to penetrate to the real depths of what is commonly hidden in the human soul and to give it universality...." (77). The common and the universal are still the desired perspectives, only this time through psychology rather than science or religion.

Whether or not Blaser read and adopted Kaiser's article, the essay catches both the feeling of collapse and the opening of opportunity that would characterize Berkeley energy for Blaser and become foundational to his thinking as a poet. The psychoanalytical response to war and all that came of it was a much bleaker view of human capacity than the older humanist one that saw the atrocities of the war as exceptional rather than chronic to the species. This psychoanalytical human subject was already under the attention of Rexroth, Miller, and Jeffers in their explorations of sexuality. When Blaser arrived at Berkeley, he thought he was leaving the "normal" of small town Idaho, but the questioning of "normal" at Berkeley was much more radical. "And if we are really artists," Kaiser writes, "then we must know that the disillusionment of Western man has become a fact: that there is hardly any real belief left, except the belief in holding on to what we have, if indeed there is anything left to hold on to" (Kaiser 1946, 74–75).

Alongside *Circle* in importance, Blaser places *Horizon*, a magazine published by Cyril Connolly from 6 Selwyn House, Lansdown Terrace, W.C., London (*AT*, 76). Founded in 1940 by Connolly and financial backer and art editor Peter Watson, *Horizon's* stunning list of contributors included W.H. Auden, Paul Bowles, T.S. Eliot, William Empson, Ian Fleming, Graham Greene, Christopher Isherwood, Randall Jarrell, Paul Klee, Arthur Koestler, André Masson, Henry Miller, Henry Moore, Edouard Roditi, Bertrand Russell, Stephen Spender, Wallace Stevens, Dylan Thomas, Eudora Welty, and Virginia Woolf, to name only some of the best known. On the *Tapes*, Blaser says that he first heard of the Marquis de Sade in *Horizon*, a lesson in human capacity if ever there was one (*AT*, 76). Like *Circle*, *Horizon* was socially progressive but not necessarily anarchist, socialist, or psychoanalytical in bent. For example, an article by Mervyn Stockwood, Vicar of St. Matthew's in Bristol, titled "The

Church and Reconstruction," makes a case for Red Tory Christianity. Stockwood writes that, "It is, of course, true that economics condition a man's character, that it is difficult for a victim of the capitalist system brought up in a poverty-stricken home, slung out on the unemployment heap and compelled to fritter away his existence in a state of enforced and embittered futility, to practice the qualities of unselfishness, patience, honesty and courtesy; but it has to be recognized that these qualities cannot be acquired through economics alone" (Stockwood 1942, 150–51). Stockwood lays out his social goals in five points:

1. Extreme inequality in wealth and possessions to be abolished.
2. Every child to have equal opportunities of education.
3. The family as a social unit to be safeguarded.
4. The sense of Divine vocation to be restored to man's daily work.
5. The resources of the earth to be used as God's gifts to the whole human race, for the needs of present and future generations. (155)

This agenda implies nothing less than the abolition of the capitalist system, the overhaul of education, and distributive justice—social measures to be built upon the pagan virtues and Christian values. Stockwood presents a best-case scenario for reviving a social Christianity. Such an agenda seems even more radical in the twenty-first century than it did in the 1940s, and even further out of reach. Ironically, Stockwood's article sits alongside Franz Kafka's "In the Penal Colony" in this issue of *Horizon*.

Stockwood's article, compared to the anarcho-pacifism of a Rexroth or the surrealist investigation into the psyche, suggests agreement on the existence of a social-existential crisis and a search for solutions, whether these would consist of charting new forms of subjectivity and new kinds of sociality or reviving and radicalizing the most progressive traditions of Christian humanism. *Circle* and *Horizon* expressed a perception among intellectuals of a historical moment of truth that Blaser had begun to experience very personally. There had been Mrs. Arpan at Northwestern and her challenge to his Whitmanesque poetry; now his entire Catholic world view would come under fire from the philosophy and arts of the twentieth century. On the "Tapes":

> I lost my sense of ground, anyway, in the language.... I simply no longer knew what it should be and found enormous dissatisfaction in it. ("AT" 5, 8–9)

How not to end up in nihilism or cynicism? More immediately, how not to despair when one's sexuality was held to be both diseased and illegal? ("AT" 3, 10). Blaser did not go home in the summer after that first 1944–1945 academic year, and in fact visited the folks very infrequently. He had made an escape and there was no turning back to the world of small town stage plays and Li'l Abner dances. Instead, he took three summer courses in 1945, one in music and two in English. Then he met Jack Spicer.

THE BERKELEY VORTEX

The Berkeley Renaissance has been narrated in a number of biographies and studies: there is Michael Davidson's *The San Francisco Renaissance*; Linda Hamalian's *A Life of Kenneth Rexroth*; Lewis Ellingham and Kevin Killian's biography of Spicer, *Poet, Be Like God*; Ekbert Faas's *The Young Robert Duncan*; and Lisa Jarnot's Duncan biography, *Ambassador from Venus*. In these accounts, Robert Duncan is the senior "master of rime" for his generation (as opposed to Rexroth's) and the impresario of the off-campus poetry scene. Blaser, however, experienced Berkeley as an apprentice, rather than a boss poet. The big events for him, as he narrates Berkeley on *The Astonishment Tapes*, were meeting Jack Spicer and Robert Duncan, and studying with Ernst Kantorowicz. As reticent as he was about Jim Felts, Blaser was loquacious about Spicer and very fond of repeating the story of their first meeting.

Unbeknownst to Blaser, Gene Wahl had a friend in Los Angeles with whom he had attended the University of Redlands. When Wahl moved to Berkeley, he encouraged Jack Spicer to do the same (Ellingham and Killian 1998, 8). Wahl had gone to Los Angeles during the summer of 1945 and directed his friend to Jim and Robin's house.

> ...it's either late-August or early-September '45 when the doorbell rings, 2520 Ridge Road, and I open the door and there is a mysterious man with a mustache, dark glasses, a trench coat, sandals, his feet painted purple for some incredible reason—it turned out later that it was purple gentian for athlete's foot—and an umbrella, and it's Jack Spicer. He so horrified me in the shadow of that hallway that I slammed the door in his face. (*AT*, 56)

Spicer had somehow landed a part-time job as a detective, checking on bartenders for knocking down drinks. The bizarre get-up was his idea of how a detective should look. It was Spicer's laughter, Blaser says, that caused him to re-open the door:

> It's not only joyous laughter but it's somehow cutting. I mean it's somehow— he's not only amused by what he's pulled, but he's also laughing at me and I couldn't stand it. I opened the door again to find out what was happening and it was Jack.... Now Big Gene had brought Jack back from Los Angeles and Jack was there, and that was it.... (*AT*, 56)

Jack "diddled" everyone's life, Blaser says, meaning that Spicer created a kind of social commotion around himself (*AT*, 56). He told outrageous stories, he read Spinoza in English and pretended to read him in Latin, he studied Buddhism, and he practiced the lotus pose, a position he could still assume years later even when he was ill with drink. He also liked to needle his friends.

Blaser and Felts invited Spicer to stay with them and he moved in for about six months. Immediately, he began to interfere with the relationship, accusing Blaser of not properly appreciating Felts's cooking (*AT*, 60–61). He then proposed to do the cooking himself, creating disasters in the kitchen. "[T]hree years later," Blaser says, "I was cleaning the spaghetti sauce off the ceiling" (*AT*, 61). Spicer would take an egg beater to it and splatter the entire kitchen, leaving the mess. Fed up with the antics, Blaser kicked him out and the two did not speak for several months (*AT*, 61). Spicer was the first to make peace, knocking on the door with three poems by Robert Duncan. Spicer had met Duncan at one of Rexroth's Wednesday night anarchist meetings. His gift of the poems brought Blaser, Spicer, and Duncan together, a meeting that Blaser would later describe as "fateful" (*Fire*, 161). In "The Practice of Outside," his essay on Spicer's *Collected Books*, Blaser notes that Spicer sometimes gave his birth year as 1946 when they all met (*Fire*, 161).

The Duncan poems Spicer had in hand, now published in *The Years as Catches*, were "Among My Friends, Love is a Great Sorrow," "An Elegiac Fragment," and "A Woman's Drunken Lament" (*AT*, 61). These poems, along with "I am a Most Fleshly Man," and "Heavenly City, Earthly City" from the same Berkeley period, turn on emotional precision, sexual exploration, and a faith in the form-giving powers of poetry to connect the individual with a company of poets to be found in the common ground of the language. In politics, Duncan was anarcho-pacifist; in poetry, he looked to reinvent community. Poetry with a capital "P," as he wrote it, was a virtual collective of all writers and artists, past and present, as they had been preserved in language or visual forms. In Poetry—the "*grand collage*" (Duncan 1968, vii)—he would "[search] out there a vision of the individual freedom and the communal commitment of man" (Duncan 1966, vii–viii).

Blaser's response to the Duncan poems was "*unbelievable* excitement" (*AT*, 62). "Finally," he says, "there was a poet that one knew. Both Jack and I suffered from disbelief in our own poetry from the beginning, at the root. Jack had a kind of assurance and bravado, but neither of us knew. And Duncan is just sheer genius. He knows, he's sure..." (*AT*, 62). After meeting Spicer and Duncan, Blaser began to drop in on the literary circles they created. A leader in poetry, Duncan also commanded the scene around the campus. Ellingham and Killian date the "Berkeley Renaissance" from the fall of 1946. This was the period when Duncan began to hold his soirées at Throckmorton Manor, a rundown boarding house on Telegraph Avenue (Ellingham and Killian 1998, 14), and it was here that Blaser had a first real encounter with the moderns, one that would destroy his faith in the transparency of language and challenge his Catholicism. At Throckmorton, the readings ranged from Joyce and Pound to Lorca, Ibsen, and Stein. Pound's *Cantos* were certainly a challenge, but in *Finnegans Wake*, Joyce got inside the Catholic world and broke it down.

In the *Tapes*, Blaser tells the story of an Easter Sunday to illustrate the impact of his initiation into modernism. It was 1947 and Blaser was in a café eating strawberry sundaes with Duncan and Leonard Wolf, a poet and graduate student on the GI Bill. Wolf leaned forward with a strawberry on his spoon, saying that the red berries were the wounds of Christ. Duncan made loud slurping noises. Blaser's response to their blasphemous banter was to run out to the street in tears. "I've not yet faced what was going to be the ultimate challenge, and that was Joyce," he says (*AT*, 171).

The Throckmorton sessions meant a new circle of literary friends. Tom Parkinson, a young poet-professor at Berkeley and mentor to student poets offered readings of Yeats; Rosario Jiménez helped the group through Lorca because she had the Spanish; and everyone contributed to the reading of Pound's *Cantos*. In this same period, 1946–1947, Spicer introduced Duncan to friends at 2029 Hearst Street, the home of a young couple, Hugh and Janie O'Neill. Hearst Street quickly became another meeting place for the literary crowd. Wolf was a member of the group and his poems, *Hamadryad Hunted*, were published by Bern Porter in 1946. The round table at the O'Neills, evocative of Camelot, was a place to plot daring acts of sex and poetry, or magic as Spicer would call it. Here, Duncan would compose the first poems of *Medieval Scenes*, later published by Centaur Press in 1950. These were composed successively over several evenings, in company with the Hearst Street habitués.

What, then, was Blaser's role in all this? In an interview with Colin Sanders in 1980, Duncan makes a point of saying that Blaser was not in the Hearst Street group: he was "a person that you read poems to or something and came to visit at times" (Duncan 2012, 75). A few years later, when Spicer was teaching in Minneapolis, Blaser contemplated writing a "Lives of the Poets" that would sort it all out. In a letter to Spicer dated 23 October 1950, Blaser refers to a discussion with Duncan and a question Duncan had posed for him: "'Who in Berkeley understands what Jack and Duncan were doing with the Berkeley myth?'" Blaser responds:

I agree with Duncan that there are categories of believers, understanders, understander-believers, and so on. And among the understander-believers, I think he's right to place Jo Fredman (irritatingly?) and me. Much as it bothers me to admit it one of the real problems in my brand of Catholicism has been the clash between that Catholicism and the belief in the world of my friends. Perhaps the reason I haven't utterly broken under the strain (I think I can call it that) is that my connection with that myth has been entirely in the realm of poetry. What I know of 2029 begins and ends in your poems and those of Duncan—with the added pleasure of a little careful listening. Gossip, if you want to call it that.

As an "understander-believer," Blaser took Berkeley to be an imaginative landscape:

The whole thing worked in two ways; the world of poetry had to reshape an alien landscape for its own purposes: Berkeley, then, became the foundation of that complex, the Berkeley myth. The people, then, had to fit the landscape. And to effect that little trick, [Wallace] Stevens' world of the imagination became more real than the real world, hence the violence of the clashes with the university world—nothing could be more like the stone that Dr. Johnson kicked than the university. (Blaser to Spicer, 23 October 1950)

In this letter, Blaser names *Medieval Scenes* and *The Venice Poem* as the culmination of the Berkeley myth in Duncan's work. *Medieval Scenes* offered an initial performance of the serial poem, a form that Blaser would take up in the early 1960s. *The Venice Poem* was a major statement of Duncan's faith in Poetry, occasioned by the infidelities of Gerald Ackerman with whom Duncan had had an affair. Later to become an art historian, Ackerman was then a student at Berkeley. When the social activist Paul Goodman came to teach in 1949, he "stole" Jerry, to Duncan's great distress. In this poem, Duncan works through elaborate constructions of love and jealousy, ranging in reference from Shakespeare's *Othello* to the *Venus of Lespuges*. He comes out the other end, reborn from the pains of his affair with Ackerman into the creative life of Poetry. Spicer disliked the poem because he thought that it was inauthentic—that poetry could not heal emotional suffering. For Spicer, personal feeling is never quite expressible in language because language is communal and transhistorical. It does not belong to its speakers and it is therefore always already an abstraction of what must be undergone by the individual. The community of Poetry for Spicer was no compensation for "all the things in nature that must fall" (Spicer 1980, 9). If Duncan was going to come out of *The Venice Poem* as the "little cross-eyed king" of his own poetic universe, Spicer would play the bad fairy at the coronation. In the letter cited above, Blaser remarks that Spicer might prefer Alcibiades to Plato, a beautiful young man to poetic Platonizing.

Spicer responded to this letter with his own kind of myth-making.

> Just as I passively created the myth at 2029 by acting as critic to Duncan's magic making, so you created the Landis myth at the later period by acting as critic of our feeble attempts at magic.
>
> Just as The Arcadia for D.B. [Dick Brown] (which you confuse with Duncan's Ode in your last letter) was a criticism of the magic, so were your three poems to God and Landis. Now it is time for you to make magic while someone else criticises [sic]—if your religion and dignity can stand this somewhat unpleasant task.
>
> …
>
> Consider the pattern of the grand myth for a minute. 2 stages. 2029—Father Duncan wants Hugh but can't have him. Son Jack wants Hugh, is wanted by Hugh, but doesn't take him. McKinley—Granfatter [sic] Duncan has the patriarchal right of first night (droit [de] seigneur), Father Jack wants L.E. but can't have him.… Son Robin wants and is wanted by L.E. but doesn't take him.
>
> Next act? The pattern demands that you play the Father (the Fool in the Tarots), I play the Grandpa (the Emperor), and some new person receive the succession by being the Son (the Hanged Man). (Spicer to Blaser, "The sequence of your letters")

L.E., in this instance, is Landis Everson. The letter gives Spicer's view of the relative distances in poetry that Spicer, Blaser, and Duncan had covered in the 1946–1948 period: Duncan was the senior, Blaser the junior, and Spicer had the middle. It also brings forward the potent mixture of sexual adventure, *mythopoiesis*, and critical battle that made Throckmorton and 2029 Hearst so compelling, and it shows how seriously these young poets took themselves.

Duncan outlines his view of the Berkeley myth in a letter to Spicer that has now been published in the back matter of Blaser's edition of Spicer's *Collected Books* (Duncan to Spicer [1975] 1980, 362–63). There, he draws attention to Berkeley professor Ernst Kantorowicz's role in his thinking, particularly the sense of history that Kantorowicz encouraged: "The poem is above all things an attempt to picture, to imagine—how gods, demons, lovers, and companions are inter-related in history; my history expanded to include the Middle-Ages" (Duncan, 362). His second point is that the lived experiences of Hearst Street were "subject to the design of the poem, REVEALD in terms of the necessities of the forces of the poem" (362). In a further comment, Duncan turns to his interpretation of the sex-and-poetry relations of the 2029 experience: "But we were all sex-stupid," he says: "that is we did not know how to make sexual love to each other. It takes intellect, imagination, to do it and our concepts were tar-baby primitive compared with the erotic concepts of anybody with any kind of know-how" (363).

This section of the letter is more than a turn from poetics to personal matters. Knowing how to love, beyond personal desires, would take on weight in the context of Ernst Kantorowicz's meditations on Dante, the great poet of cosmic love. As important as teacher–mentors such as Tom Parkinson and Josephine Miles were, it was Ernst Kantorowicz who stole the show and left a lasting imprint on all three poets. Over the 1946–1947 academic year, Blaser took courses in History, Physics, Classics, Latin, and English and he wrote poems for Josephine Miles's English class. However, by far the most vivid in-class experiences of Blaser's undergraduate years were the courses he took with Ernst Kantorowicz. After Spicer and Duncan, this was the second big astonishment.

First to hit was the charisma. A German Jewish war immigrant, Kantorowicz was elegant, haughty, erudite, and irresistibly perfumed with scandal. Did Göring himself really spirit the great scholar out of Germany as the rumor mill had it? (*AT*, 82). It was certain, at least, that he had studied with Friedrich Gundolf, the historian and *Georgkreis* habitué. Stefan George, a powerfully mesmerizing German poet and aesthete of the inter-war period, had assembled around himself a circle of gay intellectuals focused on the study of history and aesthetics. Spicer was fascinated that George had made up a language of his own (*AT*, 82); later he (Spicer) would do the same with "Martian." The *Georgkreis* also offered precedent for and affirmation of Throckmorton and 2029 Hearst Street, frequented, as they were, by the young, the gay, the beautiful, and the precocious. Blaser describes Kantorowicz's lectures on the *Tapes*:

His English was superb and he spoke in a heavily accented, highly intonated language so that you could become somewhat mesmerized as he would go "ooooh," up and down with his voice, and these words and the stories, so delicious and crazy and marvelous, and everything was just going on. (*AT*, 80)

Jack found him, Blaser says, and then all three attended his classes (*AT*, 77). There was the course on Byzantine culture where Kantorowicz "would go through whole lectures on the shape of the churches: Why is a Byzantine church different from the Roman churches? ... And then we would find out, of course, the West is full of hierarchy so that you go up through to the heavenly, whereas in the Eastern church, you've got a revelatory form" (*AT*, 78). Then there was a Renaissance course and one on the constitutional history of England, the latter designed for lawyers, Blaser recalls, who had no idea what hit them.

Blaser credits Kantorowicz with insights that would be crucial to his intellectual life and the development of his poetics. First, he says, Kantorowicz offered a view of history as process: "[a]n intellectual landscape, a history that isn't simply a system of names, but a process" (*AT*, 82). Before he began to absorb Pound or read Charles Olson, Blaser had a "special view of history" from Kantorowicz. He distinguishes this view from that of the "modern sociological historian ... who wants simply to give the patterns of social forms, where he's lost the content" (*AT*, 85). The content had to be the particularity of persons acting in carefully delineated historical contexts. Olson's "special view" was that individuals acted within, and were acted upon, by a complex world, full of limitations and yet equally rich in opportunities for agency. The individual is situated, in other words, within a moving field of acts and qualities and this field has to become visible in the poetry: hence the famous descriptor of projective poetics as "composition by field." For Blaser, Kantorowicz and Kantorowicz's teacher Friedrich Gundolf in the latter's *Mantle of Caesar*, led the way with their historians' approach to the embeddedness of the subject in a geo-historical context. For Blaser, this would open up a lifelong meditation, later to become a key element in his work, on the nature of a shareable, public world:

> Anyway, the public world, the struggle for it, was one of the big issues and it was only available if one had a sense of the way history worked and where one was in it. As a consequence then, you could then have memory that was alive rather than something which was dead. You could also have a future because you knew what way you were moving forward into the future with these materials, and this was the way in which we were able to read Pound. (*AT*, 86)

Another way of describing this "special view" might be to say that the historical world and the individual continually reverse into each other: the real is the play between them.

A second insight that Blaser attributes to Kantorowicz is that "poetry is noetic" (*AT*, 81). "We were listening to English professors talk about the bullshit of feeling," he says, "...when suddenly I had a man who knew that the poetry was noetic, that its task is knowledge, that it is always the recentering of the origin of the world, that it is always the beginning again and the dwelling of the nature of the world, of man and the world" (*AT*, 81). "[R]ecentering the origin of the world" may not count as knowledge from a technological or scientific perspective. It does, however, count for meaning in the world of lived experience. If the poet can articulate the orders and relationships that compose the real at a given moment, he or she can show how things stand with us humans—or to use Olson's phrase, what it means now to be in "the human universe." The "bullshit of feeling" that Blaser disparages in the above passage is that of the detached individual: *my* feelings, *my* sensations without the context that gives to personal feeling its necessary sitedness and therefore its shareability as a unique perspective on a common condition—a view-from-here. On the *Tapes*, Blaser says that from Kantorowicz he took the idea that "we are visibilities of a vast action and as a consequence you began reading almost everything dramatically because you saw all the men and all the events as visibilities of vast actions" (*AT*, 84). Years later, in "Image-Nation 9 (half and half," he would write of "that action / we are images of" (*HF*, 167). The idea goes back to the *Poetics*, where Aristotle says that poetry is an imitation of an action, but it was dramatically refurbished for Blaser in Kantorowicz's lectures.

One course that resonated long with Blaser was Kantorowicz's class on Dante. In the late 1940s, Kantorowicz was lecturing on the material that he would later publish as *The King's Two Bodies*, a study in medieval political theology that explores the office of kingship as distinguished from the historical persons who fill the role. The final chapter of this book focuses on Dante. Here was a connection for Blaser that went back to childhood memories of looking at Gustave Doré's fascinating illustrations of the *Inferno* and in terms that spoke to his youthful Catholicism. Kantorowicz's scholarly Dante was a way to rethink religious feeling in a world where religion had lost much of its authority. The *Commedia* was, after all, the great Catholic world poem. In his chapter titled "Man-Centered Kingship," Kantorowicz suggests that Dante secularized the Christian corporate body. The Church was understood to be unified as one body under Christ; Dante, however, extended this corporate structure to the human species. The species has the innate *capacity* to build the terrestrial paradise, if not the *will* to do it. There is precedent here for Duncan's "grand collage" and precedent as well for Blaser's view of *poiesis* as world image: if the human task on earth is to construct the terrestrial paradise, it is that of the poet to imagine it. "In the mind indestructible," Pound had written in 1945, from a cage in Pisa (Pound 1993, 450). As Duncan interpreted it, however, the human collective requires *all* of its members to actualize the potential of the species for hell, purgatory, and heaven here on earth, including the wicked, the trivial, and the silly. Hence Duncan's defense of low and high art in the *H.D. Book* and his inclusion of Sally Rand, a burlesque dancer, alongside high modernists like H.D. and canonical writers like Hawthorne (Duncan 2011, 445–46). Duncan's "grand collage," as yet unconceived in the Berkeley days, would become a postmodern response to the exclusions of modernism. The problem Blaser and his friends faced right then in the 1940s, however, was how to take the vision of collective humanity away from both Church and State: the former had collapsed under philosophical skepticism; the latter had just played out as fascism in Europe and it would unfold as social conservatism in the U.S.

Kantorowicz's lectures on Dante fed into the sense around Berkeley that the world had to be reimagined, an unexpected reinforcement from medieval studies of ideas circulating in journals like *Circle* and *Horizon*. The isolate ego somehow had to be reconnected to a larger collective in a way that dodged the obvious problems of first-generation modernism and made a meaningful life possible again. Throughout his writing life, Blaser repeatedly claimed that the postmodern was a corrective to the missteps of modernism. The project then, of searching out an image of the world as alive for the twentieth century as Dante's was for the thirteenth, was a task that each of the Berkeley three would perform differently. What they shared, however, was the enormity of the project and a fascination with the creative powers of language.

THE WRITERS' CONFERENCE

For a brief period between 1947 and 1949, the Berkeley English Department responded to student interest in creative writing by sponsoring a series of workshops and readings called the Writers' Conference. The Conference was staffed by talented students and supported by faculty (Ellingham and Killian 1998, 17). Leonard Wolf taught a section, as did faculty members Mark Schorer, Josephine Miles, and Tom Parkinson (*AT*, 204). The memorable readers for Blaser were Duncan, Spicer, and Landis Everson. Everson had transferred to Berkeley from the University of Redlands in 1947 and studied with Josephine Miles, as did Blaser and Spicer. After meeting George Haimsohn in her class, Everson moved into a house on McKinley Street, where Haimsohn, Spicer, and Duncan were living at the time. Duncan, Blaser, and Spicer all had crushes on him at various times although Landis remained charmingly unaware of his powers of attraction and diffident about his poems (Everson 2004, n.p.). A surviving program for the Spring Poetry Festival, 13 May 1949, sponsored by the Conference, features Duncan, Spicer, Wolf, Tom Parkinson, William Everson, and Richard Moore. A student of Miles and a presence at Rexroth's anarchist meetings, Moore was a poet and founder of KPFA radio in 1949, a station that featured a program on folk ballads on which Spicer would guest star (Herndon to Blaser [1975] 1980, 375). Duncan's poems for the Festival included "King Haydn of Miami Beach," and "An African Elegy." Spicer read his first three *Imaginary Elegies*, as well as "Orpheus' Song to Apollo," a poem that, at the time, he directed at Everson, dismissing him as a naif in the voice of a scornful Orpheus. "I felt used for the sake of theatre," Everson would say later in a conversation with Kevin Killian (Everson 2004, n.p.). Blaser does not appear on the program but he remembers events around the Writers' Conference as important to him. "The point in moving through this aspect of things," he says on the *Tapes*, "is that we did have a centering" (*AT*, 204).

The Conference was disbanded by English faculty in a quarrel over a proposed student literary magazine to be called *Literary Behavior*. As Ellingham and Killian tell the story, the problem was a pornographic piece submitted by a student whose name has been lost. Faculty sponsors would not countenance it, and at a student–faculty meeting over the dispute, the incivility on both sides led to departmental withdrawal of support (Ellingham and Killian 1998, 25). This incident occasioned satires from both Duncan and Spicer over student–faculty relations. For Erika Braun's Halloween party in 1948, Duncan wrote *A Poet's Masque*. It was a big party, Blaser remembers in the *Tapes*, and everybody from the literary scene was there, including young faculty like Mark Schorer.

> And then Jack arrives, because Jack had been given a part in Duncan's masque and Jack gets to read the part of the muse herself, so Jack arrives looking very pink, and he has on a very tight swimming suit. It wasn't bikini in those days, but it was extremely tight, and that's all. He arrived at my house and something had to be done.... It wasn't quite adequate for the muse, but anyway I got a lamp-shade which fit his head perfectly and got out a crystal bangle of some kind off something, it must have been a chandelier in the apartment, and hung that by string down on his forehead and then we walked all across campus, through the library with Jack as Venus the muse herself. (*AT*, 212)

This *Masque* and Spicer's *Dunkiad* (Spicer [1975] 1980, 368–73) are both cheeky pieces, but they also reveal a poetics in process and bear witness to the anti-academicism of the Berkeley poets. In the *Tapes*, Blaser spends consider-able time discussing the two satires along with *The Venice Poem* and Spicer's "Apocalypse for Three Voices" (Spicer 1980, 10–12)—all formative poems for him.

So what was Blaser writing at this time? In "The Fire" essay of 1966, a first major statement of poetics, he says that "In San Francisco, I was tied to two other poets who, it was my superstition, wrote my poems for me" (*Fire*, 9). However, neither Spicer nor Duncan could have written "Song in Four Parts for Christ the Son," a poem which first appeared in the *Occident*, the student newspaper, and is now republished in *The Holy Forest* as part of "Lake of Souls" (231–33). Blaser dated the poem variously from 1947 to 1949. "Song" turns on the idea that Christ is at once a man who dies and the "God Forever." The repeated line in the chorus is "Christ in heaven, dance with me":

> Out of the sun
> He may come
> To dance again.
>
> I shall see the rose in the tree.
> Christ, in heaven, dance with me. (*HF*, 232)

"Song" certainly draws on Blaser's Catholic adolescence, but in retrospect it looks like a first step toward later meditations on one of the big themes of his *oeuvre*: the sacred as a dimension of lived experience. The Christian narrative makes the Word transcendent to the individuals who speak it, just as a pattern of repeatable dance moves outlasts the dancers who step them out. However, the pattern only lives in its incarnation, as the Christ of "Song" dies and comes alive again. Christ is the *living* Word, the Word made flesh, and that is an important analogy with poetry as a performance. Blaser had not, and perhaps could not, articulate his poetry this way when he wrote the poem. Later, in "The Stadium of the Mirror" essay of 1974, he would say that language is "older and other" than the poet, a vastness that the poet enters and animates (*Fire*, 34). An incarnational view of language, transmuted into poetic method and distanced from the supernaturalism of religion, is performative: language abstracts and overwrites living experience (Spicer's point), but experience may also bear down on the language, inflecting, torquing, and recombining it distinctively, so to redeem words both from their ephemerality in speech and impersonality in a linguistic system.

The fit of this poem to the work of Spicer and Duncan is suggested in Spicer's 1951 open letter to Robert Duncan, included in the back matter of Blaser's edition of Spicer's *Collected Books* in which Spicer says that for him (Spicer), the king of the world is evil; for Duncan it is himself; for Blaser, Christ is king (Spicer [1975] 1980, 364). This is a shrewd assessment of how things stood between them. Duncan rules in the Kingdom of Poetry because he takes on the role of Poet and because he recognizes no other realm. Evil is the king of the world for Spicer because at the existential level, all life feeds on itself and at the poetic level, all words fail to save the loved and beautiful from death. Spicer's "Apocalypse for Three Voices" is a contrary to Duncan's *Venice Poem*: the former emphasizes the triumph of death over love; the latter the triumph of poetry over loss. Blaser's "Song" mediates these positions through an incarnational poetics: poetry does not redeem anyone from death, but it can preserve the marks of a poet's passage in the language and in this sense give meaning and durability to a life, thus "saving" the world. Christ is therefore king for Blaser, Spicer says. In a later letter, he jibes that Landis is probably Blaser's Christ (Spicer to Blaser, "Berkeley seems to be having"), and Blaser responds that Spicer is probably right (30 November 1951). "Song in Four Parts for Christ the Son" is a slender poem written by a very young poet of about 22 years, but Spicer's letter, written only three years after the Writers' Conference and long before Blaser's poetic flowering, suggests that Blaser's modest output would have been supplemented by discussion, enough for Spicer to grasp intuitively where he, Duncan, and Blaser stood in relation to each other.

GRADUATE SCHOOL

In a 15 November 1948 letter to Spicer, Hugh O'Neill writes that the energy has run out of the poetry community. The Berkeley myth was based on a few short years of youthful excitement and poetic discovery. As Throckmorton, Hearst Street, and the Writers' Conference faded, there were certainly more poems and poetry readings, but the spell was broken. In 1949, Blaser received his BA and entered graduate school. At the University, the Loyalty Oath became news in the *Daily Californian*, 15 September 1949, as students rallied to protest (Froshaug 1949, n.p.). Born of cold war paranoia, the Oath required the signer to swear that he or she was not affiliated with any organization that advised the overthrow of the U.S. Government; it was aimed, of course, at communists. On the *Tapes*, Blaser says that this measure was devastating for the intellectual community at Berkeley. Kantorowicz refused to sign. Instead, he moved on to the Princeton Institute of Advanced Studies. "It wrecked that whole intellectual basis," Blaser says (*AT*, 79).[4] Spicer, as well, would not sign, which meant that he could not work at the University. In 1950, he left for a teaching assistantship at the University of Minnesota, working for John Clark, head of the Linguistics Department, and teaching Old English and the History of the English Language (Ellingham and Killian 1998, 34). In the letter cited above from Blaser to Spicer in Minneapolis, the two were already planning their retrospective on the Berkeley scene (23 October 1950). "The wolves [are] in Europe," Blaser writes, meaning Leonard Wolf and his wife Pat. Robert Berg, as well, was leaving for Spain. Berg was the head of the Ordering Department at San Francisco State Library and managed the Campus Textbook Exchange when Robin worked there as an undergraduate (Ellingham and Killian 1998, 45). He was gay, artsy and *outre*, remarked for his literary dinner parties, as well as for getting drunk at them. Landis, as well, had departed for graduate work at Columbia University in New York. Kantorowicz, Blaser wrote to Spicer, appears "very negative about the whole oath set-up. Doesn't think that winning the court case will do us any good now" (23 October 1950). And then mournfully,

> It really does seem that the University has already lost all its charms, intellectual and fleshly.
> …
> I do feel considerable loss and each day it becomes a little harder to work.

It would take Blaser four years to finish his MA in English. During this time, he worked as a teaching assistant, took courses, studied German, and began projects that he seems to have scrapped. In an undated letter to Spicer, for example, he speaks of his "despair over [his] prose style" and mentions a "'novelette' … about a young man who, after all sorts of trials of neither the usual nor the queer sort, dedicates himself to the Church but at the moment of dedication, the figure on the cross appears to be a young man—an imaginary transubstantiation" (Blaser to Spicer, "you've no idea"). Enclosed with this description is a single paragraph from the proposed novelette; it seems to have gone no further. In the same letter, Blaser says that he has passed his French exam, but has made little progress toward the MA, although he is determined to finish the degree. The picture, then, is of self-doubt, false starts, and nostalgia over a Berkeley scene that had barely cooled in its grave. A notebook entry from 8 October 1951 speaks of unbearable loneliness:

I literally tear at the windows.

One loves so many things without touching them. I wonder that the world goes on without being crushed by all these desires.

I've promised to speak of so much and so I shall. But for now: myself. (Blaser 1951c, "I literally tear")

On Blaser's silence and self-doubt, Landis writes that it is hard to understand. Why not move away from the Berkeley style and borrowings from Duncan, he says, and cultivate your own inner voice? (Everson to Blaser, 3 December 1951).

Blaser's inner voice was active enough, but not in a public way. A notebook entry dated 28 September 1951 refers to the planned "Lives of the Poets":

It seems wise, wiser this morning than at any other time I can remember, to keep a record. A great deal of time has past [sic] and so many places gone and forgotten that it seems well to remember these, if only for their sensations.

I talk to myself and enjoy that conversation. On all sides, so many bright efforts are remembered that I can only do them the honor of a record. Before these people have fallen in their own eyes and in mine, I wish to put their lives and all their bright efforts down on paper that I (and, perhaps, we) may remember them.

And so I shall begin and though the conversation will be mine, perhaps, it will appeal to a reader or two. (Blaser 1951a, "It seems wise")

But the note stops there.

On the home front, Felts had to return to Austin in 1952 to take care of family business after the death of his father. From Austin, he wrote to end his relationship with Blaser, reproaching himself for moral cowardice before turning to the practicalities of dividing things in the apartment (16 July 1952). Robin replied with a new address and telephone number: "I've taken a place at 1571 Scenic Ave. and the new telephone number is TH3-1232" (Blaser to Felts, 30 July 1952). There are no overt signs of high emotional distress in Robin's response, however, and when Felts gave notice of his return to San Francisco, Blaser responded with pleasure. Somehow the definitive break-up that Felts planned was averted, possibly because it does not seem to have been bitter or shocking to either partner. Scenic Avenue did not last very long. By September 1953, Blaser had moved to a place on Oak Street Path and Felts with him.

In these days of the early 1950s, Duncan and Spicer were coming into their powers as poets. Spicer was working on the *Imaginary Elegies I–IV* (1950–1955) (Spicer [1975] 1980, 333–37); Duncan on *Caesar's Gate* (1949–1950), *A Book of Resemblances* (1950–1953), the Gertrude Stein derivations, *Writing Writing* (1952–1953), *Letters* (1953–1956), and *Faust Foutu* (c.1955, published 1958), all of them important pieces. As well, they had gathered around themselves communities of poets, students, painters, and gay party friends. This was not the Berkeley myth, but it was a strong creative community. In 1952, for example, Duncan and Jess Collins, the painter and collagist who would become his life companion, opened the King Ubu Gallery in a converted garage at 3119 Fillmore Street. The painter Harry Jacobus partnered with them. The Gallery exhibited work by Jess's friends and teachers at the California School of Fine Arts (Jarnot 2012, 126) and doubled as a reading space for the poets. Blaser participated, but this was not his time to flower. All that he preserved of his writing between 1950 and 1955, despite the brave plans for a "Lives of the Poets," are some school essays and a short story called "The Pacific Spectator."

Dating from 1953, "The Pacific Spectator" satirizes the Berkeley literary scene as a kind of vanity fair. Blaser's speaker is terribly self-conscious and focused on projecting himself as a sophisticate. While he lives in the art and poetry world, he does not have a very firm grasp on the content, as opposed to the superficial social forms, of that world. He cannot remember the poems he hears at readings and the books he carts around with him are selected to impress others more than for his own edification. The bar scenes he witnesses are seedy, featuring older women looking for sex and the occasional narcissistic youth. Even his own dinner party lacks companionable warmth, because the guests, like the grape soufflé he serves, are chosen for their social status rather than for friendship. Another peculiarity of the story is that some characters are satirically named and others are not. Why Duncan shows up as a Mr. Watercress is not clear, but it is Mr. Watercress who reads Stein imitations at the King Ubu Gallery and Mr. Spicer who attends. As well, elements of the story that touch on some intellectual content, like a reference to Giorgio de Chirico or abstract designs painted on the floor of the gallery (possibly inspired by the Duncan–Jess Franklin Street studio), seem to be furniture of the narrative rather than symbols or ideas to be developed. De Chirico is a fusionist of inner and outer space, twisting them in moebius fashion in *trompe d'oeil* paintings that place doors in the outdoors and feature impossible architectural spaces. But the story does not really develop this kind of elaborate folding of space as a surrealist metaphor for mind. Neither is the point clear as a satire. If the speaker is meant to be revolting, he comes off as pitiably insecure; if the social scene is supposed to seem pretentious, it appears dull and desperate.

If there is a clue to Blaser's personal state in this story, it is perhaps in the exploration of a narrator who seems insecure. This is not to identify Blaser with his fictional speaker, but to say that this kind of character drew his attention. As the title of the story says, the narrator is a spectator: his relation to the bars he visits or the reading he attends is that of someone on the outside looking in. He even smashes his face against a pane of glass in one bar incident. Blaser's project of writing a "Lives of the Poets" would have put him in a parallel position, as observer and recorder ("understander-believer") of the Berkeley scene. In a 22 September 1954 letter, Don Allen responds to what must have been yet another such project, an anthology of Berkeley poets. Spicer and Blaser had met Don Allen in the Berkeley library in 1948 and become friends. Allen would later become famous as the man who introduced the San Francisco, New York, and Black Mountain poets to the world in his *New American Poetry* anthology of 1960. In the 1950s, he worked for Grove Press and the *Evergreen Review*:

> About the anthology. Maybe we should reconsider. As you will remember, I never really did know just what the Berkeley Renaissance was for [;] what I saw seemed more nearly the afterglow. The thing I had in mind—without knowing too much about it—was to pull together a small group of poems that would somehow show the shock of discovery of POETRY. And of course Duncan and by all means Spicer but also definitely you and Landis and, too, single poems by younger and minor people which, even if not entirely successful, might reflect the spirit of the thing. (Allen to Blaser, 22 September 1954)

Allen concludes it might be best to "forget about groups and think about individual poets." The proposed anthology, then, seems to have been another attempt, like the "Lives," to give the Berkeley myth some permanent form, but as Allen's letter suggests, just what that should be was not entirely clear.

Blaser's response to Landis Everson's "The Laments of Alcibiades" speaks to his fixation on the Berkeley scene and self-doubt as a poet. Blaser described the poems to Spicer as "so perfect and austerely beautiful I'm hardly able to speak of them" (Blaser to Spicer, 30 November 1951). In this letter, Blaser mythologizes Everson and disparages himself:

> You remember you once said that the Christ of my poems was never anyone but Landis. Now, I'm afraid you were right. When he came to see me, I knew immediately that the only important thing I had to offer him was the same love I gave him four years ago. I've always been taught to be ashamed of an overbearing love, of any unrestrained emotions. But here I've given in and am my silliest self.
>
> The only thing that seems odd is that this love is more the sort one gives to a god. Everything I feel seems his due and I accept his poems as my reward. I've even noticed that in loving him I'm neither lustful nor egotistical. And at this point I should say that I'm damned sure I'm damned. (Blaser to Spicer, 30 November 1951)

Five years later, Blaser was still worrying the matter. In a letter dated 4 July 1956, Don Allen writes: "No, you never reminded me of Socrates! Is that the way you think of yourself in relation to Alcibiades Landis?" Positioned as Socrates, Blaser would be the older, philosopher–critic rather than the magical young poet. An untouchable Beauty and an abject poète maudite? Quelle misère!

Blaser received his MA in English from Berkeley on 28 January 1954. Since 1952, he had been teaching in various capacities. At San Francisco State College, he offered four summer session seminars on *Hamlet* for first- and second-year students. In 1952–1953, he was granted a teaching assistantship at Berkeley for freshman English and a more senior course on Proust, Yeats, Eliot, and Pound. He also made three PhD proposals, two of which were turned down because his supervisors did not think his subjects worthwhile. One was to have been on Sir Richard Francis Burton, a nineteenth century explorer and writer, known for his erudition and criticism of British colonial policies; the other on John Addington Symonds, a nineteenth century advocate of homosexual love, *l'amour de l'impossible* as he called it. A third choice would have been the poetic drama from Wordsworth's *The Borderers* to Hardy's *The Dynasts*, In a 1999 interview, Blaser says,

> ...of course this is far too big for any one PhD dissertation, but it made for splendid reading. And I took all of my exams, language exams and stuff and so on and so forth, and then just dipped out. Mark Schorer was then head of the department, and I went in to tell him I just had to leave. Irving Howe had written a thing in *Partisan Review* on conformity—this was the 50s you know—and I believed every word of it. (Blaser 2002, 354)

Instead of tackling the dissertation, Blaser enrolled in a one-year program in the School of Library Science.

Writing home to Ina Mae and Sophia, 16 April 1955, Blaser says that he has decided to postpone the PhD for a library job, that he has applied to Harvard and hopes for a good position "so that I can worry all of you less." The letter shows that he still depended on the family for extras, like dental care and a new suit, for which he thanks grandmother Sophia. This letter opens with the comment that "I've done very little visiting even with those friends who are closest to me," an excuse, perhaps, for not going home more often. There are no records of visits home, although in "The Fire" essay, Blaser mentions attending his grandfather Augustus's final illness, just before he died in June of 1954 (*Fire*, 8). The thing was now to get a job that paid well and claim his independence. On 16 June 1955, Blaser was awarded a Master of Library Science from Berkeley. By 30 June, he was packing for a position at the Widener library, Harvard.

Between 1944 and 1955, Blaser had been in the company of some very high-powered people—Kantorowicz, Duncan, Spicer, Josephine Miles, and Ariel and Tom Parkinson, as well as the many poets and artists that drifted in and out of the scene. In relation to Duncan and Spicer, he was the ideal reader and "understander–believer." In a notebook entry of 29 September 1951, Blaser writes, "A little later talked with Duncan over Viennese coffee and nut tartes [sic]. How much I depend upon the world he represents. Neither in that one nor in another world, I've come to hear him with considerably more respect than most. It is, perhaps, true, as Spicer says, that I know all he has to say, for he does repeat.... But the more I hear of others, the more necessary it becomes to repeat and repeat: one must look for the quality of the thing, the quality of a person" (Blaser 1951b, "A little later"). When Blaser narrated his autobiography on the "Tapes" in 1974, Spicer and Kantorowicz were the big events of Berkeley, but this diary comment is a reminder of the foundational significance of Duncan. Belief in the transformative power of *poiesis*, fraught as it would become with battles over poetics, came from Duncan. With Spicer, the relationship was not so patriarchal. Like an elder brother (they were actually the same age), Spicer cajoled and encouraged Blaser to return to poetry when both were undergraduates at Berkeley, but he had the more assured voice. On the scholarly front, there was Kantorowicz and he was a hard act to follow. It does not seem strange, then, that Blaser would want to explore a character like the one in "The Pacific Spectator" who suffers from social anxiety. At the same time, there was a lost Dauphin of France asserting himself. Blaser had come to Berkeley from Twin Falls as a gifted protegé. That kind of assurance seems to have remained in tension with feelings of inadequacy as a poet in relation to his two assertive peers. Not until Boston would Blaser begin to struggle his way through to become his own poet.

NOTES

1. In *The Astonishment Tapes*, Blaser says that there were two Genes, Big Gene and Little Gene, both involved in petty theft. Big Gene became Blaser's first lover; Little Gene went to jail (*AT*, 52–53).
2. The cemetery Blaser refers to is most likely Laurel Hill, originally the Lone Mountain Cemetery. Opened in 1854, Lone Mountain was renamed in 1867 and remained in use until 1937. World War II delayed the relocation of the cemetery until 1948, just a few years after Blaser's "happening." On the "Tapes" ("AT" 4, 12), Blaser mentions that the site was purchased by the Fireman's Fund Insurance Company, which indeed it was in 1953. Today the building is used as the Laurel Hill campus of the University of California, San Francisco.
3. For a personal narrative of what it meant to be a gay man in San Francisco in the 1950s, see Michael Rumaker's account of his arrest in *Robert Duncan in San Francisco* (66–79).
4. I have found no records that would indicate whether Blaser himself signed the Loyalty Oath or not. His teaching assistantships date from 1952 and the Oath was rescinded in 1951. On the other hand, Blaser was a graduate student between 1949 and 1955, and he may have had other campus positions that would have required him to sign.

CHAPTER 4

Boston: The Librarian

And then – a new town. Yes.
And fine brick to hit my head against. (Blaser c.1956, "Boston: The Arrival")

In July of 1955, Blaser arrived at the YMCA in Boston during a heat wave so intense that he had to rescue a pigeon stuck to the melting tar of the roof below his room (Blaser to Ina Mae Blaser, 17 July 1955). Apartment hunting was the first thing to do, and he was immediately attracted to the Beacon Hill neighborhood fronting the Charles River, a quarter with a grand history, he writes the folks, and close to excellent shopping on Charles Street. With its narrow streets and old buildings, Boston seemed like an English movie set (To Ina Mae Blaser, 17 July 1955) and Beacon Hill could claim the ghosts of the Adamses, Longfellows, Emersons, and Hawthornes (To Ina Mae Blaser, 2 October 1955). "But these old families are not many now," he wrote to his mother. "Boston is largely populated by immigrant groups – Irish, Italian, Armenian and Polish, as well as some Jews. Relations among these different nationalities are not good. There is an element of choosing sides here unless you live quite apart. And this I intend to do" (To Ina Mae Blaser and Sophia Auer, 1 August 1955). Blaser chose an apartment at 142 Chestnut Street, #2 with an impressive entrance—marble flooring and columns, a glass dome and statuary. The high double doors to the suite opened with a five-inch key and led to a spacious, high-ceilinged room with a black Italian marble fireplace (To Ina Mae Blaser, 17 July 1955). Such elegance did not come cheap. The apartment was an outrageous $110 a month (To Ina Mae and Sophia Auer, 2 October 1955) at a time when the national average was $87 a month and the average annual salary $4130 (*The People History*, n.d.). Fortunately, Jim would soon arrive to help with the rent.

Over the summer and fall, Blaser began to settle in. The apartment had to be decorated, of course, and this meant washing the walls in the 96 degree heat before painting them (To Ina Mae Blaser and Sophia Auer, 1 August 1955)—weeks of

© The Author(s) 2019
M. Nichols, *A Literary Biography of Robin Blaser*,
Modern and Contemporary Poetry and Poetics,
https://doi.org/10.1007/978-3-030-18327-1_4

work, he tells his mother and "Gran" (To Ina Mae Blaser and Sophia Auer, 2 October 1955). Then there were drapes to be sewn and furniture to buy: "It is far too expensive to have these things done for one," he writes, "so I buckle down. I go to a used furniture store called <u>The Good Will</u>, a real junk shop, buy a lamp for $1.00, rewire it, repaint it, buy an old ruined shade for a dime and recover it with a remnant I buy ... [at] a local department store" (To Ina Mae Blaser and Sophia Auer, 1 November 1955). Painting and decorating would become Blaser's way of establishing presence in new places and he would do it all his life:

> I think one's greatest problem in a new place is one of identity. You can wander down a street and though you know your own name and can number your dearest wishes and desires, all those items which add up to the real and singular world that each man is to himself are missing—old friends, family, well-known trees, paths and houses, even ideas, that in a new place are shared only with oneself—all are missing from the world around you. But this wears away as new streets and new people become familiar. (To Ina Mae Blaser and Sophia Auer, 1 November 1955)

Blaser constructed identity by making his households into strong exoskeletons. In an undated notebook from this period, he writes:

> The constant awareness of clothing, furniture—The need for these as they reflect some indefinable quality. Always, the quality outside the person, a building of the man in externals. (Undated, "Constant awareness")

In another notebook, a handwritten short story hints at some of the childhood contradictions that were back of Blaser's need for domestic elegance. The story features a character named Jack whose mother tries to coach him in habits above his social station. She wants him to be a gentleman, but the comportments she thinks appropriate for her son are forbidden by a stern father. Much of the story is taken up with how to properly set a table and negotiate byzantine arrangements of cutlery.

> The problems she bequeathed him were quite clear when she died. Years before when they had left the church after his great grandmother's funeral, walking down the 150 steps to the street below the main entrance, she had grabbed his arm and said very coldly: "So much sobbing was unnecessary my dear. A man should know how to console those who grieve, but he should not grieve overmuch himself." (Undated, "Problems")

This narrative fragment references Robin's real-life experience at the funeral of his grandfather Auer, when it was his father who had slapped him down the steps of the church in Boise for crying. The story concludes:

> She [Mother] had wanted him to be a "gentleman" like those she'd read about, but she had wanted him to have those qualities which first attracted her in her

husband, straightforwardness, hardness and force.... He was to feel without showing it, to feel like crying without really doing it. So Jack began with contradictions and we suppose he will end with them.

As it touches the autobiographical, the story suggests the close connection Blaser felt between "externals" and core identity.

Along with all the scrubbing, painting, and sewing, there was Harvard to get used to. From Chestnut Street to Harvard Yard was a convenient, 16-minute trip: eight minutes to walk to the subway and eight to cross under the Charles River with a beautiful view of it as the train emerged on the other side (Blaser to Ina Mae Blaser, 2 October 1955). Architecturally, the Widener was "what one expects of Harvard" (Blaser to Ina Mae Blaser and Sophia Auer, 1 August 1955), all white marble columns with a flight of stairs leading up to the gold doors of the library. But about his job as Administrative Assistant Librarian in Cataloging,[1] Blaser was equivocal almost from the beginning. "Harvard is a curious place," he writes home, "I am not entirely pleased with the place though a part of this dissatisfaction is due to being new. I am still training, changing jobs every few days and always learning new things. The place is loaded down with tradition, some of it noble, some idiotic" (Blaser to Ina Mae Blaser and Sophia Auer, 1 November 1955).

However irritating betimes he found his job at the Widener, Blaser seems to have excelled at it. Over the course of his four-year tenure there, he was promoted to a position of more responsibility and he remembers taking on a demanding curatorial display of American philosophy from Jonathan Edwards to Alfred North Whitehead.[2] Yet Blaser did not discuss his job much with friends. The scanty traces of his time at the Widener come from co-workers in cards and letters that followed his departure in 1959, or in one instance, a laudatory poem from "Marion the Naughty Librarian." The poem is dated 9 September 1959 and suggests that Blaser had helped the speaker in her library duties, apparently fruitlessly, because she confesses to messing up on the job. Sue Haskins, Blaser's supervisor, responded with shock to the resignation. She writes that she had no idea that Blaser had been unhappy at Harvard and mentions hiring an assistant who would free him up for "more interesting and administrative responsibilities" (Haskins to Blaser, 13 July 1958). She asks Blaser to reconsider. When he would not, Harvard offered a three-month terminal payout if he would stay on to the spring of 1959. This Blaser accepted because he needed the money for a much dreamed-of European tour before his return to San Francisco. A letter from Paul Buck, just before Robin's departure, accepts the resignation with regret and much praise for the quality of Blaser's work (23 April 1959). By other colleagues, Blaser was congratulated for making Room 89 (cataloging) run smoothly (Alfreda to Blaser, 8 December 1959) and he received an acknowledgment in the pages of *Literary Resources and Technical Services* for his binding techniques (Smith to Blaser, 21 October 1959).

Blaser was also able to help his poet friends through the library position. He worked with Jack Sweeney of the Poetry Room to arrange recordings of Olson and Duncan, lobbied unsuccessfully to get them readings, and dug up Melville manuscripts for Olson. Yet Blaser chafed at his library duties. The library meant a "small executive post" he complained to Duncan, and it interfered with his main focus which was poetry (10 February 1958). As well, Jim Felts wanted to return to San Francisco. He had a position as Assistant Professor of Physiology at Tufts with a Public Health Service Senior Research Fellowship worth $66,000, but he had come to dislike Boston.[3] By 1958, he had scouted out a job in San Francisco and Blaser prepared to follow. Writing home just before leaving Boston for his European trip, Blaser says: "Sometimes, it seems I cannot wait to get out of here. I gave a full year's notice and still the rush to wind up is on. I have really disliked this place, in spite of Harvard's efforts to please and recognize" (Blaser to Ina Mae Blaser and Sophia Auer, 10 May 1959).

THE BOSTON SCENE

Over his four years in Boston, Blaser lived two lives. He had a day job that he needed to support himself, and an unpaid night job that meant much more to him: he had to read, absorb, and process the new poetry that was coming off the typewriters of Jack Spicer, Robert Duncan, Charles Olson, Robert Creeley, Denise Levertov, Michael McClure, and Frank O'Hara, not to mention those of the Boston boys he was hanging out with—John Wieners, Steve Jonas, and Ed Marshall. And as he was processing this new work, he had to find his place in it—his own ground as a poet. This was the real job.

Blaser credits Spicer with introducing him to Wieners, Jonas, and Marshall. Shortly after Blaser left Berkeley, Spicer lost his job with the California School of Fine Art due to "organizational changes" (Ellingham and Killian 1998, 61) and set off in August for the East coast, seeking literary fame. The trip was a disaster. He had applied for a position at Black Mountain and received a polite letter from Creeley, saying that the college was in no position to hire (Creeley to Spicer, 5 September 1955). Instead, he landed a job teaching English at a New Jersey prep school and hated it (Ellingham and Killian 1998, 63). Worse, he found the New York scene uncongenial. His biographers, Lewis Ellingham and Kevin Killian, write that John Button, a painter friend that Spicer knew from Berkeley, offered a pass into the O'Hara circle (Ellingham and Killian 1998, 63), but Spicer did not thrive there. His usual way of commandeering an audience with avuncular sagacities didn't work in a circle where O'Hara was the star and cool was the thing, nor could he compete with the New York Beats for coterie (Ellingham and Killian 1998, 65). Landis Everson, by this time installed at Columbia University, reported that Spicer had called John Ashbery a "'faggot poet,'" (Ellingham and Killian 1998, 65). Spicer's dark side came out, too, in his blaming of New York Jews for controlling big business and the arts (Ellingham and Killian 1998, 66). In a letter to Blaser, poet and Berkeley friend Arthur Kloth, then living in New York, announced that Jack was putting people off with his unkempt appearance and his unwillingness to *do* things in the city (15 January 1956). Broke and unhappy, Spicer headed for Boston.

Spicer arrived at 142 Chestnut Street in December 1955, looking for a place to stay until he could find work and get his own apartment. Ellingham and Killian record the spilled red wine on Blaser's gray silk sofa and the dirty socks left about in defiance of domestic order (Ellingham and Killian 1998, 75). Yet however trying Spicer might have been as a house guest, the bond in poetry between him and Blaser was sturdy. With Blaser's help, he found work in the Rare Book Room at the Boston Public Library and it did not take him long to come up with "brilliant finds" in the poetry world (Blaser 1995e, 6)—Wieners, Dunn, Marshall, and Jonas. In other words, Spicer had sniffed out the real poets and drew Blaser into their company. Poems were written, exchanged, discussed, rewritten. Spicer would dedicate his translation of Lorca's "Ode to Walt Whitman" to Jonas, a freewheeling hipster poet (Ellingham and Killian 1998, 71); with the married Joe Dunn, he fell in love (Ellingham and Killian 1998, 73).

"News," Blaser writes to Duncan, "a charming young man named Wieners is leaving here in June to go to Black Mountain. When I first saw his app't he had <u>Song of the Border Guard</u> nailed to the wall and lines of Pound written on the paint with frames over each. He's young and new to everything and is going there for Olson and you" (28 May 1956). Born in 1934, Wieners was nine years younger than Blaser and barely out of Boston College (he graduated in 1954). After hearing Olson read at the Charles Street Meeting House, he had become an enthusiast (Petro 2003, n.p.) and hied himself off to Black Mountain, first in 1955 and again in 1956. As he would later write to Olson, Wieners was after "a living that counted" (LJW 2, 8 January 1957). Michael Seth Stewart, editor of Wieners's letters, describes him as "openly and happily gay in a dangerous time to be gay, in love with a blonde firefighter, building the friendships and networks that [would] blossom into the 'Boston Renaissance' of the late-50s, on the working-class north side of Beacon Hill" (LJW 1, Introduction). The firefighter, over whom Wieners agonized in many a letter, was Dana Durkee, a footballer in high school, a navy man, and a Boston College student on the GI bill. The two of them—"mostly John"—would organize poetry readings at their apartment (LJW 1, n. 9).

Steve Jonas, denizen of the bohemian side of Beacon Hill, also opened his door to poets, as well as various demi-monde sorts—"a gay interracial Ezra Pound devotee," Stewart describes him (LJW 1, n. 52). Writing retrospectively to Don Allen in 1997, Blaser says that

> ...Jonas, who was ambivalent about his blackness and anti-Semitic in the Pound sense, was very, very Boston underground—he was into black jazz in general & in the Boston scene— (7 June 1997)

Jonas's editor, Joseph Torra, describes him as "a generous and compassionate friend" as well as "a rootless, social renegade" (Torra 1994, 2). Surviving on a military disability pension, Jonas pursued his many curiosities through a poetry of investigation. He was interested, Torra says, in poetry, music, economics, history, mythology, philosophy, science, magic, alchemy, and politics. In his friends—"poets, artists, musicians, prostitutes, runaways, junkies, and thieves"—he had a subterranean world that gave "sustenance for his life and poetry" (Torra 1994, 3).

Jonas's roommate was Ed Marshall, a "New Hampshire-born street preacher … for the Old Catholic Church movement" (Dewhurst 2013, 12), who had moved to Boston in 1953. Jonas connected him to Wieners, Joe Dunn, and Black Mountain where Marshall would become a student and poet himself, notably contributing his 1955 long poem "Leave the Word Alone" to *Black Mountain Review* 7 to the acclaim of both Olson and Duncan (LJW 1, n. 43). Joe Dunn had grown up with Wieners in Boston and remained friends with him after both had moved to San Francisco. Stewart describes Joe and Carolyn Dunn as "perpetually poor and smoking"—in the phrasing of painter Tom Field, "'pre-punk, proto-punk,' Carolyn with green makeup, the apartment 'dumpy' and dark" (LJW 1, n. 10). They were perfect. Kevin Killian says it this way:

> These Boston poets showed the Berkeley refugees a new bohemia, one based on anarchy, drugs, cool jazz, midnight parties, broken syntax, and a vision of the page as an open field in which form is never more than an extension of content. The Berkeley bohemia, "literary and University centered" (to echo Duncan), with its beliefs in ordered ideals of purity and hierarchy, was never like this. (Killian 2002, 257)

The "Boston occult school," Gloucester poet Gerrit Lansing named it (Dewhurst 2013, 12).

In a 22 September 1956 letter to Charles Olson, Wieners writes: "Spicer, Dunn, Jonas, Blaser here, all frantic with ideas of readings and Boston Newsletters, etc." (LJW 1). The *Boston Newsletter*[4] consisted of poems from Spicer, Dunn, Wieners, Jonas, and Blaser and a missive to the Ford Foundation, signed by all five poets, requesting money so that they would "not have to be librarians and postmen any longer." The signees promise to believe in the *Hudson Review*, the "benevolence of Israelis," W.S. Merwin, the Boston Red Sox, Edward Dahlberg, and the Pound Newsletter should the Foundation decide to buy them—the poets, that is. In addition, they undertake to send vowels and become an orchestra. Such was the level of cheek. But the poems were serious enough, investigative forays into what could be thought and said in poetry. Blaser's "And when I pay death's duty" (*HF*, 9) and "Poem for Charles who is a river," later retitled "Poem by the Charles River" (*HF*, 15), for instance, are two of his best early lyrics and they open up serious questions about the nature of perception that would persist in the later major works.

Beyond the digs of Jonas and Wieners, the Poets' Theatre was also a Boston hot spot, a place where Wieners worked off-and-on as "stand-in, errand-runner, lackey, usher-type" (LJW 1, 2 December 1955), and O'Hara spent a summer in 1956. Situated over a hardware store, the Theatre operated on a shoestring budget. The Irish-born Mary Manning Howe, who had worked with William Butler Yeats and the Abbey Theatre in Dublin, was a founding member (Schneiderman 2009, 1). The idea was to resuscitate the poetic drama and retain control of production in an artist-run space. Writing to Kenneth Koch in January 1956, O'Hara describes an evening at the Theatre:

> I read miscellaneous poems, the first group including INVINCIBILITY which Hugh Amory kindly had mimeographed and ending with the hit of the evening FRESH AIR. Everyone was interested in your work and I was told some had the desired reaction, fury, but I don't know whom. Don Hall unfortunately was not with us. However, everyone laughed a great deal in general and it went over big. (Schneiderman 2009, 1–2)

An important production from the Blaser–Spicer angle was Cocteau's *Orpheus* in the spring of 1956. On the performance, Blaser writes to Duncan:

> Dear Jack—we went to Cocteau's <u>Orpheus</u> Sat. night and he was angry because it was chic and not like the movie which he didn't see because Cocteau was something else west of the Mississippi. It was good and extremely well done. (28 May 1956)

Although Spicer grumbled, the Cocteau film would become the primary reference in his *Heads of the Town Up to the Aether*, a major serial poem yet to come. The figure of Orpheus was also significant to Blaser. In "The Fire," he writes that "in the image of the scattered body and mind of Orpheus ... I place whatever I know about the poetic process—that scattering is a living reflection of the world" (*Fire*, 9).

Although Blaser did not work at the Theatre, he set himself to get his friends on the play list. The Theatre had rejected Spicer's *Troilus* (Ellingham and Killian 1998, 75) and Duncan's *Faust Foutu*, but Blaser tried to get *Medea* into production anyway. To Duncan, he says, "The fight to interest them in *Medea* is not over. I've got to get through to the script committee, which is guarded over by Hugh Amory, who believes the audience teaches and the poet entertains" (16 March 1957). Blaser adds that "It is true that no Theatre exists. And I know it is agony to make one. I'm afraid that's what you're doing". When Gerta Kennedy of the Script Committee gave Blaser a definite "no" for *Medea* (Kennedy to Blaser, 24 November 1957), he denounced the Theatre. Two years later, the slight to Duncan was still on his mind. The Theatre has been lost, he huffs, to "a bunch of anglicised actors" who "failed to understand how to do it [*Medea*]" (Blaser to Duncan, 15 August 1959).

The Boston five didn't last very long—June 1955 to November 1956, according to Stewart's reckoning, the length of Spicer's Boston stay (LJW 1, n. 77). Spicer didn't wash enough to please his employers at the Public Library and he soiled the books with dirty hands. According to Ellingham and Killian, he was also up against homophobia in the person of Miss Harriet Swift, the curator of Americana and one of his bosses. "Song for Bird and Myself" takes a poet's revenge. In the poem, two "birds" (Charlie Parker and the Holy Ghost perhaps?) get into the Rare Book Room and Miss Swift, *éminence grise* of that establishment, goes to lunch, leaving the custodians to kill them (Spicer 2008, 69–70). After some months, Jack was fired, Blaser recalls, for breaking the spine of a Bay Psalm Book, 1640—the first book printed in North America (Blaser 1995e, 6). Reporting to Duncan, Blaser writes:

> Jack isn't at all well here. The total absence of his admiring Juniors leaves him pink and shell-like. When I try to understand I get angry, and that isn't exactly payment for my many obligations to him. (28 May 1956)

Spicer and the Dunns left Boston for San Francisco in November of 1956. The departures were fêted with a final poetry reading. Wieners wrote to Blaser "that this Saturday night will be the last gathering of the Boston poets. Please come and bring all poems you want carried out in their ears to that place on the WC. I have written Spicer–Dunn, and shall write Steve, so that's all that will be present, but feel free to bring any interested parties if existent." "We will go on till dawn like the Chinese nightingale," he says (LJW 1, 4 November 1956). They did, apparently, make it until 3 am. In a letter to Robert Greene, Wieners reports:

> The Dunns have left and are in San Francisco, with Jack Spicer, and we had a large poetry festival, lasting until 3 in the morning, with most of it taped, and then and now, Robin Blaser and Steve, and I try to meet once a week to read what has been done. (LJW 1, 11 December 1956)

Left to themselves, Wieners, Blaser, and Jonas had weekly "ladies bridge" meetings (LJW 2, 8 January 1957). To Charles Olson in May of 1957, Wieners says "Blaser & I devour each other / and trying [sic] to gobble you up in it" (LJW 2, May 1957). In that year, Wieners stepped up with *Measure*. Black Mountain College was in its last days by then, and *Origin*, Cid Corman's essential little magazine for Black Mountaineers, was finished. Out of departures and endings, Wieners conceived of a new venue that would carry forward the poetic energy of his generation. As he first imagined it in a letter to Olson, *Measure* was to be edited by himself, Blaser, and Jonas. Olson replied enthusiastically, but advised him to do his own editing (Dewhurst 2013, 9). For the first issue, Blaser was to create a biography of a burlesque dancer, written as if for a girlie magazine—"[a]vec Wieners" (Blaser to Duncan, 11 July 1957). Although the biography was never completed, Blaser did begin the tale of Jennifer, a "Boston bred showgirl" of "jet black hair." She was to be "[t]he best bed-time story I've seen in Boston or anywhere for many a year" (Undated, "Jennifer").

Wieners took the title of his magazine from William Carlos Williams's "On Measure—Statement for Cid Corman" (published in *Origin* 1954) and Blake's "Proverbs of Hell": "Bring out number, weight and measure in a year of dearth" (Dewhurst 2013, 9). The editorial principle was "'to provide space for those whose advances in form / and or / whose content allow it nowhere else, or barely'" (Dewhurst 2013, 9). In a letter to Duncan, Wieners explains that "Measure is edited simply by my conviction: and it is and always will be: a thing of process also, that it is opened onto new territories by nearly every one of yr letters, that others must see as you is [sic] I think reason enuf to print yrs of the 18th" (LJW 2, 22 August 1957). The first issue came out in July 1957 with a frontispiece by artist Tom Balas, and writing by Michael Rumaker, Charles Olson, Robert Duncan, Ed Marshall, Frank O'Hara, Larry Eigner, Fielding Dawson, Jack Spicer, Robin Blaser, Steve Jonas, Jonathan Williams, James Schuyler, Ed Dorn, Allen Ginsburg [sic], George Montgomery, and John Button. In an open letter later published in *Measure* 2, Duncan explains his understanding of the journal's mandate:

THE HEART OF THE MATTER IS: THAT THIS BE NOT A SHOW-WINDOW BUT A RECORD OF WHAT IS BEING DONE; A WORKING GROUND FOR A PROCESS. (Duncan 1958, 63)

As Duncan elaborates, the journal was not to be about writers making a name for themselves, but about a poetry in the making: "if we are to have a magazine somewhere not of the created but of the process—then it is to be as all things in the Process are, primordial, unestablished in the Good" (Duncan 1958, 63). This was the page conceived as open space, a significant forerunner of Stan Persky's *Open Space* newsletter of 1964–1965 and of the open space poem as Blaser would later develop it. In the first issue of *Measure*, Blaser republished some of his best 1956 poems from *The Boston Newsletter*: "And when I pay death's duty"; "Letter to Freud"; and "Poem by the Charles River." A "silent partner" for the first two issues, Blaser read manuscripts out loud with Wieners (Dewhurst 2013, 14). In September of 1957, Michael McClure sent poems to Blaser for *Measure* 2, unsure of whether to address them to Blaser or Wieners (McClure to Blaser, 15 September 1957).

Measure 2 was at the printers when Wieners packed up in the fall of 1957. He, too, had decided to decamp to San Francisco, but just before take-off he received news that the typescripts for the second issue had not been received. Robert Dewhurst describes the moment: "Over the next five days, while crashing at Robin's for the weekend, he mailed a bevy of apologetic notes and somehow managed to reassemble the issue piece by piece—a testament, if there ever were one, to the robust postal network that existed among these poets in the predigital era" (Dewhurst 2013, 15). Would Robin box and mail a suit that he had left hanging on Tom Balas's door, please, Wieners asks (Wieners to Blaser, 26 September 1957). It was his only one. This letter includes a long story of being followed by the police and narcotics squad in New York. The next day, there is another: "Returning to life after 'Kicking' [sic] benzedrine (none for 4 days) and coming down a hill to 'rolling' green plains of Oklahoma." "I am exhilarated by the wind tillers and the fields of sunflowers/daisies," he writes. "The day's eye falls and we speed on Route 66 to reach where it's setting. New York we leave behind. Its movie house poets and its Federal men who follow us on the streets, all the streets and avenues, pursued by G-men who would pin me down behind bars, take America out of my eye, take this open car and imprison us all" (27 September 1957).

Measure 2, the Magic issue, came out finally in the spring of 1958. It included an article on the unconscious by Michael Rumaker, excerpts from Kerouac's *Mexico City Blues*, and poems by Duncan, Creeley, Dorn, Blaser, Jonas, and some of the San Francisco poets. By this time, Wieners was installed in the gay North Beach scene, sometimes attending Spicer's Sunday afternoon reading circle. The City issue he was planning for *Measure* 3, however, would be delayed for four years until 1962, partly through discouragement and partly through life circumstances. After a vacation on the coast in August 1957, Blaser had reported a negative reception among the San Francisco poets of *Measure* 1 (Dewhurst 2013, 14–15). Then Wieners and Dana Durkee broke up in the spring of 1958, and the jobless Wieners moved in with Joanne Kyger: "I stay with a lovely poet-girl named Joanne Kyger, until I get a job.... She lives too much, and that makes her easy to live with, for me" (Wieners to Blaser, 12 April 1958). In this letter, Wieners thanks Blaser for his work on *Measure* and asks for a reference for library school. Sales of the magazine, he says, are his only form of income and could Robin please try to sell some in Boston (12 April 1958). To Duncan, Blaser writes, "And Wieners? What am I to do about him. I've written. Telephoned, etc. No response" (30 June 1958). By the fall of 1958, LeRoi Jones (Amiri Baraka), then editing *Yugen* in New York, would write to Blaser, expressing regrets that *Measure* had folded and Wieners was reportedly not well (30 September 1958). Wieners produced the beautiful *Hotel Wentley Poems* in 1959 and these would launch his public presence in the poetry world, but his drug use—or was it his homosexuality?—landed him in the Medfield State Psychiatric Hospital in January 1960 (Dewhurst 2013, 17).

> I sit in Lees. At 11:40 PM with
> Jimmy the pusher. He teaches me
> Ju Ju. Hot on the table before us
> shrimp foo yong, rice and mushroom
> chow yuke. Up the street under the wheels
> of a strange car is his stash—The ritual.
> We make it. (Wieners 1986, 28)

Writing to Blaser a year later (5 February 1961), Jonas blames Wieners's family for his institutionalization: "Jack Wieners' whereabouts is a mystery. I have talked with his mother on the phone and she tells me he is in Connecticut with friends and she has no address. But a week before she told Billy Donahue that he was gone back to California. It is the old runaround. The real truth of the matter is—his father has put him away in another mental institution and they are not telling anyone where." "Brilliant" Blaser says to Duncan about *The Hotel Wentley* poems, but he did not quite follow Wieners or Jonas into the demi-monde of drugs and irregular living (27 June 1959).

In relation to his younger Boston comrades, Blaser was the socially stable one. To Olson, he says he will be up early

> ...to go with Wieners and Dana to stand with Steve Jonas in DOMESTIC COURT. Seems like Steve's been playing HiFi from 11 to 7 PMAM and the entire middle class can't sleep. Since I look middle class it was good to have me on hissss [sic] side. Rhadamanthus thought Jonas was lying, which I did too, and so lectured all of us. But did not force Jonas to move. Charges were brought by a Dr? Feinberg, so, of course, preliminaries had involved a process of names: "Fairy"—"Kike." (18 May 1957)

Again, in August 1958, Blaser worried to Duncan about the antics of his friends. Jonas and Balas had been arrested, and he, Blaser, had put up $2000 bail for them. Steve might skip, he thought, and there would be the consequent loss of the bail money. By August, however, the matter was concluded with Blaser reimbursed, and Jonas with a one-month suspended sentence and six months' probation (Blaser to Duncan, 23 August 1958). Writing to Olson, Blaser explains his view of such behavior:

> The POINT: John and Steve said poetry was on trial. The poem's in jail. Judge said you can write anywhere, can't you. Yes or no. But I saw only the weakness, the lack of meaning, the unmeeting. Justice, even in the guize [sic] of straight man did not appear. There is here for John and Steve a revolution in becoming. Not fully understood by Blaser. What he calls "image hunting." They want the fringe, the distortion, the criminal, as if this were closer to the source. If the swollen belly must always relate to abortion, is not some motion of breath lost? If a man is arrested for stealing candy and cheese (one was!) is poetry under arrest? I say the man must breath with me to form a line.
>   I've known criminals all my life. Began at 10 when I stole a flower shaped pen-wiper and had to return it. It was so beautiful. Shills, junkies, card-sharks, con-men, suicides (no murderers, but I can understand that) and I know they suffer. And when the queen who carries a hat box to stuff the loot in (Countess) offers "her" impetigo (brought straight from San Quentin). Mark of love. Breath against mine. Or the house-breaker, first floor man, nigger of the night, when I say drop it and get out, asks to use the pot—calls over the pissing sound, "I love you." Word love in prison talk.... But where's the revolution? In joy? In hate? Or am I just that much older. But then Steve's older. Confusion. (18 May 1957)

This passage explains much of Blaser's attitude toward the kind of life that Wieners and Jonas lived, and William Burroughs and Herbert Huncke, with the help of a titillated media, would make iconic. But as the above remarks to Olson say, Blaser did not think that acting out against the middle class was particularly revolutionary. While empathetic with the truly marginalized—gays pushed into the criminal underground for being gay, for instance—he was looking for something more radical than the cranking of drugs and stereos. Blaser was no prude and certainly not a purist when it came to sex and substances. In the letter to Don Allen, he remembers aiding and abetting his friends' habits:

> Twice I bailed Jonas out when he was up on mail-fraud charges—stealing door to door art book [sic] and selling them. Somewhere (?) I have poems—very long—written on toilet paper while he was in jail. Steve was a central figure in a drug-loving set, introduced to Jack and me by John Wieners—no blacks, except Steve, among them. What was that stuff for teething babies called—2 types—one with opium, the other with morphine—I remember once collecting in one day across Boston—by means of my "respectability"—something like 40 bottles for them—oh!—the result was constipation that came to look like pregnancy… (7 June 1997)

And yet the poverty that came from living without regular employment and the physical stresses of benzedrine or heroin addiction, were not, for Blaser, desirable, nor were they a route to social or intellectual revolution.

Hanging out with the Boston poets and working at the Widener might have been enough busyness for most people, but these were not Blaser's only tasks. He had always been an attentive and admiring reader of Duncan's work and he actively cheered Duncan on to publish in journals like *Measure* (Blaser to Duncan, 18 February 1958) and the *Evergreen Review* (Blaser to Duncan, 16 June 1957). He also advised Duncan on a possible "Selected Poems" for Grove Press and this task plunged him into a time-consuming re-reading of Duncan's entire *oeuvre*:

> This is a first note on the selected poems. What I've been going through with them! I had no copies of *Domestic Scenes* or the African poems available. How very good they are and what a path you've taken. I pulled out a notebook you gave me to see what you had said – that I had followed even when you were away. I hope I have. When I despair it is that there is no place to go that you haven't gone. When I am sure and joyous, working and studying it, it is the hand-clasp and the breath against breath, which is after all, among poets a kind of kissing. (Blaser to Duncan, 1 June 1957)

This letter goes on to discuss the possible aims of a "Selected" ("Is it to be the representative idea?") and what should be included? (1 June 1957). As Blaser says on "The Astonishment Tapes," he probably read Duncan more closely than Duncan ("AT" 3, 38). This sometimes led to grief, as when Blaser tried to mediate between a persnickety Duncan and Don Allen over selections for *The New American Poetry*. "My concern over your break with Don Allen is pervasive," Blaser writes. "In fact, it has put me into a panic of phone calls, notes, arguments. I can only say, the anthology makes no sense whatever without you" (23 August 1958). Chided by Duncan for giving in to "Don's pervasiveness," Blaser apologized profusely before finally rejecting the "part of middleman." "I am too often despised for it," he writes (30 August 1958). Yet even in the flurry of leaving Boston for Europe in June 1959, Blaser was talking to Jack Sweeney at the Library about a possible Duncan reading (Blaser to Duncan, 27 June 1959).

A COMPANY OF POETS

The thing about Boston, as Blaser discovered early on, was that it was close to New York. Shortly after arrival, he wrote to his mother and Gran that he was "saving up to go—it's only 215 miles away" (Blaser to Ina Mae Blaser, 2 October 1955). Over his time at the Widener, Blaser made many trips to New York and came to like and admire Frank O'Hara and John Ashbery. In a letter to Duncan, he asks: "Do you know O'Hara's little book[5] and what do you think of it. (I need to say that I adore Frank.)" (8 April 1958). With Ashbery, as well, he was friendly, although Ashbery was then based in France and the two did not get to know each other much until Blaser arrived in Paris in 1959. In a note to Blaser, Ashbery apologizes for getting drunk during Blaser's last visit (10 June 1958). He announces his trip to France and invites Blaser to visit him in New York when he returns. However, Blaser did not correspond extensively with Ashbery or O'Hara. The real New York interlocutor of the Boston years was old Berkeley friend Don Allen. Allen had moved to New York and taken a position with Grove Press and the *Evergreen Review*. This put him in a special position in relation to emerging poets. He was a reader and publisher for Blaser and for the others he famously called "New Americans" in *The New American Poetry* anthology of 1960, but he was also a personal friend and this double role caused some fuss and bother, as well as much correspondence. Allen and Blaser visited back and forth between New York and Boston; they discussed poems and upcoming publications, and they weathered Blaser's furies over Allen's editorial decisions.

In 1956, Allen wrote about the possibility of a volume featuring Blaser, Duncan, Spicer, and Landis Everson. The proposed anthology never came about; instead, Allen produced the San Francisco issue of *Evergreen*. The *Evergreen Review* was founded as a quarterly in 1957 by Barney Rosset and edited by Rosset and Allen. Unlike *Measure*, it was large, perfect-bound, and international in scope. The first issue included an essay by Jean-Paul Sartre and a story by Samuel Beckett called "Dante and the Lobster." "I've seen the first Evergreen and rather liked it. But a little safe for my money," Blaser remarks to Duncan of issue one (16 March 1957). The second issue, the landmark San Francisco special, was a topic of much discussion between Blaser and Allen. Blaser's "Hunger of Sound" was to be included in this issue, but Allen had reservations about the second section of the poem and turned it down (10 June 1957). He also let Blaser know that he would prefer to publish a group of shorter poems rather than this more ambitious longer piece that he thought was flawed (10 June 1957). Although ambivalent about the poem himself,

Blaser wrote to Spicer that exclusion from the San Francisco issue would make him feel like an exile (13 April 1957). Allen accepted a revised version of "Hunger of Sound," but then asked Blaser to put off publication until the third issue of *Evergreen*. In a letter that clumsily tries to smooth Blaser's ruffled feathers, he asks for the privilege of using the poem to make up the page count, should it be needed. Hence a Blaser fury: *Evergreen* had kept and then rejected his poem, bumped to make space for Ginsberg's "Howl," he fumes to Duncan (15 June 1957). In a huff, he refused to give Allen the shorter poems that Allen had asked for, thus cutting himself out of the San Francisco *Evergreen* entirely. So it would go. To Spicer, Blaser says that he doesn't know whether Don is an editor, cheat, or friend (19 August 1957). In his angry moments, Blaser objected to Allen's concept of a journal quite contrary to that of *Measure*, one that presented polished and representative works rather than a poetry in the making, barely dry on the page. Still the trips and dinners and letters continued between New York and Boston. In the summer of 1957, Allen and Blaser went to Gloucester together to visit Olson, and faced with Duncan's truculence about contributing to *The New American Poetry*, Blaser defended Allen and urged Duncan to contribute (Blaser to Duncan, 23 August 1958).

One of the most influential relationships to come out of the Boston period for Blaser was his friendship with Charles Olson. Blaser made the first move, writing on the morning of his birthday, 18 May 1957. In a commentary on the ensuing correspondence, written retrospectively in 1995 to accompany publication of the Olson–Blaser letters in Ralph Maud's *Minutes of the Charles Olson Society*, he says that Duncan had brought "Projective Verse" and field composition to Berkeley in 1950 (Blaser 1995e, 6). *Origin* and the *Black Mountain Review* would follow and then it was "In Cold Hell, in Thicket" in 1953 along with Jonathan Williams's edition of *The Maximus Poems 1-10* in the same year. "I recall the consternation and the dismissals at large around Berkeley and San Francisco," Blaser writes. "Something was loose" (Blaser 1995e, 6). In Boston, Wieners and Marshall insistently brought Olson to Blaser's attention:

> I do remember what was behind my writing him. Wieners had told me that Olson just plain "dismissed" Dante—of no use to poets now. I also remember that I blazed up from my usual smouldering and proposed to write Olson a blast. John objected—please, not to. But, I had a real stake in this. I'd read Dante as a very small boy by way of Gustave Doré's engravings and had never let go. Dante's hold on me was not primarily religious, which has been a problem since my earliest erotic ties; rather it was the way imagery could conduct me through the arguments of realities. Later, it would be the way many voices could enter his poem—that a poem was as much a matter of thinking as it was of personal cares.... Once I'd thought this over, I realized that I knew nothing about what Olson might be trying to tell Wieners. Thus my letter, as I try to recall it, folded my concern with Dante into my continuing attention to "Projective Verse" and The Maximus Poems. (Blaser 1995e, 7)

The letter that Blaser here recalls begins like this:

Dear Charles Olson, Sir: John Wieners says you won't mind the pink aspect and he's warned you I'd send the poem. Intended as some sort of thank you.

With Duncan and Wieners, I've been pouring over your work and whereas I hate students, I've been one. Odd that we need another REVOLUTION so soon after the last one. But we do. I once thought refinement of the Williams–Pound reel (refinement in the sense of reaching out from there) was the next step. Now, I'm not so sure. That is, everyone has to reach out from there unless he's academic. Which is settling in to dignified repetitions. But the breathing you suggest combines with Williams to suggest for me a REVOLUTION in texture. No more carried away by sound alone, which problem you will see I struggled with in Hunger of Sound. Anyway, I wish to escape the repetitions of the minds [sic] hunger for a safe beat. The projective suggests a rescue. (29 April 1957)

Olson wrote back quickly on 3 May 1957, a long letter that takes off on Blaser's characterization of the breath line as textured and on the comment about the need for another revolution, post-the-modern as Olson phrases it elsewhere. This letter anticipates the foundational pieces of his poetics: his periodizing of cultural change; his cosmology, and the fourfold structure of it as laid out in *The Special View of History* and the second volume of the *Maximus Poems*.[6] As Blaser says in his 1995 commentary, "Olson's first letter was, in the lingo of the '60's, a mind-blower" (Blaser 1995e, 11). Read in retrospect through the later *Maximus Poems* and *The Special View of History*, the letter foretells the shape of things to come, but Olson had not written these key pieces in 1957 and there was then no George Butterick to do the heavy lifting. Coming through the mail, the letter was a cryptogram that would pull Blaser deep into Olson's world.

This bullet of a letter demanded a visit and in the summer of 1957, Don Allen and Blaser called upon Olson in Gloucester.

When we arrive, Olson is waiting for Don Allen and me at a small table in The Tavern bar. We'd barely settled when Olson turned to me and asked, "Who is Matilda?" It took me some time to find my bearings. We were, it turned out, in the midst of Dante—Purgatorio, Cantos XXVIII & XXIX—gazing with him across a stream—one appears who warms herself in love's beams—she is the fourth of Dante's six guides in The Comedy. I do not remember in detail my answer. I do know that it was inadequate. (Blaser 1995e, 11)

This conversation, Blaser writes, was followed by a reading of *Maximus* 1–22, "straight through." Again, the event would stay with Blaser for a very long time. "Who is Matilda" would fold into his poetry as an ongoing meditation on Dante's *Purgatory*—a place very like the earth, Blaser would say in *Astonishments* (*AT*, 106).

Another key exchange between Olson and Blaser was a discussion about syntax. In a 13 May 1958 letter, Olson references a conversation he had had with Blaser "over the spaghetti." As Blaser records it later, the comment from Olson was, "'I'd trust you / anywhere with image, but / you've got no syntax'" (*HF*, 223). In this long letter, Olson begins with the comment, "Very struck of course by yr saying who's the image boy around hyar?" (13 May 1958). He then moves to a dream directive, later published in the *Maximus Poems*: "of rhythm is image / of image is knowing / of knowing there is / a construct" (13 May 1958). So form (image) comes out of process (rhythm, content). Olson had been reading Alfred North Whitehead's *Process and Reality* in the mid-1950s, a work of speculative philosophy that proposes subject and object are mutually constitutive manifestations of a material continuum rather than ontologically distinct entities.[7] Olson had been working toward similar ideas in his relating of form and content in "Projective Verse" (1950). In this dense letter to Blaser, Olson is "throwing dimensions around," he says, "so we can talk of it." Then he responds to Blaser's "Ten Songs for Love" (still unpublished):

> Anyhow: to get back to what I sd that night in yr living room—if you go apart from the specific object or person/ or the image floats free from such literalness of <u>source</u>, one is losing the DOUBLE (TWO FACED (fact in the universe?) which gives image its effect... (13 May 1958)

Blaser "lacks syntax," it seems, because he doesn't adequately ground "Ten Songs" in a particularized time and space; without that grounding, the image floats as fantasy or metaphysics. Hence the gem-cutter figure of Blaser's poem is "too large an observer" according to Olson's marginal notes—this coming from a Maximus who, however grand he would become in some of the poems, is discernibly a figure working on and in a cosmos that dwarfs him.

Blaser's poetic response to Olson's critique would unfold over decades. In *Syntax*, a serial poem collecting work from 1979 to 1981, it would come in the performance of multiple syntaxes among which Blaser's own voice sounds alongside others as a kind of Minimus. In 1958, however, Blaser took the "no syntax" conversation as a challenge and a task. To Olson he writes:

> Your great letter caught me on the run between New Hampshire and New York. Important. I work on it. And will continue that as I accomplish this and that. I think it is unanswerable without <u>objecta</u>.
>   On <u>Gem-Cutter</u>. I think I explained I'd cut out all "personal" – to concentrate on image. And you say, "Where are you?" I'm so damn wrong as I'd forgotten that I am myself an image. (29 May 1958)

The letter concludes with "This is thanks for what is <u>help</u>!" In letters to Spicer and Duncan, both written on the same day (29 May 1958), Blaser sounds less easy with the Olson admonition. To Duncan, he says that "Olson gave me the gun and has tried to help." To Spicer, he comments similarly that he has had the "gun" from Olson, Duncan, O'Hara, and Don Allen (29 May 1958). It was the Olson comment that he would chew on, however, and for a very long time. "I don't really understand what he means," he writes to Duncan, "but it does seem to involve elements in my poems which seem 'poetic'" (11 April 1959).

At the Widener, Blaser carried out Olson's errands, tracking down a manu-script copy of Herman Melville's poem, "After the Pleasure Party" (Blaser to Olson, 27 February 1958) and forwarding messages to Ed Marshall for Olson (Olson to Blaser, 8 December 1958). And the "no syntax" comment would continue to resonate between them. On a visit to Harvard and dinner at the Wursthaus, a German restaurant in Harvard Square, Olson kissed Blaser's hand, right in front of university officials, to Blaser's immense delight:

> This is to say your kiss burned the skin of my hand.
>
> The problem of syntax: you say it is difficult to tell me what to do. It's wrong that I ask you to. Beyond the indications given. As I don't know what this syntax is. It is an awkward word for what every poet has to find out for himself—or he ain't. (Not to be misunderstood as a threat, since, God, I'm scared, but that's a Dantesque obstruction.)
>
> Your visit was historical. My history. I've never been where we were in the winged Wursthaus. I mean to say a long period of discipline (worship) has begun. (29 March 1959)

For both poets, there was the stimulation of serious conversation about poetry. "I went right off like a jet from that conversation, and the pleasure of staying with you, and have been volant ever since," Olson writes of the above-mentioned visit (15 April 1959). And when Blaser left Harvard for Europe in 1959, Olson was there to see him off.

Blaser's widening circle over the Boston years would also include Michael McClure, Gregory Corso, LeRoi Jones, and Denise Levertov. McClure sent Blaser material for Wieners's *Measure*; Corso and Jones solicited work from Blaser for their publishing ventures. Holed up in Paris on rue Gît-le-Coeur, Corso wrote to Blaser for some "spilled angel juice" for his German anthology, *Junge Amerikanische Lyrik*, eventually published in 1961 (Postcard, 26 September 1958). Jones also asked for poems for *Yugen*, publishing Blaser's "Quitting a Job" in *Yugen* 3 (1958) and "Out to Dinner" in *Yugen* 6 (1960). Blaser's relationship with Levertov, however, was a little more detailed.

Blaser had opened an exchange with Denise Levertov in a complimentary letter in 1956 of the kind he called mash notes. Levertov responded and sub-sequently accepted Blaser's hospitality in Boston, stopping over with the whole family. The friendship, however, never really blossomed. Levertov confessed some puzzlement over Blaser's poetry and later remarked that she had read some of the poems as having a homosexual content that didn't reach her.[8] This sent Blaser into a rage because he felt that Levertov had misread him. An apol-ogy letter from Levertov (15 September 1958) never quite erased the miss between them. On *Astonishments*, Blaser remembers a later comment that Levertov made to Duncan about Duncan's reading with John Ashbery to the effect that "[y]ou don't want to read with faggots like that" (*AT*, 215). "[A]t which point," Blaser says, "it must have been my first response in gay lib at all—I just went up the wall and refused to see Denise" (*AT*, 215).

So Duncan got me to come to lunch, and Denise and I played the magic which is really literally between us whenever we're in the same room, like the time she was staying with me in Boston and so on. But she wrote that poem in the opening of that book [*O Taste and See*] to make up for that. It was about the touch between women and fairies not meaning a *fairy* but meaning—I think she calls me an elf at that point. Why is he elfin? Anyway, it fixed it for a while but it didn't [fix the problem]. (*AT*, 215)

The time of this reconciliation is not clear from *Astonishments*, but it postdates Blaser's Boston period. The poem in question, from 1964, is called "The Elves":

> Their beauty sets them aside
> from other men and from women
> unless a woman has that cold fire in her
> called poet... (Levertov 1983, 76)

As Blaser remembered it, Levertov did not publicly dedicate the poem to him because she thought it would embarrass him (*AT*, 215); Levertov's own explanation was that a dedication was unnecessary because those for whom poems in the collection were intended would know who they were (16 October 1964). Referring to the poem, Blaser says "It's how fairies speak together and so on, and she said it would embarrass me, and my rage at her for that—I think that's when my split goes. I must remember that because that's where the real anger at Denise begins to go" (*AT*, 215). Blaser was no queen but he was not in the closet either, except in front of his parents. He heard the notion that being called a fairy would or should embarrass him as homophobia. Blaser remained leery of Levertov, not only because she seemed distant in her response to homosexuality but also uncomprehending of his poems.[9] In a draft letter to Duncan, he writes of poetry as the "agony of beautiful sound and worship of divinity," but, he says, "This was not the homosexual difference. Homosexuality means much to my passion, but little to my poetry. And that poetry is not one of the passions I am convinced—moving to Shelley, Pound, Olson and you" (Undated, Blaser to Duncan).

THE BOSTON POEMS

In the first edition of Blaser's collected poems, *The Holy Forest* (1993) edited by Stan Persky and Michael Ondaatje, *The Boston Poems* appear at the end of the book under the title *Earlier, 1956–1958: The Boston Poems*. In the revised and expanded *Holy Forest*, published by the University of California Press in 2006, *The Boston Poems* appear in chronological order at the front of the volume under the title *The Boston Poems, 1956–1959*. In this position, they are the first series of *The Holy Forest* and the beginning of it all, as opposed to an appendix of lesser importance than the main body of the *Collected*. In both cases, Blaser chose the position and the change shows a long-lasting ambivalence about the poems of this period. As his editor for the second edition, I found Blaser more willing to accept *The Boston Poems* as integral to his *oeuvre* than he had been earlier and he even agreed to publish poems that had been left out of the first edition: "Poem" ("O dark haven") and "Quitting a Job" were restored to the Boston record. However, the published *Boston Poems* still conceals the extent of Blaser's output in Boston.

All serious poetry requires a view of the world and a stance on what art can do there. This is what Blaser was working out in Boston and nothing mattered more to him. From Berkeley, he brought to the task an engagement in the occult and the surreal, both of them allied to the psychoanalytical through a shared focus on what lies beyond or beneath rational, ego-centered consciousness. I have said that the surreal was available to Blaser in journals like *View*.[10] The nearer sources were Duncan and Spicer. In his commentary on Duncan's early surrealist period in *Robert Duncan and the Pragmatist Sublime*, James Maynard shows that Duncan shared many of the aims of the Parisian movement, despite his ambivalence about André Breton's orthodoxies. Even after repudiating surrealism, Duncan remained engaged with the language of dreams, the dissolution of ego boundaries, and the creative destruction of existing forms of expression in the constant venturing of the new.[11] In the mid-1940s, Spicer, too, was working with images evocative of a destabilized, post-rational surrealist world. "The Chess Game" (c.1946), for instance, combines references to *Alice in Wonderland* and the "Lord's Prayer" to advance a dystopian "wonderland" in which the Knights are "non-Euclidean," the Rooks fly "faster than the speed of light," and the pawns are headed toward some unspeakable realm below the chessboard (Spicer 1980, 4).

Blaser was still in high school when Duncan was editing the *Experimental Review* and writing surrealist pieces like "Toward the Shaman." By the time they met in Berkeley in 1946, Duncan had moved on and Spicer was only just coming into his own reckoning with what lay beneath the chessboard: his sureness of a language for it would come later in the *Imaginary Elegies* (1950–1955) and *After Lorca* (1957). In the Boston poems, Blaser began to work out his own relationship to desire and the unconscious, and he would inflect it differently than his Berkeley peers. His "Letter to Freud" (1956) takes on the psychoanalytical roots of surrealism. "A Preface to Works to Come" (1958), still unpublished, explores the occult as it comes through William Butler Yeats. "The Hunger of Sound" (1957–1958), the most polished poem of the period, takes up the epistemological questions that arise from a consideration of language as a mediator of consciousness. The foundational work of Boston, then, rests on these themes: the surreal, the occult, the language.

Blaser's Freud poem is titled "Letter to Freud" in the *Boston Newsletter* and "Letters to Freud"[12] in *The Holy Forest*. This is a poem that nods to the psychoanalysis back of surrealism and works through a confrontation with death—the ultimate Other to consciousness. Freud treated the unconscious as more than *merely* subjective because he thought it could exert an unperceived influence on thoughts, actions, and desires in the shared physical world. Writing to Duncan, Blaser expressed his interest in this line of investigative poetry:

> I think I did a straight job of describing the necessity of this stuff [.] That they [Pound, Williams] are early stuff takes me close to the unconscious which I'm trying to understand and use. Surreal. Super-real. Etc. (18 February 1958)

Freud read the inner world, particularly as manifest in dreams, through a logic of condensation and displacement (metaphor and metonymy); the surrealists picked up on the strategy. I suggest that Blaser's poem makes use of this logic. Here are the opening lines:

> ((When I—
> > yes, sleep, Mr Freud.
> > > *A crushed dog on West 9th.*
> *Sounds like a man.*
> > > Yes
> Mr Freud, if—
> > Mr Freud, if—
> Oh, damned words. Yes, Mr Freud,
> > > damned descriptive.
> My dear Mr Freud, *when I lie in the sun, a bird passes*
> *over and the wings grow on me....* (*HF*, 16)

In Freudian terms, a man with wings might refer to some prior trauma associated with a bird or condense an experience involving a man and a bird or stand in for some other object of unconscious significance. The difference between such an image and a trope employed for descriptive vivacity is in the uncanny, fraught nature of the Freudian dream image which includes something that cannot reach consciousness directly. Analogously, early surrealist imagery draws together elements that do not easily resolve into simile or metaphor and that have the uncanny feel of a "message" from beyond the conscious mind. Blaser's Freud poem does not say that the man is like a bird or wishes to become a bird or wants to fly. It fuses man and bird in a hybrid object. The strangeness of this object is expressed as wings that grow on the man without his willing them there. The image is unassimilable either to a clear dichotomy between man and bird (simile) or to the more common literary use of metaphor in which one term is understood to be a symbolic representation of the other, either of which would be more pleasing to common sense.

The narrative component of the poem is about the sufferings of a dying dog and the poet's agonized response. In a letter to Duncan and Jess, Blaser says that he had been woken by the howls of a dog that had been hit by a car and had its pelvis crushed (30 November 1956). He ran to the animal, intending to strangle it to end the suffering but found that he couldn't do it. This story of the injured dog worries the hybridity of self and other. Pain and death are limit concepts of communicability in language: everyone knows what the words mean, but no one can actually experience the suffering of another or consciously go through death. Hence the speaker of the poem is stuck with "damned words" that cannot actually translate the dog's misery into the speaker's cognition: like the unconscious, the howl of the Other does not translate directly. The speaker of the poem *does* strangle the dog—as Blaser could not—just as a poet "strangles" an event to render it in words that are inevitably abstractions. Yet the event in its suchness—in this instance, the death of a non-human creature—remains unsaid. Like a kernel of trauma in the unconscious, it *motivates* the words of the poem. Hence the repeated invectives throughout the poem against the "damned words" that circle the experience of suffering and death that here goes on in the body of the dog, beneath the words—sur-real. The Freudian connection is that death is, literally, the unsayable core of all trauma and of all erotic desire to merge with the Other. The surrealist connection is that the hybrid object stands in as a glyph of this strangeness back of the familiar. The terrain of the surreal is thus neither in the depths of the subject nor in the objects of the common world but between the two, as the poem is between the man and the dog. "In the ordered world," Walter Benjamin says in his essay, "Surrealism," "dreams hollow out individuality like the cavity in a tooth" (Benjamin 2015, 18).

Thus, Blaser would come to theorize perception in later essays like "The Practice of Outside," his Spicer essay of 1975, in which he draws on the philosophy of Maurice Merleau-Ponty (*The Visible and the Invisible*). In 1956, however, he was reading Olson and Olson was reading Alfred North Whitehead's *Process and Reality*, a work which proposes that all things express and inflect each other, that an entity is always already a composite of what seems to be Other to it. If we accept the thesis of these otherwise disparate philosophers that subjects and objects are neither separate from nor reducible to each other, then the surrealist object may begin to read as an *affective performance* of a phenomenology of perception: perception is irreducibly fraught with what it cannot fully assimilate, including the death of the perceiver and the perceived. For Olson, Whitehead's philosophy meant the end of mind-body dualism and a means to think the recovery of the familiar in what had been estranged as *merely* material in Platonic-Christian metaphysics—the body, the earth, the sky. For Blaser it was the beginning of what he called polarity—the strange in the familiar, the Other in the same. The two views are contraries. Small wonder, then, that Olson "let fly" at Blaser over "the surrealist danger" (Blaser to Duncan, 11 April 1959).

Like poems everywhere and across time, Blaser's "Letter to Freud" reaches for the world—"the flesh, / the golden earth"—but what comes back is a hybrid that is uncanny. The face in the mirror (death is "an image complete as my face"), the moon, the earth, the planet, the dying dog are the existents that the poet tries to bring to presence, but words cannot quite close on them: the intrusion of the dog's pain in the speaker's consciousness keeps the poem going (*HF*, 16–18). In other words, death keeps the form open. The poem begins with a strangling of life to end suffering, an act of compassion, but it turns into a "yes" to life and the perils of loving it.

> *My dear Mr Freud,*
>   *simply no longer.*   *Yes.*   *Light*
> *yes is after all yes like yes*
>   *an image in flight.*
> P.S.   yes. (*HF*, 18)

In these last lines, death is transmuted to "simply no longer"; it is tucked into the life process which the poem says is like "an image in flight," perpetually elusive, and the poet, echoing Molly Bloom's yes to existence at the end of James Joyce's *Ulysses*, affirms it despite the suffering and strangeness.

The Freud poem distinguishes Blaser's poetic stance from that of both Duncan and Spicer. Unlike Duncan, Blaser does not *dwell* in the inexhaustible potential of language to generate new forms and spark new modes of consciousness. In the Freud poem, death is beyond language and poetry. As Spicer was at pains to demonstrate, life and language are different orders of the real. Bodies suffer and die, words do not; bodies are particular, words are abstract. Yet Blaser also avoids locking into unsatisfiable Spicerian desire—the fixation on love lost to the death waiting beneath the chessboard and the incapacity of poetry to save it.[13] In the letter to Duncan laying out the back story, Blaser includes a comment on a quarrel with Spicer:

> Also, quarreled with Spicer violently over what I called the monomania of his poetry and the limited reference. A poem like his <u>Poem for the Reader of the Poem</u> is much changed for this insistence upon what a poem must take on. In a very crucial sense. The poem once written no longer belongs to anybody. (30 November 1956)

Spicer wanted the intimacy of a direct connection to people and things, but he also knew very well from his linguist's training that this was impossible. He therefore made present an absence that indexed his desire for immediacy. Hence in "A Poem to the Reader of the Poem," he opens with the line, "I throw a naked eagle in your throat" (Spicer [1975] 1980, 349), as if words were birds that might choke the indifferent or blasé reader into feeling what the poet feels. In a draft letter to Spicer that I have not confirmed as sent, Blaser says "Yet I do not believe in a poetry which is a construct of the desire for poetry" (Undated, "Dearest Jack – well, the sound has come"). Blaser was readier than Spicer to accept the suffering that love entails. In the spring of 1957, he was reading Antonin Artaud (Blaser to Duncan, 16 March 1957) and thinking about translating Artaud's essay on Van Gogh for Grove Press. In that essay, Artaud refers to "the pure enigma of a tortured flower" (Artaud 1965, 153). Van Gogh, he says, painted that thing with "his drunken brush" (153). Love, death, the suffering-through that is life—the Freud poem puts together the bones of it.

"A Preface to Works to Come," dated September 1958, takes Yeats as a point of departure for another study of the surreal and the occult. Much of Yeats's poetic thinking turns on relations of contrariety. To name a few, there are the dancer and dance in "Among School Children"; Hic and Ille in "Ego Dominus Tuus"; the He and She of "Michael Robartes and the Dancer"; Self and Soul in "A Dialogue of Self and Soul"; life and art in "Sailing to Byzantium" and flesh and spirit in the alchemical tales of Michael Robartes ("Rosa Alchemica") and Owen Aherne ("Tables of the Law"). In "Rosa Alchemica," for example, the speaker is drawn into a magical dance by the latter-day mystic Michael Robartes. Tranced participants are initiated into the esoteric side of the alchemical tradition as they dance with shadowy gods and goddesses that feed on their souls. As a metaphor for poetry, the dance suggests that the poet is there to give voice and form to the invisible world. If one drops belief in the literality of a spirit world, then it is the extreme Otherness of things—the invisible world that is not coincident with consciousness—that is being summoned.

Blaser engages with Yeats's contraries, but rejects the anthropomorphism of the occult. The occult view of the invisible is that it is a spirit world of gods and goddesses who look rather like us but with improved capacities. For both Blaser and Spicer, Yeats modeled the practice of dictation (poetry dictated by an "outside" source, like the car radio from the underworld in Jean Cocteau's film, *Orphée*), but it was Yeats modulated through a Berkeley version of the surreal, fraught with the uncanny. The surrealists had tried to reach beyond the cogito in order to let the depths of the unconscious manifest. However questionable the experiments in cognition (automatic writing, for example), the surrealists provided an initial spectacle of the decentered self or the self that is an Other. So in Blaser's "Preface," the juxtapositions are as strange as Meret Oppenheim's famous fur-lined teacup (1936): "The nightingales in our fingers pluck at the eyes of the man / it concerns"; "The lights whip around the Portuguese mothers herding / their unicorns home to supper"; "A tiger of foam is purring with helpless rage against / my mouth"; "The white doves in my pockets cackle"; "10,000 ancestors weep out of my thighs like salt." In such images, the unknown presses against common sense experience. In lines that seem to layer images from Yeats's "Rosa Alchemica" with the surreal, Blaser writes:

> There, out at the edge, I see the light of our skin
> dance or dazzle.
>
> The spray falls in beads of sweat on the dance. (Blaser 1958, n.p.)

The initiatory dance of Yeats's "Rosa Alchemica" takes place in the Temple of the Alchemical Rose at the end of a pier extending out into the sea (Yeats 1978, 280). When the speaker of this story awakes after the hallucinatory dance, he finds himself not in a chamber alive with spirits and a living rose, but in a bare room with crudely painted images on the walls and ceiling (Yeats 1978, 290). The speaker is drawn out of his sleep by the loud shouts of fishers who attack the building because they think the initiates have brought devil worship and bad luck to them. Daytime common sense perceives the uncanny as a threat. What Blaser's poem takes from Yeats is the "edge"—pushing the image out to a point where it becomes wild:

The language must gather in clouds. As swarming bees against
the screen-door anger. The bee opens the jaw of the snapdragon.
Tearing the hinge. And the stance must open as woman has opened
eternally to her first man. Adam has opened his hand. Thrust
the willowy language apart. (Blaser 1958, n.p.)

These images suggest a violent assault on the cogito: bees swarm a door and
tear at a snapdragon as a first lover would tear a woman's hymen. Rainer Maria
Rilke's bees of the invisible[14]—bees of perception that gather the outside into
the honey of experience—should come to mind, but these bees gather a strange
nectar. The intrusion of the unknown into one's sense of a stable reality,
whether in "messages" from the unconscious, or an unsayable real somewhere
underneath the words, or the howl of a dying dog means a dramatic assault on
one's sense of self. In section eight of "Preface," Blaser writes that poetry is a
"man-eating shark" and this would place the poet in imminent danger of being
consumed. In another Yeatsian image, the "Bright body of / my world / has
creaked on the steps / to the third floor / where we live among configurations
of a dance." *Something* mounts the steps to "where we live," and it is stranger
than gods and goddesses.

Belovèd Yeats, now I'm writing at home.
It is breakfast
amidst the glorious wallpapers of poetry.

The cats are pawing the carpet of
an intolerable future where the dance begins.
Not isolate. The fates on my ankles
twist the joy out of my mouth.

On West Cedar. Outside the houses.
Where the bricks have the teeth of flowers.
Yes. A dancer spreads his claws. (Blaser 1958, n.p.)

Danger and mystery are immanent in the mundane, morning-after "on West
Cedar." When the spirit world falls out of belief and loses its anthropomorphic
shape, Otherness becomes much more startling in secularity than it was in religion, whether occult or orthodox. In the morning light, the spirit magic disappears for Yeats's speaker, but for the poet of "A Preface," "the bricks have the
teeth of flowers" and a dancer "spreads his claws."

   "The Hunger of Sound" is Blaser's most fully realized poem of the Boston
period, but like most of the longer, unpublished poems of these years, the writing of it was fraught with anxiety. After a depressed and angry letter from Blaser
complaining that the "Olson babies" (Marshall and Wieners) had criticized the
poem for "false breath patterns, rarefied language, lack of specificity and too
many similes" (19 February 1957), Spicer advises Blaser to simply "[e]mbrace
and smother [his] weaknesses" ([21 February 1957]). If they complain of rarefied language, Spicer opines, Blaser should make it so rare they can't breathe.

On another occasion, he tells Blaser that his real problem is that he can't write a bad poem (Spicer to Blaser, "I don't see correcting poems"). Look at Duncan, Spicer says, he writes more bad poems than either of us and that is why he is ahead. There was also the history of the poem at *Evergreen* and Allen's request that publication be delayed. In fact, "Hunger of Sound" was first published in *Measure* 2 in the winter of 1958 and dedicated to Lars Balas, the young son of artist and Boston pal Tom Balas. The poem begins this way:

> I asked a man to consider poetry.
> I said
> Begin then with this image:
> A child's head bends in the light,
> slips like a star across a man's mentality.
> He and his guardian cat reach for a word.
>
> Among stars, a man becomes a giant.
> Take this image:
> > the masked face of a child,
> insatiable of light.
> > A word found,
> a child's voice—
> > this hunger of gulls
> that fish from the broken edge of ice. (*HF*, 19)

When a child reaches for the world, he or she gets a word instead, and slowly, through that medium, the human universe comes into focus. I use the verb "reach" with consideration because I think it is key to Blaser's view of language and distinguishes his thinking from that of the structuralist linguists who would become so important to poets and philosophers of later decades. For Blaser, language is a *techne* by means of which humanity reaches. Like the hands of a child or the hunger of gulls or fish breaking the surface of the water (see "Poem by the Charles River" (*HF*, 15)), it expresses a hunger for things: the child is "insatiable of light." That hunger comes from the situated nature of existence—from the infantile discovery of a not-me. In the opening lines cited above, the world comes into focus like "a tree / first planted in chaos," out of the unordered sensations of preverbal infancy. It is uprooted, though, suspended in air. It is not that words are naturally attached to things, but that they offer "a world of exact proportions" (*HF*, 19). Language fits the world as a glove fits a hand—precise, but not at all of the same stuff. (In Cocteau's *Orphée*, Orpheus passes through a mirror, from one side of the real to another, using a pair of magical gloves.) Outside the word is only "chaos," a word for what remains unthought. In the fourth stanza, the child counts and names things—"The returning birds / or the new leaves counted" (*HF*, 19). So the tree of the third stanza blossoms and becomes "the flowering peach of the orchard, / each blossom counted and named" (*HF*, 20). The whole first section of "Hunger of Sound" shows a world emerging into thingness for the first time. That freshness is, of course, every poet's dream—to say the world again in a way that makes it new. Thus Rimbaud imagined a freshly washed world emerging "après le deluge." Thus Pound's "make it new." Thus the great vision of Dante, who suddenly comes to wakefulness in a dark wood. The objects that emerge are vivid and beautiful, but as the child reaches for them, he or she grasps along with them the imminence of terror and death in living things:

> Read Dante without words.
> (By Doré)
>   I try now to remember
> what I thought of hell.
>   A small head
> bent over the big pages.
>   And now
> borrowed the terrible trees
>   and
> the whole image of Dante. (*HF*, 21–22)

Blaser's choice of this particular image from the *Inferno*—the trees are the suicides who have murdered the human form—underlines the fact that language also exacerbates suffering. It uproots us from the flow of unreflective material processes and sensations, sets us facing a world of objects, and brings the consciousness of death. Dante's suicides reject suffering by killing themselves as the poet kills the suffering dog in the Freud poem: they say "no" rather than "yes" to the pains of life.

The final section of "Hunger" opens with a repetition of the first line: "I asked a man to consider poetry" (*HF*, 24). This is perhaps the most personal section of the poem because it is where Blaser puts together the "orchard" of childhood memory, the trees of Dante, and the long years of self-doubt about being a poet.

> I said:
>   My emblem became a tree.   Stood
> tall and could both bend and straighten.   Rode
> on the hills of New Hampshire   a great hunter.
> Ice-caught gestures of the trees
> turn inward.
>
> This is a gesture. The words stopped
> there—part of the forest. (*HF*, 25)

The tree would become the central trope of *The Holy Forest*, although Blaser did not know it at the time. In this Boston poem, however, Blaser allows himself to say, "'I, poet," and to begin to use past failures and uncertainties—the "uncounted" words "killed there in the blossoming mouth"—as the "rot" that will feed the "star flowers" (*HF*, 25). In the first stanza of this section a "boatman sings" and "bends to an outward journey" (*HF*, 24). So also the poet.

In retrospect, "The Hunger of Sound" is a launching pad for *The Holy Forest*. It establishes a view of language and hence an epistemology. It draws in the poet's personal history (Orchard, Idaho), and it settles on a trope that would hold through a lifetime of writing: the world-tree, linguistic tree (roots and branches of language), poe-tree, and family tree of *The Holy Forest*. It also acknowledges Blaser's earliest and most important source in Dante and through Dante it names Blaser's project: a saying of the world for the twentieth century as Dante said it for the thirteenth. Further, the poem situates Blaser's attention in perceptual experience and an intuition of the surreal,[15] negotiating between Duncan's fascination with the generative powers of language and Spicer's sense of the inadequacy of them in the presence of death. Because some of this early work anticipates structuralist views of language, and because Blaser would engage directly with structuralist and deconstructive philosophies of language in his poems and essays of the 1970s and 80s, this situating of his attention in perceptual experience at the beginning of his poetic practice is important and it is not naively done. "The Hunger of Sound" does not contest what linguists call the unmotivated relationship of words and things—the word "tree" hangs in chaos, not on a tree—but it does suggest that language is how humanity handles the world and that what is of interest is its manner of doing so, rather than the fact of the medium itself. In a notebook, Blaser writes:

> And linguists teach
> 　　　　　　how speech is young
> 　and I teach
> 　　　　　　how we cheat the young
> Come, let me tell you what I've learned
> that it is desire burned the first bush
> turned the first kiss into a wish
> and left our leafy eyes to twist
> [in] the wind. (Undated, "And linguists teach")

The deconstructing of language as an unmediated representation of mind and world was of lesser interest to Blaser than what the poet might be able to do inside the medium. It is only from the perspective of a consciousness that the world-as-form becomes possible and the thingness of things thinkable. In this poem, the acquisition of language plays out as a violent uprooting from the flow of life that runs like "water in water" as Georges Bataille describes it,[16] but only after that uprooting is it possible to speak of a world at all, and hence of love.

THE GRAND TOUR

The urge to return to San Francisco had settled in Blaser's imagination over the course of an August 1957 visit[17] when he stayed with Duncan and Jess. The visit gave him courage, he wrote to Duncan: "I'm unable to say what that visit meant.... Your beautiful apartment, the poems, drawings—all the made things and I want you to know I MEMORIZED the whole damn place, so if I haunt you somewhat. Right now I'm hiding behind Jesse's castle, which I wish I'd bought too" (20 August 1957). Blaser turned in his resignation at Harvard a year later and planned his European trip, a much-longed-for cultural tour and a reward for library drudgery, but the last months dragged. He was asked to fire a woman who had worked at the library for 17 years. She was dull, Blaser writes to Jess, but could have been transferred instead of fired by "bourgeois swine" (14 March 1959).

After Felts returned to San Francisco in December 1958 to get ready for the new job, Blaser moved again to a room at 42 Kirkland, Cambridge, in order to save money over the months that he would have to pay the rent alone. Given the importance of dwelling space to Blaser, he found these moves anxiety producing. He was unable to finish a chapbook that Joe Dunn had asked for. By 1957, Dunn was publishing under the White Rabbit Press imprint, the *de facto* Spicer press. Blaser's book was to be illustrated by Jess and in a letter to that eminence, Blaser sent a proposed Table of Contents, but he could not get the poems revised to his satisfaction. Alone on Kirkland Street, he asked Duncan and Jess for a small Jess art piece to give courage (1 December 1958). When the package arrived in January, he says in his thank you letter that it came during "the worst depression of my life" (6 January 1959).

This impatience with Boston does not, however, adequately reflect the record of Blaser's output or the richness of the Boston experience and its long-term significance for his writing life. In the same letter to Duncan in which he expresses dissatisfaction, he describes a reading at Harvard with Ginsberg, Corso, and Peter Orlovsky, sponsored by the Harvard Poetry Society and Harvard Law Forum. Olson came to Boston for it and this was the hand-kissing occasion. "I have never been so moved," he tells Duncan (11 April 1959). The reading was followed by a night of talk: "Allen [Ginsberg] is beautiful and brilliant, but very disappointing in talk. And very political where poetry relations are concerned. Gregory is a little gangster. Peter is apart and strange," he decides (11 April 1959). This event was one of many over Blaser's four years in the east. There were excursions to New Hampshire, to the point where Don Allen suggested the possibility of getting a place there with Robin and Jim: "Am holding onto several chairs and a couple of lamps that we could use in such a house" (22 July [c.1957–1958]). There were jaunts to see Olson, including one to Provincetown with Michael Rumaker (Blaser to Duncan, 30 August 1958). There were trips to New York for parties and shows. On one such occasion, Blaser encountered Marianne Moore and Marilyn Monroe with Arthur Miller at the Academy of Arts and Letters (Blaser to Duncan, 23 June 1958). As he liked to tell the story in person, Moore was looking down Monroe's dress. There was also the collaboration with Wieners on *Measure*, despite the short life of the journal, and there was plenty of insider's input on the San Francisco issue of *Evergreen*, as well as Allen's *New American Poetry* anthology. Blaser was able to leave the Widener with head high: he had in hand stellar recommendations from Harvard and had made many friends during his

Boston gig. Most importantly from his own point of view, he had, by the end of his four years in the east, a substantial collection of poems.

Despite the endless revisions, the withdrawing of poems from private circulation among friends, coupled with a desire to publish and fear of rejection— despite the whole fandango—Blaser did the necessary thing in Boston. He had begun to seriously work through the big questions that every poet has to face about the nature of the real, the purpose of poetry, and the possibilities of his medium. In a notebook draft letter to Duncan, Blaser writes: "I can never say the agony of ten years. I knew I was a poet when others wanted to be firemen, railworkers ... The agony of beautiful sound and worship of divinity" (Undated, Blaser to Duncan). This untitled poem (now published in *The Holy Forest*) marks an exit from years of silence:

For years I've heard
others speak like birds.
                    The words
clicking.
            One day I spoke
articulate
            the words *tic-ed*
in my throat.
            It was
as if love woke
                    after anger.
The words
            sure—
                Listen.
(CHURRR)
            Love wakes
at the breakfast table
                    (CHURRR)
Not that
            the language itself has wings.
(CHURRR) Not that
                    (CHURRR)
unfortunate skill.
                Listen.
The words
            sure as a scream. (*HF*, 14)

With resignation accepted and farewell party attended, Blaser was packing by the end of June 1959, wiping out Boston, he tells Duncan (27 June 1959). "[Robert] Lowell seems the only poet in town," he complains. [Richard] Wilbur and [W.S.] Merwin had gone, and "Charles [Olson] gets no ear at all." As well, Don Allen had resigned from *Evergreen* and Blaser had heard that White Rabbit was folding (27 June 1959). "I'll send you soap and Kleenex at regular intervals," Jim writes, "but what else will you need?

Cigarettes?" (5 July 1959). For years, Blaser had dreamed of the splendors of Europe and the Harvard post had made a trip possible. "O, I expect the joy to last all summer. I'll hang on to it / with a gull's beak," says Blaser in "Quitting a Job" (*HF*, 26). He was to go by boat.

On 12 July, Blaser sent a telegram to Olson, telling him where to meet up with the ship for the send-off party. The RMS Nova Scotia was to sail from Boston to Halifax on Tuesday, 14 July 1959. Olson arrived with his wife Betty and son Charles Peter, a copy of Melville's *Redburn* to read on the voyage, and a poem. Writing to Don Allen, Olson says that Blaser was pale-faced and at first looked right through him, but there was a bottle of Cutty Sark and a little group of well-wishers from Harvard (Dick Stone, Ed Klima). Everybody went on board to drink the whiskey in Blaser's cabin. (Olson to Don Allen, 16 July 1959). "We shall miss you forever," Olson wrote him: "I feel as though my windward anchor is gone" (16 July 1959).

Blaser had planned two weeks in London to visit the great cultural sites of the city. On 28 July, he checked into the Bedford and got down to it. His itinerary included Westminster Abbey and the poets' corner with the graves of Chaucer and Ben Jonson, the British Museum "filled with superb Greek things," the National Gallery, and the Tate (Blaser to Ina Mae Blaser and Sophia Auer, 4 August 1959). Over the first week of August, he met up with his old Harvard boss, Sue Haskins, in Brighton to tour George IV's faux Indian palace (Blaser to family, 8 August 1959) and visit the Sussex countryside. A landscape "mild and protected (protective) compared with Idaho's," he says to the folks (Blaser to family, 8 August 1959). Other excursions included a boat ride on the Thames to London Tower and visits to St. Paul's Cathedral and the famous parks, Hyde, Kensington, and Regent. Evening forays were made to the theater. The real business of London, however, was inside the galleries and museums. At the British Museum, Blaser took note of Assyrian friezes, artifacts from Ninevah, and the gates of Balawat. In one display, he found a winged god, fertilizing the sacred date palm by touching it with a cone, and drew it out for Olson (Blaser to Olson, 5 August 1959). Blaser kept notebooks on his museum visits, mostly full of brief lists of pieces seen or to see and these show hours spent over Greek, Roman, Egyptian, and Middle Eastern antiquities. The Elgin marbles; the Egyptian hippopotamus, goddess of childbirth; Etruscan wall paintings from the fourth century; mosaics from Ur, and the Tablets of Gilgamesh drew his attention. On the last, "what surprises most is their delicacy—baked in clay" (Blaser 1959a, European trip notes). At the National Gallery, he exclaimed over Carlo Crivelli's "magnificent" *Saint Michael* (c.1476), Bronzino's *An Allegory with Venus and Cupid* (c.1545) and the masterworks of the European renaissance painters (Blaser 1959a, European trip notes). To the folks, he writes of Raphael's Madonnas and Leonardo da Vinci's *Madonna of the Rocks* (c.1495–1508): the "light in the most wonderful places" (To family, 8 August 1959). Such a packed itinerary was bound to result in tourist fatigue.

Out of America, dead or alive
I'm here.

In this disaster
climbing monuments to drip
ice-cream on Edward III

found the old Church Yard
of St. Peter, Paul's Wharf, burned 1666

Blackfriars Bridge has pulpit
of marble—from which I look
at the Thames— (Blaser 1959b, "Out of America")

The notation begins as a poem and tapers to a travel note. Felts comments that Blaser's letters make London sound "dreary" and cautions him against over tipping—one of Blaser's princely habits that would be lifelong. "[Y]ou don't care what they think about you, or do you?" Felts scolds, "This is your chance to see Europe so don't waste your money just because you want a cabbie or a bell hop to like you a little better" (3 August 1959). However fondly the cabbies and bellhops might have looked upon him, Blaser did not find London as pleasing as he had hoped. There were too many tourists for one thing. Westminster Abbey looked like a "circus picnic ground" (Blaser to Ina Mae Blaser and Sophia Auer, 4 August 1959) and the city was full of nationalities in native garb, "a city of visitors" he says (Blaser to family, 8 August 1959). There were also pick pockets (Blaser to Ina Mae Blaser and Sophia Auer, 4 August 1959) and the currency was a challenge, with a confusing number of coins of different sizes and denominations. For the folks in Idaho he traced the shapes of them out on paper, writing in the values of each (Blaser to family, 8 August 1959). To Duncan, Blaser later writes that "London wasn't my city" (15 August 1959). On 11 August, he was ready to move on to Paris.

The Hotel Soufflot was then located at 9, rue Touillier in the fifth arrondissement. Blaser checked into a small room that boasted hot water, a bidet, and a concierge who locked up at 10 pm. Although one had to share the toilet, it was Paris at the frugal rate of less than $2 a night (Blaser to family, 15 August 1959). The food was good and cheap, and there was *café au lait* and *pain buerre* for breakfast (Blaser to family, 15 August 1959). The Café Soufflot also specialized in ice creams decked with various sauces, liqueurs, nuts, and fruits (Fig. 4.1). For homesick Americans, there were hot dogs and hamburgers on the menu. Then there was the adventure of doing laundry secretively, late at night, because it was forbidden at the Hotel, and of swimming at a French *piscine* in a French bikini (Blaser to Widener friends, 29 August 1959).

Like many non-native speakers, however, Robin had trouble with the spoken language, and this was a disappointment, given his efforts in French through high school and university—"too literary and the Parisians speak so fast" (Blaser to family, 15 August 1959). To Duncan and Jess, he writes that he feels both joy and depression, loving the city but feeling cut off from the

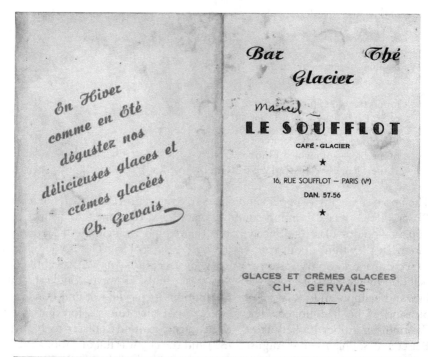

Fig. 4.1   Menu of the Café Soufflot, Paris, 1959

real life of it because of the language barrier (15 August 1959). Importantly, however, Paris brought a closer friendship with John Ashbery. Ashbery invited him for dinner (c. August 1959) and they toured Paris's art nouveau buildings (Blaser to Duncan, 17 August 1959). In a long letter to his Widener friends, Blaser writes that Paris is rich in textures in contrast to the neatness of London and that the French are difficult but not so anti-American as the British (Blaser to Widener friends, 29 August 1959). Better, unlike London, which had absorbed too many Americanisms despite whatever unfriendly sentiments its denizens may have retained about the colonies, Paris was French. Organization at the Louvre is crazy, he writes, and the paintings of Rubens are glowing, beautiful absurdities that ready one for French painting. Good modern painting, however, is American, he opined: "We seem to be the twentieth century par excellence" (Blaser to Widener friends, 29 August 1959).

At the Louvre, Blaser spent time with the impressionists and visited the Musée de l'homme where he notes the Upper Paleolithic Venus de Lespuges and Venus de Laussel (both about 25,000 years old). The famous Cimetière du Père Lachaise was a must and Blaser mapped out a route through it ("gay-mapping" Ellingham and Killian say (Ellingham and Killian 1998, 75)). Then there were films, *Orfeu Negro*, *Les 400 coups*, *Les Tricheurs*, *Les Cousins*, *Les drageurs*, *Hiroshima mon amour*, *Moi, un noir*, and *Un drôle de drame*, doubt-less to help with the French, as well as to entertain. In a sketch of a Paris poem:

> This moment I opened the foliage
> and thrust my tongue among the leaves
> where the animal breath endures.
>
> This was a beginning out of naked arms
> and a blaze of myself. Dying, I said,
> the blood will quit me when I've touched
>
> This monument or that. Cutting my hand
> on the Pont Neuf, there was only a blaze of flesh
> The blood stood thus in its secrecy.
>
> Don't push. The guide books are filled
> with catastrophes and facts. The sorrow
> of this voyage is that I don't see it. (Undated, "This moment")

If the poem doesn't quite speak to Blaser's capacities as a poet, it does suggest a state of mind. A French kiss on the foliage of the city would have to stand in for other kinds of communication. The last three lines sound like a note to self: "don't push." What remains of the poem turns up in *The Faerie Queene* of 1961: "This monument / has torn to pieces our guide book / of facts" (*HF*, 59).

In an itinerary sketched out for the folks, Blaser writes that it was going to be Rome for two weeks at the beginning of September and then a week each for Venice and Florence. He would return for another two weeks to Paris and then sail back to New York from Le Havre on the Flandre, 15 October (Blaser to family, 3 September 1959). In Rome, Blaser found the colors of the city and the night lighting magnificent and was proud to be mistaken for French or Arab with his olive skin (To family, 3 September 1959). However, the notes thin out on this part of the journey. In Venice, there were postcards to the folks from the Ducal Palace, the Basilica di San Marco, and the Rialto Bridge, a great shopping district for clothes and jewelry he finds it and this was no small attraction (Postcard to family, 2 October 1959). Always drawn to pretty things, Blaser loved to shop. To Duncan, however, he writes that Venice is "odd and beautiful" but "a little set apart for the tourist" (29 September 1959).

Back in Paris at the beginning of October, Blaser seems to have felt more at ease, perhaps because return brings familiarity. Writing home, he says:

> ...here once again in Paris which I love and at the same address as before. If it weren't for pressing personal contacts in San Francisco I'd stay here. Get a job, that is, and stay here. Perhaps one day I can bring a friend with me and move to Paris for several years. Its beauty is extraordinary, even apart from the old things. Each morning I get up and go to a small café where the employees shake hands with me, and my lovely café au lait (coffee with hot milk) arrives. And croissant, those wonderful, unsweetened, flaky, [sic] buttery rolls the French serve at breakfast.
>
> Then, I whip down to the Seine and sit in the sun, watching the river and listening to the clatter of the French, always very excitable in the A.M., before I decide which museum or bookstore or whatever I want to go to. Sometimes I just sit over coffee trying to write or I return to my hotel and read. Often I meet friends for walks through odd parts of the city.
>
> Anyway, I'll soon sail for New York aboard a French ship, The <u>Flandre</u>, and arrive in New York Oct. 22. (Blaser to family, 6 October 1959)

Blaser again dined with Ashbery and the two parted with the promise to exchange poems (Ashbery to Blaser, 22 October 1959). Paris would remain a city of the heart for Blaser, although he never found occasion to live there. Back at the Soufflot, however, he complained to Don Allen that the trip had destroyed his ear: "And that's no small matter. The most essential of all my belongings, words, words, have now been packed away for nearly three months.... I turn out to be abnormally sensitive to the voices around me" (8 October 1959). Lacking the fluency in French for intimate contact, Blaser chafed. On the trip, he wrote letters, sketches, museum notes, and drafts of poems. "Ode for Museums," a poem that Blaser hoped to publish in *Yugen* (Blaser to Don Allen, 8 October 1959), came out of this. Although it was not published at the time, "Ode" turned up years later in a serial called *Notes 1994–2000*, where it was included as new material in the second edition of *The Holy Forest* under the title "Ode for Museums, All of Them!" and dated 1995.

> We are so tired of museums. Even prehistory
> is monumental. Who more so, than these
> scraggly natives picking sponge out of their
> eyes. Is it true we've seen anything but
> animals, two by two? (*HF*, 418)

By the sounds of it—I am merely speculating—this verse was probably carried over from 1959.

On 22 October, the Flandre docked in New York. After a brief stay with Don Allen, Blaser was off to San Francisco (Allen to Blaser, 27 October 1959). Felts, in the meantime, had quit his job at the Research Institute because it was doing poorly financially and had found a new position at the University of California Medical Center in San Francisco under Julius Comroe, a distinguished research physician and Head of the Cardiovascular Institute. Moneywise things are shaky, Jim writes, "[b]ut I see no reason why you will have to take a full time job. We can easily get ourselves solvent within about 90 days" (Felts to Blaser, 6 October 1959). There was, nonetheless, the task of finding suitable lodgings since Blaser didn't quite trust Felts's discrimination in domestic matters—and of course the inevitable job hunt. So home again it was to San Francisco.

NOTES

1. In a draft of a job-seeking letter dated 11 November 1959 from Clay Street in San Francisco, Blaser describes his position at Harvard as "Administrative Assistant" (Blaser 1959c, Application for Employment); in a *CV* prepared for Simon Fraser University in 1972, however, Blaser lists the position as "Administrative Librarian," a supervisory post (1 May 1972, *Curriculum Vitae*).

2. In a letter to Michael Boughn, 6 May 1999, Blaser describes the exhibit:

   > When I did the exhibit at Harvard in 1958 of American Philosophy for the American Philosophical Association (which Olson saw) I opened with Jonathan Edwards, then moved directly to Emerson—and Olson knew or understood what I meant to do—meandering through the depths—until I reached Whitehead—cases upon cases down the staircase in Widener—

3. Blaser preserved a news clipping announcing Felts's fellowship, but the name of the newspaper and the date have been cut out. The clipping is in MsA1 Box 8, Folder 7, Blaser fonds.

4. *The Boston Newsletter* is a very rare hand-produced publication. Michael Seth Stewart has provided me with photographs of a private copy and this is where I have found the Ford Foundation letter. I have no archival reference for the *Newsletter*.

5. Blaser does not mention the title of O'Hara's "little book" in this letter to Duncan, but in terms of timing it is likely that he was referring to *Meditations in an Emergency*, published by Grove Press in 1957.

6. One of the most difficult points of the Olson letter dates the postwar "revolution" in poetry to 1875:

   > ((date 1875 I'd take to be something like 1300
   > and not, say, 1429 which was the Renaissance, and the change of 1875 was on
   > an order to establish premises which go out the back door of Athens at 500 and
   > probably the change is only, as I remember once preaching in "Gate and
   > Center", the 2nd heave! (Olson to Blaser, 3 May 1957)

Writing in retrospect, Blaser says, "This letter still leaves me with problems that were never settled in conversation. These are involved in Olson's fundamental concern with historical change, more clearly outlined in his <u>Special View of History</u> (many have noted the play on Einstein's famous title), which was not published until 1970" (Blaser 1995e, 7).

   In another section of the letter, Olson turns to his theme of the fourfold which he would develop in the *Special View* and in the second volume of *Maximus*. In the *Special View*, Olson lays out a cosmology in series of fours, each series an analogue of the others: nature, man, civilization, culture; love, beauty, idea, will; space, time, history, and discourse; form as primordial, consequent, structural, and creative (Olson 1970, 60–61).

 7. Many years later, Blaser would write an essay called "The Violets" on Olson's reading of Whitehead's *Process and Reality*. In this essay, he cites a Black Mountain lecture in which Olson dates his study of Whitehead to 1955, just a few years before writing that letter to Blaser (*Fire*, 202). Working through the marginal notes in Olson's copy of *Process and Reality*, Blaser shows that Olson connected the dream message, "of rhythm is image" to Whitehead's philosophy (*Fire*, 209) and to the "'end of the subject-object thing'" (*Fire*, 218).

 8. This comment is in an undated letter from Levertov to Blaser, marked "Tuesday" (see Archival References).

 9. In 1964 while she was poetry editor at the *Nation*, Levertov wrote to Blaser that she would like to publish one of his poems, but that she would not be able to explain it should anyone ask (15 December 1964).

10. James Maynard points to the essay "Reviewing *View*, An Attack," published in 1947, as evidence of Duncan's impatience with what he saw as a growing conservatism in the journal (Maynard 2018, 53–54).

11. See James Maynard's discussion of Duncan's early surrealist explorations in the chapter "'Seas of Desire'" in *Robert Duncan and the Pragmatist Sublime* (Maynard 2018, 35–73).

12. From references he made to it in various letters, I believe the title intended was "Letter to Freud." The plural "Letters to Freud" was an editorial mistake (my mistake) in the second edition of *The Holy Forest* (16).

13. Spicer's sur-real anticipates the neo-Freudian writings of Jacques Lacan, especially in Lacan's essay, "Subversion of the subject and dialectic of desire" (Lacan 1977, 292–325). Lacan proposes that consciousness, enabled through language, forever cuts the mind off from a perceptual immediacy that is, in fact, an effect of language and never available to begin with. The result is incurable desire for an intimacy with "the real," the satisfaction of which is impossible and the pursuit of which would logically lead to madness or death (one would have to think outside one's own means of thinking). Spicer's logic is similar, but he is emotionally very far from the kind of theoretical joy that some Lacanians took (take) in the critique of perception. Spicer's and Blaser's use of the word "real" should not be confused with that of Lacan: for both poets, the real has an unsayable component, but it also connotes the "human universe" (Olson's term)— the world as humanity experiences it.

14. In a 1925 letter to his Polish translator, Witold Von Hulewicz, Rilke writes: "*We are the bees of the Invisible* ... at the work of these continual conversions of the beloved visible and tangible into the invisible vibrations and excitations of our own nature...." (Rilke 1948, 374).

15. The phenomenological and the surreal need not contradict each other if we take seriously Maurice Merleau-Ponty's idea of the entanglement of perceiver and perceived (see the concept of the "chiasm" in *The Visible and the Invisible*, a book Blaser came to after Boston). The surreal image literalizes the hybridity of perception as both familiar and strange, conscious and unconscious. The *drama* of surrealism (the shock of the imagery) comes from the challenge it represents to the assumption that reality must be *either* subjective *or* objective. Once that assumption is dropped, the hybrid loses its power to astonish. Perhaps this is why Blaser did not pursue the kind of imagery he was exploring in "A Preface" and other early poems. What remained of the experiment, however, was a life-long pursuit of the Other—the strange in the familiar that would morph into a long meditation on the de-anthropomorphized sacred.

16. Georges Bataille proposes that the animal is in the world like "water in water" (Bataille 1992, 25), meaning, I think, that the animal is continuous with the flow of life: the creature does not face the world as not-me in quite the same way as does humanity. I realize that this view might be disputed by contemporary animal researchers. My point, however, is about the myth of language acquisition rather than current science on animal cognition. For humanity, individuation is bound up with language acquisition and because we cannot get behind or underneath that process, our account of it amounts to an origin myth: at some point or another we crawl(ed) out of the womb/ocean without language and then we acquire(d) it. After the fact, we imagine the preverbal state through the mediation of language.

17. On this August 1957 visit, Blaser managed to seriously hurt Spicer's feelings by failing to stop by The Place, Spicer's watering hole and unofficial office. Here is Spicer's response to the apology letter that followed:

> As far as the personal hurt feelings, I know myself well enough to know that they will disappear whenever I see you regularly again. Our friendship has never stood up well to the sudden—it almost (because we are so different) has to be a day to day thing or nothing. In the meanwhile—you know me well enough to know that I'd be lying to tell you that the hurt won't stay. I think (hope) that you'd be insulted if it didn't. ("Thanks for your letter," n.d.)

CHAPTER 5

San Francisco: The Artist of the Beautiful

Poetry Wars

By the time Blaser arrived in New York on 22 October 1959, Jim Felts had taken an apartment at 622 Golden Gate Avenue in Richmond, with the idea of moving when his more domestically discriminating partner returned—"something old that we can fix up," he thought (6 October 1959). With a new job and expectations of improved finances, he offered to jet Blaser home "as the final touch to your trip" (6 October 1959). While Blaser was in Europe, he had bought a sky-blue Jaguar convertible with the Widener Library savings that Robin had sent for safekeeping. "The car you will just love," he had written, "It will take you a month or two to learn how to drive it, just as it has taken me" (Felts to Blaser, 5 July 1959). Hilde Burton remembers that with their good looks and the Jaguar, Robin and Jim would stop sidewalk traffic (Burton interview, 30 December 2008). The change in living arrangements wasn't long in coming. By the end of November 1959, Jim and Robin had a vintage 1924 apartment at 3101 Clay Street in the upscale Pacific Heights neighborhood.

As usual, Blaser set about arranging things. "His apartment," wrote cousin Eleanor Easley after a visit, "is a minor masterpiece—distinctive, spotless, everything in good taste & well put together. His library was amazing.... As I looked at mother's rug on his living room floor, I had repeatedly a sense of satisfaction—mother would have approved of Robin, his apartment & his way of life—That her rug which she loved should end up there is altogether fitting and proper" (Easley to Ina Mae Blaser, 16 July 1961). "Mother" was Blaser's Aunt Mae, his music teacher from Twin Falls and Sophia's sister. Mae died on 20 January 1960, leaving a lovely wine-colored Persian rug to Blaser that would become a centerpiece in this and subsequent households. On the walls were the paintings Blaser had collected from the artists he knew and cared about. The art was a passion, not an investment, often paid for in small installments. By the end of his stay in San Francisco, Blaser not only had numerous

© The Author(s) 2019
M. Nichols, *A Literary Biography of Robin Blaser*,
Modern and Contemporary Poetry and Poetics,
https://doi.org/10.1007/978-3-030-18327-1_5

Jesses that he had been collecting for years but also works by a number of San Franciscan painters who hung out with the poets—Paul Alexander, Lyn Brockway, Tom Field, Fran Herndon, and Harry Jacobus.

There was also the job to worry about. Although Blaser never acknowledged the position on his *Curriculum Vitaes*, he took a part-time job at a children's bookstore as a tide-me-over and the experience would leave a trace in the children's rhymes in *Cups*, the first serial poem Blaser completed in San Francisco (Persky interview with author, 11 November 2013). The immediate task, however, was to find more lucrative employment. In March of 1960, Blaser wrote a librarian's exam at the Civil Service Commission of San Francisco which put him at number two on a list of librarians eligible for work in the state of California (Civil Service Commission, 1960). His first post was as Assistant Librarian at the California Historical Society, a position that he held in 1960 before taking up more permanent work at San Francisco State College Library in Acquisitions with Robert Berg from the Berkeley days. He would remain at the College until he left San Francisco for Vancouver in 1966. The job was a ticket to financial stability, but like the Widener position, it was dull work and a constant distraction from Blaser's focus on poetry: ergo the old cognitive dissonance.

When Blaser returned to San Francisco in 1959, a new Bohemia was in full swing. Through magazines like the *Evergreen* special issue on San Francisco poetry, novels like John Clellon Holmes's *Go* (1952), and popular media coverage (*Life* did a negative article on the Beats in 1959[1] and Kerouac appeared on the Steve Allen show the same year), the nation knew that there were beatniks and bongos out there somewhere and that some such were to be found in San Francisco. Blaser, Spicer, and Duncan had departed just short of the fuss that began with Allen Ginsberg's historic reading of *Howl* at the Six Gallery, Friday, 7 October 1955. Reading that night were Philip Lamantia, Michael McClure, Allen Ginsberg, Philip Whalen, and Gary Snyder, introduced by Rexroth. Ginsberg stole the show, however, and the obscenity trial that followed the publication of *Howl* guaranteed it a prolonged buzz. In retrospect, the Six Gallery reading signposts a poetry scene that would find its center in Lawrence Ferlinghetti's City Lights Books. In a letter to Blaser in Boston, Duncan comments:

> Well, Ginsberg's *HOWL* is the San Francisco poem of all poems for 1955–1956. When we were in Mallorca everybody from San Francisco was affected by it. (Qtd in Jarnot 2012, 144)

In an indignant letter to Blaser, Arthur Kloth wondered in writing who this Ginsberg fellow *was* (2 September 1956). Spicer's friend, Myrsam Wixman, gave this account of the evening to Spicer in New York:

> Finally, a somebody named Ginsburg or -berg read a long rhetorical (Freudianslip) protest against all the best minds of his generation having gone to pot or worse.

It was in 85 choruses with a number of strophes and antistrophes that I couldn't
identify because I've never been an English major, but Mason said that they were
there....

Rexroth was master of ceremonies. He mumbled, and goosed McClure. He
was not drunk, they say, because his liver has gone bad....

However, Ginsbuerg's [sic] lover was very drunk, and sat on the floor behind
Rexroth and shouted a running commentary on everybody's poetry. Ginsbuerg
himself fell off the platform several times, and altogether gave a grand performance. He said that 30,000 of his friends were playing ping-pong in Rockland.
Later, he came to The Place and knocked three paintings off the wall after falling
downstairs. Ginsbuerg is currently the busboy at Robbie's. (23 October 1955)

He might have added that Gregory Corso and Jack Kerouac were at the Gallery
that evening as well, passing the jug.

However, sniffly the locals greeted the Beats, the publicity they generated
made San Francisco a magnet for the young and restless and not all of them
ended up at City Lights. Black Mountain painter Knute Stiles and painter-
photographer Leo Krikorian opened The Place in 1953, a bar that would
become Spicer's office for a while. When Black Mountain closed in 1957, many
of its alumni moved to San Francisco. Painters Tom Field and Paul Alexander
arrived, as did the young poet, Ebbe Borregaard who had literally caught Black
Mountain in its last moments. Poet Joanne Kyger and painter Nemi Frost
would soon join. Wieners was on the scene between 1957 and his "breakdown" in 1959, and Jim Herndon, a fellow student of Spicer's from the
Berkeley days, returned to San Francisco in 1957 after seven years in Europe
with new wife Fran. Both of them became essential to Spicer's North Beach
circle: Jim would become Spicer's Boswell, Ellingham and Killian say (Ellingham
and Killian 1998, 102), and Fran would engage in an intense dialogue with
Spicer through paintings and lithographs while Spicer was writing *Heads of the
Town*. A teen-aged Stan Persky, still in employ of the U.S. Navy, arrived in
1959 looking for love and poetry. With his youthful energy and nose for action,
Persky soon found his way into the Spicer circle,[2] introduced by George Stanley.

The Spicer–Duncan circle functioned alongside that of the Beats, sometimes
overlapping through poets like Bob Kaufman, Michael McClure, and Joanne
Kyger. Interviewed for *The Capilano Review*, George Stanley remembers that
"There were two groups in San Francisco at the time. There were the Beats,
and there was the Spicer–Duncan group, which didn't have a name at that
time. Later on people began calling it the Spicer Circle. But there was not
much contact between those two groups" (Stanley 2011, 6). In this interview,
Stanley remarks that one big difference between the Beats and the Spicer–
Duncan crowd was that the former were coming out of an interest in eastern
culture. Joanne Kyger, for instance, lived in a Buddhist-oriented commune, the
East–West House. Spicer and Duncan, on the other hand, were grounded in
western culture through their education at Berkeley and their classes with Ernst
Kantorowicz (Stanley 2011, 6–7). Other differences were the high proportion

of gay poets around Spicer and Duncan and the preference of the Blaser–Spicer–Duncan crew for alcohol over drugs. Neither Duncan nor Spicer liked drugs and Blaser had already distanced himself from that side of the action in Boston.

Back from Mallorca and Black Mountain in 1956, Duncan had taken a position as Assistant Director of the Poetry Center at San Francisco State College, working with Director Ruth Witt-Diamant and office assistant Ida Hodes. He was responsible for arranging readings, introducing poets, and managing correspondence (Jarnot 2012, 161). This position allowed him to launch readings and workshops such as his "Basic Techniques in Poetry" which ran in 1958. When Spicer returned from Boston, Duncan helped to set up a workshop at the San Francisco Public Library for him, the one that would turn into the now famous Magic Workshop that Blaser would later document in his edition of Spicer's *Collected Books*. On the social side, Duncan and Jess participated in a reading group called the Maidens with old friends James Broughton, Madeline Gleason, Helen Adam, and Eve Triem (Ellingham and Killian 1998, 92). Blaser was made an honorary member during his visit to San Francisco in the summer of 1957 (Broughton to Blaser, 18 August 1957). Out of these and other workshops and reading groups, a community evolved, a contentious one perhaps, but a community nonetheless.

One significant outlet for these energies was White Rabbit Press. Joe Dunn had attended Spicer's Magic Workshop, and at Spicer's suggestion, he began a press in 1957 (Ellingham and Killian 1998, 112). He had a job in the Print Department of the Greyhound Bus Company and the head of the department was Jack Sutherland, a former student at the California Art Institute who had studied alongside Jess and the painter John Allen Ryan. Sutherland cooperated by letting Dunn use the Company's equipment during off hours. Between November 1957 and September 1958 (Ellingham and Killian 1998, 113), Dunn produced ten chapbooks under the sign of the Rabbit, a stylized colophon drawn by Robert Duncan. When Dunn teetered into methedrine and alcohol addiction—to Spicer's disapproval—subscription money got spent on drugs and White Rabbit stock got sold to City Lights. Needless to say, production stopped (Ellingham and Killian 1998, 142). Duncan brought out two of the chapbooks lined up for White Rabbit under the imprint Enkidu Surrogate (Ellingham and Killian 1998, 142), Spicer's *Billy the Kid* and his own *Faust Foutu*, both with drawings by Jess. With prodding from Spicer, however, Graham Mackintosh, a former student of Spicer's at the California School of Fine Arts where Spicer had worked before moving to Boston, resurrected White Rabbit. Years later, Blaser would still identify the press as "ours" and occasionally talk of reviving it.

In addition to the Press, there was also *J* magazine in 1959, a venture of Spicer's and Fran Herndon's. *J* responded obliquely to the launch of *Beatitude*, a Beat journal that inspired Spicer to scorn and envy (Ellingham and Killian 1998, 165). *J* was coincident with Spicer's romantic enthusiasm for James Alexander (Paul's brother); when the affair faded so did the journal (Ellingham and Killian 1998, 165). It ran for five issues under Spicer's editorship, manuscripts to be dropped off in a box at The Place. After that, George Stanley brought out two and Persky and Harold Dull a final issue. Persky had been posted to Naples in 1959, and produced the last *J* from there. His first communication with Blaser was to ask whether Robin had received copies: "Heard from the Dulls that J-8-Italy possibly dint [sic] get to you, so here is ten more" (14 March 1961). When Spicer began to publish *J*, Blaser was still wrapping up in Boston and Spicer was still offended that Blaser had not turned up at The Place during his summer of 1957 visit. Writing to Blaser in Paris, Don Allen says of the incident,

> His resentment against you is at bottom I believe his terrible disappointment in not seeing as much of you, not getting as much of your love, as he had strongly counted on when you visited SF two years ago. I was with him later that last night and felt all of his terrible agony. (11 October 1959)

Blaser offered a conciliatory contribution to *J* 1: "Two Astronomers with Notebooks" (now reprinted in *The Holy Forest* (5–6)). In a letter responding to this olive branch, Spicer acknowledges his hurt over the missed visit and goes on to worry about Blaser's lack of detailed response to his Lorca translations, wondering if his poetry has become for Blaser as Duncan's had for him: beautiful but not astonishing (Spicer n.d., "Thanks for your letter"). At this point, Spicer sounds warm and reasonable, very much the intimate friend and companion in poetry. But he had his insecurities, and his doubts about Blaser and Duncan worsened as his alcoholism increased.

These, then, were some of the energies swirling about as Blaser settled into the Clay Street apartment. From a distance, San Francisco may have seemed an enticing Bohemia of creativity, but up close it could be cantankerous. *Poetry mattered*—this is the outstanding fact about the San Francisco of the 1950s and 1960s—and the kind of poetry one wrote and paid attention to was what determined who one's friends were going to be. It was one thing to enjoy insulting the Beats, and Spicer did not hold back when it came to Ferlinghetti, but the scene around Blaser, Spicer, and Duncan was not homogeneous at all, but a whirl of conflicts. Some of this, George Stanley remembers, was just the way gay men related to each other at the time, with a witty sharpness learned early as a defense against omnipresent homophobia—a Bette-Davis-*All-About-Eve* bitchiness (Stanley interview, 8 March 2014). But some of it had to do with ongoing discussions about the nature of language and poetry. In interviews with me, both Stanley and Persky remained adamant that poetry always trumped social rivalry, that beneath the fuss was a mutual respect. However, this was also the period when differences in poetics really began to show as Blaser, Spicer, and Duncan wrote some of their signature works.

Once housed and employed, Blaser plunged into a number of poetry events and projects. One of these was a reading circle held once a week at the Clay Street apartment or at the Herndons, with Spicer, Jim Herndon, and Landis

Everson. This move, Ellingham and Killian suggest, was the beginning of discord between Blaser and Duncan because Duncan was excluded (Ellingham and Killian 1998, 182). As well, Jess had never really taken to Spicer, despite periods of détente, and Spicer vented his envy of Duncan's success with *The Opening of the Field* by calling Robert a whore—a sell-out, he meant, to establishment literary publishing. Blaser's first serial poem of 1960 was *Cups* and it is full of the imagery of dismembered or mutilated bodies. This imagery has theoretical content in the idea of the decentered self (the Other in the self) that Blaser had been working through via surrealism in Boston, but it also resonates with the social wounds regularly inflicted in the poetry circles he frequented.

Another project was the opening of a new Black Mountain style college to be called White Rabbit College. Writing to Jess, Blaser says that "Jack and I want to open a College, offering courses this Summer (June 15 to 20 beginning, for 9 weeks), and then, if successful, we'll continue in the Fall" (7 May 1960). Duncan was to teach mythology, Jess modern painting, Spicer Elizabethan poetry, and Blaser French poetry (Blaser to Jess, 7 May 1960). The venue was to be Ebbe Borregaard's Museum. Borregaard had an apartment at 1713 Buchanan Street in Japan Town with living quarters and a gallery space where he proposed to mount exhibits and give readings. The Museum would house White Rabbit Press and serve as a venue for all that was new and exciting. Unfortunately, no one could agree on the program or how the school was to be managed or whether it was to be free or not. All that survived of White Rabbit College was a Duncan course on the History of Poetry, already running at the time of the dust-up, but like the Press, the idea lingered in Blaser's imagination, manifesting in off-campus study groups for the big poets like Pound and Blake, decades later in Vancouver.

In the fall of 1960, Blaser ran a Poet's Seminar at San Francisco State College where he was working in the library. It was a non-credit course that met on Monday nights for 15 weeks, beginning 26 September (Lola Chardon to Blaser, 2 September 1960). From suggestive sketches, it seems that Blaser intended to focus on a poetics that would include discussions of Yeats, Spicer, and dictated poetry; Pound and economics; and Jean Cocteau.[3] These notes are attached to more on Dickinson, Emerson, Thoreau, Whitman, Josephine Miles, and Eliot, implying discussion of the American tradition back of the moderns. Although the workshop did not generate a social circle as did Spicer's Magic Workshop, Blaser impressed his students and was still receiving notes from them several years later.[4] However, Blaser did not make himself available as did Spicer, in part because, unlike Spicer, he had a full-time day job, but also because he had the habit of putting off response until he could offer full attention and this often meant not responding at all. The same habit of delay applied to his work. Despite the offer from Joe Dunn to publish the Boston poems as a chapbook, Blaser held back because he did not feel that they were ready.

Despite his complaints about a chronic time crunch, Blaser was productive in the years between 1960 and 1966. During this period, he wrote *Cups, The Park, The Faerie Queene, The Moth Poem, Les Chimères*, and much of the original *Holy Forest* section of *The Holy Forest*. He also began the ongoing *Image-Nations* series with *Image-Nations* 1–4, a serial that, like Duncan's *Passages* and *Structure of Rime*, was meant to be interspersed with other sequences. In addition to the chapbooks, Blaser published in a range of little magazines and anthologies, including *The New American Poetry*. Solicitations from *The Floating Bear* (Diane di Prima and LeRoi Jones/Amiri Baraka); *The Elephant in the Room* (DiPrima and Andrew Spellman); *magick* (Dale Landers); *M* (Lewis Ellingham); *The Nation* (Levertov); and *The Paris Review* bear witness to the vibrancy of the poetry scene and Blaser's role in it. Blaser was known among the "avant" poets of the 1960s even as he remained a secret to academics and to the kind of popular audience that Ginsberg was able to draw.

On the social front, Blaser had to find his own place in the rough and tumble of the poetry circles around Spicer and Duncan. His relationship with George Stanley, for example, was a bumpy one. Stanley was one of the most promising young poets in the Spicer circle and his initial interactions with Blaser seem to have been cordial. In the spring of 1960, he moved to New York for a time and corresponded with Blaser from there, sending back the New York gossip. However, like others of Spicer's circle, Stanley was practiced in oppositional dynamics. When Duncan gave his workshop the year following Spicer's, it fell flat and the Spicereans disrupted the class. As Stanley remembers it,

> After the Spicer workshop, the very next year Duncan did the same thing. Duncan had a class—it was the very same room, I think, of the San Francisco Public Library—but it was a kind of fizzle. It just didn't work. And by that time Joanne [Kyger] and I had become totally disrespectful, so we were very disruptive in the Duncan class and made Duncan very angry. Spicer, of course, was gleeful to see us acting up.... (Stanley 2011, 7)

The kind of mischief Stanley describes here would escalate and eventually contribute to some serious rifts between Duncan, Blaser, and Spicer. In retrospect, Stanley sees his relationship with Blaser then as prickly because he did not really accept Robin as an equal to Spicer and Duncan and therefore of mentor status (Stanley interview, 8 March 2014). As well, Blaser looked and acted middle class in relation to the North Beach poets. Stanley remembers a lunch at Clay Street when he and artist Bill Brodecky Moore mocked the soufflé along with Blaser's pretensions. Pacific Heights, according to Stanley, was just bourgeois (Stanley interview, 8 March 2014). In one divisive incident, Blaser became embroiled in a Spicer circle mockery of Duncan. Blaser read Duncan's "Night Scenes" at the bar and the work occasioned some raillery. In a letter to Spicer, an angry Duncan writes:

> Robin tells me 'Night Scenes' in the Bear was the occasion of a ridicule.... "Let someone else read it," George said—"we're not laughing at you, Robin, but at the poem." (Duncan to Spicer, 22 May 1962)

Then there was the picketing incident, recounted by Ellingham and Killian in the Spicer biography. Spicer encouraged his juniors to picket the dress rehearsal of Duncan's *Adam's Way*, held at the Tape Music Center in 1962, because he thought the work no better than "early Swinburne." Stan Persky, Harold Dull, and Stanley obliged, carrying signs that said "Fuck Duncan, Fuck Jess, Fuck Chi-Chi" (Ellingham and Killian 1998, 239–40). Blaser was Chi-Chi, lampooned for his habitual elegance and perhaps for his costumed role in the play. And yet the dinners and meetings continued. Somewhere along the line, Blaser and Stanley even tried a one-night stand, although Stanley recalls it didn't work very well (Interview, 8 March 2014).

Typically, Blaser would try to smooth things over. In an attempt to mend the Duncan–Spicer rift over *Adam's Way*, Blaser unintentionally made it worse. He arranged a dinner with Duncan and Jess that was to give Jack a chance to read from *Heads of the Town* and let the poetry work its magic. Poetry trumped bitchery, or it was supposed to. Unfortunately, Jack arrived late with Ron Primack (then his current love), Stanley, and Bill Brodecky. The gang was already drunk and Jack refused to read. Jess walked out. The evening was a disaster that no one would soon forget. At the time, Jess was apologetic to Blaser: "I should have begged off when learning at dessert that Jack was due. I thot after having a breath of air I could return, but even then I knew it was futile. How I ever missd [sic] hearing or registering what was planned is beyond me & I feel really mortified at my obtuseness covered with ambivalence" (28 August 1962). In another account of the party, however, Jarnot writes that it marked a "final impasse" from which Duncan and Spicer could not recover the friendship (Jarnot 2012, 217). A few months later, there were fresh injuries. Jess accused Blaser of a "need to seek literary excitement. Why else have you made use of Robert's poetry to gall those idiots, knowing as you well do it does disservice to the art so exposed, or are you pleased just to create an atmosphere of ridicule?" (19 October 1962).

The year 1962 seems to have been Blaser's *annus horribilis* and his *magnificat* at the same time. Not only was there quarreling that strained old friendships but this was the year that Blaser began an affair with Stan Persky that would end his relationship with Jim. It was the year in which Blaser's beloved grandmother, Sophia Nichols, died on 12 September—no priests, no bishops, she said, just tell him to read poems. It was the year that Robin and Jim bought a house in the Bernal Heights area on Waltham Street, only to split up shortly after. It was the year that Blanche Jantzen, Blaser's colleague at the library, fell hopelessly in love with him and pressed her unwanted suit with infuriating persistence. It was the year of Auerhahn Press, when Blaser facilitated the publication of Spicer's *Heads of the Town* only to have Jack turn against him for it. It was also one of Blaser's most creative periods (Fig. 5.1).

Fig. 5.1 Robin Blaser in San Francisco, 1962. Photo by Helen Adam. Copyright the Poetry Collection of the University Libraries, University at Buffalo, SUNY. Reproduced with permission

The Handsome Sailor: Stan Persky

In 1958, Stan Persky was a 17-year-old sailor with the U.S. Navy, stationed at Treasure Island in the Bay area. He was doing a clerical job and getting his military service out of the way early, but there were evenings and weekends and he was interested in finding out what was there to be found. He was impossibly young, beautiful, and energetic. He had read about Beatniks and he knew about the Hotel Wentley before John Wieners made it famous. He knew about John Wieners and Jimmy the pusher too: the three of them were the sailor, the queen, and the dealer. Perksy also knew about Co-Existence Bagel, owned by Leo of The Place fame, and about the Bread and Wine Mission on Grant Avenue, run by the radical preacher Pierre Delattre who was an editor of *Beatitude*. The Mission was a drop-in center for Beats and a venue for poetry readings. Persky cannot quite remember where he met George Stanley, but

Stanley invited him to the Spicer Sunday reading circle which he was then hosting.

Persky was transferred to Naples in Italy that year where he served out his stint with the Navy until the end of 1961. Harold and Dora Dull were also there on an extended stay in Europe, and they became Stan's mentors. The Dulls, he recalls, showed him "civilization"—art, music, literature (Persky interview, 19 October 2013). There were also weekend leaves to Paris. Allen Ginsberg was there with Peter Orlovsky and Gregory Corso. William Burroughs and Brion Gysin lived at 9, rue Gît-le-Coeur, the Beat hotel. James Baldwin and John Ashbery were in Paris, Ashbery as an art critic for the *Herald Tribune*. Through the Dulls, Persky kept in touch with San Francisco. He had read Donald Allen's *New American Poetry* and seen a copy of Blaser's *Cups*. To Blaser, John Ashbery wrote:

> A be-dungareed poet named Stu [sic] Persky was telling me how great he thought it [*Cups*] was the other day in the <u>caves</u> of La Grande Séverine, a restaurant owned by dirty book tycoon Maurice Girodias, where a champagne party for Gregory Corso's novel "American Express" was in full swing. (10 May 1961)

When Persky was discharged from military service in January 1962, he returned to San Francisco and immediately rejoined the Spicer circle.

Persky and Blaser met that January. Persky remembers that he was sitting in Gino and Carlo's with Spicer and Spicer mentioned that Blaser had returned to San Francisco from Boston:

> As much to relieve Spicer's boredom and to forestall his complaints that "no one was coming around to the bar," I suggested that we call Blaser up and get him to join us in Gino's.
>
> "Oh no, Robin never comes out to the bar," Spicer groused.
>
> "He will if I call him," the arrogance of youth replied.
>
> Spicer bet me a quarter I couldn't get Blaser down to the bar, and even supplied me with the nickel for the telephone call.
>
> "Hi," I said to Blaser, giving my name and announcing, "I'm twenty-one years old, I've just come back from the Navy, and I'm here in Gino's with Jack Spicer. Jack says you don't come out to the bar, but I told him he's wrong. So why don't you come down here and have a drink with us like a regular guy?" (Persky 2010, 10)

In about half an hour Jack had to pay up.

The affair between Blaser and Persky began shortly after with a dinner invitation to Clay Street in Jim's absence. Persky remembers getting the full Blaser treatment with a dinner of filet mignon and fois gras on pumpernickel (Persky interview, 11 November 2013). He thought Blaser handsome, but what really attracted Stan was the household. The library, for instance, was impressive but not for antiquarian reasons. It was not primarily about first editions or fancy binding, although small press editions collected for pennies brand new would quickly become rare as they went out of print; rather it was impressive because it was a working library tailored specifically to Blaser's imagination. From Hawthorne's *Tanglewood Tales* and the Doré illustrated *Divine Comedy* dating from childhood to the most recent issue of *J*, Blaser's books fit him like his well-tailored clothes. In a tribute written after Blaser's death in 2009, Persky says that the "order of objects, art, furniture, carpets, books, [was] deliberately chosen and arranged, so that their inter-relations set up a sort of field of activity. The old notion of household gods was treated literally" (Persky 2010, 12).

In 1962, Jim was still in the picture, but Persky does not remember any high drama over the affair. Blaser and Felts seem to have been more like dear companions at this stage than a committed couple. In October of 1962, they moved from Clay Street to purchase a home in Bernal Heights at 73 Waltham that allowed for an up–down arrangement—Blaser on the upper floor and Felts below. Even after Blaser had moved out to live with Persky at 24 Allen Street, the correspondence with Felts remained cordial. Jim would compliment Robin on work published and Robin would send little birthday gifts. In contrast, Blaser's affair with Persky was stormy and it drew Blaser deeper into the dynamics of the Spicer circle (Fig. 5.2). Persky was cheeky and it wasn't just Duncan that came in for needling. In a note to Jess just before his move to Waltham Street, Blaser writes:

Fig. 5.2 Stan Persky and Robin Blaser at Stinson Beach, c.1964. Photo by Helen Adam. Copyright the Poetry Collection of the University Libraries, University at Buffalo, SUNY. Reproduced with permission

I've just bugged out. The attack on me in North Beach has been vicious and pointless.
Samples–Personal
    George: "You are deeply middle-aged."
    Stan: "I'll sleep with you anytime. That's good. All the rest of you stinks."
And on it goes from Jack and against the establishment which seems to be Duncan and myself. So I'm hiding out.
Jack is reduced to lying or he's gone completely <u>kook</u>. (10 October 1962)

The steady job and the middle-class address were easy targets for the satirically minded young, egged on by Spicer. In the view of his biographers, Spicer both wanted and rejected recognition as a poet, wanted and rejected the sustaining space of a household. This default position was to accuse others who had these things of betraying poetry for money and fame—and of course this made them legitimate targets of verbal warfare.

On the Duncan front, Blaser's relationship with Persky was a sticking point. On a telegram in which Blaser had excused himself from a Duncan reading of the *HD Book*, Duncan hand writes: "But Saturday morning (the reading from the book had been on Friday evening) we saw Robin and Persky in line for the Stinson Beach bus at 11:40. Aie! He had only to say, after all, that he had a previous engagement. Why lie? But for once, I mean to let Robin go—to call him to order on the lie would only be to claim a friendship I don't think rightly exists" (Duncan on Blaser to Duncan telegram, 15 March 1963). On the occasion of Persky's return from a trip to Mexico, Blaser wrote to Duncan, "Stan arrived unexpectedly will be in touch later." And Duncan at the bottom: "Of course. But we have our own peculiarities. We shall not presume to invite you again" (Blaser to Duncan, 14 May 1963). And on another occasion, spelling it out:

> ...that you make it a condition of accepting invitations at all that Stan Persky also be invited and that, being aware that we do not enjoy Persky's company and being thoughtful of us as friends, you make it an added condition that we not be embarrassed by being invited at the same time.... you have set up a formula of total acceptance of Stan Persky and total rejection of Jess and me. (Duncan to Blaser, 8 June 1963)

Blaser's attention to Persky even ruffled the feathers of Don Allen on the occasion of a visit. Blaser's apology suggests how compelling the affair had become:

> Dear Donald, you are right, I haven't been a good friend for sometime.
>
> I fear that I've thrown myself into this Persky thing headlong, as if there were nothing else....
> Missing Friday night with you has no real excuse, since I should have checked on bus schedules and didn't. And allowing Persky to keep me to a movie-date at this cost is madness. I suppose I presumed too much that you would know the desire to see him controls me.

> He came at a time when James, Jack, Duncan and Jess had all turned on me. And from outside, it is clear that I used him to heal what I couldn't understand. And there his power begins. He has received every available minute. (24 November 1962)

As this letter implies, there were temperamental differences between Blaser and Persky. Blaser was insecure in the relationship, unable to accept that Stan might really be attracted to him, given the age difference between them. Persky's quick eye for beautiful boys was not exactly reassuring. While attracted to the richness of Blaser's household and poetic imagination, Persky was more interested sexually in younger men closer to his own age. Tony Aste, a young "Jet" as Spicer called him, after the handsome punks in the 1961 film, *West Side Story*, had drifted into the Spicer scene and with his good looks and whiff of danger, he was a strong attraction (Persky interview, 11 November 2013). Persky also had a looser attitude toward sex than did Blaser, although Blaser did his best to cultivate nonchalance. In April of 1963, Stan spent a month in Mexico City and his correspondence with Blaser during this time—sometimes as many as two or three letters a day—shows the genuine affection between them as well as the asymmetry of the relationship. Persky's letters were frequent and loving, usually with a "wish you were here" line or two and an "I love you" to sign off. Blaser tried not to hover, but he was obviously uneasy about all the possibilities down south. "Yes, the people here are very handsome," Stan wrote.

> By the number of times you've mentioned it and the way you treated it almost as a reason for not being here I see you still don't understand this business of boys as being equatable with a supreme candy, a delightful entertainment. Isn't there any place in your 'aesthetic line' where one is able to do things with full interest and yet not commit some emotional betrayal? (11 April 1963)

Blaser's long response to this letter is a study in the nuances of attraction and suppressed jealousy. A sample:

> "Isn't there any place in your 'aesthetic line' where one is able to do things with full interest and yet not commit some emotional betrayal?" I think you can hardly mean this, but I remain frightened. If this is your view of the strings which I've tried to drop around you, I'm speechless. (16 April 1963)

In another letter the next day, Blaser tells Persky that his way of working the poems has begun to shift; instead of a solitary activity it has become "the poetry circle the two of us made out of whole cloth" (17 April 1963). That Persky had found his way into Blaser's poetic practice was serious indeed, and in fact, despite sending Blaser on an emotional roller coaster, Persky was the companion of some of Blaser's best statement pieces, including the signature *Moth Poem*. In *Astonishments*, Blaser recalls Spicer's interference in his relationship with Jim way back in 1946: Spicer knew that the relationship wasn't "vital," Blaser says (*AT*, 60). With Persky, things were plenty vital.

In May 1963, when Persky returned to San Francisco after Mexico and a visit with his family in Chicago, he and Blaser were still living separately. Stan wrote to Robin that he would stay with the Dulls or possibly Landis Everson and Landis's partner Bob until he could earn some money for a place (9 May 1963). The job Persky found was with Merchandizing Methods, a mail order firm that had a small print operation in the back. Ebbe Borregaard, James Alexander, and the painter Bill McNeill also worked there; Bill helped Stan get the job. Stan had been helping Graham Mackintosh with White Rabbit, but by the end of 1963, he had another idea for a publishing venture. It would be called *Open Space*. For one year, the magazine would publish the work of an invited group of poets and artists, plus whoever else might find their way into the drop box in Spicer's bar. Duncan, Spicer, Blaser, Kyger, Harold Dull, Stanley, and Borregaard had carte blanche. Jess contributed some of the covers and published a serialized prose piece called "Critical Dreams." To be noted is that Duncan and Jess, despite the feuding with the Spicer circle, agreed to contribute at Persky's invitation, showing that poetry could indeed triumph over personal drama when it mattered. Every month, the magazine would circulate the art and poetry news of the community. Merchandising Methods provided the means. Persky would type manuscripts on a stencil-like machine and the resulting plates would be run on an offset press. In this, he was helped by Mike Coomer, the printer at Merchandizing Methods, who worked the press and would run off 100 to 150 copies of *Open Space* on weekends. Persky would then collate these by hand, staple them, and deliver the result to the bar. His energy was seemingly boundless. Not only did he control every step in the production of the magazine and provide comical monthly reviews of the material, he also organized a union at Merchandizing Methods, worked on the docks, bartended on Green Street, and continued to write (Persky interview, 16 November 2013).

The record of *Open Space* from January to December 1964 is impressive. Duncan published parts of his *Structure of Rime* and *Passages* as well as the stunning poem, "My Mother Would be a Falconress." Olson's admonitory essay to Duncan, "Against Wisdom as Such," came out in *OS* 8 along with Duncan's reply to it. Spicer's contributions included the poems now published as the *Language* series. David Bromige published in the journal, as did George Stanley, Gary Snyder, Joanne Kyger, Helen Adam, and many more. Blaser contributed *The Moth Poem*, *The Holy Forest* section of what would become *The Holy Forest*, "Sophia Nichols," and *Image-Nations* 3 and 4. Spicer, of course, wasn't entirely happy. By *OS* 7, he was complaining that *Open Space* wasn't a happening enough place—too homogeneous (Spicer 1964, n.p.). Persky's response in the same issue is revealing of Spicer's impossible-to-please behavior at this point. The letter, under the header "A CHANGE," distinguishes Dirty Jack from Radiant Jack, the two sides of Spicer as Persky saw him:

It isn't that you've given little or withheld too much—only last week you led me
to a new friend, among the dead, where one has more luck with friendship than
here—but it seems to me you want a world small enough so that wherever you
spit you'll hit something, a world you can control. Though you've often shown
how this can serve poetry, more and more often now it seems to exclude the
music, paintings, statues, objects, adventures, I want in my poems, my life—and
the world isn't fixed....

    I think you're wrong about the poems, the problem is not so much in them,
as in the range of your interest. (Persky 1964, n.p.)

Despite his grumbling, Spicer continued to publish in *Open Space*. By creating
this forum, Persky had found a way of making a community of poets present to
itself, despite who wasn't talking to whom. *Open Space* anticipates the kind of
community that Blaser would assemble in his poetry and suggests a precedent
for what would become the open space poem. In 1964, entangled with Persky
in both love and poetry, Blaser moved out of 75 Waltham and into an apartment with him at 24 Allen Street.

THE BLANCHE JANTZEN AFFAIR

Persky was not the only romance on Blaser's horizon in the early 1960s,
although he was most likely the only desired one. Shortly after Blaser began to
work at the San Francisco State College Library, a colleague, Blanche Jantzen,
fell in love with him. Blaser rejected her suit, but Jantzen would not take "no"
for an answer. When she could not get to first base with Blaser, she began to
contact his friends. A long letter from Denise Levertov to Blaser explains that
Jantzen has written several times, asking Levertov to assist in the pursuit and
suggesting that Blaser needs a "good woman" (Levertov to Blaser, 21 July
1962). Blaser was, of course, angry that his tormentor had contacted one of his
literary friends behind his back and he let her know it, but she continued to
write and to encroach on his life. She interested herself in the poetry world
around Blaser and began to turn up at poetry events like the Vancouver festival
of 1963 at the University of British Columbia.[5] Although Blaser did not make
it to Vancouver, his community certainly did and Jantzen memorialized the
event in comic rhyming portraits of Creeley, Olson, and Ginsberg. Her more
sober work, as sent to Blaser, is what I would call sentimental and signed with
the name "Fire Bird."

    Jantzen's main theme in letters between 1962 and 1965 is that Blaser is a
better poet than all of his friends and simply doesn't realize it. She therefore
urges him to publish. Her letters suggest that she knows Blaser better than he
knows himself. On one occasion, after Jantzen had been discussing Blaser again
behind his back with her friend Sandy Boucher, she writes that she and her
friend agree that Blaser's poetry is "superior" to that of his contemporaries in
San Francisco (12 March 1964). She goes on to say that Blaser has an obliga-
tion to share his light as a visionary and fellow Catholic. Jantzen's claim to

camaraderie in poetry and religion, especially when Blaser had had to wrestle his way out of doctrinal Catholicism, cannot have been welcome and Jantzen anticipates this, acknowledging that her gossip annoys Blaser but declaring herself incapable of prudence (Jantzen to Blaser, 12 March 1964).

Blanche Jantzen's infatuation with Blaser might have slipped from the record if she had not been so insistent on contributing some inheritance money to the literary world. At first, she offered it to Blaser for a trip to Europe. When he turned her down, she suggested he take the money anyway for the community. In her 1962 letter to Blaser about Jantzen, Levertov takes up the issue of the cash. She tells Blaser that in a second letter, sent about two months after the first, Jantzen says that she is recovering from her passion and wants the money Blaser has rejected to be used for some other purpose than the trip to Paris she had proposed. Subsequent letters from Jantzen to Blaser suggest that the "recovery" was feigned, but she persuaded Blaser to accept the money as an anonymous donation to the local arts. While the sum was not grand—$2500 in some accounts, $3000 in others[6]—it went a long way in chronically cash-strapped alternative art circles. Hence Blaser's involvement with Auerhahn Press. Some of Jantzen's money was handed off to Don Allen for his Four Seasons Foundation publishing venture; the rest went to Auerhahn Press to fund the publication of Spicer's *Heads of the Town up to the Aether*, and to launch Blaser's Peacock Gallery.

The Auerhahn Press was founded in 1958 by Dave Haselwood, later assisted by Andrew Hoyem. The first title was John Wieners's *Hotel Wentley Poems*. Between 1958 and 1964, Haselwood brought out work by Diane di Prima, Philip Lamantia, Michael McClure, Philip Whalen, David Meltzer, William Everson, Charles Olson, William Burroughs, and Jack Spicer, earning a reputation for publishing the best new stuff. In the spring of 1962, Blaser joined the Board of Directors with James McIlroy, Philip Whalen, artist Robert LaVigne, and Haselwood. At a June meeting, the Board approved the publication of Spicer's *Heads of the Town Up to the Aether*. With Jantzen's money, the book was beautifully produced—perfect-bound in hard cover, with lithos by Fran Herndon tipped in. Spicer added a crayon drawing to each of 100 limited edition copies. (My copy informs the reader that "Don Allen eats shit.") Yet Jack was not happy with the publication. Ellingham and Killian suggest that he was conflicted about his stand against fame and copyright. The Auerhahn book was the first Spicer book to be copyrighted (Ellingham and Killian 1998, 235) and hence a "sell-out." Yet at the same time, Spicer was unhappy about the poor distribution, even though he contributed to it by refusing to let City Lights or Discovery Bookstore carry the book. In a letter to the Board, Haselwood gives an account of the number of copies sold and placed with reviewers, implying that he had been questioned about distribution: "Upon your request," the letter begins (22 October 1962). At this time, Spicer was entering a more advanced phase of alcoholism that pushed even his close friends to question his sanity:

"When Dave Haselwood was publishing *Heads of the Town Up to the Aether*, Jack was as close to insane as I ever saw him," Dora Geissler [Dull] recalled. "He was convinced that Dave was out to destroy him, ruining his poetry and killing any possibility of future writing." (Ellingham and Killian 1998, 235)

Spicer was "disturbed," Ellingham and Killian write, "that he had compromised his own integrity to achieve the fame he both wanted and reviled" (Ellingham and Killian 1998, 235).

Spicer's response to the Auerhahn publication left some real scars on his relationship with Blaser. Blaser withdrew from the Press and revoked plans to publish his own book with Auerhahn, thus angering Jess.

Dear Robin—it is a cruel disappointment to me to learn today from Robert that you have capitulated and cancelled your Auerhahn project. We must thereupon now wipe the slate clear, so I take this occasion to withdraw my request to illustrate your poems. The future will adjust itself. I know you must be under personal pressures as well as artistic and probably feel the inevitable in your chosen course. I can only assert my sorrow and lack of comprehension. Pass on. (Jess Collins to Blaser, [?] October 1962)

This note has the final ring of a good-bye and Blaser responded with grief and apologies, defending himself against the charge of capitulating to Spicer.

But then I also capitulate to you and Robert—there is doubtless hidden away the old weakness—to please. Which I've always restricted to adored friends and they were always poets or painters. I rather doubt that I could want to please Jack now. I have made it clear that it is his turn to look for me. Instead, he charges that he's supported my poetry for years and I've given nothing. There has been the public charge that I successfully (he apparently allowed that) took the serial form from him.

It is a very bad year. Your 'pass on' strikes as sharply as you wished.... The whole of my world of friendships, loyalties and artistic devotions seems breaking away from me without my having the ability to understand the causes. (17 October 1962)

Spicer confirmed *his* displeasure by changing the executorship of his estate from Blaser to Jim Herndon. In an improvised document sent to Herndon, Spicer writes, "My previous verbal agreement with Robin Blaser is null and void" (Spicer to Herndon, 6 October 1962). An anguished letter from Blaser to Spicer in October of 1962 says, "I'm so unused to writing for enemies, the result is to give me a new breath. And I'm not sure of it." And in a P.S.:

Jack, following two conversations with you, I have tried to imagine a world without you, and have even made small efforts to build one. I cannot see it. (30 October 1962)

THE PEACOCK GALLERY: PAINTERS AND POETS

The next project that Jantzen's money funded was the Peacock Gallery. In a 1986 interview with Christopher Wagstaff, Blaser says that he started the Gallery because his painter friends could not get shows in San Francisco (Wagstaff 1986, n.p.). The Peacock opened on 11 October 1963 at 1906 Union Street and the show ran from 12 October to 23 November. Blaser chose to exhibit six painters: Paul Alexander, Lyn Brockway (née Brown), Tom Field, Fran Herndon, Harry Jacobus, and Jess. The Gallery was distinguished by the context that Blaser created for the artists: it was a rented antique shop, already furnished with fine armoires, side tables, chairs, and Persian rugs. Rather than hang the works in gallery fashion on white walls, Blaser painted the space in rich colors and hung the paintings floor to ceiling. In other words, the Gallery was a version of his household. Remembering the Peacock in a 1991 film featuring him (*Robin Blaser in Vancouver*, produced by Ralph Maud), Blaser compares his Gallery to the Dilexi just up the street. The Dilexi Gallery (1958–1970) featured white walls and paintings hung with lots of space around them—outrageously expensive, Blaser remarks.

Despite the accolades of friends, the show was not a commercial success: no significant reviews and meager sales. Blaser writes:

> The exhibition was a bust except for the insiders; the newspapers chose to ignore us except for a jobber's notice published after the official closing date. But who the outsiders are drags one down a rain-barrell [sic] of commerce, success and notice. Somehow we hoped to be public—to make a point (in the organization of so large a collection and in the hanging where Harry [Jacobus] and I placed the paintings richly to allow for complements, enlargements and structures). We were frankly avoiding the tone of the museums and spareness of the galleries by placing the show among furnishings, objects, rugs. You moved through the shop, two small rooms, a back porch, a kitchen, two sitting/rooms and a hall, all very high ceilinged, all hung from eye level to many feet above the talest [sic] viewer. The point was not lost on the insiders. The only demand on the others was the care to see. But this care implies ability and that in turn implies knowledge. (Blaser 1963a, "La Richesse Necessaire")

The Gallery closed after its inaugural show because with no prospective buyers and Jantzen's money gone, Blaser could not afford to keep it open. Bill Brodecky Moore wrote a complaint to the editors of *Artforum* (Brodecky Moore, 28 December 1963) and Persky decried the lack of critical notice in the "Prospectus" issue of *Open Space*: "The six painter group show at the Peacock Gallery (1906 Union) is almost over, and except for a completely stupid review by Mr & Mrs Dean Wallace, has been largely ignored, instead of creating the excitement that the best show of paintings in a decade should have made in this city" (Persky 1963, n.p.). Such complaints, however, fell on deaf ears.

Expectably so. In 1960, Clement Greenberg had broadcast an essay called "Modernist Painting" as one of a series of *Forum Lectures* for the program

Voice of America (Greenberg 1993, 93). The essay was printed in *Arts Yearbook* 4 in 1961 and then reprinted numerous times in journals and anthologies between 1965 and 1982. One of the most influential assessments of modernist art to come out of the mid-century American art world, it articulated a formalist aesthetic. Greenberg argues that modernism means "the use of characteristic methods of a discipline to criticize the discipline itself, not in order to subvert it but in order to entrench it more firmly in its area of competence" (Greenberg 1993, 85). Painting, if it was to rise above sentiment or entertainment, had to focus on the "unique in the nature of its medium" (Greenberg 1993, 86) by distinguishing itself from the other arts. This meant drawing attention to the flat surface of the canvas, because "flatness was the only condition painting shared with no other art" (Greenberg 1993, 87). Figural representation would detract from this reflexive focus. Perhaps it was Greenbergian formalism[7] that led Philip Leider, editor of *Artforum*, in a 1967 essay on Vancouver artists, to remark in passing on the "disastrous history of the San Francisco figurative school" (Leider 1967, 2). Later in the same essay, Leider writes that "San Francisco artists, for the last decade or so, have remained consistently indifferent, when not hostile, to developments in painting as they have manifested themselves in the east, while pop art, for example, as well as the structurist paintings of Stella, Noland and company were accepted with immediate enthusiasm by the younger artists in Los Angeles" (Leider 1967, 3).

From the perspective offered by these leading art critics, Jess's collages as well as the figurative abstractions of Alexander, Brockway, Field, Herndon, and Jacobus drop out of sight because they are so bent to the literary, figurative, and semiotic and so out of tune with the cool ironies of pop art and minimalism. In the exhibition brochure for the show, Blaser comments: "These painters are associated by recognitions among them. They comprise no group or movement" (Blaser 1963b, *Peacock Gallery Exhibition*). I know of no artists who consent to generalization, and yet something kept the San Francisco artists circulating in the same community, despite broad differences in technique, scale, color, and subject. The essential connections, I think, would have to include narrativity and a sense of immanence. There is an analogy to be made to "composition by field," the poetic method that Olson presented in "Projective Verse" and other essays. The "field" of the poem or art work is to be imagined as a space—a landscape, let's say—where various events may occur and forms emerge. Within this space is a dynamic interplay between figure and ground, such that the former is neither reducible to nor separate from the latter. The poem or painting as a field of moving energies conveyed to the reader or viewer through the artist's point of view is a much "hotter," more emotional construct than abstractions that court the elegance of geometry. Not only were the San Francisco painters out of step with such formalism, but from a pop art perspective, they were lacking in the requisite awareness of the commodifying effects of the art market on the image. Alive with emotional energy and immanent meaning, their paintings were too sincere, too romantic, too available for cooption—too uncool.

Jess and Fran Herndon were the most literary artists of the group. In an essay on Jess's work in *An Opening of the Field*, Michael Duncan cites an exhibition statement written by Jess or Duncan (he is not sure which) that the artist depicts "the spirit's track recorded" (Duncan 2013, 38) and that sense of "track recorded" or narrative movement is significant. Like a Duncan poem, a Jess painting or collage is multiphasic and eventful—a *happening* differently activated by each viewer, like a park that one might walk through dozens of different ways. The Greenberg-era contrast would be something more like Stella's *Black Paintings* (1958–1960), a series of canvases with black-striped parallel lines—a move that inspired the minimalist artists of the 1960s. The art world's lack of interest in the Peacock show or in the artists closest to Blaser, Spicer, and Duncan was not just a lapse of attention, but rather indifference in the face of an art form—figurative abstraction—that did not fit into the most admired trends and current discourses of the moment. So San Francisco bucked the trend and the artists had to arrange their own exhibits if they were to see and be seen.

Of the painters that Blaser was close to, none were so near to him as Jess. Even in relation to his immediate peers, Jess's work was an anomaly—openly romantic and frank about quotations from a wide range of literatures and art practices, including children's books, fairytales, pre-Raphaelite artists, and symbolists like Gustave Moreau, Odilon Redon, and Pierre Bonnard. Like the symbolist painters, Jess was interested in the invisible world as it might flicker in the visible, not as mystical transcendence but as the secret life of common things. If something of this strangeness of things can be called upon—here, again, is the surrealist thread, the strange in the familiar—the artist may then very well find him or herself on a great venture in the Wonderland of his or her backyard. Christopher Wagstaff has noted Jess's literary bent and his use of literary elements such as puns in his work (Wagstaff 2013, 63). In this, Jess was strictly in accord with Duncan, for whom the poem or art work was a revelatory event: stories come out of stories, forms out of forms, and letters, in both senses of the term, out of words.

Jess's art hung on Blaser's various walls for life. In particular, Blaser loved the three oval paintings that Jess had lifted from Hawthorne's stories. "The Birth Mark," "The Snow Maiden," and "Young Goodman Brown" are highly literary paintings, each with a strong sense of narrative drama. Jess delayed the painting of a planned fourth, "The Artist of the Beautiful," past the point when Blaser had quarreled with Duncan and left San Francisco, so Blaser never did acquire the coveted fourth oval. But perhaps in the spirit of romance that Hawthorne so cultivated and Jess too it was right that he should not own a painting that he had begun to live.

During the early 1960s, Blaser also painted and collaged. In a piece called *Triptych*, from 1960, the year that he wrote *Cups* and *The Park*, mythic elements and dismembered body parts are scattered across the canvas. In the upper left-hand corner, the Parthenon overlays the arm of a large figure, the eyes highlighted as if through a mask. A four-poster canopy, minus the bed,

Fig. 5.3 *Triptych*, by Robin Blaser, 1960. Collage, 14 × 24½". Collection of Anne and Robert J. Bertholf. Reproduced courtesy of the Blaser estate

floats in the middle of the collage while on the right-hand side, an eye, a nose and part of a face drift alongside the Virgin and Child and a Greek column. The collage manifests a shattering of the sacred in Greek and Christian myth and the dismemberment of the body, one of Blaser's recurring tropes. Another painting of this period features a chalice-shaped Cup, overflowing with water, in a green, heavily brushed space. These are pieces in which presence and absence are continually at play, echoing the ongoing chiaroscuro of *The Holy Forest* (Figs. 5.3 and 5.4).

Following the closing of the Peacock, Paul Alexander and Bill Brodecky (name changed to Moore) opened Buzz Gallery in Ebbe Borregaard's old live-work space, and with Larry Fagin renting the apartment alongside, the Gallery was set for parties. Buzz functioned on the same principles as Persky's *Open Space*: it was to run for a year and feature one unedited group show a month. There would also be solo shows for all of the artists in the community. When everyone had had a turn, the Gallery would close. Over 1964, Buzz showed the work of David Allen, Ken Botto, Jack Boyce, Ernie Edwards, Tom Field, Nemi Frost, Fran Herndon, Jess, Harry Jacobus, Larry Jordan, Lori Lawyer, Bill McNeill, Knute Stiles, Bill Wheeler, and of course that of Alexander and Brodecky. Like *Open Space*, the Gallery accommodated a community that was full of dissent. Bill Brodecky Moore remembers Jess arguing with Paul Alexander over Gustav Moreau: Alexander was critical while Jess identified with Moreau (Brodecky Moore 2003, n.p.). Spicer would not attend openings because he did not allow himself to go west of Van Ness Street and Buzz was in Duncan territory (Brodecky Moore 2003, n.p.). George Stanley, however,

Fig. 5.4 *Cups*, by Robin Blaser, c.1960. Oil on canvas, 20 × 24". Collection of Alan Franey. Photo by Alan Franey. Reproduced courtesy of Alan Franey and the Blaser estate

was enthused about the Gallery and broke with Spicer on this point. Buzz also served as a party space (gallons of red wine had to be served at openings) and a venue for readings. Richard Brautigan packed the place when he read *Watermelon Sugar* and LeRoi Jones fascinated when he arrived with body guards. One special event was the Poets' Show, featuring work by Helen Adam, Duncan, and Fran Herndon. Buzz and *Open Space* showed that despite the dissonance, the participants of this San Franciscan community of poets and artists remained deeply attentive to each other.

THE ARTIST OF THE BEAUTIFUL: THE FIRST SERIAL POEMS

Between 1960 and 1966, and despite the personal turmoil of that period, Blaser produced the foundation pieces of his *oeuvre*. Building on his work in Boston, he wrote *Cups, The Park, The Faerie Queene, The Moth Poem, Les Chimères,* and the first of the *Image-Nation* poems, all of them serials that would eventually go into the making of his lifelong poem, *The Holy Forest*. In "The Fire" (1967), Blaser writes retrospectively of his interest in "a particular kind of narrative—what Jack Spicer and I agreed to call in our work the serial poem—this is a narrative which refuses to adopt an imposed story line, and completes itself only in the sequence of poems, if, in fact, a reader insists upon a definition of completion which is separate from the activity of the poems themselves" (*Fire*, 5). Spicer compared the serial to the kind of weekly narrative he found in cartoon series like *Dick Tracy* and Duncan had provided the initial performance of it back in the Berkeley days with *Medieval Scenes*.[8] Blaser's serials, like those of his companions, unfold over time as a record of the poet's attention to certain "persons, events, activities, [or] images" that "tell the tale of the spirit" (*Fire*, 5)—"a *carmen perpetuum*," Blaser calls it, "a continuous song" (*Fire*, 5). While he shares the form with Duncan and Spicer, his version of it is distinctive. Uniqueness, in fact, is simply built in to the method: as long as the poet stays with the "sequence of energies" (*Fire*, 5) recorded in the poem, the result will be true to his or her capacities and circumstances—a constant reversal of person and world into each other. No two poets can tell the truth about this process and write the same kind of poem.

Cups is the first of Blaser's serials, consisting of twelve poems that move between childhood landscapes of Idaho and those of 1960s San Francisco. On one level, it is an autobiographical poem about making poetry. In *Cups* 1, two poets sit in a tree—Spicer and Blaser—and the point "is to make others see / that two men in a tree is clearly / the same thing as poetry" (*HF*, 31). The easy rhymes in these lines and throughout the series recall the children's literature that Blaser was selling in the bookstore where he worked on first return to San Francisco. This explanation of *Cups*, however, does not account for images and references drawn from the high art of the classical–Christian tradition. A cup is a vessel to be given and received—hence an emblem of communion, with all attendant symbolic freighting. As such, it might evoke the Holy Grail or, back of that, emblems of female fertility. In the context of the *homoeros* that unfolds in these poems, it brings to mind the Platonic male womb of *The Symposium*—male fertility in the realm of art and ideas. "Cups" might also suggest the Cups suite of the Tarot cards, in which case the temptation is to read the poems as corresponding to the cards. At the literal level, a cup gives shape to the fluids it contains and these are of a different substance than the vessel itself; it is thus an apt metaphor for the way that language holds the world, and so makes an epistemological point. The problem is that the poems evoke, and then fail to confirm, all these readings and more. What distinguishes them from symbolist poems is that they do not refer to something beyond the page like the Grail but are rather *haunted* by cultural traditions embedded in the language, ghostly now, or present-as-absence, because they have fallen out of belief.

There are at least two outstanding precedents for the ghostly in Blaser's early works, beyond the early Catholicism. Hawthorne is one of them, a life-long passion of Blaser's and beloved since boyhood. In a short prose piece titled "The Haunted Mind," Hawthorne conjures up an hour between waking and sleeping "when the mind has a passive sensibility, but no active strength; when the imagination is a mirror, imparting vividness to all ideas, without the power of selecting or controlling them" (Hawthorne 1987, 57). In such a state, the artist is visited by memory in the form of a parade of personified "things of the mind" (Hawthorne 1987, 57). So in Hawthorne's tales and novels, the ghosts of Puritan New England rise again, filtered through the emotions of the characters and the imagination of the narrator. The stories are tense with an imagined Puritanism that has no correlate in living practice yet continues to haunt the living. In a notebook entry on Hawthorne, Blaser writes that "[h]is philosophy, point of view is broadly Christian – heaven, earth, and hell whether these are 'real' or subjective, psychological facts is one of 'Hawthorne's crucial ambiguit[ies]' – But for Hawthorne there would be no separation between the reality and the psychological fact" (Undated, "His philosophy").

A nearer and more narrowly focused source for the haunted mind in *Cups* is Mary Butts (1890–1937). Butts was an enthusiasm of Duncan's, shared with Spicer and Blaser at Berkeley. In *Armed with Madness*, there is a mysterious cup that may or may not be the Grail and a character, Picus, who may or may not be Zeus. Blaser knew Butts's work well; years later he would edit a reprint of her *Imaginary Letters* for Talonbooks in Vancouver and write an extended essay on *Armed with Madness* (see Chap. 7). In *Cups*, the narrative elements of the poem are fraught with a sense of immanence similar to that in Butts's novels.

The most important presence of *Cups*, however, is Amor, taken from Dante's *Vita Nuova*. Nine years after first seeing Beatrice, his Beloved, Dante receives a greeting from her that has the *gravitas* of a heavenly blessing. The poet is then visited in a vision by "a lordly man" who holds his (Dante's) flaming heart which he gives to Beatrice to eat. The man is Amor, and with the gift of the poet's heart to the Lady, he binds Dante to her service. Beatrice is the origin and end of the journey in *The Divine Comedy*; through her mediation, Dante receives the permission of heaven to make his way through hell and purgatory until he reaches paradise.

Amor comes to Blaser not only through his love of Dante and his Berkeley studies of the poet with Kantorowicz, but also Pound's fascination with the courtly love lyrics of medieval Provence. Blaser had been studying Pound for years by the time he came to write *Cups*. In "Psychology and Troubadours" from *The Spirit of Romance*, Pound compares Love in the troubadour tradition of the thirteenth century to Baruch Spinoza's understanding of it: "'the intellectual love of a thing consists in the understanding of its perfections … all creatures whatsoever desire this love,'" he says (Pound 1968, 91). Pound suggests that the Provençal poets leaned toward a view of the happy life as one in accord with nature's orders. The Lady who was the subject of their poems became a kind of shorthand for the perfections of such an accord ("a sort of *mantram*" (Pound 1968, 97)). So Amor, re-routed through a thirteenth century Florentine poet like Guido Cavalcanti and transported to the twentieth century, displaces religious mysticism with a feeling for nature's creative energy. Pound writes that there are only two kinds of religion—the exoteric kind that aims at social control through fear (God is a "disagreeable bogie") or the more esoteric sort that aims at "a sort of confidence in the life-force," such that people of the right temperament might "live at greatest peace with 'the order,' with man and nature" (Pound 1968, 95). In my view, Blaser accepts these steps toward an Amor that is love of the world and intellectual attention to its particularities.

In *Cups* 3, Blaser rewrites the scene in the *Vita Nuova* where Amor appears to Dante and offers the poet's heart to Beatrice, combining it with Pound's god in the rock (the energy in matter):

> We opened the rock.   This
> time I saw the god
> offer with out-stretched hand
> the heart to be devoured.   The
> lake flowed into my hands.
> Dante would say the lake
> of the heart. (*HF*, 33)

"We have about us the universe of fluid force," Pound writes, "and below us the germinal universe of wood alive, of stone alive" (Pound 1968, 92). Given the new Einsteinian physics, Pound could plausibly suggest that noun is verb— matter is energy—but an Amor so embedded in the world would have to mean a love of life's processes rather than a completion of the world in paradise. This would then imply a tearing open of the detached mind—the mind understood as separate from the body and the human creature as standing apart from the physical universe.

Blaser had begun this mental work of decentering the cogito in Boston through his forays into surrealism; in *Cups*, as in many of the serials that follow, this work is enacted as dismemberment. When Amor gives the poet's heart to Beatrice in the *Vita Nuova*, the literal image is violent: Love rips the heart out of the poet, as the bees of Blaser's "A Preface" rip "the jaw of a snapdragon." Dante's cosmos had a *paradiso*, of course, and the poet's prospect at the end of life was reunion with the Beloved and the healing of his heart in a state of bless-edness beyond loss and death. But the cosmos available to poets of Blaser's generation had already been riven by Nietzsche and Freud: one had declared the death of God; the other had attacked the transparency of consciousness to itself. And then James Joyce, as Blaser says on *Astonishments*, had written the ruin of the metaphysical tradition—"the death of the modern world, the death of God" (*AT*, 174). Without the Dantean hierarchy, the content of the Christian humanist tradition simply spills out in *Finnegans Wake*. Hence the need for "cups"—something to hold the spill, as the Grail once held Christ's blood.

Blaser's *Cups* holds these ambient ghosts of myth, literature, and religion in tension with a number of autobiographical stories. The landscape of Blaser's childhood Idaho appears in desert scenes, sage brush fires, and cameo appear-ances by family members such as Uncle Mitch[9] and Robert Blaser. These homely images are then shadowed by those drawn from the high narratives of the western tradition. For example, in *Cups 2*, the Catholic world appears in an interdiction against masturbation ("If he does not masturbate, / the promise is a second chance" (*HF*, 32)). In *Cups 7*, however, the spilled seed evokes a Jewish creation story from the *Zohar* (the world of Merkabah mysticism): "in service to love, / your hands dip out of the water / the shell or sperm, dropped there in passing / by some *ashen likeness*" (*HF*, 37). The "shell," grammatically apposite to "sperm," recalls the rabbinical account of creation as an outflowing of God's creative power into a series of vessels (cups). These, on first receiving the divine energy, crack and the "shells" of the broken vessels make up the material world. This Hebraic creation story then bumps up against the Catholic *contra dictum* against spilling the seed; the spilling here, however, is transmuted into a world-making act. The "*ashen likeness*" of the above lines is a phrase Blaser takes from Pound's translation of Cavalcanti's Sonnet XXVI: "thou knowest well I am Amor / Who leave with thee mine ashen likeness here / And bear away from thee thine every thought" (Pound 1963, 77). In the Cavalcanti sonnet, Love stands before the poet like a ghost, an "ashen vision," asserting his authority. So in *Cups*, the ghost of Amor binds the poet to the world. Hence a marriage poem, but it is a marriage in which the poet weds the world-tree rather than the Lady:

> Upon that tree there was a ring.
> HI   HO   HUM
> The ring surrounded the darkest part.
> HA   HA   HA
> The ring imagined a marriage bout.
> FIRE   FIRE   FIRE. (*HF*, 40)

Of this marriage ceremony, anticipated in "A Preface" and repeated in "Image-Nation 6" (*HF*, 156) and "Image-Nation 11" (*HF*, 177), Blaser says that he had in mind a Coptic myth in which one actually marries the world when one marries a woman. In this ceremony, "you go up and put rings on the tree not on one another's hands" ("AT" 8.27, 20). In the context of the myth, Blaser's retelling of an old joke of his father's about sheepherders choosing the goat with the best pelt to make love to (*HF*, 37) takes on a new resonance. Marriage leads to consummation, but if the Beloved is the world and the Lover is the poet, then intercourse would mean spilling the seed on the ground or perhaps a coupling with the creaturely. Whether so precise a metaphorical spin can be put on the *homoeros* of the poem or not, *Cups 10* records the springing up of new life, apparently in the middle of a desert:

> High on stilts, the black water tank
> leaks.   A pond rises by the railbed.
>   ....
> Willows, starwort,
> water striders appear in the desert. (*HF*, 41)

The water tank in Orchard, Idaho did literally leak and as Blaser remarks on *Astonishments*, he was perpetually amazed at the appearance of insects or even frogs on the pond and the mystery of where they might have come from in the middle of the desert (*AT*, 20). The striders in the above passage appear as if by magic—after the poets have fertilized the ground, perhaps—followed by Amor:

> Amor entered disguised as grass.   You both
> hoped your seed would fall among the roots
> of this tree and there grow up a second tree
> and guardian.
>
> WHAT IS THAT WRINKLES UNDER THE ROOT?
>
> SKIN, SEMEN, AN ARM AND A FOOT. (*HF*, 41)

To put this series of images together, *Cups* offers a number of autobiographical memories that begin when the poet finds himself up a tree "where Amor sits" (*HF*, 33). This is a world tree/language tree in which constellations of literary and mythical images hover over the personal stories. These ghosts in the language attach to fertility emblems (the titular cup, the teeming puddle of *Cups* 10, the snakes of *Cups* 11), rituals (the marriage ceremony in *Cups* 6, the spell-like chant of *Cups* 8, the Dionysian rites in *Cups* 12), and creation stories. They are presided over by an Amor who leads the poet into a spiritual marriage as Amor led Dante to Beatrice, but for this poet, it is a marriage to the world rather than the Lady. Consummation takes the form of masturbation—the insemination of the ground—an act that secularizes and redirects the Catholic universe of Dante at the same time as it introduces a *homoeros* into the poem since the act appears to be shared with another male poet up the same tree ("Jack" is named in *Cups* 1). Instead of the censure that masturbation might invite in a heteronormative or Catholic context, *Cups* offers the fruits of the male womb. Adapted to poetry, male creativity rests on the poet's capacity for wedding the world—or, to carry forward the plot of the *Vita Nuova* and *Commedia*, for following his Love all the way to hell and back through the saying of the Cosmos. The marriage is inspired by passion (the flaming heart), Blaser's signature element for creative energy and an emotional tie-back to childhood when it was Ina Mae's schoolbooks, imprinted with the flaming heart of the Sacred Heart Academy, that inspired a feeling for the life of the spirit and the imagination.

In retrospect, then, the plot of *The Holy Forest* is there in *Cups*. The poem is to be a *Vita Nuova* and the aim is a holy forest. In Dante, that forest, as opposed to the dark wood of the *Inferno*, comes at the end of the *Purgatory*. The earthly paradise is a limit concept of human potentiality—it is what lies within the imaginative range of intellectual love. And so back to Amor and the commitment to his service. Hence the priestly tone at the end of *Cups* 12: the poets are "among the thyrsus bearers"; they are "initiates [of the Muse]"; "they stamp on the ground / where her skin has fallen" (*HF*, 45). The ritualistic passages of *Cups* that sound like spells carry this whiff of the priestly, which is to say that the poetic venture was, for Blaser, a calling, a vocation, and a transmutation of his adolescent interest in the priesthood. And finally, haunting the broken order of the cosmos—the Joycean rubble of it—is Hawthorne's story, "The Artist of the Beautiful,"[10] a ghost image back of the whole of Blaser's *oeuvre*. The beautiful mechanical butterfly that Hawthorne's watchmaker–artist creates so laboriously, all for love, might have flown in a metaphysical tradition that hid its cunning device, but it had long shattered into small glittering pieces under the pressure of skepticisms that demanded that the illusion be unmasked and the magic debunked. Any artist post-the-modern would have to work with that skepticism of beauty and the perils of it. This would be Blaser's task throughout *The Holy Forest*.

The serials composed immediately after *Cups*—*The Park* (1960), *The Faerie Queene* (1961), and *The Moth Poem* (1962–1964)—extend and rework the territory of *Cups*. In fact, every serial reworks and modifies the poems that precede it, so that the scope and meaning of the whole evolves through difference-in-repetition. *The Park*, for example, unfolds in image-strings that have the same haunted quality as those in *Cups*. At the autobiographical level, Cleo Adams appears as a first Beloved and instance of the shared "male womb"; the magically multiplying desert rabbits of *The Park* are analogous to the water striders that materialize on the pond under the dripping water tower in *Cups*: "Cleo swears / the god-damned rabbits / mate with the sagebrush" (*HF*, 49). In both cases, creatures emerge from the desert without an evident source unless the reader remembers that the poet has married the world (tree) and that his spilling of the seed metaphorically inseminates the ground of poetry. In these early poems, Blaser *unnames* the old mythical powers because they have lost their force and credence in a secular time, even though they hover over the poems. In *The Park*, the alphabet burns (*HF*, 54); in *The Faerie Queene*, "the gods / [are] severed and loose / like architectural adornments" (*HF*, 61) and in the final poem ("For Gustave Moreau"), "the lips [twist] to allow / the tongue to play in / the broken mirror on the floor" (*HF*, 64). So the gods die and the poet must then re-articulate the relations they once named: the potencies of nature and the chronic human emotions.

One of Blaser's best-known serials, *The Moth Poem*, begins to put together some of the broken pieces of culture that litter the earlier poems. Stan Persky writes that it began "[o]ne day in 1962, in [the] Baker Street apartment":

> [Blaser] heard an eerie sound emanating from the baby grand piano, as if the instrument itself was playing. When he lifted the lid of the piano, he discovered the source of the sound, a moth trapped in the piano strings. The moth was duly rescued and the poem began. Once the first moth appeared, so did others, over a year or more, inexplicably turning up in the most unexpected ways, to provide the images or metaphors upon which successive poems in the serial were predicated. (Persky 2010, 13–14)

Blaser gave a private reading of *The Moth Poem* late in 1964 at Lew Ellingham's apartment. It was a gala affair with golden candles. In a letter to Persky, Helen Adam reports that "Lew wrote that he gave a dinner for twenty poets & Robin read it, & the rain rattled the windows, & Lew felt it was me trying to get in & listen..." (29 January 1965). The poem was first published in *Open Space* in 1964 and it turned out to be a signature piece, a series of sixteen poems, or seventeen counting the musical notes that take up a page (C D ♭E G A ♭B B D (*HF*, 85)).

Like *Cups*, *The Moth Poem* has some strong autobiographical elements, this time referencing the social swirl of San Francisco poetry circles. In "The Medium,"

> ...the story is of a man
> who lost his way in the holy wood
>
> because the way had never been taken without
> at least two friends, one on each side. (*HF*, 73)

This poem, says Persky, "was written one weekend while we were staying at a friend's summer cabin on the Russian River, north of San Francisco" (Persky 2010, 16–17) and it includes "an oblique reference to Spicer and Robert Duncan, their long friendship now strained by quarrels over poetry and flare-ups of personality" (Persky 2010, 17). "Supper Guest," as well, seems to reference the San Francisco social scene: "tin flowers" and "castles" float out of the mouths of the guests in table talk. These are like "magic juices / on the eyelids" (*HF*, 72)—and if these juices be like those concocted for Titania by Oberon in Shakespeare's *Midsummer Night's Dream*, they confer the capacity to fall in love with the asinine. "O-friend" is another such poem where the guest leaves "a kind of music, / la-de-da and stink // in the air" (*HF*, 75). Meanwhile, the moth in this series tries its "way into corners" (*HF*, 72).

In addition to these poems that protest the "daimon of mediocrity" (*HF*, 84), *The Moth Poem* includes some that move past the breakage and loss of the first three serials into the constructedness of collage. "Paradise Quotations" is a poem made entirely of quotations, all of them about things *forming* or *transforming* from one state to another. Blaser references a story from George MacDonald's *Phantastes*, for example, in which a poet literally sings a marble Lady into life (*HF*, 80). A Coleridge fragment catches the form of a rose in an eddy of water ("*the white rose of Eddy-foam*" (*HF*, 80)), and a citation from Erasmus Darwin's *The Botanic Garden* traces the growth of a crocodile from embryo to adult ("*edge over edge expands the hardening scale, / and sheathes his slimy skin in silver mail*" (*HF*, 81)). These instances of form in the process of articulation complement the many scenes of dismemberment in the earlier serials. Moving through the broken vessels, cut bodies, burning alphabets, and shattered mirrors, the poet begins to pick up the pieces.

Les Chimères

Among the big events of Blaser's last years in San Francisco was *Les Chimères*. The choice of these poems of Gérard de Nerval for translation was not accidental. Even at the level of biography, there were affinities. Both Nerval and Blaser were gracious and well-liked socially, yet both suffered from depression and self-doubt. Both poets grappled with an authoritarian father from whom they sought approval, and both wrote with difficulty. Nerval's themes were also Blaser's: the eight poems that make up *Les Chimères* explore questions of identity, religious feeling, and cosmic order through a mélange of classical and Christian myth and historical references that give the poems that haunted feeling of *Cups*. Blaser's bookishness also had a correlate in Nerval's, as did the combining of emotional inner landscapes and the outer.

Designed by Graham Mackintosh, Blaser's *Les Chimères* was first published as a chapbook in 1965 under the Open Space imprint. Before it came out, Blaser read the series on 18 July 1965 at the Berkeley Poetry Conference. By the late fall of 1965, he was embroiled in a serious argument with Duncan over the poems. This quarrel had been building for some time, fed by growing tensions in the friendship. As quoted in a letter Blaser sent to Duncan, Ebbe Borregaard had expressed his admiration of the poems to Duncan and praised them as "'removing the hermetic'" (Blaser to Duncan, 16 November 1965). Duncan, of course, took this as disparagement of the "lore" that was so close to his heart. Another sore point was a one-night stand with Jess. As Blaser used to tell the story orally, Duncan was traveling and had written to Blaser. Blaser had put the unopened letter in his pocket and then joined Jess for dinner. He gave the letter to Jess to read, discovering later in the evening that Duncan had been writing about a sexual conquest. Blaser put his arms around Jess to comfort him and one thing led to another. Jess told all when Duncan returned and Duncan was furious. Yet Blaser, too, had accumulated grievances. By the time the quarrel really broke, he had lived through Spicer's death, an event that shook him profoundly. Duncan had not been on good terms with Spicer and his casual behavior through Spicer's final days and at the memorial wake angered Blaser. *Les Chimères* thus became a flash point for all the rages and rivalries that had been simmering since Blaser had returned to San Francisco.

The Blaser–Duncan exchange over the Nerval translations unfolded in letters, and finally became public when Duncan published these with his own commentary and translation of Nerval in *Poetry/Audit* in 1967. Two major areas of conflict emerge from the *Chimères* episode. First, the personal. To add to the above cited grievances, there was the history of the Blaser–Duncan friendship. Blaser had always deferred to Duncan, accepting the position of junior acolyte and ideal reader. In 1965, he was still in this position in the eyes of the poetry world, and in Duncan's eyes too, having published much less than Duncan. Given this history, Duncan's public re-translation of Nerval was a humiliating public put down from someone who had long been in the position of an adored mentor.

A second and, in my view, more enduring conflict to come out of the *Chimères* episode had to do with poetics and Blaser's finding of his own direction, separate from that of Duncan. Duncan heard a challenge in Blaser's translations:

> It is because I hold these basic concepts [of Nerval's] most essential to the good of our art as poets, because I find these to be truths and Nerval's text to be gospel, that I undertake to restore them and to contest the text which you present.... If I attack you for substituting "that hill" for "Posilipo," it is because I believe Nerval to be of such an order in Poetry that the Posilipo, El Desdichado out of Scott's **Ivanhoe**, Lusignan and Biron, are not literary or personal references to be let go, but, like Dante's Beatrice, eternal places and persons, revealed places and persons of Poetry. (Duncan 1967, 48)

At issue are two different views of poetry. For Duncan, Nerval's "constellated lute" lives on in the vast collage that is the story of the species as preserved in art. This collage is what he calls Poetry with a capital "P," a place that the poet enters and to which she or he contributes. As Duncan says in "A FOOTNOTE, April 1966" to the *Chimères* essay, "there is no real me, only the process of derivations in which I have my existence" (Duncan 1967, 49). Very strictly speaking, he is right and Blaser would agree: poetic discourse as discourse and language qua language belongs to everyone and no one. The disagreement, however, is in defining the individual poet's relationship to that great human saying. From Blaser's point of view, a translation of the distinctive time, space, and perspective of a poet from a different era and a different language requires the kind of correspondence that Spicer had imagined in his conversation with Federico García Lorca. The poet has to become a "time mechanic not an embalmer," Spicer says, translating the energies of his source into his own moment (Spicer 2008, 122). What Blaser brings across from Nerval is not a precise rendition of the architecture of Nerval's poem, but the experience of it as it might still be lived in 1960s San Francisco—the feelings of metaphysical loss, the struggle with existential anguish, the inquiry into the nature of love, and the search for relationship within a civilization that had experienced the death of God. From Duncan's point of view, "Blaser as an artist aims at signature or style; I aim at meaning..." (Duncan 1967, 49). But signature is the diachronic component that the poet brings to the poem—his singular acts in the vast field of language and Poetry: "signature" signs the poet into his personal and historical situatedness. There is an analogy to be made here to the "king's two bodies" as Kantorowicz explicates it in a European medieval context: the person who fills the role of King is a fallible individual; the office of King, however, is a deathless, divinely ordained public institution. Adapted to describe poetry, that dichotomy inserts a distance between the poet and Poet. What Duncan might see as humility on his part, as a participant in the community of Poetry, reverses into the arrogance of a commander of the field if poet and Poet become indistinguishable—"the little cross-eyed king" of a thousand lines as he has it in *The Venice Poem* (Duncan 1975, n.p.). Duncan's response to Blaser suggests that he saw the difference in perspective between them and defended his right to the high office of Poet with vigor. In a letter from 23 April 1966, also published in *Poetry/Audit* Duncan writes:

> If I had taken your "translations" as separate from Nerval and separate from my own work, I would have been cut off indeed from the syncretism in Poetry I seek, from what make the Hellenistic syncretism in religion so fascinating: the structure containing its contraries. (Duncan 1967, 61)

In the *Chimères* affair, Duncan handles an unkind gesture—his public put down of a longtime friend and a vulnerable poet just coming into his own—as a matter of poetics. Duncan and Denise Levertov would part company over a similar incident: Duncan criticized her poems of the Vietnam era for allowing politics to dominate poetry. In response to her emotional and wounded defense, he "read" her letter as a hermeneutical exercise, commenting on her poems much as he does on Blaser's translations in *Poetry/Audit*.[11] The gesture resembles that of a teacher correcting the grammar in a student's love letter and sending it back.

Blaser was deeply affected by Duncan's response to *Les Chimères*, more so than Duncan appears to have been over the affair. In *The Astonishment Tapes*, nine years after the event, Blaser gives over large sections of the discussion to his differences with Duncan. For Duncan, the quarrel seems to have been over with *Poetry/Audit*. Blaser, on the other hand—once established in Vancouver where he would move in 1966—practiced a polished civility and respectful attention to Duncan's writing that included little congratulatory notes on new work. He also praised Duncan consistently as a great poet. Somewhat nervous about joining Blaser in Buffalo for a March 1968 Festival of the Arts, Duncan was reassured by Blaser's manners, writing to Barbara Joseph "'that in the end there was good cheer on all sides'" (Jarnot 2012, 275).

But Blaser did not forget and the relationship with Duncan never returned to what it had been. Vancouver friend Karen Tallman remembers Duncan's "poisoned chocolate" encounters with Blaser years later in the 1970s (Karen Tallman interview, 3 May 2014). On visits to Vancouver, Duncan would sometimes stay with Ellen Tallman, Karen's mother, downstairs from Blaser in the up-down duplex that Ellen and Robin had bought together in 1977. Duncan would be "nice" to Blaser in a way calculated to wind him up, snickering over Blaser's imagined response to his poisonous "sweets."

SPICER'S DEATH

When *Chimères* was ready, Blaser wanted Spicer's ear. Stan Persky remembers conveying the message and Spicer's immediate response—his attentive listening and unreserved praise of the poem (Persky 2010, 24–25). This incident, Persky stresses, demonstrates the bond between Spicer and Blaser in poetry, despite their fallings out. By 1965, however, Spicer's body was beginning to go. Writing to John Button, Blaser relayed the news:

> Spicer—he's now lost his last one-day-a-week-job, following alarums and threats of suicide. He's made some effort to see me <u>cordially</u> again—after two years (you will remember his denouncements after I got <u>Heads of the Town</u> out). It's odd that there is now no way to make up these things—I don't think I'm less fond, certainly not less interested, but there's no way to patch up with someone who's too alcoholic to remember the hatred he pours out. He's writing again, and well, so that, I suppose, will save him, but he does come very close to leaving his imagination for the world of insanity. (22 February 1965)

In May of 1965, Spicer, Blaser, and Persky took a bus to Vancouver to read, with Blaser babysitting Jack's brandy habit all the way, ducking out for refills at every stop. When they finally got to the Canadian border, they appeared sufficiently reprobate that their hosts, Ellen and Warren Tallman, had to go down and bail them out (Karen Tallman interview, 3 May 2014). Spicer stayed with the Tallmans, and Blaser and Persky with Vancouver writer Maria (Gladys) Hindmarch. At the New Design Gallery, Blaser read *Cups, The Moth Poem* and *The Park*; Spicer read *Billy the Kid*; and Persky, *The Lives of French Symbolist Poets*. Blaser remarks in an interview with Lew Ellingham for the Spicer biography that Spicer very much wanted Vancouver to be his scene (Ellingham and Killian 1998, 335), and according to Ellen and Karen Tallman's recollections, he did better for a while in Vancouver. Ellen wanted to save Spicer's life. The plan was that he would live with the family until his health improved and for a time, it seemed as though the plan might work. Spicer was still drinking a bottle of brandy a day, but he was at least eating and playing with Karen's cat, Greedy Guts. In June of 1965, Spicer gave his *Vancouver Lectures* at the Tallmans' home with a crowd of young poets sitting on the floor in the packed-out living room. During this trip, Spicer met Ron Baker, then the Chair of the Department of English at Simon Fraser University (SFU), the brand new, soon-to-be-radicalized campus, and Baker offered him a job (Ron Baker interview, 23 February 2015). Spicer was quite incapable of holding down a faculty position at this point, but the invitation pleased him and it unintentionally opened the door to SFU for Blaser later on.

When Spicer flew back to San Francisco, the idea was that he would return after the Berkeley Poetry Conference. The Conference took place in July 1965 and Spicer gave his "Poetry and Politics" lecture, although Blaser remembers that he had to get Jack to the event (*AT*, 216). Over the month of July, he still showed up at Aquatic Park in the afternoons and at the bar in the evening, but he was getting sicker, and those close to him noticed a farewell in his responses to friends that summer (Ellingham and Killian 1998, 355). Spicer collapsed on 31 July 1965 and was taken by strangers to the poverty ward of the San Francisco General Hospital.

Blaser's account of the end in his Spicer essay, "The Practice of Outside," is legendary in poetry circles: "*My vocabulary did this to me. Your love will let you go on*" (*Fire*, 163). In the eyes of the doctors at San Francisco General, Spicer died of acute alcoholism. Perhaps, as Ebbe Borregaard said, it was the nineteenth century and his "idiot friends" that killed Jack Spicer (Ellingham and Killian 1998, 363). But in the land of poetry, Blaser was surely right. The only real way to win the game against language that Spicer had been playing for so many years was to die—a pyrrhic victory if ever there was one. I do not mean to imply that Spicer sought death, although he refused to acknowledge the consequences of his drinking. Rather, in the breakdown of his body, he lived the difference that he had insisted on so often in his poetry between bodies and words. The "absolutely temporary" he wanted until it claimed him. In *Astonishments*, Blaser says, "I don't think we have to die the way Jack did. I don't think we have to. I do not think we any longer—I think the task of Jack's recognition is complete and as a consequence we no longer have to die in order to bring that language forward" (*AT*, 73). In the land of poetry, Blaser could allow for the flight of life and love (recall the "Freud" poem) as Spicer could not. As his biographers record it, Spicer died at 3 am, 17 August 1965 (Ellingham and Killian, 360). In a notebook, Blaser wrote a poem–letter to him:

> Dear Jack, now you're dead, I'll
> write that letter.
> When I asked what you believed,
> You said "Despair." – How puzzled
> I was. And afraid.
> We were drinking – our first
> meeting apart. Dinner & talk.
> And I said, "Love."
> Despair & Love.
> And you said in the guise
> of a raven, Despair. (Undated, "Dear Jack, now you're dead")

In *Astonishments*, Blaser describes the wake.

When Jack's mother and brother came [Dorothy and Holt Spicer] and asked me to invite Jack's friends to meet them, they said that they were simply cremating him and it was going to be the end. There was no funeral, there was nothing, but they'd like to meet his friends and of course they thought he had two—me and maybe somebody they'd never heard of. He had hundreds. People canceled everything—my house filled—you couldn't walk down the hallway, you fell over buckets of roses. There were drawings, there were books, there was—the door-bell rang and I opened the door and Duncan says, "Sorry, Jess doesn't come to parties." (*AT*, 65–66)

As condolences rolled in over the late summer and fall, Blaser was made literary executor of Spicer's estate by arrangement with Dorothy and Holt Spicer.[12] This had been Spicer's long-held intention, despite his revocation of it in the midst of the quarrel over Auerhahn. The executorship would soon bring new responsibilities in the form of multiple requests for permission to publish Spicer poems and the task of editing Spicer's *Collected Books*, a job that would take Blaser another decade.

In the meantime, Blaser received an invitation from Warren Tallman to read at the Vancouver Poetry Festival in February of 1966 and to act in a Festival staging of Duncan's *Adam's Way* (Tallman to Blaser, 9 December 1965). The occasion, Tallman says, could serve for lunch interviews with Stanley Reed, Chair of English at the University of British Columbia (UBC) and Ron Baker at SFU, the point being a soft introduction that might lead to a faculty position. Blaser had applied for a Guggenheim fellowship in October of 1965 to give himself time to complete *The Boston Poems* and *The Holy Forest* sequence (Blaser 1965a, "Guggenheim"). "Even if the Guggenheim comes through, it would be well worth," says Tallman encouragingly (9 December 1965).

Alienated from Duncan and struggling to process Spicer's death, Blaser was looking for change. He was tired of poetry circle squabbles and fed-up with the tedium of the library job and the time it took from poetry. And there was Jantzen's pestering. According to a notebook entry dated 4 August 1965, just after Spicer was hospitalized, Blaser turned to the Kenkyusha. The Kenkyusha is a Japanese-English dictionary, the second edition of which—and only the second—is thought to have divinatory powers. One asks the Kenkyusha a question and opens the dictionary at random, placing a finger on an entry without first looking at it. The entry is the response to the question. In a notebook, Blaser recorded a session with the Kenkyusha in which he asks about Jack and his own future in San Francisco. "What of Jack's illness," he asks and the Kenkyusha replies, "a main attack, a frontal attack." "Shall I pick Vancouver," Blaser asks, and the Kenkyusha answers "an approved lodging house" (Blaser 1965b, "Kenkyusha").

By July of 1966, Robin and Stan were packing. Unwilling to completely sever ties with San Francisco, Blaser arranged a one-year leave of absence with San Francisco State College, allowing himself the option of returning if Vancouver didn't work out. Stan went ahead to find a place for them while a stressed-out Blaser was undergoing psychiatric examination. In a letter to Persky, dated 26 August 1966, Dr. R.M. Grissom of the Langley Porter Clinic in San Francisco writes that Blaser is undergoing tests at the Neuropsychiatric Institute, but that these will not change the plans. Apparently, they did not. In September 1966, Blaser left San Francisco to take up a temporary, one-year appointment as lecturer in Simon Fraser University's brand new English Department.

NOTES

1. Paul O'Neil published his article on the Beats, "The Only Rebellion Around," in *Life* magazine in 1959. The article included a staged photograph of a Beat "pad" with actors dressed in black, a pair of bongo drums and a guitar, and a vase of sprigs representing marijuana. Kerouac's appearance on the Steve Allen show in 1959 also drew attention to the word "beat" and to *On the Road*. The publicity, however, focused on lifestyle, not on the substance of what the poets were saying.

2. Stan Persky remembers that the Spicer circle in 1959 consisted of himself, Duncan, George Stanley, Joanne Kyger, Ebbe Borregaard, and Harold Dull. Later, Ron Primack and James Alexander (brother of the painter Paul Alexander) joined. (Persky interview, 19 October 2013). George Stanley, in an interview with Brenda Houglum and Jenny Penberthy, adds David Meltzer, James Broughton, and Michael Rumaker to the list. Joe and Carolyn Dunn hosted some of the Sunday sessions; some were held at Stanley and Borregaard's apartment (Stanley 2011, 5).

3. Blaser's notes for the workshop are in MsA1 Box 45, Folder 1, Blaser fonds.

4. A postcard from "Joe" dated 6 March 1961 complains that Blaser is neglecting his students and a note from Blaser to Parker Hodges dated 2 October 1962 comments on poems that Hodges has sent. Both notes are dated well past the end of the Poet's Seminar.

5. The Vancouver poetry festival of 1963 has morphed into legendary status. See Chap. 6 for a description.

6. Accounts of the sum that Jantzen proposed to donate vary in the correspondence of the period. In a filmed interview with Blaser, produced by Ralph Maud in 1991, Blaser remembers the amount in question as $3000. In an undated letter to Blaser from Jantzen it is $2500 (Jantzen n.d., "It would be better").

7. In 1978, Greenberg added a note to his famous essay, saying that he had intended it to be descriptive rather than prescriptive, but the effect, as least in some art circles, was similar.

8. See *The Astonishment Tapes* on Duncan's *Medieval Scenes* as a first performance of seriality (Blaser 2015, 68, 167–68). Spicer also points to *Medieval Scenes* as an early serial (Spicer 1998, 52).

9. In *The Astonishment Tapes*, Blaser says that his Uncle Mitch, a figure from his Idaho childhood, was "kooky" to the point of incarceration in an asylum. Among his eccentricities was a habit of whistling between words. He was also a writer of westerns. When Mitch committed suicide, Robert Blaser burned the trunkful of writings (*AT*, 32–33). This story turns up in *Cups* 10, where musical notes, like Mitch's whistles, punctuate Blaser's "western," a family story about an Aunt Celestia's presence at the Mountain Meadows Massacre in 1857. In that massacre, a group of California-bound emigrants was slaughtered by the Utah Territorial Militia and their Paiute allies.

10. In "The Artist of the Beautiful," watchmaker Owen Warland falls in love with local girl Annie Hovenden. She, however, chooses a blacksmith to marry, preferring a practical man to one she considers a dreamer. Warland creates an exquisite mechanical butterfly for her nonetheless, a masterwork that takes years to create and that flies through the air as if by magic. When he presents his gift to Annie and her husband, however, the couple's child grabs it, crushing it to shards.

11. The Duncan–Levertov exchange over Levertov's antiwar poems has been published in *The Letters of Robert Duncan and Denise Levertov*, edited by Robert Bertholf and Albert Gelpi. The relevant letters run from pages 660 to 693; they are numbered 449 to 456.
12. The documents passing the literary executorship of Spicer's estate to Blaser are in the Blaser fonds, MsA1 Box 55, Folder 1.

CHAPTER 6

Vancouver in the Sixties: Context as Explanation

In the 1960s, Vancouver still had the feel of a biggish town rather than a gateway city as it has now become. The economy was resource-based (logging, mining, fishing, hydro power) and there was a sawmill on False Creek at the center of town where there are now multimillion-dollar condominiums. Wages and prices were still oriented to the resident work force and this meant a mostly modest middle class with commensurately modest amenities. Hippie culture had arrived and was centered in Kitsilano, the neighborhood where Blaser eventually settled. Now an upscale destination for international cash, Kitsilano was then awash in tie-died T-shirts, "head" shops selling paraphernalia for marijuana smoking, organic grocery stores, and vegetarian restaurants like the Naam (opened in 1968). While the art scene was hip, it was relatively small and undiscovered.

This provincialism was a source of anxiety for the incoming San Franciscans. In a letter to Blaser, Persky complains of the square box houses, likely "Vancouver specials" as they are still called, built in quantity between 1965 and 1985. The special is a two-story duplex, designed for utility rather than beauty. It is often faced in inexpensive plaster and brick and decorated with wrought iron railings around the upper decks. The awkward dimensions of these houses and cheap, pretentious materials add up to ugly. To someone accustomed to vintage, Spanish-inflected San Franciscan architecture or funky brown-shingled Berkeley cottages, they must have looked dreary indeed. On the up side, however, Vancouver had beautiful beaches. Persky settled for a place at 1854 West 5th Avenue (Persky to Blaser, 5 August 1966)—not exactly ideal because it was off the water, but a stop gap until Blaser arrived: "If you're totally unsatisfied we can find another place," he wrote (5 August 1966).

Despite its shortcomings, Vancouver offered a context for Blaser's kind of poetry. Ellen and Warren Tallman were important facilitators in connecting local writers with poets stateside. Ellen knew Blaser, Spicer, and Duncan from

© The Author(s) 2019
M. Nichols, *A Literary Biography of Robin Blaser*,
Modern and Contemporary Poetry and Poetics,
https://doi.org/10.1007/978-3-030-18327-1_6

Berkeley where she had studied music. Through this connection and the faculty positions that both she and Warren held at UBC, the Tallmans did much to bring the New American poetry to town. Warren had an engaged set of students in his poetry class, who, with the Tallmans' help, arranged for Duncan to give readings in December 1959 and February 1961. After the second reading, Tallman encouraged a number of his students to raise money to invite Duncan for another "lecture visit" (Davey 1975, 7). In his introduction to *TISH 1-19*, Frank Davey recalls the inception of the seminal little magazine that came out of Tallman's classes:

> In May, 1961, the amount of writing produced by our unofficial circle had reached such proportions that Wah and Lionel Kearns were half-seriously proposing the founding of a little magazine to be named **COCK**. But the main push toward a magazine was Duncan's. His accounts of the histories of little mags such as **ORIGIN, BLACK MOUNTAIN REVIEW**, and **THE FLOATING BEAR** began to promise freedom from received standards and establishment bias should we venture to create a similar publication. (Davey 1975, 8)

The "unofficial circle" consisted of George Bowering, David Dawson, James (Jamie) Reid, Lionel Kearns, Davey, and Fred Wah. Maria (Gladys) Hindmarch was an important friend to them and Daphne Marlatt contributed to the magazine after the initial group began to scatter to jobs after graduation. The five-member editorial board of *TISH* consisted of Davey, Reid, Bowering, Wah, and Dawson.

In his essay "The Wonder Merchants," on Vancouver poetry and the New Americans, Warren Tallman describes two obvious centers of literary activity in 1960s Vancouver. There were the *TISH* editors and their slightly younger counterparts at UBC, and there was a downtown group that included Gerry Gilbert, Judy Copithorne, Maxine Gadd, Bill Bissett, Roy Kiyooka, and John Newlove. The downtowners were less academically oriented but interested in the contemporary arts and in the New Americans (Tallman 1977, 196). These communities of poets were seed beds for the growth of a Canadian, West Coast postmodernism. Of the original editorial crew, Davey, Bowering, Wah, and Kearns went on to long writing lives and influential teaching practices. Reid would become a poet and political activist. Daphne Marlatt, a little too young for the first round of *TISH*, would develop a rich feminist poetics. On the downtown front, there were Bill Bissett's blewointment press, Gerry Gilbert's *B.C. Monthly* newsletter, and Roy Kiyooka's multidisciplinary work in poetry, mixed media visual art, and pedagogy. At the same time, the publishing venture that would become Talonbooks, one of the most ambitious and enduring literary presses in Canada, progressed from a gestetnered magazine at Magee High School in 1963 under the collective editorship of David Robinson and friends to a quarterly journal, then a collaboration with Very Stone House Press, and finally Talonbooks in 1968.

Of particular, interest to the poetry crowd in Vancouver was a festival in the summer of 1963, 24 July to 16 August, that featured a credit course, an extension (non-credit) course in poetry, and a series of readings. Organized by Warren Tallman and Creeley, English 410, the credit course, was taught by Ginsberg, Olson, and Creeley, the last of whom was already teaching at UBC as a sessional. Morning sessions consisted of lectures and discussions; the afternoon was given to workshops. Contributing poets were Margaret Avison, Duncan, and Levertov. Registered students were also expected to attend evening readings. Among those who signed up for English 410 were George Bowering, David Bromige, Daphne Buckle (Marlatt), Clark Coolidge, Judith Copithorne, David Dawson, Gladys Hindmarch, Robert Hogg, Lionel Kearns, Dan McLeod, Michael Palmer (registered as George Palmer), Sam Perry, Jamie Reid, Linda Wagner, and Fred Wah, to name a few who stayed with the arts (Vidaver 1999, 15–18). Don Allen, Bobbie Louise Hawkins, and Philip Whalen were in attendance. The intensity of these three weeks has drifted into legendary status, helped along by Robert McTavish's 2013 film, *The Line Has Shattered: Vancouver's Landmark 1963 Poetry Conference*.[1]

In addition to the poetry events, a series of annual arts festivals at UBC provided another convergence of locals and out of towners. Initiated by a Fine Arts Committee chaired by the painter B.C. Binning, the UBC Festival of the Contemporary Arts, kicked off in 1961, was an annual event until it began to flag in 1966, eventually ending in 1971 (Rogatnick 2006, 33–38). When Blaser landed in Vancouver in August of 1966, he chose a neighborhood that housed a who's who of local talent, some of whom were festival organizers. The house that Persky had found that summer at 1854 West 5th was on "a quiet street of old houses," but it had no fireplace and it housed other people in two single rooms (Persky to Blaser, 5 August 1966). Ergo, inadequate by Blaser's standards. By October, he and Persky had moved to 4570 West 1st Avenue, the Jericho Beach neighborhood of Vancouver, close to UBC.

On West 1st, Blaser's neighbors included Michael Morris, Helen Goodwin, Jane Rule and Helen Sonthoff, Alvin Balkind, and Victor and Audrey Capel Doray. Morris was a visual artist of various media (paint, plexi, wood, text, environments). Helen Goodwin was an experimental dancer who had worked with Anna Halprin; she was active in organizing UBC's arts festivals and she participated in Intermedia, an important Vancouver art collective initiated in 1967 to explore film, performance art, painting, sculpture, sound, poetry, and new media (Rogatnick 2006, 36). Jane Rule was a novelist and an out-of-the-closet lesbian; her partner, Helen Sonthoff taught at UBC and was also a festival organizer. Victor Doray was Director of Medical Illustration for UBC and Audrey Capel Doray was a visual artist of multiple media. Alvin Balkind curated UBC's Fine Arts Gallery; with Abraham Rogatnick, a professor of architecture there, he had founded the New Design Gallery in the mid-1950s, where Blaser, Persky, and Spicer had read on their 1965 trip to Vancouver. Both Balkind and Rogatnick contributed to the UBC festivals, and they mightily bolstered the local art scene by setting up the Arts Club Theatre, still an important venue in Vancouver. Of this venture, Rogatnick says in an interview with Marian Penner Bancroft,

...Alvin Balkind and myself ... we started the Arts Club—it opened in '58, and it was a fantastic club. Marshall McLuhan gave his first lecture in Vancouver at the Arts Club. And because the Tallmans had brought in all these wonderful poets from San Francisco (Ferlinghetti gave a performance with his orchestra at the Arts Club), we had all kinds of events. (Bancroft, "UBC in the Sixties")

Blaser's neighborhood, in other words, offered a significant sample of what was new and exciting in Vancouver art in the 1960s. The scene was small because the city did not have a network of galleries or buyers capable of supporting a world class art market. However, it did have some very forward-looking poets, artists, and educators who, with the help of Canada Council funding,[2] were able to engage with their international counterparts.

At mid-century, modernist Canadian art and poetry was associated with landscape. Sometimes the land was sublime, sometimes mysterious, and sometimes it was hostile. Writing of the 1950s, curator and art historian Scott Watson says that "the dominant look of painting in Vancouver had become a lyrical, painterly abstraction with a landscape reference" (Watson 1983, 90). In the 1960s, however, younger artists began to move in other directions. Some of the most memorable shows of the 1960s were built environments. Intermedia was an artists' collective put together to explore art-making in multiple media. During its short life, its artists organized three large exhibitions at the Vancouver Art Gallery (VAG). For *Intermedia Nights* in 1968, Michael Morris and Gary Lee-Nova, the latter a painter and filmmaker, were commissioned by the VAG to create an installation. *Prisma* was "a seven-sided room of plate glass mirrors, its floor of faceted plate glass, its domed ceiling of black plexiglass." Lighting made the room pulse with rainbow color and a sound track incorporated chanting and drums (Lowndes 1983, 145). Elsewhere and otherwise, Iain and Ingrid Baxter created the N.E. Thing Company (NETCO) an umbrella name for their experiments in environments and information technologies. Provincial policy in British Columbia was schizophrenic: on one hand, the province promoted full throttle resource extraction (forestry, fishing, mining, hydroelectric power); on the other, it sold B.C. as a pristine wilderness to tourists in magazines such as *Beautiful B.C.* The Baxters ironized the latter and put a new spin on Canadian landscape art.[3]

Scott Watson gathers up these trends in Vancouver art to point to certain discussions of the times that emerged from the idea of communication in art—whether or not art was to be "about" something (Watson, "Transmission"). The Clement Greenberg inspired anti-narrative line that had marginalized San Franciscan figurative abstraction was also used against "Minimalism, Pop Art, and Duchampism" because these art forms worked through irony and idea (Watson, "Transmission"). Watson suggests that New York modernism was read in Vancouver as a "high cultural form of imperialism in sync with the terror being unleashed in Southeast Asia"—the Vietnam war. Hence Canadian support for art currents that had a semiotic content ("Transmission"). On one memorable occasion in December of 1969, Robert Smithson arrived in

Vancouver to perform his *Glue Pour*, a conceptual art piece that consisted of dumping a barrel of orange glue over a clay embankment near UBC.[4] Christos Dikeakos photographed the performance and it became an off-site component of a large conceptual art show at the VAG in winter 1970. The show was guest curated by New York art critic Lucy Lippard and titled 955,000, the population figure of Vancouver at the time.

In Vancouver, as in San Francisco, Blaser actively engaged in the visual arts community. He went to parties and openings and he became friends with some of the key artists in town. Dikeakos, a collagist and photo-based artist, remembers that Dennis Wheeler was instrumental in connecting him with Blaser, who would become a lifelong friend and mentor. A writer, educator, and filmmaker, Wheeler was a blue-eyed wunderkind that Spicer, Blaser, and Persky had met at the Tallmans on the 1965 trip. Blaser was coming out of an art environment that was intensely semiotic, painterly, and oriented to wall art, yet he was open to all manner of art forms and embraced the Vancouver "scene with no scene" (Leider 1967, 1). When celebrity art critic Lucy Lippard came to Vancouver, Blaser was at the party, dallying with a young man in a back room, as Morris remembers it (Michael Morris interview, 21 March 2014).

Both Dikeakos and Wheeler were interested in First Nations art and this was another important strand in Vancouver alongside Canadian and American postmodernisms. When Doris Shadbolt took over as interim Acting Director of the VAG, she mounted the *Arts of the Raven* show in 1967, a game-changer in terms of how First Nations art was perceived. Encouraging the interest, Blaser brought Jerome Rothenberg's anthology of multi-ethnic and aboriginal writings to Dikeakos's attention and he followed Dennis Wheeler's engagements with First Nations cultures (Dikeakos interview with author, 24 May 2014). For instance, Wheeler documented the potlatch ceremony of the Kwakwaka'waka in a film titled *a strict law bids us dance* (1975). In a catalog essay on Christos Dikeakos, Vancouver artist Jeff Wall says of this period that there was "the esotericism of Duchampian symbolism, the fusion of the literary and the visual in collage and page design, the reminiscence of mythic language and its startling presence in both the prehistory of B.C. and its immediate present [and] the new omnipresence of photography and its challenge to the whole structure of western modernist pictorial art" (Wall 2014, 4). Wall knew Blaser as a colleague at SFU and in fact, Blaser had helped Wall to get a faculty position there (Dikeakos interview, 24 May 2014). When Blaser came to teach the modernist version of his Arts in Context course at SFU, Wall would be called upon to lecture on visual arts.

Two key drivers of change behind Vancouver art and poetry in the late 1960s and 70s were technology and politics. Marshall McLuhan had drawn attention to the *media* of art and communication, and the big 1965 UBC arts festival had drawn attention to McLuhan: new media were in, painting was on the way out. In combination with McLuhanism, was a growing Canadian nationalism that had been building since the 1950s. Canada celebrated its centenary in 1967 and Montréal hosted a spectacular world's fair that year. That international exposition, replete with techno wonders and futuristic sensoria, put a provincial backwater—the city and the country—on the world stage. At the same time, the Vietnam war was on under sustained U.S. domestic protest; in Canada the mood was anti-American. Abraham Rogatnick writes that the UBC arts festivals petered out by 1971 in part because of "aggressive aspects of 'Hippy' philosophy" that manifested in political activism and anti-American sentiment (Rogatnick 2006, 37).

In the 1970s, this combination of political awareness and attention to the medium would extend beyond McLuhanism through the currency of cultural theorists such as Theodor Adorno, Max Horkheimer, Walter Benjamin, and Herbert Marcuse who offered leftist critiques of capitalism and the culture industry. These energies would also find expression in the barely emergent English translations of new continental theory, a blend of linguistics, philosophy, Marxism, and psychoanalysis. Blaser was reading "theory" (Maurice Merleau-Ponty, Jacques Lacan, Michel Foucault, Roland Barthes) very early on in relation to widespread academic awareness of it. His book orders for the university and for his own library, dumped in boxes that have made their way to the SFU archives, record a storm of orderings of this kind. Yet Blaser never took critical reflexivity as invalidating perceptual experience because he never understood experience as an authoritative claim on the truth: perception, however mediated, is how we receive and interact with the world rather than what we can know about it. Neither did Blaser ever look to technology as redemptive as did some McLuhanists.

Once settled in his new town, Blaser was attentive to the local poets, assiduous in his academic reading, and engaged in the art world. He could welcome into his home a Glenn Lewis sculpture or a plexiglass Michael Morris hard-edged piece or a Roy Lichtenstein alongside a Jess or Tom Field painting, wondering at the sensoria of each and setting them in conversation with each other. He would greet the paintings and *objets* each morning, just to say hello and see how everybody was getting along. About this time, Christos and Sophie Dikeakos ran one of Vancouver's first authentic Greek restaurants, Kozmas—a gathering place for the hip as well as for folks who just liked Greek food. Their kind of hospitality was both social and intellectual, an analog of the hospitality that Blaser had begun to enact as a poetic practice. For all this, and despite the social charm, Blaser was swimming against the currents of the time and place, particularly those of Canadian nationalism and the theoretical *putsch*.

Professor Blaser

Mr. Blaser: Thank you for the introduction to Ezra Pound. (Tracy Hearst to Blaser, 1967)

Vancouver's art galleries and festivals created buzz, but the really big news in town in the mid-1960s was out in the 'burbs on Burnaby Mountain. Simon Fraser University, the "instant university" as historian Hugh Johnston calls it

(Johnson 2005, 5), was created by the right-wing Social Credit government[5] then in power to answer the postwar demand for more access to postsecondary education. In this, it was similar to many new universities of the 1960s in Canada, the U.K., and the U.S. But in *Radical Campus*, Johnston says that SFU was unique in that it did not come about as a result of a community-based process but rather by government fiat (Johnston 2005, 11–12). Premier W.A.C. Bennett tasked Gordon Shrum, a retired Physics professor at UBC, with building a university in two years. Shrum had a reputation for getting things done with military efficiency. His top down way of proceeding was fast and effective, but it led to a governance structure that would later draw opposition from students and activist faculty.

In addition to the haste with which it was conceived and constructed, SFU's other peculiarities were its independence from existing institutions and its mandate to develop graduate studies (Johnston 2005, 30). Other new universities of the time got their starts as branch plants of existing institutions; usually focused on undergraduate degrees, they were expected to develop sedately, over time, into research universities. This was the path that UBC had envisioned for the new campus at the other end of town: it would handle undergraduate teaching under the supervision of UBC (Johnston 2005, 22–23). Bennett, however, had other ideas. He was unfriendly to UBC, and he took from the plan what he wanted, ignoring the rest (Johnston 2005, 29). SFU was mandated for innovation and it was not to be tied to UBC. This mandate was to be expressed both in the architecture of the institution and in its academic structure.

Arthur Erickson's winning design for SFU embodied the aims of the university: innovation, interdisciplinarity, democracy, and growth (Stouck 2013, 184–86). Instead of a series of discipline-specific buildings, Erickson designed a central quadrangle, housing offices and classrooms for all disciplines, and a covered central mall or agora which could serve as a gathering place for students and faculty. The rectangle of the mall would house a theater, a library, and student services, as indeed it still does. Perched on top of Burnaby Mountain, the university was to embody "'vistas of human knowledge and experience'" (Erickson quoted in Stouck 2013, 196). At the same time, the low-rise plan of the whole and the central agora impressed some reviewers as a classless commons (Stouck 2013, 197).

When SFU opened in September of 1965, its first 2578 students had the look of good clean 1950s kids. Consulting early issues of the student newspaper, *The Peak*, Johnston remarks that the men had "clean-shaven faces and hair cut short on back and sides"; some of them wore jackets and ties to school. The girls were coiffed in bobs or pageboys and wore minidresses that caught the mod London look (Johnston 2005, 123). It wasn't long, however, before all that would change. The hair got long and the politics longer. In the summer of 1966, just a year after the doors opened, SFU students protested the construction of a service station on top of the hill and this would be the first of many such actions. Very soon, the trappings of university life as it looked in the

1950s—the shirts and ties, the faculty lounges, the President's fancy dress ball at the end of the year, and the cute year books would disappear. In the spring of 1967, students reacted to the firing of five Teaching Assistants (TAs) for their part in picketing Templeton Secondary School over an incident that, from the student view, was about free speech. A high school student had been suspended for "a parody of the school's literary magazine" (Johnston 2005, 262); the TAs took up the cause. SFU fired them for behavior unbecoming to the university. The student body organized a strike. When the administration backed down, the students celebrated victory. Student activism accelerated from there. The hastily conceived governance structure of the university was authoritarian in the eyes of students and some faculty—out of key with the times—and it came back to bite administrators in the Political Science, Sociology and Anthropology (PSA) Affair of 1968–1969. Political Science, Sociology and Anthropology (PSA) were grouped in one department. When activist faculty and students tried to democratize key committees like the Tenure and Promotion Committee, the administration reacted strongly. The ensuing confrontations—faculty contracts not renewed, the department placed under an appointed trusteeship—drew formal censure from the Canadian Association of University Teachers (CAUT) in February of 1968. In an internal report on the affair, PSA members cited the CAUT statement:

> A University is not a business, a government or an army, it is a democratic community. The notion that all power should be concentrated at the top simply won't work. Fifty years ago it might have done so, but ideas of community and democracy have changed in that interval; a failure to meet this change fairly and squarely will only prolong and intensify unrest. (Quoted in Douglas, Hollibaugh, Lees, Lockhard et al., 30 September 1969)

The battle that followed continued for months, with faculty firings, student demonstrations, and strikes. Berkeley North, Johnston calls it, drawing a parallel between Berkeley's Free Speech Movement of 1964 and student activism at SFU.

The backstory of Blaser's hiring illustrates the combination of conservatism and 1960-era radicalism that lit up the place in its few years as an activist campus. Ron Baker, Chair of the English Department, was mandated to fill it with new hires, and he wanted a solidly traditional department. With a background in linguistics, he was not taken with the philosophically-based literary studies which were then on the horizon, and which aligned literary exegesis with political radicalism (Baker interview, 23 February 2015). When Spicer came to Vancouver in 1965, Baker offered him a job for two reasons: first, Spicer had training in linguistics; and secondly, Baker thought the department could handle a wild poet because it was otherwise sturdily grounded in traditional scholarship. He did not recognize the severity of Spicer's alcoholism and simply felt that university discipline would kick in if there were a problem. When Spicer died before he could take up a post he was in no condition to fill,

Blaser was there for the wild poet job and even better, he had some sober credentials. He was a trained librarian, he had had a position at Harvard, and he came recommended by Ralph Maud and Warren Tallman. Maud was hired when SFU opened its doors in 1965 as a Dylan Thomas scholar, although by that time, he had already shifted his formidable, Harvard-trained scholarly attentions to Olson. Tallman's position at UBC was based on his Henry James dissertation. So the New American poetry walked in the front door, draped in academic drag.

Blaser came with the allure of 1960s San Francisco and the charisma of that world of art and ideas he had lived so intensely that it had become a kind of second skin. Within months, his classes at SFU were jammed, often with people who were not enrolled in the courses but who came to sit in on the lectures (Scott Watson interview, 1 March 2014). Tom Grieve, one among Blaser's first wave of students, remembers the drama. Lectures were held in rooms that seated about 50 and they were full to the point where people were sitting on the floor. Blaser would usually arrive a little late with a briefcase stuffed with books and a few more under his arm. Then there would be the ritual of laying everything out. When the lecture began, it would include citations from these sources, threaded into a narrative (Thomas Grieve interview, 11 April 2014). Blaser's signature lecture style was to present context as explanation. Kantorowicz is a shadow figure here for the historical sensibility that he instilled in his students. The text never stood alone for Blaser, as it did, say, for the New Critics, still very much in business in the mid-1960s; rather it was a part of a conversation between the discourses operative in a given historical time and space. The meaning of a work depended on its place in that conversation.

In Ralph Maud's filmed interview, *Robin Blaser in Vancouver* (1991), Blaser comments on this method. Art is not transcendent to its place in history, he says, and the problem with contemporary culture is that it allows itself to forget its past. As Blaser developed his teaching method and pedagogical focus, he began to specialize in the classical backgrounds of contemporary poetry. Dante, Homer, Virgil, the Bible—these would become integral to his effort to cultivate cultural memory in his students. In the Maud film, Blaser is asked just where he might stop, since his method seems to imply that the student has to know everything. This brings a laugh and a yes. As a poet-scholar, however, Blaser went about his own descents to the Hades of history differently than the academic focused on exhaustive treatment of an author or area of specialization. Like Pound, he ransacked the past for items of present use in his lifelong effort to construct a response to the events of his times. This would later earn him the disapproval of some colleagues who thought such forays a form of charlatanism because they were not informed by scholarly field studies.

As a teacher, Blaser was demanding, but he often pushed his students to stellar results. Tom Grieve would wind up a Pound scholar with a PhD from Johns Hopkins and a faculty position at Simon Fraser teaching modernism. Brian Fawcett, also among the first wave of students, would become a prolific writer and public intellectual and Sharon Thesen a major Canadian poet, scholar, editor, and professor. Karl Siegler, after translating Rilke's *Duino Elegies* for his MA thesis, would go on to steer Talonbooks to prominence among Canada's literary presses. Poet and teacher Susan McCaslin remembers arriving at SFU in 1969, age 22.

> It was one of the most blessed days of my life when I walked into Robin's course on classical backgrounds, team-taught with Romantics scholar Rob Dunham. Robin was impeccably dressed with silver hair, aquiline nose, dark brows, and an elegant bearing. He seemed more European than American; yet was, strangely enough, originally from Idaho though part of the San Francisco poetry Renaissance. I had been reading fairy tales and myths since I was a child, but Robin re-opened myth for me in a radically transformative way. Good criticism, he remarked, honours the text by "providing entrance"; judgement has to await this honouring of the text. (McCaslin 2015, n.p.)

Brian Fawcett has also described his student encounter with Blaser in an essay published on the occasion of Blaser's death in 2009.

> Blaser didn't disappoint. He was just turned forty, handsome and sophisticated enough to be called, not entirely tongue-in-cheek, the Marlon Brando of American poetry. He was immensely well-read, not just on my terms, and he was just reaching full command of his intellectual powers: pretty much a god to a twenty-two year old wanting to be a writer, in other words. (Fawcett 2010, 69)

Charles Bernstein was another student, although much more briefly, of Blaser's first teaching decade. A graduate of the Bronx High School of Science and a student of philosophy at Harvard, Bernstein had a William Lyon MacKenzie King Fellowship to study in Canada for a year and wound up in Blaser's class at SFU. Often associated with Language poetry, so-named after the journal L=A=N=G=U=A=G=E that he published with Bruce Andrews between 1978 and 1981, Bernstein would soon become a leading practitioner of experimental American poetry. In a conversation with visual artist and wife Susan Bee and editor Andrea Actis, transcribed for *The Capilano Review*, Bernstein recalls attending Blaser's Emily Dickinson seminar in 1973. Despite differences of "generation and temperament," Bernstein says, he found a poetic connection with Blaser: "I loved the idea that a poem was a starting point for a discussion that could take you anywhere; and with Dickinson, the closer you stayed to her words, the farthest distance you'd be able to travel. Robin saw the poems as cosmologies, so I guess you could say I entered his galaxy that Winter in Burnaby, BC" (Bernstein 2010, 12).

Blaser would typically throw students into the deep end of readings that were often over their heads. Sometimes he would not complete the syllabus of a course because the first readings on the list required so much contextualizing that later readings would fall off the end of the semester. Many students had to request extra time for assignments, and some of them got caught up in the largeness of the projects they developed under Blaser's supervision. One such student, Charles Watts, wound up writing an MA thesis on Pound that topped 500 pages. Watts became an important curator in the Contemporary Literature Collection at SFU and remained a lifelong friend. Others were not so sanguine, resentful of receiving an MA for what was surely PhD level labor. But Blaser was not attuned to the exigencies of academic careers, partly because he had never had to face the rigors of the job market during the economic contraction of the 1970s. He himself had spent 11 years at Berkeley following his interests, come away without a doctorate, and done just fine with finding work. As well, his model of the pedagogue had been Ernst Kantorowicz, whose aristocratic manners had been sharpened by the unapologetic elitism of the Stefan George circle of German intellectuals.[6] Blaser's focus was on following the masters—the "great companions" of his poetic thinking, like Dante—and students were supposed to go along for the ride. When they rose to Blaser's occasions, the results could be stunning—undergraduate and MA papers sophisticated beyond the level assumed for apprenticeship work.

I do not mean to imply that Blaser did not have his nay-sayers. As a practicing poet and busy professor, he did not always respond to everyone with as much attention as they wished from him, and some complained of neglect. His popularity also generated complaints of cultic status among skeptical faculty and students.[7] One group of young men who orbited Blaser for a time were snidely called the Red Guard in reference to the paramilitary movement of young people in 1966–1968 China, bent on carrying out Mao's cultural revolution through attacks on the intelligentsia. Then there were the social risks built into an academic culture that, in the 1960s, still allowed for mentorship. The fraternizing of faculty and students at parties and the intimacy of off-campus study groups—Maria Hindmarch remembers one such reading group on Pound—always held the possibility of mismatched expectations. Blaser was openly gay and expressing one's sexuality was part of the social revolution then in swing. Some of the male students around him later reported discomfort with the "pressure" to tolerate gay flirtation (Hindmarch interview, 23 March 2014); others reveled in it. The sure thing, however, was that Blaser left few students or colleagues indifferent.

When SFU opened its doors in 1965, the soft structure of the University was still under construction. This included the governance structure within departments and most importantly, the programming to be offered. Blaser sat on a number of key committees and contributed to some important initiatives. Ralph Maud had recruited him for the library committee before Blaser had even arrived from San Francisco (Maud to Blaser, 12 June 1966). In addition to supporting the acquisition of small magazines for the Contemporary Literature Collection, Blaser ordered numerous books that reflected his interests, including many volumes on mythology and esoteric religion for the circulating stacks. In the Department, Blaser's administrative initiatives suggest that he saw the university as a place for exploratory intellectual endeavor rather than academic job training, a view that seems more wild and wonderful today than

perhaps it did in the 1960s and 1970s, before the massification of postsecond-
ary education had fully taken hold. Supportive as he was of interdisciplinarity,
Blaser was also involved in the push to establish a Centre for the Fine and
Performing Arts at SFU.

As a member of the Programme Steering Committee for Studies in Creative
and Performing Arts, Blaser put forward a proposal for an Arts in Context
course, that was, in retrospect, a jaw-dropping extravagance, both in the experience it offered and—I am making an assumption—the cost of it. The course
would focus on a historical period, in this case the Renaissance. It would involve
a number of disciplines, predominantly literature and visual art in the original
plan, but with provision for supplementary workshops in music, dance, and
drama. When the course actually ran, it was divided into lectures that moved
across the disciplines and seminars that focused on one of them. So, for example, one student might take the course with a drama focus; another might
choose the literature or visual art seminar. Blaser did the lectures, and he led
the literary seminar; other faculty took up seminars in dance, music, visual art,
and drama. In November 1975, Nini Baird, who would become Director of
the Centre of Communications and Art, sent a memo to the Steering Committee
outlining a complementary program of performances to go along with the
Renaissance Arts in Context course. It would feature Angene Feves, a
Renaissance dancer from San Francisco, as artist-in-residence. It would also
include a series of noon hour and evening events by the Vancouver Chamber
Choir (Renaissance choral music); lutenists Ray Nurse and Brian Fitzgibbon;
the Elizabethan Trio; the SFU Repertory Ensemble (theater); the SFU
Madrigal Singers and SFU Early Music Ensemble as well as shows organized by
the SFU student society (Baird to Arts Steering Committee, 13 November 1975).

In his 26 May 1975 course proposal, Blaser says that the course should be
"intellectually penetrating" even at the first-year level. An historical overview
was to be carefully related to "selected examples of painting, sculpture and
architecture which would be studied in depth" (Blaser 1975, "The Arts in
Context"). The whole trick would be to offer intensity and breadth at the same
time—to avoid the superficiality of a survey without sacrificing interdisciplinarity: "Every effort should be made not to turn this into aesthetic theory or
aesthetic judgment after the event—such is, in my view, a modern misunder-
standing of the crucial place of art in thought—but rather, the course should
present the way in which the art of the period entangles men and women with
the world—their beliefs and disbeliefs included." The same principles that
Blaser used in his lectures would inform his conception of the course as a pursuit of the imaginative relations of a given epoch. So, he proposes to follow
"[t]he complex movement of Renaissance humanism worked from the
fragmentation of the so-called medieval vision toward a new vision of the past,
which then became a reformation of the present." After putting together the
Renaissance version of this course, Blaser designed another one on the same
principles for modernism.

This contextualizing approach to art very importantly defines not only Blaser's teaching style, but also his poetic project. As a teaching practice, the method led students into rich cultural worlds proposed as imaginative responses to a historical time and place. As a poetic method, it gave Blaser the haunted language of the early poems and the practice of "companionability" in the later ones, where the poem becomes a forum or open space for many voices. Whether it was through courses that asked students to attend to the imaginations of an epoch, or through poems that gathered the living and the dead, or through a household filled with handled *objets* and beloved books, Blaser created a world that, in Whitman's phrasing, provided a "path between reality and [the soul]."[8] It was the tantalizing possibility of entrance to this richly imaginative world that filled the seats in his lectures.

With his ability to attract students and willingness to participate in the making of the university, Blaser rose meteorically in the department in the late 1960s. By the end of August, 1969, he was offered tenure, much earlier in his teaching life than most professors, and on receipt of same, 3 September 1969, he was made a full professor, a very rare leap in status.[9] He had, of course, let the job at San Francisco State Library go in 1967, and had made some strong new collegial friendships. Ralph Maud was one such, a friendly rival in the teaching of the New American poetry (Maud interview, 7 April 2014). In a note to Maud dated 2 April 1972, Blaser writes that "If anything should happen to me, you are to receive my book collection in lieu of my debt to you."[10] Coleridge scholar Rob Dunham also became a close friend, as did poet George Bowering. Blaser would become Dunham's executor and Bowering's editor for the *Selected Poems* of 1980. Kafka scholar Jerry Zaslove was not only a co-conspirator in bringing "arts in context" to SFU, but a companion in intellectual curiosity and historical consciousness. Ed Harden, a distinguished interpreter of Thackeray, became a beloved and lifelong friend; Harden made Blaser the godfather of his son, Edgar. Roy Miki, a Williams scholar who would go on to become a major mover in Canada's Japanese redress movement, was in conversation with Blaser from his days as an MA student through his tenure as SFU faculty. During the late 1960s and early 1970s, Blaser's salary improved with annual raises and merit increments of mind-boggling size by current standards. As he was fond of saying later in conversation, the university "bought my ass" and he enjoyed the financial freedom, however, much he complained of the workload. An Eaton's department store credit card was one of his first acquisitions in Vancouver.

In June 1970, Blaser won a President's Research Grant to further develop his courses on the classical backgrounds of contemporary poetry,[11] and he was granted a sabbatical leave in 1972. Greece was a must-see and Blaser had not managed to get there on the European trip of 1959. For three weeks, from 4 to 26 April 1972, he toured the sacred places, making daytrips from a base at the Athenée Palace Hotel. By chance, he ran into teen-aged Karen Tallman in Athens on arrival. Karen was working as an *au pair* for Mary Eliot, an archeologist then at the American School of Classical Studies. She caught Blaser heading toward the Parthenon in the wrong direction and got him turned around. They saw the Parthenon together and Karen, Robin, and Mary drove to Delphi for a day trip. From his tours, Blaser preserved a collection of post-cards, a number of which suggest that it was archaic Greece that held his attention. From Heraclion, an image of the snake goddess; from Epidauros, the Throne of Minos; from Mycenae, the Lion's Gate and secret exit; and from Eleusis an image of a neolithic female.[12] In Maud's film, Blaser comments on this trip, recalling his first foray to Eleusis by bus. No one could understand where he wanted to go because the word is pronounced "Elefthis" in modern Greek. Blaser got the whole bus involved: problem finally solved when a priest recognized the archaic pronunciation. Of the sacred way to Eleusis, Blaser said that it looked like Kingsway, then a dreadful through-street between suburban Burnaby and Vancouver, lined with fast food restaurants, car lots, and seedy motels. The sacred places were jammed with tourists, but nonetheless, Blaser found an old Greek hospitality at Hesiod's birthplace that fed and honored strangers. Blaser remarks in the film that the Mediterranean belief in a chthonic mother is one of its oldest—that such a belief teaches that life and death are of the same order of the world, not negations of each other. The contemporary quarrel with dualism that Blaser had encountered in Whitehead and then in the new theory coming from France rhymed with the archaic.

PACIFIC NATION: POETRY AND POLITICS

Blaser would face the political hubbub of his first years at SFU—for him, a question of the relationship between poetry and politics—in his own little magazine, *Pacific Nation*, and the essay "Particles." Before Blaser and Persky left San Francisco, Blaser had taken on the project of starting a poetry journal to be called *Pacific Republic*. The idea, Persky recalls, was actually Spicer's (Persky interview, 14 December 2013). During the Vancouver trip of 1965, Spicer had imagined a nation extending from San Francisco to Vancouver, a community of congenial spirits who had detached themselves from U.S. imperialism. This kind of mythical mapping was an extension of the anarchic local-ism Spicer practiced in North Beach. The pun on the word "pacific" suggests a critique of the U.S. position in Vietnam and the geographical trope a loose way to imagine an open space for those like-minded enough to find it. In 1965, Persky and Blaser picked up the myth of such a nation. By spring 1966, *The Pacific Republic* had a letterhead and Olson was among the first to be solicited for material (Blaser to Olson, 16 May 1966). The journal was to be printed by Graham Mackintosh and published under the imprint of Open Space and White Rabbit. In the letter, Blaser writes that "The point is to do something with our real and imagined geography," and he asks Olson for notes on Carl Sauer's *The Early Spanish Main*. Olson responded with encouragement and sent "[to get the rituals straight." He also steered Blaser toward a name change:

Just (in fact) to celebrate—or greet what I have felt ever since getting your letter, with its letterhead ((even though I <u>wish</u> in fact you all had thought to get the same result—and a better future!—by calling it THE PACIFIC NATION! (Olson to Blaser, 21 June 1966)

Blaser replied enthusiastically about the poem, but told Olson he was "dead stopped" because he wanted something more than another little magazine.

And here's where I don't have the material. I do have good prose, and some poems, and I hope you'll send more to make a group, but so far, I lack what you would call <u>discourse</u>. The search is on. The shitiest [sic] thing about this San Francisco scene is that we've been cut off from discourse except among ourselves, and I wanted <u>The Pacific Republic</u> to open up.

This is only a note to respond, because I've been away and am again at work, so more will follow. Your note on <u>The</u> <u>Pacific Nation</u> is on me. As, if I understand you, it is what I'm up to, if I can. (14 July 1966)

As the date on Blaser's letter says, he was just a month away from the move to Vancouver; the disruption would delay the first issue and affect the content of it.

Pacific Nation 1 came out in 1967, a 6 × 9½, 114-page journal, stapled rather than perfect-bound, with an ink-drawn landscape by Fran Herndon on the cover. Blaser's "Preface" is dated 3 June 1967:

I wish to put together an imaginary nation. It is my belief that no other nation is possible, or rather, I believe that authors who count take responsibility for a map which is addressed to travellers of the earth, the world, and the spirit. Each issue is composed as a map of this land and this glory. Images of our cities and of our politics must join our poetry. I want a nation in which discourse is active and scholarship is understood as it should be, the mode of our understanding and the ground of our derivations. (Blaser 1967, 3)

The pieces selected for this issue suggest the kind of discourse that Blaser was after and register as well his move to Vancouver. Charles Olson contributed "A comprehension (a / measure" and "[to get the rituals straight," both poems that find the archaic in the contemporary. Spicer's "A Poem to the Reader of the Poem" appears in this issue as does Richard Brautigan's "Trout Fishing in America (1–5)." George Stanley contributed "You" which begins "The enemy in the Vietnam war is you. You as I see you; 'you' defined by my seeing you" (Stanley 1967b, 47), and "On Strangers," a witty prose piece on the death of God (1967a, 101–05). In "California Sociology," Persky reviewed two books of the moment, *Huelga* by Eugene Nelson on the grape pickers' strike in Delano and *Burn, Baby, Burn!* by Jerry Cohen and William Murphy on the Watts riot, both events from 1965 (Persky 1967a, 98–100). Persky also contributed "Orpheus Editor" (Persky 1967b, 108–13), a comic rendition of editorial ennui written in New York slang and featuring the characters of Cocteau's film, *Orphée*. Pieces by Jim Herndon, Harold Dull, John Button, Jonathan

Greene (of Gnomon Press), and Michael McClure rounded out the American contingent. From Vancouver, Blaser chose poems by Colin Stuart, Rick Byrne, and Gerry Gilbert. Karen Tallman contributed "Story," and Randy Enomoto, a first wave student of Blaser's at SFU, had a piece on Pound's *Jefferson and/or Mussolini* titled "A Recovery of Intelligence (Ezra Pound and Fascism)" (Enomoto 1967, 83–91). John Mills, a colleague and political activist at SFU, contributed an account of student protests over the firing of the five teaching assistants for their part in the Templeton High School incident.

Blaser's own contributions to the first issue of *Pacific Nation* were significant. "The Fire" essay appears there for the first time, and the poems "Out of the Window" and "Image-Nation 6," the latter "a marriage poem for Gladys Hindmarch [now Maria Hindmarch] & Cliff Andstein." "Out of the Window," now included in *Charms* (*HF*, 133) is an anti-Vietnam war poem and it foreshadows the way that Blaser would manage poetry and politics in "Particles," a key poetics essay first published in the *Georgia Straight* in 1967, and then in *Pacific Nation* 2 in 1969. In "Out of the Window," Blaser returns to the image of the burning heart:

> I would have the betrayers eat of it,
> because afire, the heart has that
> permission   to desire   because out
> of the rock and brush of the first place
> toward the land of this *sight*,
> *sound and intellect*, the consumed heart
> has the courage to be lost   half
> earth,   half sea   burning. (*HF*, 133)

As in *Cups*, the flaming heart of the *Vita Nuova* is back of the imagery. In this context, the heart married to the world is an eloquent protest against the burning napalm that floated on water and flowed over land to create terrible suffering in Vietnam: "the sea is afire," the poem begins.

"Particles," written in 1967 for an Arts Council Symposium on Art and Politics held at UBC, was published in *Pacific Nation* 2 in 1969 and reprinted in *The Fire* (13–25). It is a response to the leftist position that art cannot be considered separately from politics. Blaser names Kantorowicz and Hannah Arendt as his guides in political thinking at the beginning of the essay. From Kantorowicz, he takes a reading of history as "events, actions, and men in relation to ideas, rather than as a process and generality" (*Fire*, 13). From Arendt, he accepts a distinction between the social and political realms of life. Controversially, Arendt designates matters concerning human necessities (health, welfare, public works) as social and susceptible to rational administration. Politics she defines as a public activity where individuals see and say the world to each other; public space is "a space of appearance"[13] where people come together to make the reality they are to inhabit. Arendt has been strongly challenged on the division she makes between the social and political on the grounds that it is both impossible to separate them and anti-democratic to try.[14] Her view, however, is that matters of distributive justice concerning food, clothing, and shelter are chronic; human need is not up for debate because it will always be with us and because necessity is something that we can and should resolve rationally. Only when need has been satisfied can people begin to participate creatively in the world; the freedom *to act*, as opposed to the freedom *from* want and oppression, supposes the prior satisfaction of need.

This argument is back of Blaser's position on poetry and politics, adapted from Arendt to the exigencies of *poiesis*. People who are in need are doubly oppressed: they suffer crippling social injustice, but they are also excluded from creative participation in the making of the human universe. In effect, they are denied voice and historical visibility, limited, as they are, to a merely statistical presence. On the expectation that poetry should have a particular political content if it is to be progressive, Blaser writes that this is to treat poetry "as an opinionated sponge" (*Fire*, 13). Arguing with Ernst Fischer's *The Necessity of Art, A Marxist Approach*, a critical book current when "Particles" was written, Blaser says that "I am disturbed by the lack of attention to the kind of knowledge in poetry and by the whole implication that the content of human life is drawn up into something called the collective will" (*Fire*, 15). The "collective will" is problematic for who it excludes and what it conceals. In short, Blaser says that poets are either excused from politics (consigned to sentiment) or "used by wiser men to propagandize and support either the status quo, which the poet by the nature of his work will know to be a lie, or the revolution, which the poet by the nature of his work will try to understand" (*Fire*, 16).

So what, then, is the alternative relationship between poetry and politics? In poetry, to follow the argument of the essay, a singular encounter with the world is re-enacted in a discourse that gives it some permanence and transmissibility. One singularity calls to another, so that what we share is our particularity. Things don't connect; they correspond, Spicer had said, and Olson agreed with Keats that "a man's life … is an allegory" (Olson 1970, 17). If the performance in poetry of "particles"—singular points of view—seems elitist or of small interest to non-poets, consider the chronic ubiquity of the desire to be seen and heard—twisted now, as it was then, in celebrity culture and in violent grabs for power and respect from the streets to heads of state. Blaser is clear that his defense of particularity is an alternative to this constant din of thwarted egos: it does not mean self-expression and aggrandizement, but rather entrance to an ongoing conversation that is the human way of gathering the world up. Entry to that conversation requires intense listening (this, rather than wealth, is the price of the ticket in the land of poetry): the poet addresses a shareable world of common concerns, not one of private fantasy or personal or collective will, and this requires much attentive scholarship. While it is possible to sustain life, even luxuriously, without such a conversation, it is difficult to live meaningfully without it. "We are after 'meaning and thing,'" Blaser says, "and the intensity of that activity is what is at stake" (*Fire*, 24). *Pacific Nation* was an effort to perform such a public discourse, unavailable and conceptually problematic in real world politics. Poignantly, Blaser ends the essay with a quotation from Walt Whitman's "Repondez!": "Let me bring this to a close – I pronounce openly for a new distribution of roles" (*Fire*, 25). Then he reprints the Whitman poem (not reproduced in *The Fire*). "Repondez!" addresses the American Civil War, itemizing the perfidies that enabled that war. Reprinted in a journal tuned to 1969, the poem addresses a U.S. society once again at war, this time in Vietnam.

Blaser managed only two issues of *Pacific Nation* before giving up the venture. Although the second issue was planned for 1967, it did not come out until 1969 and then only with Persky's assistance. Persky's "Program Notes" at the back of this issue comment drolly on the delay:

> ROBIN BLASER'S lightning editing job of Pacific Nation 2 was moving brilliantly into its 17th month, when he was unfortunately struck down by a severe case of Hong Kong mysticism; the issue was thereupon rescued by
>
> STAN PERSKY, an anthropologist from Dagger Lake, British Columbia. (Persky 1969, 107)

Blaser abandoned *Pacific Nation* partly because of the busyness of being a poet-professor, but he also lost a large chunk of the nation he thought to build when Olson died in 1970 of liver cancer. In a transcribed conversation years later with Michael Smoler, recorded at Naropa University in 1999, Blaser describes Olson's death. Creeley had contacted him and said to come, that Olson would like him to. Harvey Brown, an Olson student, was putting people up at the Plaza. Brown had come into some inheritance money and was generous in his support of poetry and the arts, particularly touching Olson. Ashbery was there, and Wieners and Jack Clarke. Creeley had come and gone. Blaser brought three pieces of jade, one for Olson, one for Creeley, and one for himself. "'[Y]ou've brought me a whole fucking mountain,'" Olson said (Smoler–Blaser 1999, 16): "And he had it and he took my other hand and he had all these things sticking in him and he left touches of the blood fluid on my hand, I've never forgotten, and then suddenly he was in pain and it looked like something under the bed was pulling him." Olson was talking then about wanting a female liver transplant, "'talking his mythology,'" Clarke said:

> ...well the doctor heard this too and the doctor accused all of us of feeding him dope. So, Harvey Brown gets up, walks right out of there, and goes to North Carolina and finds a psychiatrist who he knows, who also knows Olson's work and brings him back as a go-between the doctor and Olson. Well, that's the story. I had to leave and go back home and he died shortly after that, January 10, 1970? And they weren't able to get word to me in time, I don't know how that happened, but I wasn't able to get to the funeral. But there was all this craziness and it was heartbreaking and we were all indebted.... (Smoler–Blaser 1999, 17)

Olson is "just ground" (12), Blaser says in this conversation.

IMAGE-NATIONS 1-12 AND THE STADIUM OF THE MIRROR

Between 1966 and 1976, Blaser wrote the poems of *Charms* (the original "Holy Forest" serial of *The Holy Forest*), three poetics essays—"The Fire," "Particles," "The Stadium of the Mirror"—and the first 14 *Image-Nation* poems. He also edited Spicer's *Collected Books* and wrote a lengthy essay for it, "The Practice of Outside." In the spring of 1974, he recorded "The Astonishment Tapes." A major accomplishment of the decade was the launching of the *Image-Nations* series in *Image-Nations 1-12 and The Stadium of the Mirror*. Like Duncan's *Passages* and *Structure of Rime*, the *Image-Nations* are an ongoing serial interspersed among other sequences. The thought of alternative ways of living and thinking had been a source of excitement in the Berkeley days. *Open Space* and *Pacific Nation* had then come out of the idea of community building and public conversation through the little magazine. The *Image-Nations* poems extend this concept of the poem as a performance of an ongoing symposium inclusive of the dead as well as the living.

In "The Stadium of the Mirror," Blaser writes that "Form is alive," and he says that he has "let the image speak out of the absence the Other [has] become" (*Fire*, 27). This essay and sequence of poems move Blaser into an extended exploration of how the sacred might function as experience, rather than dogma. The proposition is that the sacred is not a form but a relationship with the cosmos that must find its shape in every historical epoch. If we dismiss it entirely, we are stuck with an anthropocentrism that reduces the world to the human. Hence Blaser's hostility to the social sciences: psychology, anthropology, and sociology situate the world in the human; poetry situates the human in the world. If the gods once expressed living relationships with the planet, then they must be historical and capable of death. This leaves the poet to do "the work of it" again.

> ...a reopening of words—toward the violence and dynamism of Language—the work of it is in Pound's return to Homer, Egypt, Na-Khi and in Olson's ultimate return to Pleistocene,—his curriculum. A beginning again with everything. This reopening of words lets us see their solidifications—the crystals FORMing in the work—(a crust, akin to *cruor*—blood, *Kryos*—icy-cold, a coagulation that is the "external expression of a definite internal structure." (*Fire*, 31)

Like the first serials, this run of *Image-Nations* repeatedly "[begins] again with everything" by unnaming ossified forms of the sacred while at the same time inviting the strangeness of the familiar into the poems: the surrealism of the Boston poems persists here. To cite a few examples, "Image-Nation 7 (l'air,"[15] pushes off from Jean Cocteau's surrealist film, *Blood of a Poet* (1932). The film begins with the poet–artist drawing a self-portrait. When he hears a sudden loud knock at the door, he tries to erase what he has drawn, but the mouth of the drawing rubs off on his hand and begins to speak, crying for air. With much effort, the poet is able to transfer his other mouth to a statue in his studio, which then directs him to pass through a mirror (an image Cocteau used in *Orphée* as well). Cocteau's vision of self-becoming-other, and no longer obedient to the will of the poet, is precise to the uncanniness of this *Image-Nation*.

> the fearful noise   and
> the archaic smile
> who is the physical
> source of all things
> gods and men included. (*HF*, 160)

In these lines, an indeterminate event precedes the gods and men that rise out of it: something has "passed out there" (*Fire*, 3).

Similarly, "Image-Nation 9 (half and half" imagines an encounter with powers that have been unnamed:

> they come from the dark   under
> many names   the blue   wind
> they are not ourselves.... (*HF*, 168)

In this same poem, lying around as if only just tossed aside, are "*a bone, a ball, a top / an apple, a mirror, a skein of wool*" (*HF*, 168). Blaser sometimes uses italics to indicate quotation, and this list of toys, slightly misquoted, comes from W.K.C. Guthrie's discussion of Greek mythology (Guthrie 1966, 121). They belonged to the infant Zagreus, son of Zeus and Persephone. According to Orphic myth, Hera was jealous of the birth and persuaded the Titans to kill the child. They distracted him with toys in order to seize and dismember him. Zeus took the beating heart of the dismembered god and implanted it into Semele, who gave birth to Dionysus. The story, then, is about a god who dies and is reborn; at the level of *poiesis*, it is a story about a divine energy that has moved on. We see the traces of the god's passage (the abandoned toys) left around like litter in the language.

So, it goes throughout this series. In "Image-Nation 5 (erasure," "god moves to the end / of our sentences" (*HF*, 153). In "Image-Nation 6 (epithalamium," "the powers are brought / to birth and again the vocabulary / loses them" (*HF*, 156). In "Image-Nation 8 (morphe," "the words were the attributes / of what we were out there / watching the sun swim" (*HF*, 164). "Image-Nation 10 (marriage clothes" "[tries] to say what the soul is" (*HF*, 174) now that the word has fallen out of belief. The etymologies Blaser evokes in this poem, like the god's toys, are the historical leavings that have congealed in language, consulted not for authenticity—etymological meanings as somehow less mediated than contemporary usage—but for a genealogy of human encounters with the otherness of things. The first twelve *Image-Nations* end with "(Actus," a poem that again traces the "gods and goddesses at the ends of our words, / dead or alive" (*HF*, 179). The poem presents the soul as a boat and introduces the word "suddenness" to the concept of form. The "sudden," Blaser says, is "like a hillside" or a horizon (*HF*, 181)—it comes as the *thereness* of a distinct perception of form. This trope then works into later serials through poems like "Suddenly" (*HF*, 195). "Image-Nation 12" bends and extends the language of the preceding eleven poems and of "Stadium" too. Phrases like the "operational language," "the wild-logos," and "the fold" (the last from *Image-Nation* 1) come into the poet's "masked procession" (*HF*, 181), the parade of thoughts and images that, as in *Cups*, pass through the haunted mind.

An evolution of his early Catholicism, Blaser's fascination with the sacred and his insistence that it remains in poetic discourse as an Other seemingly flies in the face of the critical theory that he was reading and quoting at this time. Certainly, it was contrary to the direction poetry and art were taking in the 1970s when the Language[16] poets began to emerge as the next wave of experimenters after the New Americans, when visual artists turned away from expressionism, and when philosophers began to deconstruct phenomenology. Blaser was not insensible to these trends. In "The Stadium of the Mirror" he says that the essay was named after Jacques Lacan's description of the mirror stage in the child's ego development—"*le stade de miroir*," "translated for the metaphor" (*Fire*, 32). Lacan proposed that the sense we have of the self as a unified whole comes from a misidentification of the psyche with the mirror image of the body. For Lacan, the exposure of this *méconnaissance* is meant to ironize and deconstruct the experiential "imaginary." Lacan's suspicion of perceptual experience was shared by other theorists active in the 1970s, even though they differed on the details: the point was to loosen the grip of the mind on its supposed certainties.[17] But Blaser wanted just that perceptual experience that theory places under erasure: "Poetry," he writes, "always has to do with consciousness. Its restlessness is what we have called the unconscious..." (*Fire*, 29). This is why he proposes that the Other must accompany the telling of experience. Rather than deconstruct, Blaser positions perception alongside the "unthought" (Foucault's term). This move limits and relativizes the mind's claim to "know" the real while acknowledging that experience is irreducibly the way that we receive the world. Through skeptical philosophies and critiques of the culture industry, we may suspect our instruments, but we must nonetheless live with them. This question of *how to live*, rather than *what can be known* with certainty is the one that engages Blaser.

Blaser knew, however, that experience could not be engaged in a naïve fashion, by simply avoiding or denouncing the propositions of philosophical skepticism. He had already worked out a position on language in "The Hunger of Sound"; in "The Stadium of the Mirror," he turns for intellectual companionship on this position to Merleau-Ponty, Merleau-Ponty's editor, Claude Lefort, and translator, Alphonso Lingis in *The Visible and the Invisible*. The concept he wants is that of the *wild-logos* and its apposite, the "operational language":

> *the reversability of experience and language*
> *neither experience nor language is a reality that*
> *will suffice to itself alone*

> *two aspects of the reversability which is ultimate*
> *truth*
> *there is no frontier between language and the world*
> A wild-logos   *to recognize the movement that*
> *prevents the fixing of the meaning of the thing,*
> *visible or invisible, and makes arise indefinitely,*
> *beyond the present given, the latent content of the*
> *world.*[18] (*Fire*, 28–29, original emphasis)

Blaser adapts these phrases from *The Visible and the Invisible* to distinguish between language experienced as memory, thought, and perception on one hand and the structuralist view of language as a system of linguistic relations on the other. What we feel to be experience may reverse into linguistic structure as the philosophers of language proposed, but the contrary is also true. Blaser had worked it out in "Hunger of Sound" (see Chap. 4): language *as a whole* reverses into experience because *as a whole* it is an affective, historically fraught response to things, always already embedded in the world. In other words, Blaser balances the synchrony of structuralism with the diachrony of language as a historical, affective action. Language is how the species relates to things, a tool that fits the human grasp at one end and the thing reached for at the other, even though tool and thing are different orders of the real. The *wild-logos* further suggests that there is no hard boundary between language and the world, no point at which we can separate words and things any more than we can reduce them to each other. A *wild-logos* keeps the interchange between language and experience moving. Hence the usefulness of etymology which Blaser repeatedly turns to, as in his meditations on the soul in "Image-Nation 10." Etymology is the historical sediment in language of various encounters with things, which is to say, "*the latent content of the world.*"

In 1973, when Blaser was finishing the *Image-Nations* and "Stadium" essay, he wrote to Ralph Maud about a publisher:

> Now I've all but finished <u>Image-Nations</u> 1-12, only have to revise 5—there's an essay to reword them called <u>The Stadium of the Mirror</u> all done—I want these to go out now—there's no real problem of a publisher—but I don't want most—I'd thought to give it to Coach House, but Stan writes to say he can't stand that so, I think London—could you ask Jeremy [Prynne] about small presses that are "said" to be interested in my work? (5 June 1973)

In the same letter, Blaser describes the kind of publication he wants: "It is to look like a regular Gallimard paperback—cheap, off-white paper, and the red & black lined notes on the cover." Maud apparently contacted Andrew Crozier at the Ferry Press. About a month later, Blaser wrote to Maud again that "Andrew Crozier has written nicely—and he's keyed me in that you are underwriting—it seems to me I should be able to get a publisher these days who could take the chance himself" (11 July 1973).

Despite the reservation about having Maud subsidize the publication, Blaser sent the manuscript to Ferry Press. Poet and editor Andrew Crozier had ties with Jeremy Prynne; in fact, Crozier had published Prynne's *Brass* in 1971. That same year, Prynne and Ed Dorn had come to SFU, Dorn to read *Gunslinger* and Prynne to give a lecture on Olson's *Maximus* IV, V, VI. Prynne subsequently invited Blaser to Cambridge as a visiting scholar (Prynne to Blaser, 15 November 1971). The visit never came off (Prynne to Maud, 21 August 1972), but Prynne makes an appearance in "Image-Nation 7" where Blaser cites him "explaining / the abstract" (*HF*, 160). Crozier passed a copy of the *Image-Nations* manuscript to Prynne and Prynne sent Blaser an "excoriating" review (Blaser's word). Writing to Crozier, Blaser says that "Not one of his points is recognizably what the book says or performs.... Jeremy's letter reduces the only indication that uneasy book gives of a next move—a relearned love—to 'sexual posturing'" (7 September 1973). Blaser acknowledges that Prynne's disapproval puts Crozier in an awkward position and suggests that he (Crozier) reject the manuscript if he is uncomfortable with it: "I will not withdraw the book on my own—as I cannot withdraw my interest in what Jeremy wishes to do in his own work—I prefer to have the book rejected as a record of its adventure" (7 September 1973). Crozier went ahead with publication, but the Prynne response prompted the addition of what is now the first paragraph of "The Stadium of the Mirror," beginning with the line: "Unless the *Image-Nations* are read by image, there is no saving grace" (*Fire*, 26). Blaser also wrote a long letter to Prynne on the poetics of the *Image-Nations* (21 September 1973). Among the points of explication is a statement of commitment to "a narrative of spiritual energy"; he will, Blaser says, "face into the decline of the sacred in order to reopen in the narrative of the poems its primordial, original data" (21 September 1973). Blaser kept multiple drafts of this eloquent, wounded letter. In an undated note to Crozier, apologizing for a number of late additions to the "Stadium" essay, Blaser writes:

> Andrew—This is absolutely the last—but it has to be added because I'm bugged—
> (blame Jeremy and bill him for the extra pages)—this finally answers the misreading—Now I'll be silent. I know I've been troublesome. (Blaser, "This is absolutely the last")

THE COLLECTED BOOKS OF JACK SPICER AND "THE PRACTICE OF OUTSIDE"

> In the meantime, I washed my bathrobe, vacuumed the rug, watered the plants, worked on an essay called The Practice of Outside, ate yesterday's macaroni & cheese, washed the dishes, checked the phone bill, sat waiting for someone, and worried over the phrases—credo quia absurdum, credo quia impossibile est, credo ut intelligam, centum est quia impossibile est, est—could anything be more polar? And yet an ordinary day—200 AD—1109—where-when. (Undated, "In the meantime")

As Spicer's literary executor, Blaser was tasked with bringing out Spicer's works and passing on the royalties to the family. Almost immediately, he began to receive permission requests from journal editors and the longer the *Collected Books* were delayed, the shriller these became. Blaser had opened up talks with Harcourt, Brace & World as early as 1967, but before the due date of 30 November 1967, he was also talking to Nathaniel Tarn at Jonathan Cape Limited (London) about the *Collected* and a second book to be called *Of Things and Angels* (Tarn to Blaser, 1 July 1967). In December of 1967, he was negotiating with both Tarn and Penguin Books (Tarn to Blaser, 31 December 1967). Characteristically, Blaser retreated when pressure mounted. Toronto poet and Coach House Press founder Victor Coleman expressed frustration over Blaser's lack of response to requests for permission to publish Spicer (Coleman to Blaser, 9 November 1969), writing that if he does not hear from Blaser, he will print the Spicer poems anyway.

As the book languished, the project grew, notably with the writing of "The Practice of Outside." In 1974, with the Spicer still not out, Blaser received a pointed letter from Stephen Vincent of *Shocks: A Critical Magazine of Poetry*.

> Whatever might be the complications, a public statement at this time is really of necessity. Otherwise you stand guilty of a censorship of which you have no larger right. (Vincent 1975, n.p.)

In *Shocks 5*, Vincent published Blaser's explanation: Harcourt had declined after eight months, citing cost; New Directions had turned down the project for the same reason, advising Blaser that "the only poetry publishing possible now is underground" (Blaser 1975, n.p.). However, by the time Vincent had published the letter exchange, Blaser had an agreement with John Martin of Black Sparrow Press and the Spicer was on its way. The first handsome edition came out in 1975 and was subsequently reprinted in 1980.

In "The Practice of Outside," Blaser had contextualized Spicer's dictated practice with a deep plunge into theory—Merleau-Ponty and Foucault in particular—and reactions were mixed. Opening the essay, Blaser writes that "At first this essay was short and simple—about Jack. But that became a reduction which every twist and turn of the work denied—a biography without the world the poet earned…" (*Fire*, 113). Context as explanation demanded a mapping of that earned world. This is exactly what happens in the essay, where Blaser drags his theoretical sources onto poetry's territory to argue that dictation proposes "a polarity and experienced dialectic with something other than ourselves" (*Fire*, 117). "Polarity" was Blaser's way of giving theory an affective reading: dictation is a "*practice* of outside" (my emphasis). In Foucault's discussion of the "unthought" in *The Order of Things*, Blaser found a companion in this idea of the outside. Blaser ordered and read Foucault's book in 1971, but not all of Spicer's friends were on board with the high language coming out of France. Bill Brodecky Moore commented that the cool reception might be coming from the notion that Blaser had commandeered Spicer's "remains"

(17 September 1975). Persky and George Stanley were apparently among the unimpressed, possibly because they felt that the essay was not true to Spicer's rejection of academic theorizing. Blaser, however, had come into the sureness of his practice. In a letter to Brian Fawcett, he writes:

> Item: "The Practice of Outside" precedes that essay ["Stadium"] by 2 years, 1971–1972, but it does have a serial relation to The Stadium. "The Practice" is a scholarly study of the context and task of Spicer's poetry, not an exegesis of the poems, and I learned from it. Stan's viscious [sic] accusations that I am assimilating Spicer to my poetics is an ad hominem, ideological ploy, hardly forgiveable [sic].
>
> Item: The dramatic aspect of the definition of the Other in the Stadium is backed up by the careful definition of its naturalness and democraticness in "The Practice." "The Stadium" is carefully staged to make the personal and the other both dynamic and dialectical. The implied but unstated position is that poesis must take dramatic form in order to become public—finally. (11 June 1976)

This comment defends the essay against the reproach of over-theorizing Spicer, but it also shows the weight that Blaser threw on performance. In a postmodern world, where the order of things cannot be taken for granted, the poet, Blaser says, must dramatize the kind of relational thinking that goes into making a view-from-here—so that others might see and form their own view. To repeat: "a man's life ... is an allegory" (Olson 1970, 17). In "Image-Nation 9 (half and half," Blaser writes that "the astonishment is / that it is *kosmos* / *playing out with one man*" (*HF*, 169).

PERSONAL AFFAIRS

While Blaser was hobnobbing with local artists, finding his feet as a poet-professor, and building a poetics, his personal life was falling apart. In 1966, Persky enrolled at UBC as an undergraduate in Anthropology and Sociology and very quickly became involved in radical student politics. This was a natural move because he had already been engaged in leftist activism in San Francisco. And with *Open Space*, he had launched himself as a publisher and public intellectual. Persky had leadership qualities and these began to show at UBC. With his usual energy, he began to write for the *Georgia Straight*, then an alternative newspaper rather than the entertainment what's-on it is now, and to teach at a Free School. Persky recalls one incident in 1968 when he was delivering an anti-capitalist lecture at a public meeting in downtown Vancouver outside the Hudson's Bay department store. He was arrested for loitering and refusing to sign a peace bond (Persky interview, 11 November 2013). Persky brought energy and activism to the UBC campus and his freewheeling attitude toward sex as well. In this era of pre-AIDS sexual liberation and gay rights, promiscuity came close to political protest against compulsory heterosexuality, homophobic straight people, and *Father Knows Best*[19] family life. At this point, the Persky–Blaser relationship included affairs on the side. Rick Byrne, a handsome

UBC student, attracted them both and unbeknownst to each other, they both slept with him. Persky remembers such matters with equanimity, but Maria Hindmarch recalls a strain showing when she unwittingly walked in on Robin and Stan at a delicate moment when each had just realized what the other had done (Hindmarch interview, 23 March 2014).

In addition to the infidelities, Blaser and Persky had begun to drift apart in their interests after the move to Vancouver. While Stan pursued a whirlwind of activities, Blaser was occupied with poetry and his professorial role at Simon Fraser. He had also begun to get involved in Cold Mountain, an institute for personal growth based on Cortes Island, off the coast of B.C. By 1968, he and Persky were headed in different directions. As Persky remembers, Blaser was interested in an intense SFU student by the name of Colin Stuart. After an all-nighter himself, Persky came home to find Stuart sitting on the edge of the bed and decided to move out (Persky interview, 11 November 2013). Blaser would later complain that he took the curtains.

Stuart was a brilliant student who had studied with Blaser at SFU and a poet himself. He was precocious beyond his years and handsome in what his acquaintances remember as an Edwardian way, with dark hair and pale skin. He was lyrical and witty; according to some, he could also be sarcastic. Stuart had left SFU without completing a degree. When Blaser moved from West 1st to 2247 Bellevue Street in West Vancouver in May 1969, Stuart moved in with him, although the terms of the relationship were not very clear. Notes from Stuart to Blaser ask to be woken at certain times, hinting at separate sleeping arrangements (Stuart to Blaser, n.d.). The West Vancouver home was a Blaser marvel with deep red walls covered in paintings and shelves of books. There was also a garden that Stuart particularly liked (Susan Knutson interview with author, 12 April 2014). Stuart planned to be a Pound scholar as well as his own poet and in the spring of 1970 he applied to UBC with a project on Pound and the troubadour poets. He also had an interest in classical backgrounds, and he was beginning to be noted for it. Poet Jack Clarke had set up the Institute for Further Studies in 1965 with George Butterick, Fred Wah, and Albert Glover to oversee a series of chapbook publications suggested by Olson under the series title, *Curriculum of the Soul*. Clarke asked Stuart to contribute (Clarke to Stuart, 4 December 1971). Stuart never followed through, but Clarke's vote of confidence points to his talent.

By the fall of 1972, Stuart had moved out and begun a friendship with Susan Knutson, a student of Fred Wah's at Selkirk College, who had moved to Vancouver and was attending SFU. With Knutson, Stuart went to Europe in 1973 to read at the School of Classical Studies in Athens and then at the Oriental Institute of the University of Chicago at Luxor. He and Knutson returned at different times, but they wound up living together for about five years. Knutson remembers a place in Vancouver's Point Grey neighborhood that Stuart altered with a hole in the wall between a writing studio and dining room and then plastered in Greek fashion as a kind of holograph of his classical interests. For a while, Susan and Colin would visit Robin and he them. He was supportive, Knutson recalls, and gave the couple a small Chinese goddess figurine as a house blessing (Knutson interview, 12 April 2014). The friendship continued for some time, and then ended in a verbal fight. Knutson remembers the quarrel at her and Colin's Point Grey home—something loud and out on the street, but not intelligible to those inside the house. Whatever the argument, it seems to have stopped the visits. Knutson lost track of Stuart when they broke up and at some point, he slipped from the public poetry scene. From time to time, he would reappear. David Farwell, Blaser's partner from 1976 onward, remembers Stuart throwing rocks at the window and Blaser used to tell the story of Stuart's showing up once with an offering of raw chicken in a bag—promptly tossed as "very dangerous."

This period in Blaser's life was not an easy one at the personal level. When Stuart left, Scott Watson moved into the picture. This is the same Watson I have quoted above, but in 1971, he was a student in UBC's Bachelor of Fine Arts program, rather than a professional art historian and curator. He had taken Ellen Tallman's Arts One course and knew Robin by reputation. They met through Stan Persky, when Scott was in his early 20s and Blaser his mid-40s, still living with Stuart. Like Stan and Colin, Scott was attracted to the Blaser world. As he recalls now, he lived down the street from the Bellevue Street house and moved in around 1972, to his own space in the basement. Unlike Stuart, Watson was not ambivalent about his sexuality, but he was not ready for commitment to a mature man who came with baggage and expectations. In one story about the relationship, Brian Fawcett, by that time a close friend, tells of Blaser laying out a gift of three cashmere sweaters and the complete works of Freud by Scott's bedside, with a note saying that he would be back at five to administer the exam (Fawcett to author, email, 9 May 2014). The story, Fawcett says, was deliberately apocryphal, meant to illustrate the pressure that Blaser could apply without always meaning to. The house, Watson remembers, was immaculate and this kind of controlled domestic space was not particularly congenial. He describes the relationship as "stormy" and it was fairly short-lived. Miriam Ulrych, a friend of Blaser and the Tallmans, remembers a game of "Essences." The purpose of the game was to give a description of someone present and have people guess who it was. Her description of Scott was "a fast lane through a small town" (Ulrych interview, 23 April 2014). Everyone got it, she says. Scott moved out in 1973, while Blaser was working on Spicer's *Collected Poems* and "The Practice of Outside." In *The Astonishment Tapes*, Blaser's comments about Watson suggest that he was still stinging from the relationship in 1974. It also brought him ill-feeling from George Stanley who had been interested in Scott before Robin. Brian Fawcett describes the break-up with Scott as particularly hard:

> [Blaser] didn't sleep or eat for about a week. George Bowering, Tom Grieve and I sat up with him on alternate nights to keep him from going right off the edge, and it was really hard work. He'd be discussing some technicality of Olson or Elaine Pagels one minute, and the next he'd be weeping uncontrollably, and wailing about how much he loved Scott and simply couldn't go on, etc.—and then back onto Olson/Pagels. (Fawcett, 9 May 2014, email to author)

In *Astonishments*, Blaser says it this way:

> In the recent silliness and melodrama of my life as it stands, as it stood, stupidly
> and silently and suddenly apart from the real, another trap in the piled up stories
> of my love of young men, I wanted in that silent way to die. It just wasn't worth
> it. Two months with nearly no sleep. A loss of thirty pounds weight on a man not
> very heavy anyway. The body broke out in hemorrhages. Was the blood flow then
> too close to the surface? The body's SOSs were real. Friends moved forward,
> literally. Colin Stuart, being the best example on the most extreme evening of all,
> arrived as though he were in a trance at the backdoor, not knowing why he was
> there, but he was there to stop something that he didn't know he was stopping.
> (*AT*, 184–85)

Blaser had two ways of getting past emotional trauma. One was liquor. The more constructive method was art and poetry and he would turn to both of these loves in times of stress with a logic analogous to that of the Christian argument against despair. Despair, and its realization in suicide, amounts to saying that individual misery is greater than God's grace. Blaser would adapt this logic to say that the world cannot be reduced to one's own unhappiness, the cure for which lies in an expansion of one's worldly relationships. Hence the good sense of facing up to heartbreak with the help of Olson and Pagels.

Miriam Ulrych saw yet another side of Blaser during this unsettled period. She became an important lifelong friend and a mover in the therapy community in which Blaser would participate. An English student at UBC in the early 1960s, she had gotten to know the Tallmans and sometimes babysat for them. She had met Blaser at a Tallman party in 1966 and thought him terribly handsome, but did not get to know him very well at that time. With her husband Tad, a geophysicist, she left Vancouver in the late 1960s for the University of Western Ontario, where both she and Tad taught for a few years. On returning to Vancouver, she began an MA at UBC and then entered the School of Social Work. By this time, Ellen Tallman had abandoned UBC and begun to give personal growth workshops. Cold Mountain was an institute founded in 1968 with the aim of "exploring and developing those trends within the humanistic, or third force movement which held promise for the enhancement of human personal growth, for contributing to social change, for humanizing education, social services and other helping professions" (*Cold Mountain* 1975, inside cover). Miriam and Ellen both ran workshops on Cortes and built up private therapy practices in Vancouver. In affiliation with Antioch College, Cold Mountain launched an undergraduate independent study program in 1971. The Institute offered courses in bioenergetics, psychosynthesis, sex and identity, meditation, Tibetan mysticism, body intelligence, psychology, philosophy, ecology and environmental studies, and more. Blaser was invited to give Tarot card readings. He had the capacity to understand other people's reality very quickly, Ulrych remembers, and he would use the Tarot images to organize these insights (Ulrych interview, 23 April 2014).

When Blaser was between partners, he would cruise the bars, sometimes showing up late at Miriam and Tad's afterward. The late 1960s and early 1970s were the glory days of party sex for both gays and straights. On one occasion Miriam, Tad, and Robin tried a threesome. Tad had never had a same-sex experience before, and the next day he was all for moving in with Robin. As Miriam recalls, Robin said that, "If it's the right thing for you to do today, it will be the right thing tomorrow." When the sex magic had worn off, however, Tad "forgot" the whole incident and everyone went back to being friends (Ulrych interview, 23 April 2014).

Blaser's close ties with the therapy community would remain a contradiction. Some of his best friends were involved in therapy and David Farwell, Blaser's about-to-be partner, would become a therapist at St. Paul's hospital. As a poet, however, Blaser remained intellectually hostile to what he thought was the reductiveness of the social sciences. The imagery of the Tarot worked for him because the cards present relational thought in cosmic terms. And yet Blaser did seek therapy for himself at certain points, although he was always careful to draw the curtain between that component of his life and the public professor and poet. His unsettled domestic life, however, was about to take a turn for the better.

NOTES

1. In the essay "The Conference that Never Was: The 'Landmark' 1963 Vancouver Poetry Conference," Frank Davey challenges the way in which this 1963 event has been historicized as a "conference," suggesting that "Tallman's jamboree would seem to have been permanently normalized into the polite and legitimizing academic event he so much wanted it not to be" to the professional advantage of some (Davey n.d., 20).
2. Established in 1957, the Canada Council for the Arts is a Crown Corporation with a mandate to support the arts in Canada. In the 1950s, Canadian culture was overshadowed by American imports; the establishment of this arts funding body was coincident with a Canadian push toward more autonomy, not only in the arts but in the economy and the management of natural resources.
3. For a more detailed discussion of NETCO, see Nancy Shaw's article, "Siting the Banal: The Expanded Landscapes of the N.E. Thing Co."
4. See Adam Lauder's essay, "Robert Smithson's Vancouver Sojourn: *Glue Pour*, 1970."
5. The British Columbia Social Credit party dominated B.C. politics from 1952 to 1991, with only one break between 1972 and 1975. The party had roots going back to the Alberta Social Credit Party (founded in 1935), which combined the monetary theory of Major Clifford Hugh Douglas with Christian fundamentalism. In B.C., it became a right-wing "free enterprise" party, fiscally and socially conservative. After severe defeat in the 1991 B.C. election, the party dissolved. Its policies have since found a home in the deceptively named B.C. Liberal Party, a party distinct from the more centrist federal Liberal Party of Canada.
6. Blaser describes Kantorowicz's style in *The Astonishment Tapes* (77).

7. For a skeptical view of Blaser's teaching practices, see Stephen Bett's memoir, *So Got Schooled: In the Tower, On the Field*.
8. This famous remark of Whitman's comes in the 1855 "Preface to Leaves of Grass": "folks expect of the poet to indicate more than the beauty and dignity which always attach to dumb real objects ... they expect him to indicate the path between reality and their souls" (Whitman 1977, 10–11).
9. Memo to Blaser from G[erald] M. Newman, Acting Head of the English Department (Newman, 3 September 1969).
10. Maud financed Blaser's trip to Greece in 1972 and never asked for repayment. David Farwell remembers that Blaser never forgot and often mentioned this debt to Maud.
11. An outline for a graduate course, dated spring 1970, is titled "Classical Sources and Mythology for the Study of Contemporary American Poetry." The required reading list is as follows: Henry Frankfort, *Kingship and the Gods*; Hesiod, *Works and Days: Theogony*; Homer, *The Illiad*; Károly Kerényi, *Promethus*; Charles Olson, *Causal Mythology*; James Pritchard, *The Ancient Near East: An Anthology of Texts and Pictures*. This list is followed by a much longer one of books reserved for the course.
12. Postcards and trip material are archived in MsA1 Box 43, Folder 7, Blaser fonds.
13. Arendt says in *The Human Condition*: "The space of appearance comes into being wherever men are together in the manner of speech and action, and therefore predates and precedes all formal constitution of the public realm and the various forms of government, that is, the various forms in which the public realm can be organized" (Arendt [1958] 1959, 178).
14. See Sheldon Wolin's essay, "Hannah Arendt: Democracy and the Political" for a critique of Arendt's division of the social and political. She "never succeeded in grasping the basic lesson taught not only by Marx but by the classical economists as well, that an economy is not merely work, property, productivity, and consumption: it is a structure of power, a system of ongoing relationships in which power and dependence tend to become cumulative, and inequalities are reproduced in forms that are ever grosser and ever more sophisticated" (Wolin 1994, 295). At issue for Wolin in this argument is that Arendt does not seem to adequately recognize that the means to social justice stand between most people and political freedom in her sense of it. Hence Wolin finds her anti-democratic. Even more friendly critics like Margaret Canovan pick up a conservative strand in her thinking (Canovan 1997, 11–32).
15. Like Olson, Blaser uses an open bracket to suggest a thought-vector. All the *Image-Nation* poems are subtitled with an open bracket.
16. The Language poets were so-called after a journal titled *L=A=N=G=U=A=G=E*, edited by Charles Bernstein and Bruce Andrews from 1978 to 1982. Like *Measure* or *Origin* or *Open Space*, *L=A=N=G=U=A=G=E* gathered the interests of a new generation of writers and poets who came to be called, not always to their pleasure, *L=A=N=G=U=A=G=E* poets. In their preface to a book-length publication of selections from the first three volumes, titled *The L=A=N=G=U=A=G=E Book*, Andrews and Bernstein note that labels are "troublesome" but that "our project, if it can be summarized at all, has involved exploring the numerous ways that meanings and values can be (& are) realized—revealed—produced in writing" (Andrews and Bernstein 1984, ix).

17. I have in mind Jean-François Lyotard's comment that the postmodern marks "a kind of flight of reality out of the metaphysical, religious, and political certainties that the mind believed it held" (Lyotard 1984, 77).

18. The phrases in this passage come from Claude Lefort's "Editor's Foreword" to *The Visible and the Invisible* (Lefort 1968, xxx–xxxii). Alphonso Lingis uses the terms "wild-*logos*" and "operative language" in his "Translator's Preface" (Lingis 1968, liii). The "operative language" is that of "literature, of poetry, of conversation, and of philosophy, which possesses meaning less than it is possessed by it, does not speak of it, but speaks *it*, or speaks *according to it*, or lets it speak and be spoken within us, breaks through our present" (Lingis 1968, liii). Lingis is discussing the embeddedness of perception in the world and the chiasmatic, mutually constitutive relationship between perceiver and perceived. The italics in the passages that Blaser's quotes are his; they indicate quotation rather than emphasis.

19. *Father Knows Best* was a television comedy about family life, starring Robert Young and Jane Wyatt. It ran from 1954 to 1960.

CHAPTER 7

Cher Maître

Trafalgar Street

On May 18, 1975, Blaser celebrated his 50th birthday with a crowded party at
Christos and Sophie's Kozmas restaurant. People ate and drank and smoked
and there was cake on paper Superman plates. By some accounts, Blaser danced
on the table. At this point, he was an established presence in at least three communities in addition to that of the university—the poetry scene, visual arts, and
therapy community. These connections would serendipitously bring him to
Trafalgar Street and a permanent home. Through his tarot readings at Cold
Mountain, Blaser had met Darryl Goldberg, a beautiful man, Miriam Ulrych
recalls—a golden boy—but uncommitted to a relationship. Ulrych remembers
that he kept running off to Israel (Ulrych interview, 23 April 2014). On one
occasion, Blaser babysat his dog, a major sacrifice given Blaser's domestic fas-
tidiousness. On Goldberg's return, Blaser cooked a roast beef dinner but
Goldberg wouldn't stay. Just came to pick up the dog. The affair, needless to
say, was another disaster. One side effect, however, was that Goldberg led
Blaser to Trafalgar Street. When Goldberg moved out of his upstairs suite in
the Trafalgar Street duplex in 1976, Blaser moved in.

The Trafalgar Street house is in Kitsilano, now one of Vancouver's toniest
neighborhoods, but then redolent of fading hippy glory. The house is a gracious yellow plaster affair with a garden and a spectacular view of the North
Shore Mountains. In 1976, the downstairs suite was occupied by feminist art
historian, editor, and filmmaker Ardele Lister and her boyfriend, David Baert.
In the basement was Svetlana Zylin, a director for the Women's Theatre Co-op
and her partner David Smith. When Lister and Baert broke up, Ardele dated
David Robinson, founding member of Talonbooks. Blaser and Lister hit it off.
She was the initiator in 1973 of ReelFeelings, a feminist film cooperative, and
in 1974 of the arts journal *Criteria*, in which she published Blaser's review of
Jack Burnham's *Great Western Saltworks: Essays on the Meaning of Post-Formalist*

© The Author(s) 2019
M. Nichols, *A Literary Biography of Robin Blaser*,
Modern and Contemporary Poetry and Poetics,
https://doi.org/10.1007/978-3-030-18327-1_7

Fig. 7.1 Blaser in *Criteria* T-Shirt, c. 1976. Photo by Ardele Lister and Bill Jones. Reproduced courtesy of Ardele Lister and the Blaser estate

Art (Blaser 1974, 3–5). *Criteria* was printed at B.C. Monthly Press, run by Gerry and Linda Gilbert (Fig. 7.1). Gilbert used the press to put out his arts newsletter *B.C. Monthly*, but he would also print for others. For a short time, Trafalgar Street was buzzing with art and poetry. The downstairs crew, however, did not hold together long. Lister, who would remain a lifelong friend, moved to New York, leaving the lower half of Trafalgar Street available. By this time, Ellen Tallman had left Warren and come out as a lesbian. She was living in the same Kitsilano neighborhood with Wendy Barrett, a physiotherapist turned therapist specializing in body work. Ellen and Wendy moved into the lower suite and a year later, in 1977, she and Blaser bought the duplex together. Both would remain there until death.

In the meantime, a young man from New Brunswick with strawberry blonde hair and a winning smile was undergoing therapy with Miriam Ulyrch. David Farwell came from a conservative banking family and he had entered the Faculty of Arts at Mount Allison University in Sackville with the aim of becoming an Anglican priest. By the third year, however, he had lost his faith and his heterosexuality too. This led to a series of disastrous treatments aimed at "curing" his gayness. After flunking out of Mount Allison in a severe depression, Farwell worked at several jobs of expediency, took a trip to Europe, and finally headed west by train, because, as he tells it, there was nothing to do in the Maritimes. The west, however, wasn't much better. Through his father's connections, he landed a job at the Bank of Nova Scotia in New Westminster until he was transferred to the small interior town of Fernie, British Columbia. There he was given the task of repossessing mobile homes from unemployed miners stuck in a downturn in coal prices, a job he detested. Next, there was work at a pulp mill in coastal Gibsons as a chemical analyst and therapy sessions with a traveling psychiatrist who serviced the Sunshine Coast of B.C. Recidivist weekends were to be had at the gay steam baths in Vancouver. After an injury in a car accident, Farwell rehabilitated in Vancouver where he continued his treatments. The problem, it seemed, was that he wanted a quiet family life—he just didn't want the wife that went along with it. His therapy treatments included electric shock at Riverview, an asylum for the mentally ill, and more anti-gay therapy at the Burnaby Centre for Mental Health. Finally, he ended up at Cold Mountain, where he met Ellen Tallman and wanted to work with her. Ellen's client list was full and so she referred him to Ulrych. Miriam was simply not about aversion therapy and she encouraged David to accept his sexuality as it was. Farwell recalls that at the end of their sessions, Ulrych wished three things for him: that he complete his university degree, that he attend Cold Mountain, and that he meet Robin Blaser (Farwell interview, 11 November 2014).

Ulrych arranged the last item over dinner at Eye Scream restaurant, a trendy eatery in Blaser's neighborhood run by artist Iain Baxter of NETCO (N.E. Thing Company, an experimental arts initiative). It featured dishes like Cubist salad, group of seven snails, and a filet mignon with mushroom wheels that made it look like a little Volkswagen. Blaser was a regular, eyeing the waiters as some of them still remember. At that dinner, Blaser offered Farwell an audit of his Renaissance course at SFU and David took him up on it. However, this was the period when Blaser was courting Darryl Goldberg. Farwell remembers that Blaser turned up one day for class looking absolutely terrible and this was unusual. Blaser was a careful dresser and his thick white hair was always impeccably coiffed. Farwell made inquiries of Miriam Ulrych and learned about the crash of the Goldberg affair. With Ulrych's encouragement, he made a house-call. "I've come to commiserate," he remembers saying, and then never went home. "Just to get my clothes," he says, "he was the most exciting person I had ever met" (Farwell interview, 11 November 2014).

Blaser and Farwell settled into Trafalgar Street with a domestic flurry. After the purchase of the place with Ellen (mortgage approved 10 June 1977), there had to be skylights (invoiced 18 February 1978), roof decking to take advantage of the spectacular view of the inlet and mountains, new fencing, a garden, and jewel-toned paint of a deep forest green in the halls and bedroom. Not that the relationship was easy. Farwell recalls that Blaser had trouble trusting his new love's constancy after the string of short-term relationships and disappointments that he had experienced since Felts. For the first while, Blaser treated him like a "bauble" that might break at the slightest touch. "He wouldn't let me do anything," Farwell remembers (Farwell interview, 11 November 2014). One night, however, about four months into the relationship, Farwell took a gold chain from around his own neck and placed it on Blaser's. The next morning, they both went down to Birks, Vancouver's fanciest jeweler at the time, and Blaser bought a matching chain for David. And so they married each other.

David and Trafalgar Street stabilized Blaser's domestic life, but other fronts were more turbulent. Dennis Wheeler contracted leukemia and Blaser carried on a dialogue with him through the illness—a "death work," he called it. Writing to Brian Fawcett, he speaks of this turn his work had taken (11 June 1976). Like "The Astonishment Tapes," the exchange with Wheeler was to be recorded as an oral dialogue. Neither piece was ever completed or published in Blaser's lifetime, although Wheeler's notes mention a film on the Bardo Thodol as a project to be worked through with Blaser.[1] In an interview with Lister published in *Criteria*, Wheeler mentions his work with Blaser and makes it plain that he wants to face his cancer and impending death in a conscious, public way. The interview is dated 10 February 1977:

> One of the things I've been trying to do is practise meditation (deep breathing) slowing down and seeing myself ... watching my own inner dialogue and that whole practice. And some of the work with Robin (Blaser) was set up specifically to start returning our whole relationship with our being which was more like ... I sometimes had the image of my being as being tied on the hood of a powerful automobile, driving down a freeway ... that was my energy, rather than being at the wheel and being discretionary and ... I had the energy behind me and was being shoved through the universe ... and I very definitely want to change that relationship to my own sources but it's not so easily done even when you have the giant lever of cancer—it's a big handle. (Wheeler 1977, 16, original ellipses)

Later in the same interview, Wheeler says that he wants to create a trilogy of films about his disease and "the usurpation of power from the individual by the institutions"; the films would be about "taking back responsibility for your own health and hence society's onto your own shoulders, rather than giving it up to someone else" (Wheeler 1977, 17). Wheeler did not have time to realize these projects, but he did do a filmed interview with Nancy Holt called *Revolve* in which he talks about his cancer and the prospect of dying.

In addition to the "death work" with Wheeler, Blaser had to face up to the illness and death of his father. In 1976, Robert Blaser was diagnosed with dementia and had to be placed under the guardianship of Ina Mae. He would die two years later on 20 April 1978. In February of that year, only months before the death of his father, Blaser had participated in a sex therapy workshop with Miriam and Ellen designed to explore the connection between family relationships and homosexuality. One of the exercises the men were asked to do was to imagine what life would have been like if they had lost their mothers and had grown up alone with their fathers. As Ulrych remembers, Blaser's response to this question was a shockingly violent story in which his father catches him dressed in drag and acting out an opera on a train platform. In punishment, he is forced to watch the castration of a pig. In the fantasy, his father says that if he catches Robin again in such attire, Robin will share the pig's fate (Ulrych interview with author, 23 April 2014). Fellow participant John Hulcoop, a poet and professor in English Language and Literature at UBC, refers to this fantasy in a poem written for Blaser and Farwell four years later in 1982:

                    surviving
a father's fearful rage by assuming disguises,
playing private parts in wholly public places,
acting out his desire on the deserted platform
of an old whistle-stop somewhere in the middle
of nowhere, patiently waiting for the occasional train
to provide a passing audience, momentary applause
loud enough to muffle the screams of a boy
forced to watch farm-hands hacking the balls off pigs.
(Hulcoop 1982, n.p.)

Blaser flew home to Twin Falls for Robert's funeral with a ticket dated 23 April 1978—after the death, not before. "Tumble-Weed" (see Chap. 2) mourns the "desert father" (*HF*, 200) even as it registers the high difficulty of the relationship:

and which desert father lay his head
on a mummified-body-pillow whose
voice was a ghost of a woman
and which dreamed sadly he
knew better the perspective of his
landscape—windowless farms
and winds
and which cried out, 'father
of wax' and kissed his forehead
of lost lives   of cold florists
at last? (*HF*, 200)

CANADIAN CONTENT

Blaser had taken out Canadian citizenship in 1974, but the coincidence of his arrival in the country with the academic shift in focus toward theory on one front and the building of a Canadian canon on another meant that his reputation in Canada would remain modest throughout most of his life. In the universities, Canadian literature had hitherto been given less space than British and American studies; the 1960s and 1970s became the period of redress. If Blaser's San Francisco and Black Mountain connections had worked for him on arrival in Vancouver, they worked against him for the rest of his professional life at SFU. However, while Blaser was sidelined by the mainstreaming of CanLit in academic circles, his relationships with individual Canadian poets were another matter. Although he vehemently resisted nationalist rhetoric and border drawing,[2] Blaser was alert to the Canadian poetry scene and he was known among poets. To some, he had become a "*cher maître*": so George Bowering introduced him at a 1981 poetry reading at SFU.[3]

Between the mid-1970s and the late 1980s, Blaser completed two editorial projects that involved him in a careful reading of Canadian poetry. The first project was the selected poems of George Bowering for a series put out by

Talonbooks. Blaser's edition of *Particular Accidents: Selected Poems [of] George Bowering* was released in 1980 with an introductory essay. Bowering was already close to Blaser as a colleague and fellow poet at SFU and he had aligned himself with the New American poetry since the *TISH* days (see Chap. 6). He would go on to become a key maker of the Canadian postmodern. He raised eyebrows, however, not only for his embrace of what some critics saw as American poetics,[4] but also for his polemical and sometimes hilarious response to eastern (Ontario) writers and the University of Toronto take on CanLit as exemplified by the thematizing of "Canadian content" in Northrop Frye's *The Bush Garden* and Margaret Atwood's *Survival*. On one side of the east–west argument was a nationalist desire to claim a Canadian tradition distinct from the British or American; on the other, was a refusal to stop poetic *methods* at the border. In a section of *A Short Sad Book*—the title is a humorous response to Gertrude Stein's *A Long Gay Book*—that Blaser includes in *Particular Accidents*, Bowering writes: "Canadian literature was once written by fake Hurons & now it is written by the Immigrant Experience. It is never written by the Black Mountain Influence. It is written by anthropologists who know what a maple leaf looks like but dont [sic] know how it speaks" (Bowering 1980, 146). From Bowering's point of view, what the nationalist critics were calling a Canadian tradition was actually BritLit and it accounted neither for language as it lived in people's mouths nor indigenous perspectives. Olson's "Projective Verse" resonates in Bowering's work as a *methodological* backbeat (poetry as a transfer of energy from wherever the poet gets it), although the nearer influences would be Williams, Duncan, Ginsberg, and Spicer.

Blaser's introductory essay, titled "George Bowering's Plain Song" (reprinted in *The Fire*, 177–95) is a defense of an art that comes "out of the 'darkness of the lived instant' into form" (*Fire*, 182). The "plain song" of the title refers to Bowering's choice of a deceptively simple lexicon and syntax. In Blaser's phrasing: "The distinction here is between the authentic and the conventional in the language and the result is a forbidding honesty and irreducible simplicity" (*Fire*, 179). The "authentic," as Blaser elaborates, comes out of Bowering's attention to the "condition of writing" (*Fire*, 179)—to the occasion in life and language from which the text comes. Addressing a criticism of Bowering that he "never shows 'the results of his thinking,' but only 'the barren chess game of the mind itself'" (*Fire*, 179), Blaser cites Bowering's response: "'I'm not interested in the results of thinking—I'm interested in the process of thinking itself.'" Then he comments:

> Here, Bowering throws the emphasis in the artistic act on a kind of thinking and thus upon a careful consciousness of language. The charge itself implies a lack of objectivity which the result of thinking is assumed to be. Other charges have been of a self-indulgence and an unevenness. The unwitting demand is that Bowering give us a unity—this is the word for a nostalgia or sentiment of form in so many writers and readers—which in his work is not lacking, but is relentlessly questioned. The lack of objectivity in Bowering's work has "nothing whatsoever to do with subjectivity because it is always framed not in terms of the self but in terms of the relationship" to the world and consequently to language. (*Fire*, 179–80)

This passage tells us two things. First, the fact that Blaser repeatedly takes up *critiques* of Bowering in this essay speaks to the embattled nature of CanLit at that moment. In terms of academic literary discourse, the Northrop Frye–Margaret Atwood thematic approach to what was to count as Canadian was much stronger than the projective method that the *TISH* poets adapted to their own purposes. Blaser notes that Bowering credits Kenneth Rexroth, Kenneth Patchen, and William Carlos Williams with "a part in finding his own voice—the plain song of it" (*Fire*, 185) and then comments that "Bowering has been blamed for this first language; it is said to be American in a critical rejection of what this poet is and what he witnesses" (*Fire*, 185–86). Here is the crux of the CanLit debate in the 1970s: a clash of vocabularies between writers and critics who demanded Canadian *content* and a distinctive Canadian cultural tradition, and those who defended a *method* of writing that paid attention to the writerly process as rooted in a specific time–place rather than a theme identifiable as Canadian. Blaser's position and Bowering's too, I venture, is that the local is the poet's view-from-here, and if the "here" is Canada, and if the poet is honest and thorough, the view will be Canadian. Bowering's *Short Sad Book* satirizes the contrary quest for Canadian-ness as a hopeless search for an identity that always somehow turns out to be contaminated with an elsewhere. From a contemporary point of view which includes indigenous perspectives (marginal in Canadian Literature courses in the 1970s and 1980s), the argument for a distinctive Canadian identity largely focused on settler literature sharpens the irony.

The next Canadian project was an edition of Louis Dudek's poetry. With Dudek's permission and the support of Véhicule Press, Blaser undertook the editing of a selected poems in 1982, published, finally, in 1988: *Infinite Worlds: The Poetry of Louis Dudek*. Dudek (1918–2001) was an Anglophone Montréal poet, later to become a McGill professor. Frustrated with what he saw as Canada's literary provincialism in the 1940s, Dudek read the Anglo-American moderns and did postgraduate work at Columbia University in New York after graduating from McGill; later he corresponded with Pound. With a few others, like John Sutherland of *First Statement* (a pioneering journal of Canadian modernism) and poet Irving Layton, he saw his task as creating a Canadian modernism.

As was his wont, Blaser comments on Dudek by contextualizing his work. Dudek has inherited, he says, "that whirlwind of meaning which identifies the modern project in art, philosophy and science" (*Fire*, 263). He then claims for Dudek "a practice of openness, [that is] a correction of those aspects of modernism that thought to solve the order of things by authoritarian structures" (*Fire*, 264). In an indirect dissent from postmodern theory—the "great divide" between the modern and postmodern[5]—Blaser says that "All of post-modernism, in contrast to the current reaction against modernism, can be understood in terms of this correction" (*Fire*, 264). In Dudek, he writes, "we come upon one of the distinguished voices of it" (*Fire*, 264). While acknowledging Dudek's relationship to Pound, Blaser goes on to situate Dudek "side by side with the intellectual energies of Marshall McLuhan, Northrop Frye, George Grant, and George Whalley, all of them cultural modernists and international in scope" (*Fire*, 265). Blaser then engages Dudek's polemical response to McLuhan and Frye. To follow the argument, McLuhan is insufficiently historical for Dudek; technoculture forgets human history in the glitter of the future-forms it promises. For Dudek, Blaser writes, "this ideology of progress" has to be measured against "the ceremony of passage characteristic of the mentality of poetry" (*Fire*, 266). Blaser had always associated poetry with the keeping of cultural memory; in Dudek, he sees a fellow traveler whose work is haunted by a worldliness that all but vanishes in the anthropocentrism of technologies that extend the human will, but not the heart or mind.

Alongside the Dudek–McLuhan tiff he references, Blaser records another disagreement between Dudek and Northrop Frye. Blaser notes Frye's social concerns as a point of intersection with Dudek and he remarks on Frye's critique of McLuhan's "'determinism' among 'the latest of the illusions of progress'" (*Fire*, 267). However, he also distinguishes between Frye's archetypal view of poetic form and Dudek's more processive practice. Once again, Blaser claims that for Dudek, as for Bowering and himself, "form is alive" (*Fire*, 268):

> Frye's distanced view of writer and writing—doubtless fully aware of its Platonic aegis ("mathematics and myth")—derives from the fundamental problem with temporality in his theory of structure and form. And this is exactly Dudek's point. Time is, of course, the poet's thought, however metaphorical and imaged, as it moves into form; it is the life of his form. So that, for a modern poet like Dudek, form is alive. When the poem is there, it can be understood as an affective space, not merely as words on the page or a surface called language. (*Fire*, 268)

Quoting Dudek, Blaser writes that for Frye, "'all the meaning is to be found in the poet, or elsewhere than right there on the page'" (*Fire*, 271). Dudek says that he, in contrast, is after "multiplicity, and actuality, and a forever-expanding field of unpredictable useful meanings" (*Fire*, 271). Blaser then triangulates this argument through George Grant, Canada's great resister of techno-optimism and consumer culture:

> Within the practical liberalism of our past, techniques could be set within some context other than themselves—even if that context was shallow. We now move towards the position where technological progress becomes itself the sole context within which all that is other to it must attempt to be present. (Quoted in *Fire*, 271)

I have noted that in the Vancouver art community of the 1970s, new media such as film and video staked their claims, edging out painting, but as Blaser recognizes here and elsewhere, technology by itself does not resolve the problems of modernity: "the sources of barbarism—the bourgeois dead end from which modernism begins; the consumerism that claims reality by ownership; an anthropocentric view that closes into itself meaninglessly; the continuing, political postponement of a true commitment to social justice; the way poetry disappears in public thought" (*Fire*, 275). Neither postmodern theory nor technological innovation adequately addresses these problems. This essay claims for Dudek a different strategy akin to Blaser's own: the nurturing of cultural memory and of a sensibility capable of decentering not just the cogito—a task theory could handle—but the *anthropos* as well. "We must not stumble over the word 'religious,'" Blaser says, "That, too, is a matter of relationship" (*Fire*, 272).

The backbeat of Blaser's Dudek essay is his ongoing pursuit of the sacred, of cultural memory, and of the dynamics of form. These elements of poetics, broadly stated, Blaser could share with Dudek, even though Dudek rejected Olson and Creeley, two of Blaser's dearest companions in poetry. Blaser typically sought points of agreement rather than argument in his relations with other poets. In George Whalley's comments on poetic process, he finds a place where he and Dudek can meet:

> A poem is inexhaustible to analysis because it terminates in 'a vision of reality.' Reality is a matter of relationships; *we cannot refer a particular poem simply to 'reality,' because reality is not a determinate entity. Reality is the great unknown and unknowable.* We are constantly in quest of it, yet we can never fully know it and certainly we cannot possess it; the best we can hope for is to preserve our capacity for encountering reality in some of its aspects. (Quoted in *Fire*, 272)

And Dudek in the "Epilogue" to his long poem *Atlantis*:

> Talking, gladly, of the long journey ahead.
>   And all the future.
> It's always a new beginning.
> The real, or the unreal—
>   beginning where you are. (Dudek 1988, 197)

"Beginning where you are"—out of the "darkness of the lived instant."

Blaser's Canadian essays and editorial work show him reaching out to poets in his adopted country; they show familiarity with major voices in Canadian poetry and an awareness of the debates over Canadian literary identity. However, the essays are also components of Blaser's larger project of the period: an ongoing pursuit of the sacred and a resistance to the theoretical and nationalist positions then current.

THE SCHOLAR-POET

Blaser never really identified with the role of professor; he preferred that of poet. However, over his last decade at Simon Fraser, he participated in a number of conferences that resulted in some of his most scholarly work. His conference papers, and the essays that came of them, map out important cultural contexts of the period and show as well Blaser's push against the academic mainstream. "The Violets" got its start in January 1980 with an invitation to give a reading at a conference on process theology at the Co-operative Christian Campus Ministry at UBC. The conference was attended by a number of notable scholars, and afterward, Blaser was invited to submit an essay to the journal *Process Studies*. Donald Sherburne, a key Whitehead interpreter and guest editor for the conference issue of the journal, read the essay and wrote to Blaser praising it. The resulting piece on Charles Olson's reading of Whitehead's *Process and Reality* first appeared in this journal before it was reprinted in *The Fire*.

"The Violets" begins with a state-of-the-arts address. "Poets have repeatedly in this century turned philosophers, so to speak," Blaser writes, "in order to argue the value of poetry and its practice within the disturbed meanings of our time" (*Fire*, 197). Neither skeptical philosophies nor "scientism" can acknowledge poetry, he says. The latter is popularized science or "'scientific angelism,'" a phrase of René Girard's that means "an apocalypse of the objective or of a generalized humanity which can be seen as an objectivity" (*Fire*, 198). These two discourses, philosophical and pseudoscientific, are no more compatible with each other than with poetry, but they do seem to agree at least that poetry is not to be taken seriously—that it has lost the power to compel belief.

Blaser's introduction to this essay summarizes the difficult climate for the arts at the beginning of the 1980s when philosophy, critical theory, science, and the culture industry had effectively sidelined poetry as one of the composing discourses of the world. In "The Violets," Blaser battles to make poetry audible again. The essay is about Olson's adaptations of Whitehead's view of an interdependent, processive cosmos, but also about the importance of myth.

> It is one of the curiosities and discomforts of conversation and of lecturing, when one is involved in the presentation of, say, Dante or Giotto or Michelangelo that one meets embarrassment, even hostility, before the contents among so many people. It is necessary for them to relearn the old, natural calendar of the tradition. Many have fallen into time, so to speak, and seem unable to go forwards or backwards. (*Fire*, 214)

Embarrassment in the face of historical or religious content in art leads to cultural amnesia and the subsequent loss of a respected language for lived experience. This is a crisis in modernity that Blaser turns to again and again. In "The Violets," he argues that Olson takes "the fluency of the world" (*Fire*, 209) from Whitehead as a way to repose "a living sense of the relational" (*Fire*, 213). But then, as he once complained in Boston, Olson gets no ear.

In 1983, Blaser was invited to participate in a fall lecture series at the New College of California on Sappho. Duncan McNaughton was the contact person for the series and Blaser's talks, gathered under the title "Sappho, The Contemporary, and The Sacred: The Reappearance of Process" was in a line-up that included three lectures by feminist writer and scholar Judy Grahn on "Homopoetics: American Lesbian Poets in the Sapphic Tradition" and three by Stanford classicist Jack Winkler on Sappho's world.[6] Lew Ellingham announced Blaser's lectures in *Poetry Flash*, with a write-up on Blaser's San Francisco days. The notes Blaser has preserved on Sappho are spotty (that is to say, they are notes), and he never worked them up into publishable form. However, they do make clear that he was pursuing "a living sense of the relational" through the study of Sappho and pre-Socratic philosophies. One set of notes (there are several) begins like this:

> I am interested in a curious quality in the love poems of Sappho. I'll call it a sacred physicality because the realm of desire expressed in her poems is never simply self-expression; rather the otherness of the beloved is constantly present. The desire of her poems brings forward the actual other again and again. Desire is the activity or dynamic drawn out by the qualities of the other. (Undated, "Aphrodite")

In this passage, Blaser takes Sapphic love as the essential openness of being. If love is centered in a subject, then the object of the love is an object-for-me and something to be possessed; if love is a response to the "otherness of the beloved" then it is the relation itself, rather than the property of either one of the lovers. Sapphic love draws into question the discreteness of subject and object, mind and body, as, in fact, does Whiteheadian philosophy, although by different means; love is an imaginative power that dissolves, recreates, and implicates us in the "fluency of the world." Hence, love is another way of naming the capacity for marrying the world, as Blaser had done in *Cups*. Anne Carson, translating a fragment of Sappho, writes: "'Eros the melter of limbs (now again) stirs me—/sweetbitter unmanageable creature who steals in'" (Carson 2002, 265).

In Blaser's essays of this period, eros, homoeros, poetry, process, and the sacred form a nexus of related concepts. These again come into play again in Blaser's work on Mary Butts. In 1979, Talonbooks reprinted an edition of Butts's *Imaginary Letters*, a series of letters about a beautiful, difficult young man—"underhanded, unstable, lost, homosexual, unavailable" in Blaser's phrasing, who "somehow starts the imaginary process" (*Fire*, 173). In the first letter, written as if to Boris's mother, Butts says "Boris, your son, will be—one might say, he is—the cause of art in others" (Butts 1979, 9). Blaser wrote an "Afterword" to the Talonbooks edition in which he contextualizes Butts in her world of 1920–1930s writers, artists, and occultists. He acknowledges the elements of Butts's work that have caused readers "impatience" and left her in obscurity—"political naiveté, a very English allegiance to her class, the country-gentry, an elegiac stance toward that very modern condition of loss of 'meaning' and 'belief'" (*Fire*, 165–66)—but he also connects her to the Berkeley project of the 1940s.

> Mary Butts was one of many introductions Duncan prepared for us in those young days—William Carlos Williams, Stein, Joyce and H.D. Brilliant young Jack Spicer gave his first lecture on *Armed with Madness* (1928) during the Fall term, 1949, even then interested in the "sacred game" or an excuse for it such as the

Grail. Thus, Mary Butts became a figure inside the imagination of what was later to be called the "Berkeley Renaissance," and then, with important changes of emphasis, the "San Francisco Renaissance." Initially, or so I read the work of Duncan and Spicer, an imaginary landscape was at stake, a map that would not leave the world out. A principle of transformation is at work in all the art we knew, and present to our own thereby, without utopian ignorance of meanness, desperation or the contemporary revelation of human affairs. The "real" in this sense is both possible and impossible. Certainly a composition and a task. (*Fire*, 167–68)

The recognition of Butts comes because she, like the Berkeley poets, takes on a geography of the imagination.

In 1984, Christopher and Barbara Wagstaff organized a Butts conference at the University of California, Davis, 23–24 February. Blaser was invited to speak. It was a very small conference, but Camilla Baggs, Butts's daughter came, as did Robert Duncan, Ken Irby, and the Wagstaffs. Blaser gave a lecture on Butts's *Armed with Madness* that eventually became the essay, "Here Lies the Woodpecker Who Was Zeus," (first published in Wagstaff's collection, *A Sacred Quest*, in 1995). The title of the essay he took from a phrase in Butts's book. The novel presents a landscape fraught with immanence, like Blaser's early serials, and a character, Picus, who may or may not be a god. In a passage from Jane Harrison's *Themis* that Blaser quotes, Picus was a trickster and bird-spirit, a woodpecker who "'enshrines a beautiful lost faith, the faith that birds and beasts had *mana* other and sometimes stronger than the *mana* of man'" (*Fire*, 330). In *Traps for Unbelievers*, Butts says that "'We are back in the historical situation which Nietzsche described of a people 'for whom God is dead, and for whom no baby-god is yet lying in his cradle'" (Quoted in *Fire*, 337). This, for Blaser, would be an astute assessment of the contemporary situation, and Butts's quest for the sacred, unpopular as it helped to make her, suggests a response to this condition congenial to his own.

In 1984, Blaser began to make notes for an essay on the work of his old friend, Christos Dikeakos. Scott Watson, then a curator at the Vancouver Art Gallery, had invited him to write a catalog essay for a large, Dikeakos retrospective, an exhibition that took place from 1 February to 16 March 1986. By this time, the hurt over the past relationship with Watson had healed and he and Blaser could be friends. Blaser's "Mind Canaries" was first published in the catalog accompanying the show. Dikeakos drew on his Greek heritage to thread classical myth through the eyehole of the contemporary and vice versa. One focus of the show was the myth of Icarus: the story is of a boy who thought to escape from an imprisoning labyrinth with wings of feathers and wax. Like Icarus, the figures in Dikeakos's collages try and fail to fly. Fragmented images of mythic figures (Icarus, Medusa, the Muses, Ares, Nemesis, the Sphinx, Hera, Apollo) are intercut with photographs and images that attest to the seedy exploitation of the ancient sacred places for the tourist industry. Many of the

Fig. 7.2 *IKARIA: POEM = ESPACE, EXPLORER I*, 1976–1984. Hand-colored photograph and collage, 48 × 69″ by Christos Dikeakos. Collection of Brian DeBeck and Karen Tallman. Photo by Christos Dikeakos, reproduced courtesy of Christos Dikeakos

pieces include nude figures with collaged-on wings. At the center of the show was a triptych of Duchamp titled *Ikaria: Poem = Espace, Explorer I*. For this piece, Dikeakos photocopied Frederick J. Kiesler's photomontage, *Les Larves d'Imagie d'Henri Robert Marcel Duchamp: M.D. emeritus for chronic diseases of the Arts* (*Fire*, 241–42), hand-colored the copy, and counter-signed it. The montage shows a winged Duchamp, seated and facing away from the viewer, in a cluttered studio that opens into outer space. Objects from the studio float and disperse (Fig. 7.2).

Blaser opens the essay with his customary narrative of modernity as the loss of relational thought and then situates Dikeakos in this narrative. Unique to this essay, however, is the focus on technology, a topic touched on in the Dudek piece. Blaser characterizes his culture as "increasingly technological" (*Fire*, 237) and draws on Octavio Paz to distinguish between technology as an extension of the human will and art as a reach for the world. Technology, Blaser says, "pushes us toward the 'unknown' and the 'formless'" (*Fire*, 237) because it treats the world as an obstacle to be overcome rather than a vision to be composed. Quoting a passage from *The Bow and the Lyre*, he writes:

> Technology is neither an image nor a vision of the world: it is not an image because its aim is not to represent or reproduce reality; it is not a vision because it does not conceive the world as shape but as something more or less malleable to the human will. For technology, the world presents itself as resistance, not as archetype: it has reality, not shape. (Quoted in *Fire*, 237)

The comments on technology in "Mind Canaries" extend Blaser's critique of "scientific angelism" in "The Violets": even the sciences are largely constrained under global capitalism to immediate use—all cultural privilege given over to marketable technologies—and this state of affairs simply intensifies the amnesia and anthropocentric bent of contemporary culture. If, as Paz and Blaser say, technology is an extension of the will, the wonder of nature's things and the human relationship to them are set aside. The tie-in with Dikeakos is the Icarus theme: Icarus's wings were meant to allow him to escape his entrapment in a labyrinth designed by his father, Daedalus. The wings are a form of technology meant to solve the problems that come with technology. The story speaks to contemporary efforts to escape social problems and meaninglessness through technodazzle.

Duchamp comes into the picture via the triptych. Dikeakos's meditation on Duchamp in this collection, Blaser says, is "part of an intellectual honesty that is also an effort to return art to its place in public thought" (*Fire*, 248): Duchamp's "'criticism' of art [as in his readymades] is ... a return to the oldest tradition of art—before it lost its meaning by becoming *objets d'art*, only an aspect of the mercantilism that controls us" (*Fire*, 248). What Blaser claims here for Duchamp, with support from his readings of Paz, is the dramatization of a cultural condition. The readymades and *Great Glass* are important not as objects, even though they have been fetishized since their making, but as commentary on the world. Analogously, Blaser says of Dikeakos that his exhibition is a kind of "mind canary," like a bird in a coal mine, sent down to test the breathability of the air. Dikeakos's show tests the contemporary cultural atmosphere with an exploration of what can be thought and envisioned in the post-industrial landscapes of technoculture, here littered with the oracular shards of Greek myth and history.

Phrases like "world image," dear to Blaser and generously used in "Mind Canaries" and other essays, had no currency in the mid-1980s. In the poetry world, this was a decade when a new generation of exploratory poets, the Language writers, suspended such large coherencies as overdetermined, unreflexive, and culturally contaminated. In Vancouver, the Kootenay School of Writing (KSW) provided a venue for the new poetry. A progressive writing program at David Thompson University Centre in Nelson, B.C. closed in 1984 by order of B.C.'s Social Credit government, ostensibly for lack of funds. Following the closure, some of the teachers and students moved to Vancouver and set up the KSW as a writer-run venue. The first mandate of the school was to offer inexpensive writing programs and workshops, and its first major event was the New Poetics Colloquium, held at Emily Carr College of Art and

Design, 21–25 August 1985. Like the Vancouver poetry festival of 1963 that had brought New Americans to Vancouver, the New Poetics Colloquium brought American Language writers together with locals. Panel topics included "New Feminist Theory and Practice," "Language and Philosophy," "Translation," "New Narrative," "Post Language Writing," "Documentary/ Identity/Rhetoric," "Language and Performance," "The Book," "Language and Ideology," "Long Forms," "Music and Language," "Dissemination: Publishing and Distribution." This list of panel titles documents the concerns of writers then with poetry and language, feminist theory, new forms of narrative or anti-narrative, and the means of poetic dissemination. In 1985, practical dissemination still meant small presses. Tsunami Editions, a local press run by Larry Bremner, would provide a venue for the books and chapbooks of younger Vancouver writers into the 1990s. The KSW web describes the Colloquium as "a defining event in the development of the KSW"; the school had been leftist from its inception, but this event turned it toward Language writing as opposed to "straightforward protest-writing."[7]

Significantly, Blaser did not participate in the Colloquium: the event, in the commotion of its moment, was meant to make space for a new generation and that implied a side-lining of the previous one, of which Blaser was a prominent local member. However, he attended the Colloquium and took notes on Perelman, Silliman, Bernstein, McCaffery, and Watten. These include phrases like "Derrida – 'God is dead so any word can mean anything,'" or "Ron Silliman: High priest of the death of God." On McCaffery, Blaser makes a note that the arts "need to be shocked into recognition" (Blaser 1985, New Poetics Colloquium notes). Yet his own "discourse of cosmos" ran counter to the emphasis on reflexivity, irony, and anti-narrative strategies that drew the attention of younger poets.

Blaser expressed his differences from the younger generation more directly the following year at the Spicer symposium, 16–21 June 1986. He had received an invitation from organizer Dawn Kolokithas to participate in a Spicer memorial conference, the White Rabbit Symposium, to be held in San Francisco. The Symposium brought next generation writers Bruce Boone, Lori Chamberlain, Michael Davidson, Benjamin Hollander, Kevin Killian, Michael Palmer, Jed Rasula, Ron Silliman, David Levi Strauss, and many more together with Blaser, Duncan, McClure, Joanne Kyger, and Joe Dunn—the generation that had known Spicer personally. Blaser and Ron Silliman were on the same panel and both had titled their papers after Spicer's last words, "'My Vocabulary Did This To Me.'" Silliman emphasizes Spicer's linguistic training and consequent attention to the structure of language as "a primary antecedent for much that has come about in writing in the two decades since his [Spicer's] death" (Silliman 1987, 67). He concludes his talk with a commentary on the naming function of language, calling it "part of the violence of birth, complete with the signature of the father's surname, and the relation of our names to ourselves … not unlike that of scars to a body" (Silliman 1987, 70). This kind of analysis is apposite to Derridean deconstruction: deconstruction suspends the naming of things, thus to honor their indeterminate liveliness; naming then comes to seem a violence. So Silliman circles back to the title of the talk, "'My Vocabulary Did This To Me.'"

Blaser's talk of the same title could not have been more different. After warming up the crowd with some stories from the Berkeley days and a reading from Spicer's *Book of Galahad* in *The Holy Grail*, Blaser gets to the point. "The sacred, in my view," he says, "is a central problem of the modern condition" (*Fire*, 256). A few paragraphs later he says that "what is missing [from the contemporary] is a discourse of cosmos, and this is the reason I'm drawing attention to this element of the sacred in Spicer..." (*Fire*, 258). Rather than focus on Spicer's language play, Blaser draws out parallels between Spicer's practice and that of Christian mystics such as St. Theresa of Avila and St. John of the Cross (*Fire*, 259) who made a spiritual discipline of unknowing. Dictation, in other words, was Spicer's way of engaging with the unknown. In a rather sly move, Blaser links a counter tradition that unnames the Other with "Nietzsche, Heidegger, Bataille, Blanchot, [and] Derrida" (*Fire*, 258): "Fundamental here is the question of the Other—in Spicer's language, the Unknown, the Outside, and so forth" (*Fire* 258). In a series of "propositions" following this comment, Blaser outlines the difference between his reading of these philosophers and the more common academic reception of them.

> Our tradition sees the Other, in Michel de Certeau's words, as a *threat*, to be reduced—the Other as the realm of the dead, as in [Spicer's] Galahad. A proposition, then: we cannot appropriate the Other, even as a realm of knowledge. Proposition: there is no autonomy of poetic knowledge—it is a discourse among others, but a very real one. Nevertheless, as Levinas has said, we are involved in the *lived* experience of the Other. Proposition: that is, the reason that we cannot, as writers, simply turn poetry *over* to language—to adapt de Certeau's point again—it is unlike language (literature), unlike language which, as an object of knowledge, is a construct of philosophers and linguists; whereas poetic language—along with all the other discourses—constitutes "forms of active social interactions and practice." That is a quotation from Certeau. (*Fire*, 258–59)

An important move in the above passage is the idea of the proposition itself. The proposition is a conditional rhetorical form: it frames declaratives as up for revision. However, the indeterminacy of language, thematized in some Language writing and in deconstruction, is not taken as a proposition but as a condition of all utterances. Blaser brackets this emphasis on linguistic indeterminacy with a move he takes from Wlad Godzich's preface to de Certeau's *Heterologies*. With Godzich, he argues the necessity of a language for the "*lived* experience of the Other" and for discourses understood as modes of "active social interactions and practice." Thus he pulls the discussion back to experience via philosophers who, in the 1980s, were more often associated with suspicion of it. A little later in the talk, he addresses the philosophies of language directly:

These new methods of reading that sometimes lead us into marvels of a changed intelligence—linguistic, structural, deconstructionist—rich and challenging as they are, become dangerous when they become hegemonic, and to my reading thereby *ahistorical*. The materiality of language can be turned into an ahistorical system easily by limp wrist or limp mind. The elements of the sexual, the discourse of the Other, the otherness of language in Jack's work cannot be set aside. They date back to the beginning of modernity, what de Certeau calls "the mystic speech" of the sixteenth and seventeenth centuries. (*Fire*, 259)

Blaser thus places Spicer among the saints and mystics, so to emphasize the poetics of dictation as belonging to a genealogy of "the discourse of the Other."

The two "'My Vocabulary'" talks might have ended in disagreement; instead, Blaser turned on the charm. Steve Abbott and Kevin Killian describe the incident in their review of the conference in *Poetry Flash*:

Afterwards, Bruce Boone asked the panel at large what comes beyond Spicer. Given that Spicer's work captures perfectly X amount of negativity, can he help us today in the world of X squared? At this Blaser clutched Silliman in mock fear, like Jack Lemmon grabbing Tony Curtis at the sight of Sugar Kane in *Some Like It Hot*, Siamese twins joined at the waist. "We are the same person," he avowed to a crowd stunned into disbelief. (Abbott and Killian 1986, 16)

In my view, this was likely a deflective move on Blaser's part, meant to avert a possibly tense discussion. To align Spicer with mystical thought seems contrary to the proto-Language direction in which Silliman takes him. Introducing this special issue of *Acts*, David Levi Strauss notices that Blaser "objects not to what is *included* in these new readings ... [readings coming out of Language-based poetry and deconstructive philosophy] but to what is left out" (Strauss 1987, 2, original emphasis). Again, this is a gracious way of managing what might have been a head-on collision. The collision never happened at the White Rabbit Symposium; instead, Blaser's performance received lively praise in *Poetry Flash* from Abbott and Killian:

Robin Blaser, casually dressed in a mauve jacket and white shirt open at the collar, concluded the reading with a pyrotechnical performance. Brushing back his mane of white hair, Blaser said he'd decided to read only new work and began with a long poem honoring Allen Ginsberg on his 60th birthday. The poem ranged from song, to philosophical erudition, to humor. Blaser managed his transitional shifts with split-second timing, subtle voice modulations and a deft self-confidence all the more impressive for its relaxed, off-hand manner. (Abbott and Killian 1986, 14)

Notice the society page style. Ginsberg, be it noted, was almost as out of fashion in the mid-1980s as mysticism, but Abbott focuses on Blaser's performance rather than his decision to honor Ginsberg. In the same *Poetry Flash*, Kevin Killian describes the panel talk:

Next Robin Blaser took the floor, and held it. Half theory, half reminiscence, all presence, studded with loud announcements of "Proposition!"—like Luther— his talk proved hypnotic. The whole Conference might have been given for Blaser, the way that *Ragtime* became a film simply to lure Cagney back to the screen. Blaser has the star quality of—say—Cary Grant and uses it exquisitely. (Killian 1986)

These write-ups are a delight in the detail and color with which they recall the occasion and they are appropriate for the venue: *Poetry Flash* is a circular of poetry news, not an academic journal. But the polemical implications of Blaser's position remained uncommented not only in the aftermath of the Symposium, but in any sustained way while theory and Language writing held the forefront of investigative poetics. I will return to these implications in the "Big Poetry" section of Chap. 8.

THE TURNER TOUR

Blaser had been promising his beloved a trip for some time, a tour that would introduce David to the art and poetry of San Francisco and beyond. In 1980–1981, Blaser had a sabbatical year, so he had the time, but there remained the question of money. Blaser never traveled light or cheap, and if this voyage were to answer to the promises he had made to David, it had to be something special. Some time before, Blaser had bought a little painting in an antique store in West Vancouver for $10. The painting, he discovered afterwards, was a J.M.W. Turner. It hung in the house for a while, but Blaser found it a sorry example of a Turner and never really liked it. After gallantly offering to share the booty with the woman who sold the painting to him (she just as gallantly refused), he unloaded his find for enough to pay for a trip in high style.

On this trip, as on many subsequent voyages, David took daily notes. The tour began on 4 May 1981 with a flight to San Francisco and a stay at Landis Everson's house, Blaser's old friend from the Berkeley days. Everson was out, so Blaser took David to Russian Hill, his former neighborhood, and then lunch at the San Franciscan. His first Margaritas, Farwell writes, and then prawn cocktails and Crab Louis washed down with Chablis, Blaser's preferred white. The San Francisco leg of the trip lasted four days: Aquatic Park, lunch at Via Veneto, a dirty bookstore on Polk Street, the De Young Museum, and dinner with James Felts and Felts's lover, Joseph, "who has the mind of a 13-year old," David decided (Farwell 1981, notebook). Rather like Gertrude Stein's Alice who was tasked with entertaining the wives of painters at the Paris atelier, David was assigned to play computer baseball with Joseph while Blaser and Felts talked.

The Turner Tour took Blaser and Farwell from San Francisco to Philadelphia; Washington, DC; New York; Boston; Gloucester; Saint John, New Brunswick; Québec City; Ottawa; and finally back home by train, to arrive on 6 June 1981. The trip was all about the great American museums and the pleasures of good restaurants. In Philadelphia, it was the Barnes Foundation to look at the modern painters, the Rodin Museum, the Philadelphia Museum of Art for Duchamp's *Great Glass* and the Shiva Show, and The Art Museum for twentieth century American painters. In Washington, Farwell duly noted a hotel full of what looked to him like South American dictators, "everyone in dark suits and sunglasses. Conversations around us at breakfast were all in Spanish" (Farwell 1981, notebook). The Washington stay included a demanding tour of the National Gallery to see the moderns, and then the Hirshhorn ("Robin not pleased—too much of a mishmash"). Then they took in a pre-Columbian exhibit at Dumbarton Oaks: "So much gold!" David writes, "Wonderful Mayan bowls—death beads, jade masks" (Farwell 1981, notebook). At the Freer, they saw a collection of Bodhisattavas and Japanese screens; at the Phillips, more paintings—Puvis de Chavannes, Diebenkorn, Winslow Homer, Chagall, El Greco, Gauguin, Constable, Vuillard, Redon, Daumier, Delacroix, Bonnard, de Stael, Rothko, and Matisse, among others. David recorded the inscription on the Jefferson Memorial: "I have sworn upon the altar of God eternal hostility against every form of tyranny over the mind of man" (Farwell 1981, notebook).

From Washington, Blaser and Farwell took a train to New York. "Robin has two dozen pairs of socks strung around the bathroom drying," Farwell writes. "It's hot and muggy. His cigarettes smell worse than usual." On the up side, "the people move faster and look better than in Washington—even the drunks and bag-ladies look more interesting" (Farwell 1981, notebook). Blaser and Farwell visited Ardele Lister and her husband, artist Bill Jones. For Blaser's birthday on 18 May, they found books on Bonnard and Vuillard at Rizzoli and for David four volumes of the Cambridge Ancient History at Scribners. The birthday dinner was in the Oak Room at the Plaza: oysters Rockefeller, steamed mussels, bouillabaisse, and a half bottle of Pouilly-Fuissé—then over to Ardele's for cake. New York meant more museums—MOMA, the Whitney, the Frick, the Metropolitan, the Guggenheim—punctuated with espressos and Bloody Mary's. "Robin has a cold," David writes, "and is going to be bitchy for a while."

Blaser and Farwell departed for Boston on day 19 of the trip, 22 May, beginning with "[a] scary wait at Penn Station" (Farwell, 1981, notebook). A white war vet followed them asking for money, a black one sang at the top of his lungs, and a cop with a nightstick tapped the feet of everyone sleeping. Penn Station apparently took three Bloody Maries to recover from on the train. In Boston, they wandered through Blaser's old neighborhood by the Charles River and strolled around Harvard. To tramp the city and tour the museums, they met up with Juliet McLaren, one of Blaser's former graduate students. The three of them had a lobster dinner, served by an obliging Greek waiter who cracked Blaser's crustacean for him ("He got a *very* good tip," David writes). From Boston, Blaser and Farwell took a train to Gloucester to walk the Olson sites—the Portuguese Church with the statue of Our Lady of Good Voyage, Olson's house, the Tavern, and finally the Beechbrook Cemetery in West Gloucester. Although Blaser couldn't find Olson's grave, he poured some

Cutty Sark on the ground and took a pull himself, paying respects. Then it was a rushed taxi ride back to the station and Boston again for the train to Saint John.

The New Brunswick leg of the trip was to introduce Blaser to Farwell's home turf:

> A good snooze in a cool room even if Robin was insulted by the décor. A look at the Saint John Market—lots of fish; dulse by the brown paper bag. A tour through Loyalist House, then hopped in the car (after R. found his house keys) and drove up to Moncton. Dropped Robin at the Beausejour Hotel and I went off to spend an hour and half with Mom and Dad. Though I explained I was with Robin and where he was at the moment, they expressed no desire to lay eyes on him. Their loss! Dad looked pretty skinny. Picked up Robin at the hotel where he was stuffing his face with lobster rolls; then off to the airport and the flight to Montréal with 20 Expo fans. (Farwell 1981, notebook)

Neither Farwell's family nor Blaser's openly acknowledged that their sons were a couple, although they both tacitly accepted the presence of a male "companion." During subsequent trips to Idaho, Blaser would introduce David quite implausibly as his "driver," so to spare his aging Catholic mother a confrontation with what she doubtless knew to be so.

The stops in Québec City and Ottawa for museum tours and a look at the architecture seem to have come from Blaser's curiosity about his adopted country. Although he had no past connections with either city, he wanted to visit the historic sites and experience the francophone culture of Canada. In Ottawa, he delighted in the National Gallery and he and David attended Question Period in Parliament: a "wonderful afternoon," David writes, "we watched Pierre Trudeau utterly demolish Joe Clark several times. Both of us left feeling sorry for the Leader of the Opposition."

On the train back to Vancouver, Robin struck up a conversation with an American who happened to be ex-CIA and "who regaled Robin with horrific stories about Vietnam." Robin was "so fascinated," David writes, "that he never let the man know how he actually felt about the war." Some of the time was also spent with a four-year-old who preferred Blaser and Farwell's cabin to his own: "His mother would check on him every half hour to make sure he wasn't being molested," David writes. "Robin enjoyed it all—when he wasn't having drinks with the CIA agent or talking up a storm in the observation car." In Vancouver, I had been housesitting and picked them up at the train station in the biggest car they had ever seen, Farwell says. It was a 1973 Chevrolet Impala, an 8-cylinder, gas-guzzling Chariot of the Empire.

Farwell's notes include long lists of paintings viewed, dinners eaten, and drinks quaffed. They are entirely accurate to the kind of life he and Blaser led together. Art was oxygen to Blaser and as much a part of his world as his social circles, his academic work, his poetry, and his private life with David—an integral part of his daily thinking and a major source of pleasure. Although there would be many future trips, the Turner Tour was typical of Blaser's style. As well, it was a consummation of the relationship with David because it was meant to invite David to fully enter Robin's world. For Blaser, it was a regathering of where he had been and an acknowledgment of where he was now as a Canadian citizen in an adopted country. A settling in, finally. The gourmandizing, as well, was part of the fabric of Blaser's life. Never trust anyone who doesn't like food, he once said to me. A nicely turned out lobster, preferably shelled by a handsome server, a perfectly glazed chicken, a very good Bloody Mary, or a nice Chablis were among the joys of life. Blaser also had a real love of comfort food like meat loaf or chicken pot pie. Lunch was an ongoing passion and he was generous with friends and students, usually picking up the check and leaving a big tip. The hearts of waiters everywhere gladdened at the sight of him. Such habits might have had roots in a youth and adolescence starved of graceful living, but by the 1980s they were rooted in the man Blaser had become. The university had never turned him into a career academic; he was a poet who reached for life with both hands and enjoyed it in all its dimensions—in friendship, love, food, nature, and the beautiful, made things he routinely coveted and loved to collect. Passing over the border from the U.S. to Canada on this trip, Blaser had to display his treasures to the customs agent. David writes: "No problem at all at Canadian Customs—the agents were all fascinated by the Mexican folk art piece—had to turn the crank to see the dog wag its tail, the woman sweep the floor, the man hammer the nail, etc." (Farwell 1981, notebook). Blaser delighted in such pieces as much as in the highly serious, meditative paintings and sculptures that he and David had seen so much of on their tour. He loved whatever reached for the world, large or small, profound or funny—whatever sparkled and proposed.

SYNTAX

Blaser was working on *Pell Mell* from 1981 onward, a major statement kind of a serial, but it would not come out until 1988. The principal collection of poems for the mid-1970s to 1980s was *Syntax*, written between 1979 and 1981, and published by Talonbooks. *Syntax* is a slender book, dedicated to David Farwell, and in fact some of its found poems come from material that Farwell brought home from the St. Roch National Historic Site, Maritime Museum, where he was working at the time. It looks back on Blaser's life in poetry and forward to an assured statement of the poetics he had been building for 30 years. "Diary, April 11, 1981," returns to Boston with the Olson comment from 1958.

> Olson said, 'I'd trust you
> anywhere with image, but
> you've got no syntax' (1958) (*HF*, 223)

All of *Syntax* responds to this remark. From Blaser's point of view, one does not "have" syntax; rather multiple syntaxes are what one is among. The book is full of collage work and found poems that Blaser had discovered in his readings and travels, including this impressive one from Joe Panipakuttuk:

> *all I could see were huge rocks*
> *Mr. Larsen said that these were*
> *musk oxen, the very things I thought*
> *to be rocks   so I looked again*
> *through the telescope and the rocks*
> *began to move...* (*HF*, 218, original emphasis)

The poem ends with the lines, "*when you see musk oxen for the first time / they have a huge back on them*" (*HF*, 218). Panipakuttuk's poem brings forward the sharply perspectival nature of perception and hence the impossibility of a single syntax. Olson drew on many sources in *The Maximus Poems*, and sometimes included them by quotation, but the dominant sensibility is that of Maximus. From Olson's point of view, singularity of perspective is inevitable and the performance of it is simple honesty. Duncan describes himself as a derivative poet, but when he impersonates (Duncan's word) his sources, they become unmistakably Duncan. Blaser performs his version of the scholar-poet differently, staging his voice as one of many—a kind of Minimus in a crowded space. This he does both in the essays and the poems.

In *Syntax*, Blaser launches a new series, called *The Truth is Laughter* that, like the *Image-Nations*, is meant to be interspersed throughout multiple books. Many of these poems are found pieces that record wonderments like Panipakuttuk's observation. One piece, titled "The Mystic East," consists of nothing but place names from Newfoundland, taken from a tourist book that Farwell had brought home from the east coast: Jerry's Nose, Come-by-Chance, Blow-me-down, Bumble Bee Bight, and so on (*HF*, 228–29). The last poem of *Syntax* ("further") lifts a passage from *The Story of Opal* (1920), the journal of child prodigy and nature writer Opal Whiteley (1897–1992). Blaser had a connection to Opal Whiteley through Sophia Nichols; Whiteley was an acquaintance and had once sent a postcard to Sophia.[8] Here is the beginning of the poem.

> *after I did look looks at the clock, I did*
> *look looks out the front window. There are*
> *calf-tracks by our front window. These tracks*
> *are there because when I went walking with*
> *Elizabeth Barrett Browning on yesterday, I*
> *had her wait by the front step while I did go*
> *into the kitchen to get her some sugar-lumps.* (*HF*, 240, original emphasis)

Elizabeth Barrett Browning is a cow of whom Whiteley says "*there is / poetry in her tracks*" (*HF*, 240). These tracks she digs up and saves "*in the back part of the / cook-table drawer*" (*HF*, 240). Whiteley's musings are drawn from a childhood diary in which she recorded her daily life in rural Oregon. The diary is striking in the manner of Joe Panipakuttuk's observations, for the intense, curious perceptual interfacing with ordinary things. Introducing *Syntax*, Blaser writes:

> I read, walk, listen, dream, and write among companions. These pieces
> do not belong to me. *Syntax*, a personification, looking for a predicate and
> *vice versa*. (*HF*, 203)

Here, then, is the difference in performance. Blaser, Olson, Duncan, and Spicer all practiced a version of composition by field, but each had his variously peopled territories and each shaped them through a singular vision: it was the broad spaces of geo-history and cosmic myth for Olson, a hag-ridden *homoeros* for Spicer, and *mythopoiesis* for Duncan. Blaser was the one who went furthest in performing *mitsein* as collage.

In San Francisco, the actuality of the *Open Space* community of 1964–1965 was coterie, although the concept is suggestive of more. In *Pacific Nation*, Blaser had thought to seek out new voices, but the journal fell apart under the pressures of his professorial day job. In *Syntax*, he performs the poem as open space. The virtual community of the earlier poems already included the living and the dead; the *trouvés* of *Syntax* extend the range from bathroom graffiti to the latest voices in high theory. "Lake of Souls," an anchor poem for the collection, is composed of such a community and it furthers Blaser's meditation on the loss of the sacred to public thought. The voices of this poem include Cavafy in *Waiting for the Barbarians*; René Girard in *Violence and the Sacred*; Blake on poetic genius; Bernard-Henri Lévy in *Barbarism with a Human Face*; Geoffrey Hartman in *Beyond Formalism*; Shelley in "The Triumph of Life"; Henry Corbin in *The Man of Light in Iranian Sufism*, and Heraclitus in a fragment translated by Thomas Merton. The same poem records this comment from the men's washroom at Leo's Fish House: "*Born on a mountain / Raised in a cave / Bikin' and Fuckin' / Are all I crave*" (*HF*, 235). The graffito, another Farwell discovery, makes the point about the diminishment of life without the Blakean poetic genius rather more brusquely than the poets and philosophers who speak in this poem, but the point is that both kinds of voices are needed if the poet is to think with and through the times. If there is any principle of selection at work in *Syntax*, beyond the inevitable limitations of the poet's view-from-here, it is perhaps sincerity.

The contrast to the voices of Joe Panipattutuk, Opal Whiteley, and the anonymous graffiti artist is the pseudosophistication of ungenerous forms of postmodern irony in the culture industry. To return to "Diary, April 11, 1981," Blaser remarks that "pop-art doesn't / ring twice" (*HF*, 222), referring to Andy Warhol's electric chair, now sitting "comfy" in the kitchen. Director John Boorman also comes in for some sharp words. Boorman's film *Excalibur* of 1981 retells Malory's *Mort d'Arthur*. In Blaser's view, the film makes Arthur look like an idiot and Merlin a charlatan.

> ...it is true you can get art
> out of anything as it comes to be
> the backside of itself   you see
> the actor acting   in an anti-novel
> you see the novel novelling   in the
> anti-poem, an aesthetic raspberry is
> thrilling or worn-out   if all
> civilization is somebody's childhood

and somebody sits there forever x-ing
it out   civilization   it's called
de-construction   it is there
and not there,   so his this-isn't-it
is exactly what it is   perhaps (*HF*, 222–23)

There is humor in the "perhaps," but the serious point is that whatever narratives the mind can dream up can be critiqued as structures of the mind. There is no exit from radical skepticism: irony simply steps around the problem of finding poetic forms adequate to the world as it must be lived. The Barthesian thought that all order implies repression[9] is essentially unanswerable, but once the "this-isn't-it" has been registered there is still the problem of "what it is." "'[W]hat language do / you choose for the really Good News?'" the poem asks, and then turns to an etymological definition of syntax: "*to put together in order* the / simplicity, the wings" (*HF*, 223), twisting the question back to the hubbub of the whole series.

RETIREMENT

On 12 July 1984, Blaser wrote a letter of resignation to his old friend at SFU, Jerry Zaslove, then Chair of the English Department. "I am struck by the odd context that the university now offers—," he writes, "to stay is meaningless and to leave is meaningless, except in the most private sense of things":

> "They"—the mystery of them—seem to have forgotten that scholarship and thought (literature, in my view, is thought and the best of it scholarly in the most natural way) require a place from which to be active in the world. But that freshness I call place (like a delicious garden come upon, surprisingly, among skyscrapers) depends upon the value of persons. Never before have I felt like a number, except when I was up for the draft—...Nevertheless, I want to say that I am grateful for having been there. The learning of what I tried to do and of what I shared with a few was, for me, alive and wonderful. And I am grateful for the generous side of this early retirement policy that allows me to go when I should. I am particularly indebted to you for, in my view, single-handedly keeping the English Dept. civilized and sensitive. I've long kept in mind your wise remark: "Never ask an institution to love you." Civilization is an individual and life-long task—not the same as professionalism—and the labour of it within an institution is greatly aided when guarded over by a real person. (12 July 1984)

The letter was written two years in advance of Blaser's actual retirement on 1 September 1986 to give the university time to find a replacement. It hints of the changes that had taken place in universities since Blaser's hire in 1966. With the pull-back of arts funding in the 1970s and 1980s, institutional patience for exploration in the arts had shortened considerably and the race to professionalize was on. More degrees, more publications, more conferencing, more reprintable kudos were needed to get hired and promoted. In the 1980s, jobs in academia were tight all over North America. Professionalization meant that the time needed to think and experiment without actually producing publishable work had evaporated, at least for all but the most privileged and bankable of academics. Blaser's way of working—copious note-taking, heavy reading lists, plenty of meditation time, and small press publication—did not fly; it is very unlikely that he would have been hired on such pickings in the 1980s, let alone given a full professorship. The university as a place where the humanities were active and alive and curious was disappearing into a place where degrees were earned and careers sought in a fiercely competitive atmosphere. Blaser's sense that faculty members were numbers (each with a long line-up of young graduates behind them, waiting for a job) and that it was time for him to go seems accurate to the zeitgeist. By 1984, when he wrote his resignation, his Arts in Context courses as originally conceived—multidisciplinary, supported by faculty-led seminars, supplemented with on-campus performances in music and theater, and shows in visual arts—already seemed utopian. In the letter to Zaslove, Blaser says that he would like to be asked back to teach a *"specialité"* once in a while, but the terms had become too hard: he would have been paid a sessional's wages and accommodated like a sessional too. There was to be no respect of persons: academics of both the right and left agreed at least on that. Twenty years after it opened its doors, Simon Fraser offered a golden handshake to expensive senior faculty, clearing the way for younger, cheaper, and more pliable labor. Blaser took it. He had been well-paid during his years at SFU—the flush years—and he was canny with his money despite an incorrigible propensity for good living. At age 61, he could manage financially without the Academy and he left it for good.

NOTES

1. Wheeler's notes, dated 3 February 1976, sketch a film called "Death-Work," that is to include the sessions with Blaser.

2. In "out of the velvet," a piece Blaser wrote for Charles Bernstein's special edition of *boundary 2, 99 Poets/1999: An International Poetics Symposium*, he is explicit on the subject of nationalism:

   > I do not see my work in the context of a national state, though I hold, with conscience, dual citizenship by birth in the United States and by responsibility to Canada, where I have lived and earned my living during the last thirty-two years. Oh, yes, I worry about nationalisms, their mythic destinies borrowed from religion, and the endangered democracies here and abroad. (*Fire*, 96)

   This brief essay postdates the period under discussion in this chapter, but it expresses a long-held view.

3. This reading was held as one of a series in an SFU summer event called *The Coast is Only a Line*, featuring credit courses and a reading series. SFU faculty Roy Miki and Kathy Mezei were festival organizers. At the Blaser reading, 14 August 1981, Miki introduced George Bowering who introduced Blaser. *"Cher maître"* is Bowering's phrase (Bowering 1981, "Introduction to Blaser reading").

4. For a nuanced description of nationalist and anti-nationalist arguments in Canadian literary circles at mid-century and the source of them in Canada's branch plant economy (65% of Canada's economy was foreign owned in 1958 (Dart 7)) see Ron Dart's *Robin Mathews: Crown Prince of Canadian Political Poets* (7–8). Mathews was a more radical champion of CanLit than Margaret Atwood (*Survival*) or Northrop Frye (*The Bush Garden*), these latter often taken as the standard bearers of Canadian literature in universities. Mathews was particularly outraged by Tallman and *TISH*, American imports from his perspective, to the point of initiating a protest against George Bowering's Governor General's Award in 1970.

5. Andreas Huyssen challenged the narrative of rupture between the modern, postmodern, and avant garde in his *After the Great Divide* of 1986. My phrasing plays on Huyssen's book title. Huyssen argues that American postmodernism offers formal experimentation disconnected from the aim of the social justice he connects with an older European avant garde (170), but he also questions the possibility of retying art to a progressive real-world agenda when cultures everywhere have become heterogeneous (175–76). More bluntly said, the modernist Habermasian argument for the continuation of the enlightenment project runs aground on postmodern conditions such as globalized economics, social heterogeneity, and the balkanizing effect of identity politics.

6. Grahn and Winkler were not at New College at the same time as was Blaser, but Blaser did receive (and save) copies of their lectures.

7. The KSW website has changed since I took this list of panels from it. However, kswnet.org offers a link to "Poetics Statements" given at the New Poetics Colloquium.

8. The postcard from Opal Whiteley to Sophia Nichols Auer is in MsA1a Box 9, Folder 1, Blaser fonds. It is brief and now illegible because the ink has faded.

9. In *Writing Degree Zero*, Barthes says, "we know, for example, that the content of the word 'Order' always indicates repression" (26). The context of this remark is a discussion of "police-state writing," but there is no sure way to separate one mode of language use from another under the vigilance of a self-reflexive practice. Barthes himself writes of this very eloquently later in the book: "There is therefore in every present mode of writing a double postulation: there is the impetus of a break and the impetus of a coming to power, there is the very shape of every revolutionary situation, the fundamental ambiguity of which is that Revolution must of necessity borrow, from what it wants to destroy..." (Barthes [1968] 1980, 87).

CHAPTER 8

Big Poetry

Freed from teaching after his retirement from Simon Fraser at summer's end, 1986, 20 years to the day after hiring on, Blaser turned first toward collecting his work. In an application for a Guggenheim fellowship, sent off in September, he writes that his project is to be the completion of a *Collected Poems, The Holy Forest*, and a *Collected Essays* to be called *Astonishments*. The two volumes are to cover 30 years of work (Blaser 1986, Guggenheim application) as well as new poems for the "Great Companions" series. The Guggenheim, however, was not to be, and in the absence of this support, it would take another seven years for *The Holy Forest* to issue under the editorship of Stan Persky and Michael Ondaatje and 20 years for the essays to appear as *The Fire: Collected Essays of Robin Blaser* (2006) under my editorship. In the meantime, Blaser found himself working overtime in retirement. Peter Quartermain writes in his support of Blaser's Guggenheim application: "There are currently so many demands on his time, from ex-students who refuse to become ex, from universities (like SUNY Buffalo, inviting him to give the Olson lecture this winter), from poets, painters, museum curators, critics, scholars, and editors, that his work is seriously impeded" (Quartermain, 14 December 1986). Impeded or not, Blaser's life over the decade following retirement was rich in new writing and packed with trips and public appearances. In the serials *Pell Mell* (1988) and *Exody* (1993), themes and images nascent in earlier works open out. The essays "Poetry and Positivisms" and "The Recovery of the Public World," two of the most important poetics pieces of this period, elaborate on and consolidate Blaser's major themes: the sacred, open space, and the distinctiveness of poetry as a discourse among others. As Blaser writes humorously, he is "in the tree tops" at this point in his writing life, peering above the branches of the *Forest* (*HF*, 376) (Fig. 8.1).

© The Author(s) 2019
M. Nichols, *A Literary Biography of Robin Blaser*,
Modern and Contemporary Poetry and Poetics,
https://doi.org/10.1007/978-3-030-18327-1_8

Fig. 8.1   Left to right: Brian Fawcett, Stan Persky, and Robin Blaser at Persky's home in Vancouver, 1995. Photo by David Farwell, reproduced courtesy of David Farwell

AIDS

Blaser's work of this period, however, must be contextualized not only in terms of established themes but also as a response to the realpolitik of the 1980s. Ronald Reagan was President of the United States between 1981 and 1989; George Bush Sr. from 1989 to 1993. This was the era in which neo-conservative economic and social policies were being glued into place, the era in which the Christian right made an overt entrance on the political mainstage, and in which President Bush initiated operation Desert Storm following Saddam Hussein's invasion of Kuwait. It was also the era of AIDS. On 5 June 1981, the U.S. Center for Disease Control and Prevention issued its Morbidity and Mortality Weekly Report on five cases of homosexual men with a rare form of pneumonia, usually only found in immune-suppressed patients. Shortly thereafter, on 3 July 1981, the same body reported on 26 cases of Kaposi's sarcoma, a rare form of cancer, in homosexual men in New York and California. Then the *New York Times* published a first news article about the "new" disease. The AIDS epidemic that would soon unfold—159 U.S. cases reported in 1981, 771 in 1982, 2807 in 1983, then upward from there—fueled an already robust homophobia and stoked the anti-gay rhetoric of social conservatives.[1] It is worth remembering that in 1986, the Supreme Court of the United States upheld the anti-sodomy laws of Georgia in Bowers v. Hardwick. Not until 2003, when the same body struck down the constitutionality of state sodomy laws in Lawrence v. Texas did such laws become invalid in the states of Alabama, Florida, Idaho, Kansas, Louisiana, Michigan, Mississippi, Missouri, North Carolina, Oklahoma, South Carolina, Texas, Utah, and Virginia.

In Canada, the tone of anti-gay sentiment was less strident. Pierre Trudeau's Liberal government had decriminalized buggery and abortion in the omnibus bill, C-150, of 1969. Trudeau famously declared that the government had no business in the bedrooms of the nation. However, in the 1980s, police were still raiding bathhouses in Montréal and Toronto on the grounds of indecency and suspected prostitution, and social homophobia was very much alive. For instance, Kenneth Zeller a public-school teacher and librarian was murdered in Toronto's High Park in 1985, beaten to death by five youths. This hate crime prompted his employer, the Toronto District School Board, to implement one of Canada's first programs to combat anti-gay violence.[2]

Blaser's response to the homophobia that surged with the AIDS epidemic of the 1980s was multifaceted. To Paul Monette, a writer who had published a moving account of his lover's, Roger Horwitz's, death from AIDS in 1986, Blaser writes that the books Monette had sent him are "wonders of the heart": *Taking Care of Mrs. Carroll* (1978); *Love Alone: 18 Elegies for Rog* (1987); *Borrowed Time: An AIDS Memoir* (1988), and *Afterlife* (1990). "I do not have aids—," he says to Monette, "age is my only explanation—my thanks for your books which will help me watch over others" (14 March 1990). Blaser was to have plenty of opportunities to watch over others. As David Farwell remembers, AIDS ripped through the gay community around him and Blaser in Vancouver as it did everywhere else. A number of male nurses at St. Paul's hospital where Farwell worked as a therapist died of the disease or committed suicide (Farwell interview, 12 February 2016). At Simon Fraser, Rob Dunham, one of Blaser's closest friends and collaborators[3] in the English Department, first lost a lover, Luis Posse, to AIDS before succumbing himself in 1990. Posse died in 1984. He was a professional interior designer "of such originality and color-intensity that I dubbed him a painter," Blaser says (Blaser 1986, 3). In his last years, Posse turned out to be a poet as well. Blaser and Dunham edited his collection, *Freeing the Shadows*; Blaser wrote the introduction, "No Matter," and Dunham the afterword, "Finisterre." Blaser says in "No Matter" that Posse does not simply speak with a "dying voice"—"self-declaiming and self-descrying," but out of a dis-order of sensibility and syntax that releases him into "a writing that is the other of the boy or man," close to a dictated poetry (Blaser 1986, 5). Dunham comments, citing a poem, that Posse's "'disorder is understanding / chaos by order'" (Dunham 1986, 172). In these commentaries, the hurts of disease and death for both the sufferer and the bereaved are addressed through connection with something larger than the isolating power of pain. This was Blaser's habitual way of consoling himself and others facing personal loss: to remind, and to perform as a poet, his conviction that the cosmos was larger than the individual and the individual was larger than the suffering, thus to diminish pain and create relationships other than those defined by it. Blaser remembers Posse as well in *Pell Mell*. "There-abouts" is dedicated to him, a short little poem stuffed with an offering of spring blooms, in which Blaser acknowledges Posse's isolation in the disease but then drops in to say "hello hello hello" (*HF*, 312).

When Rob Dunham died four years later on Blaser's birthday, 18 May 1990, Blaser was immediately occupied as executor of his estate, a labor that took him some months, sorting out Dunham's beautiful furnishings, kitchen equipment, and large art books, as well as the inevitable paperwork. He also gave a moving tribute to Dunham at the funeral. Dunham taught generations of perplexed students how to read poetry and was much loved for it, winning the SFU Teacher of Excellence Award in 1986 and the 3M Teaching Fellowship in 1988. Always the gentleman, low-voiced, unfailingly courteous, and impeccably dressed, Dunham inspired devotion in the classroom and sartorial envy. One graffito in a men's room at SFU reportedly demanded the name of his tailor. His most assertive act at Simon Fraser was one of frustration at the University's reluctance to grant George Bowering a full professorship: Rob reportedly threw his beloved and much-thumbed Perkins anthology[4] down the hall. The program for the funeral service led with a quotation from Blake's *Milton*:

> There is a Moment in each Day that Satan cannot find
> Nor can his Watch Fiends find it, but the Industrious find
> This Moment & it multiply, & when it once is found
> It renovates every Moment of the Day if rightly placed. (Blake 2008, 194)

The service concluded with one of Dunham's favorite songs, Sam Cooke's "A Change is Gonna Come," poignant in the context of the official indifference and unofficial homophobia to which AIDS gave rise. In a 1991 lecture at the State University of New York (SUNY), Buffalo, Blaser cites a B.C. politician he does not name to the effect that "they"—homosexuals—chose their lifestyle and might as well die in it (Blaser 1991c, n.p.).

Four years later, in 1994, Blaser and friends buried Rory Ralston, a dear friend and neighbor who lived across the street with his partner Grant Wood. As Farwell remembers, the news came after Rory had returned from Edmonton where he had moved for a time to accept a job. Coming home from work, Farwell found Rory and Robin sitting on the back steps. Robin said that they had something to tell. At the funeral, Blaser spoke of Rory's courage, French *coeur*, keeping Rory at the heart of things. Rory was friends with both the upstairs and downstairs of Trafalgar Street, attending therapy sessions with Ellen in Seattle and dropping Ecstasy with her, or popping in for a drink and a chat with Robin and David. Before a trip to New York to take in the theater, he received a scolding from Blaser because he had not included the museums in his itinerary, and, Blaser argued, he, Rory, had pretensions to culture. Shame! Rory mended his ways, Farwell remembers, returning to report on his findings in New York's mega-galleries (Farwell interview, 12 February 2016). The funeral was at the First Nations House of Learning at UBC, 4 December 1994.

Blaser read a passage from Shelley's *Prometheus Unbound* that Rory always liked—"My soul is an enchanted boat"—and then took his listeners to Giorgio Agamben's concept of the "irreparable"—that things are as they *are*, both utterly contingent and necessary at the same time. "In this sense, the world is irreparable, Rory," he writes in his notes for the service, "and strangely joyous" (Blaser 1994b, Eulogy for Ralston).

"Even on Sunday," written for the Gay Games III, held in Vancouver in 1990, 4–11 August, is Blaser's poetic response to the homophobia that accompanied the advent of AIDS. The Games featured 7300 athletes, 27 sports, and an additional 1500 cultural participants. Then provincial Premier Bill Vander Zalm, a populist and social conservative, refused to fund it. Conservatives from a Fraser Valley church took out full page ads in *The Vancouver Sun* and *The Province*, asking followers to gather in prayer at Vancouver's Empire Stadium to stop the "sodomite invasion."[5] The phrase was quickly "turned" as the title of a literary journal: *The Sodomite Invasion Review* ran for four years and six issues as a venue for gay writers. Dodie Bellamy, Kevin Killian, Michael Morris, Stan Persky, George Stanley, and Scott Watson were among the contributors. Editor Don Larventz introduces the journal in its inaugural August 1990 issue as "a collection of gay men's writing, photographs and drawings put together to coincide with the unfolding of the Celebration 90, the Gay and Lesbian Olympics and Cultural and Literary Festival" (Larventz 1990, 1). Blaser contributed "Rose" to that first issue (Blaser 1990, 5), "Even on Sunday" to the Summer 1991 issue (Blaser 1991b, 24–26), and "Image-Nation 24 ('oh, pshaw,'" to Summer 1994 (Blaser 1994, 24–25). "Even on Sunday" begins with this prose passage:

> I don't know anything about God but what the human record tells
> me—in whatever languages I can muster—or by turning to
> translators—or the centuries—of that blasphemy which defines god's
> nature by our own hatred and prayers for vengeance and dominance—
> that *he* (lower case and questionable pronoun) would destroy by a
> hideous disease one lover of another   or by war, a nation for what
> uprightness and economic hide-and-seek—and *he* (lower case and
> questionable pronoun) is on the side of the always-ignorance of politics
> in which we trust—the *polis* is at the 'bottom of the sea,' as Hannah
> Arendt noticed—and *he* (lower case and interrogated pronoun) walks
> among the manipulated incompetences of public thought
>
> where I had hoped to find myself ordinary among others in the
>   streets— (*HF*, 370)

Blaser refers here to rhetoric by the Christian right attributing AIDS to God's punishment of homosexuals.[6] Such cruelty in God's name Blaser calls a blasphemy against the "*existential / given*" (*HF*, 372).

"Even on Sunday" breaks down the language of religious fundamentalism in several ways. First, as the opening of the poem proposes, is the argument that no one knows what God is and claims to the contrary are projections of the human will—"prayers for vengeance and dominance." Secondly, Blaser brings historical context to contemporary homophobia by collaging in passages from Hans Mayer's *Outsiders*. Mayer discusses the construction of majorities and minorities along with the persecution of the latter as "'worthless life'": *"Worthless are the Jews, there the blacks [and / aboriginals], somewhere else (and everywhere) the homosexuals, women / of the type of Judith and Delilah, not least the intellectuals keen on individuation"* (Quoted in *HF*, 373). Back of the long, historical litany of discriminations shorthanded in the poem is an idea of *"unified mankind"* (*HF*, 373), and the history of that effort to unify is a catalog of barbarisms. "[N]ormed existence" (*HF*, 372) creates outsiders by definition, many by fact of birth. The poem makes very clear that Blaser takes homosexuality to be a birthright rather than a lifestyle choice as the Christian right did and does claim it to be.

As part of his SUNY visit in April 1991, Blaser spoke to Charles Bernstein's class. The class was studying "homotextuality" and Blaser's talk is so titled (Blaser 1991c, n.p.). Blaser does not, however, fully engage in the identity politics the topic would seem to indicate. Citing Spicer's jabberwocky nights at the bar, he says that the bar was Spicer's public space, his performance space, and while being gay was a significant component of that social circle, it was not the only one. Jabberwocky night was not just for gays but for poets of any persuasion who could stand up to the occasion. Two considerations, then, distinguish Blaser's position from that of a gay identity politics. The first is that Blaser always refused to let a social role define complex individuals. As he writes in "Utopia," from *Pell Mell*, "what was once called / *being is complexity*—of reunions— / of act—of quality— // of the world" (*HF*, 304). This is a stance that goes back to "Particles" and it is consistent with Blaser's strategy of attacking stereotypes by breaking them down. In the 1991 lecture (Blaser 1991a, n.p.), Blaser makes clear that he is pleased that sexuality can be woven into intellectual and poetic discourses more easily than it could in the 1950s, but he is not comfortable with being solely defined as a gay writer. Secondly, Blaser staked his poetics on a relationship with othernesses. Although feminist language was and is against the term, Blaser says that for him, women are other and that this is a desirable state of affairs. This usage of the word "other" in this context is worth a pause, I think, because it is not the othering of women in the patriarchy Blaser is talking about, or the existential Other that is the unthought, but a nuanced and built relationship between a singular gay man and the singular women in his life—living and dead—that is based on the wonder and mystery of a mode of being that is not one's own. Sappho, he says, offers a world-sized sexuality—sexuality as mode of the world—and an opportunity to engage with that distinctive female energy.

In 1992, Blaser was invited to participate in the summer writing program at Naropa University in Denver, Colorado, an invitation that would soon enough involve him in more thought about AIDS-fueled homophobia. Each week of the summer program was differently themed. That first year, Blaser's week (July 12–18) was titled "Re-Search and Investigative Poetics: The Political

Front." Anne Waldman and Andrew Schelling directed the program; other participants there at the same time as Blaser were Lorna Dee Cervantes, Rachel Blau DuPlessis, Clayton Eshleman, Bobbie Louise Hawkins, Linda Hogan, Anselm Hollo, Erica Hunt, Robert Kelly, Judith Johnson, Pierre Joris, Ted Pearson, Ishmael Reed, Diane Rothenberg, Jerome Rothenberg, David Levi Strauss, and Peter Lamborn Wilson. Blaser gave a lecture titled "Belief, Doubt, and Politics" in which he again interrogates fundamentalist religious beliefs. As soon as one begins to think of the meaning and history of the word "cosmos," he says, or "book" or "God" for that matter, dogmatism breaks down. "Belief" itself is a word that is "a plain effort to name—in order to be able to point at—a condition of <u>holding dear</u>—something or another, even ourselves. And the violence of it, the sacrifice to or for or of it—the dogmatics of it—even the <u>hypertely of immortality</u> of it—ah these!—are, at least, evidence of anthropological stampedes in our running about to arrange things. Our Dis-courses! (<u>dis-currare</u>—<u>to run to</u> and fro)" (Blaser 1992a, "Belief").

The evidence in his correspondence suggests that Blaser enjoyed this teaching gig at Naropa and he would return many times, right up until his health began to fail in 2005. Writing to Waldman and Schelling in August after his visit, he says, "How rich my return from Boulder was—weighted with books by both of you—by Bobbie, Jerome, Diane, Kelly, Tarn—mss. by David L-S [Levi Strauss]—letters in the mail from Nathaniel and Rachel—important! for me—to which I'll now take time to turn—" (21 August 1992). In 1993, however, he refused what would become an annual invitation for reasons political as well as personal. To Waldman and Schelling, he apologizes for not being able to get an edited version of his talk to them for publication. He is exhausted, he says, from other commitments—a catalog essay for the Duncan exhibition at Berkeley,[7] an essay for the first volume of a Duncan collected poems,[8] and executor's duties to the Spicer estate. He was also working on "Bach's Belief," an essay that Olson had requested nearly 25 years prior as Blaser's contribution to the *Curriculum of the Soul* series.[9] Then in the midst of it all, his mother died. These personal challenges I will come back to, but Blaser also refused the Naropa invitation for political reasons. To Waldman and Schelling, he writes:

> ...I was taken off guard, that the Republican Convention—not mindless, but certainly vicious of mind—would become percussive in my mind's belief—embodied, as it must be, if we are to understand this empowerment of the most vicious Christianism—loose, many-headed, American horror that it is. Watch democracy become the shadow of our concern. And this, during the few days I'm trying to explain in terms of exhaustion, is joined by the Vatican advisory that it is acceptable to "discriminate" against homosexuals.... What is <u>existentially given</u> is once again viciously attacked (just as I read it there in "Even on Sunday"). Now, you may well recognize another reason I have, especially, had to stop—in order to find my way. I <u>rage</u>. I sit here, writing you, fighting my rage. I wish to throw the trash of this tradition out. We've long stood in the empowerment of this anthropological fear and ignorance, which attracts all definitions of outsiders and outsiderness. (21 August 1992)

The homophobic Christianism Blaser references here would, in the fall of 1992, manifest in the Colorado passage of Amendment 2 to the State constitution that denied homosexuals protection against discrimination. In the terms of the Supreme Court ruling that eventually struck it down in 1996, this Amendment had first "the peculiar property of imposing a broad and undifferentiated disability on a single named group, an exceptional and, as we shall explain, invalid form of legislation. Second, its sheer breadth is so discontinuous with the reasons offered for it that the amendment seems inexplicable by anything but animus toward the class that it affects; it lacks a rational relationship to legitimate state interests" (Romer v. Evans 1996).

Colorado's anti-gay legislation touched Blaser at the nerve centers of his thought—his lifelong work on the sacred, his recent thinking of Sappho and Anne Carson for the New School lectures in the early 1980s, and his Arendtian understanding of the division between public and private life that went back to "Particles." Arendt speaks to the necessity of private space for the individual as a place for personal regeneration away from the glare of public scrutiny (Arendt 1959, 62–64). This, Blaser notes, the anti-sodomy laws would deny to homosexuals because such laws open the bedroom practices of gays—but not heterosexuals—to public scrutiny. The upshot of this Blaser rage was that he did not go to Naropa in 1993, despite pleas from Schelling and Ginsberg not to desert the resistance there. However, he did give an interview on KGNU, an alternative radio station in Boulder in July of that year, in which he says that homophobic legislation comes from "religion turned political power—ancient, hieratic, a kingdom—not democratic or inclusive—but theocratic—" (Blaser 1993b, n.p.). The interview reprises Blaser's position as explicated in his correspondence with Waldman and Schelling, and in "Even on Sunday."

Great Companion: Robert Duncan

In 1993, under the editorship of Stan Persky and Michael Ondaatje, Blaser's poems were made available in collected form for the first time (Blaser 1993a). One important tonal through-line in the later series, interwoven with the major Blaser themes, is the elegiac. I have mentioned the poem for Luis Posse; Canadian poet bp Nichol (1944–1988) is also remembered in "'the universe is part of ourselves'" from *Pell Mell* (*HF*, 269), in which Blaser celebrates the "dis-creation, the kindness of fragments" (*HF*, 269) in Nichol's work.[10] Nichol died of complications from a surgery at the age of 44. In another elegy, "For Barry Clinton, d. 17 June 1984, of aids," Blaser pays tribute to a "dear blue-eyed / painter" with bunches of flowers—"iris, columbine—your favorite" (*HF*, 314). "[D]emi-tasse (an elegy," dated 18 April 1988, is a requiem for poetry itself as one of the composing discourses of public life:

> the silence surrounds me   political silence   where
>   the words were deeds once upon a time and space
>   social silence   where a fragile good composes   bankruptcies

of ideas run through two centuries   my centuries, watching
the poets sit on the shelves. (*HF*, 330)

Blaser's obituary tribute to Robert Graves, "Image-Nation 22 (in memoriam" is another elegy. Graves's excavation of Mediterranean myth revises its goddesses and "give[s] Jesus / back to time" (*HF*, 345). This kind of work parallels Blaser's own in its breakdown of mythic figures and events into mobile historical relations rather than elements of dogma. Graves gets back behind Judeo-Christianity to find that "*the Female on whom Jesus declared war was Aggrath Bat Machlat / (Alukah, by cacophemism, the horse-leech) whose daughters / Womb and Grave*—are / ISHTAR" (*HF*, 345).

Blaser's major elegiac effort of the late 1980s, however, was "Great Companion: Robert Duncan." Duncan died of kidney disease on 3 February 1988 after a long struggle on dialysis. In *The Astonishment Tapes*, Blaser is clear that his debt to Duncan is "enormous" (*AT*, 66), but he is equally clear that their relationship was fraught. The two had managed many social occasions since the *Les Chimères* dust-up, but these did not erase that event. "Robert Duncan: Great Companion" is a sort-through of Blaser's complex feelings for this important friend as well as a tribute. Many of the allusions in the poem are double-edged: they refer to and honor key poems and components of Duncan's poetic practice, but they also serve to draw out the dissonances between Duncan and Blaser. Then, layered over and under the memorial, is a meditation on poetry, death, and the heart. The poem begins by thinking about poetry ("the continuous / *carmen*")—rather than eternity[11]—as the place where dead poets meet and then picks up movement as "Berkeley shimmers and shakes" in memory. Suddenly, Rosario Jiménez pops out from behind a hedge at a gas station:

> ...Lady Rosario among us   of Spanish and Greek
>   rushes
> from the hedges around the gas station,
>   swirled with Lawrence's medlars and
> sorb-apples. (*HF*, 335)

This passage is based on an incident that Blaser recounts in *The Astonishment Tapes*. Jiménez had not only steered Duncan's Throckmorton reading circle through Lorca, but had given Blaser Greek lessons.

> She went quite crazy often, and I remember once when she took her entire library and threw it out on Union Street, stopping all traffic, and wound up in the hoosegow. Duncan and I went and got her out. And then another time she went kooky and I was walking down Telegraph Avenue and this incredible woman came flying out of the bushes at me and it terrified me, quite literally, even though I'd suddenly recognized who it was. She had the little Penguin edition of *The Selected Poems of D.H. Lawrence* and wanted to read me that wonderful one about the bruised apple, and so we went to a Standard gas station and stood there, oblivious

to traffic, and the gas station attendant is furious at us while she read this
D.H. Lawrence poem on the bruised apple with the interior, you know that marvelous poem—the bruise will open to let everything spill out. (*AT,* 199)

From this memory of Jiménez, Blaser moves associatively to the Greek lessons
and the "*white gods*" of mythology, letting the scent of the bruised apple from
the Lawrence poem carry him from one memory to the next:

<blockquote>
What

is it reminds us of white gods
flesh-fragrant
as if with sweat   *the delicious rottenness* that teems with
the life of the mind's heart   κρατήρ of an agreement, a mixing vessel,
a chasm, a threshold—βάθρον—stair of
brazen steps, hollow wild pear tree—κοίλεσ τάχέρδου
—between   among
sat down. (*HF,* 335)
</blockquote>

The very ancient gods, Ernst Cassirer once proposed, were momentary. They
appeared whenever humanity invested emotionally in some encounter (Cassirer
1953, 17–18). Blaser had considered poetic form in similar terms in "The
Fire" where he says that poetry retains the record of "meetings" with the world
(*Fire,* 4). Like Jiménez jumping out from behind the bushes or a god suddenly
manifesting, form, he thought, rises up when inner and outer worlds converge
in a memorable way and then it passes away again in the entwined flights of life
and language from that moment. This was an important difference in focus
between Blaser and Duncan: Duncan understood form as evolving multifari-
ously from "primordial patterns" as he says in "The Truth and Life of Myth"
(Duncan 1985, 34), not as a temporary coalescence of energies. Blaser puts
forward his side of this poetics story in "Image-Nation 5 (erasure," a poem
responding to the *Les Chimères* episode, where he writes of "the old Bedouin
poets" and their "encampments of / what was / a movement" (*HF,* 151). In
this Jiménez passage, Blaser gets in a memory of early Berkeley, a salute to
Duncan's love of myth, and an oblique nod toward their long-running
disagreement.

From "*white gods,*" Blaser moves to another Greek lesson: the death of
Oedipus in *Oedipus at Colonus.* The mixing vessel, the threshold, the "stair /
of brazen steps" and the "hollow wild pear tree" come from the last scene of
the play where Oedipus must be left alone to die. The scene of his death, or of
the gods taking him, cannot be spectated or spoken. He is there and then he is
not there. The astonishment of death is that it is so common and yet so utterly
mysterious. After Oedipus has gone, Antigone says that "something invisible
and strange / Caught him up—or down— / Into a space unseen" (Sophocles
1954, 151). So too, Duncan is there and then not. In this, as in other elegies,
Blaser loiters in the place of death, pondering.

So the poem advances in a series of dense, clotted allusions. The next lines return to Berkeley and the dynamics of those 1940s friendships.

> I am only leonine in the
> breath of night   awakening blurred neighbours   as your
> faces move   Jack writing the Italian underground   *we*
> *are too tired to live like lions*   on john walls   and gay-bars (*HF*, 335)

Duncan references the lion repeatedly. In *Caesar's Gate*, a swarm of bees emerge from the body of a lion (Duncan 1972, 66), just as Duncan would pull word out of word from his *lines*. The bees are "the swarm of our thought," he says (Duncan 1972, 66), and the image of the swarm (words, letters, meanings) emerging from a lion / line catches his method. In his "Preface for the Early Poems of Robert Duncan," Blaser cites Duncan's note on lions from the poetics statement in Donald Allen's *The New American Poetry*:

> For me, the Lion is the Child, the unfettered intellect that knows in his nobility none of the convictions and dogmas which human mind inflicts itself with—what is the human desire to humiliate even its own being?
>   For me, the Lion is the sexual appetite that knows no contradiction within itself. (Quoted in *Fire*, 301)

The lion sequence separates Duncan and Blaser as it relates them. In an interview with Samuel Truitt a decade later, Blaser responds to a question about the lion in this poem.

> Well certainly the lion for me is not a totem. That is I do not see myself as the lion…. The leonine is just a momentary condition of great force and fury. And power. And that I would not claim for myself very often. But it's also one of the great images that come to mind out of memory, whether it be the great walls from Assyria or elsewhere. And it's also one that Duncan liked very much. And Spicer very much liked that phrase "we are too tired to live like lions." (Truitt 1996, 20–21)

Blaser explains in this interview that Spicer had found the phrase in a history of Italian fascism. Mussolini liked to say, "'We must be lions'"; the Italian resistance responded with "'we are too tired to live like lions.'" Spicer "loved it," Blaser says, and "he liked to pin things on john walls" (Truitt 1996, 20). In the context of early Berkeley, with Duncan assuming leadership of the poetry scene and Spicer coming up as the challenger, this reference to Mussolini and the resistance resonates humorously with the local situation, even as it celebrates Duncan as a lion of poetry.

    In the next sequence, the heart sequence, Blaser pushes off from the first Duncan poem he ever read in Berkeley, 1946:

> the first of your poems
> I read: *Among my friends love is a great sorrow* (brought to me
> in typescript by Jack,   1946,   that we three should meet)—no voice
> like it   turns, turns   in the body of thought   *Among*
> *my friends love is a wage / that one might have for an honest living*
>   turns, turns
>   in thought's body   becomes
> *Oh Lovers, I am only one of you!*
> *We, convivial in what is ours!*
>   this ringing
> with Dante's voice before the comedy
>
> sorrow   and guide-dance   the courage of the work   the language
> is a lion   sentinels are owls   of work's body   glamouring passages
> the poem WHOSE alongside James Hillman's *thought of the heart*
> (*HF*, 336)

Shared with Duncan back then were the excitements of learning, making, and falling in love—the soirées at Throckmorton and the composition of *Medieval Scenes* at the O'Neills'. But as the thought "turns, turns," a more mature Duncan comes into focus with the "Dante Études" (Duncan 1984, 94–134) and Duncan's variation on the *Convivio* in that series (Duncan 1984, 120–21). The "Études" belong to Duncan's later work, but in the context of Blaser's poem, the lines "*Oh Lovers, I am only one of you! / We, convivial in what is ours!*" evoke the Berkeley companionships. The "*thought of the heart*" is the connective tissue in the above passage. Duncan's poem "WHOSE," from *Ground Work II*, is dedicated to James Hillman's book of that title (*The Thought of the Heart*). Duncan writes that the heart is "door-man double-hinge[d]," an "ex- / change artist" (Duncan 1987, 81), where the inner and outer worlds meet. In *Cups* 3, Blaser had imagined the poet with "two small windows / cut in his skin" (*HF*, 33). "[W]hose / heart"? Blaser asks, reading the poem. The question returns to the "Dante Études" because the venture of the *Commedia* pushes off when Amor gives the poet's heart away to the Beloved. Venturing the heart takes courage and it is Duncan's *coeur-age* as a writer and a public intellectual that is to be celebrated.

> Jess tells me you just went, having the heart to   whose
> heart?   I wish to say mine   impertinence   yours   that too
> is impertinence   nevertheless, always against the heart
> failures: *cowardice, nostalgia, sentimentalism, aestheticizing, doubt,*
> *vanity, withdrawal, trepidation*
>   fierce, you
>
> *name many times this uprising*
> *—political, mental, sexual, social—you name it—mounting rung by*
> *rung*

> *this climax to what overview*
>
> > *under the double axe*
> >
> > > whose heart. (*HF*, 336)

Duncan's political poetry comes in with the word "uprising," the title of "Up Rising," his best-known anti-Vietnam war poem (Duncan 1968, 81–83). In lines taken from "WHOSE," Blaser celebrates Duncan's courage in the "mental, sexual, social" dimensions as well as the political (Duncan 1987, 82). One thinks of Duncan's "The Homosexual in Society," published in 1944 at a time when homosexuality was illegal, or of his courage as a poet in exploring the language in ways that literary culture had not then prepared for. In "WHOSE," Duncan refers to his own excitability in the steps mounting to a "climax": "my heart was in my throat … my blood / pressure crested as if to arrest // I will name many times this uprising" (Duncan 1987, 82). Resituated in Blaser's poem, the steps *"mounting rung by / rung"* circle back to the "brazen steps" and the place of death.

As he does do in his elegies, Blaser brings flowers to this occasion. The next segment kicks off with "lilies" that "burn rose-orange and yellow" (*HF*, 337), a fiery bouquet from a poet who had made fire his element. These flowers bring to mind Blaser's "The Fire," the essay that Blaser wrote in response to the *Les Chimères* quarrel. There is some edgy humor in what follows:

> stopped over the 'Instant Mythology,' knowing
> an old language from you   one-inch capsules in the hot water
> break at both ends, then burst   purple, green, red, blue,
> 'pour enfants ages 5 ans et plus, pas comestible, chaque
> capsule peut contenir: Centaure, Dragon, Pégase, Licorne,
> Sirène—calling—mettez la capsule dans l'eau tiede / chaude
> et regardez un caractère mythologique apparaître'   techno-myth
> translates out of the real book into the way language
> works   regardez! (*HF*, 337)

George MacDonald (*Phantastes, At the Back of the North Wind*), Charles Kingsley (*The Water-Babies*), Mary Butts (*Armed with Madness*) are just a few from the "old language" that Duncan loved and shared with his friends. These are books of "lore"—children's fairy tales or in Butts's case a re-do of the Grail legend. Blaser brings an "'Instant Mythology'" kit to the memory, literally a child's toy. Add water to the packaged capsules and watch the creatures emerge! Blaser gets in a sly dig at Duncan's fascination with drawing much from little by closely listening to the built-in ambiguities and sensual properties of language. "'[P]our enfants ages 5 ans et plus,'" as per instructions on the packet. With some heat from the fiery flowers and a little water, Blaser tries the same trick, albeit in his own style:

>   the travois of the poetic mind,
>   the drag-load harnessed to the body,   fierily, through
>   the glowing flowers   warm and hot, the watery spell of
>   any reel of language   *poluphloisboíous sea-coast*
>
>   window-rain is *Heimat*.... (*HF*, 337)

The "reel of language" might bring to mind language unreeling itself frame by frame like an analog film, or language reeling in dance or drunkenness, reeling the world in. The "real" is there as a homonym in the word as well, and few words were more important to Duncan, Spicer, and Blaser. Spicer was "devoted" to the real[12]; Duncan, in "An Alternate Life" from *Ground Work II*, says, "So I love what is 'real.' How awkwardly we name it: / the 'actual', the 'real', the 'authentic'—What Is" (Duncan 1987, 4). The "real" is a word that, like a magic capsule, expands into the life's work of all three poets. The Greek word "*poluphloisboíous*" is another such. It is a word anglicized from Homer, meaning "loud, resounding." In a letter to W. H. D. Rouse, 1935, Pound glossed it as "the turn of the wave and the scutter of receding pebbles" (Ruthven 1969, 172–73). In the context of Blaser's poem, the word evokes the coastlines in Berkeley and Vancouver. It also brings to mind Odysseus as a figure of the twentieth-century poet. Pound's *Cantos* begin this way, with a retelling of Odysseus's journey to Hades to inquire of Tiresias the way home. In his "Author's Note" to the second edition of *The Holy Forest*, Blaser writes: "The whole thing: just trying to be at home. That's the plot" (Blaser 2006b, xxv). Another key word in the above cited passage is "Heimat": home is the ultimate aim of the Odyssean poet who has to go to hell first to find out how to get there. The German word brings Heidegger into the poem associatively, through the essays in *Poetry, Language, Thought*: "Poetically Man Dwells," for instance, is a meditation on a poem by Hölderin in which Heidegger thinks about how humanity might learn to make homely its place on earth, under sky. But then the word "Heimat" and the Heideggerian resonance of it brings in a whisper of the terrible war—and Heidegger's rectorship under the Third Reich[13]—that literally destroyed the "Heimat" of so many and created so much hell, so many homeless.

So the poem remembers, praises, mourns for, and quarrels with Duncan. "I gather as I must images of *independent realities*," Blaser writes (*HF*, 339). At the end of the poem, he brings in the Greek word *kēr* which Duncan had translated by sound in "WHOSE" as "care," noting that "the etymology is false" (Duncan 1987, 81). Blaser gives another false etymology in "core" (*HF*, 339) before correcting himself. The word "heart" is related etymologically to the Greek *kēr*; the *Keres*, however, are the Greek death goddesses.

> Care—κήρ—κήρ   together the heart and the goddess, who
> is κήρες plural among things. (*HF*, 340)

This word belongs to the nexus of key words that the poem orbits: death, heart, core, care. Blaser returns at the end to the last lines of "WHOSE." Duncan writes:

> Who then   is this passion
> that returns for me?   who then
> that remembers and goes back for me?
> "I"   –   "me"   no longer mine   —your
> sudden call   I did not mean
> to climb the ladder of. (Duncan 1987, 82)

And Blaser writes:

> *a sudden call*   *to climb the ladder of*   which you
> *did not mean*   because it does not mean, though
> it is recited   *'Never' being the name of what is infinite*
>
> of cross-ways
> of brazen
> steps (*HF*, 340)

To the question, "who goes back for me," Blaser answers with this poem, "I do," walking "cross-ways," alongside and athwart Duncan, to the place of death.

THE HOLY FOREST TOURS

The first edition of *The Holy Forest* (Blaser 1993a) allowed Blaser, as well as his readers and friends, to see the curve of his thinking and writing. Creeley did the "Foreword" to the collection and this occasioned a flurry of faxes before the fall release of the book in 1993. In the era of faxes, these became Blaser's preferred way of communicating with everyone. He liked the written record, and the control it gave him over a conversation (not too long). To Creeley, he writes, "The book is called The Holy Forest—it turns out that I've been writing just one long 'thing,' since 1959—so it is collected, rather than selected, but I've asked Coach House not to use the word collected as part of the title— it misrepresents the ongoing busyness that I just happened to collect as far as it goes" (3 May 1993). On receiving Creeley's "Afterword,"

> Dear Bob, it's JUST RIGHT—leading into—and intimate in the finest way. For the 'reader' I pretended to be, it's exactly what I need to know (for me myself, it's a thrill of reassurance). (23 July 1993)

So *The Holy Forest* inched its way into the world. On receiving his copy, Creeley sent warm compliments and Blaser was equally pleased. Writing to Margaret McClintock at Coach House Press, he says "The Holy Forest is beautiful in my eyes, and I didn't want to wait until Monday to fax you saying so. I'm sitting here leafing through Stan's copy—celebrating" (6 November 1993).

Blaser had been traveling extensively since his release from teaching duties, and the trips around *The Holy Forest* began before the book was actually out, with a reading tour of SUNY Buffalo, Boston, and Brown University in Providence. The Buffalo reading, which Creeley introduced, was recorded, 15 September 1993, and has been made publically available on PennSound (Blaser 1993c). In Boston, Michael Franco hosted Blaser in a reading series called "Word of Mouth" on 19 September 1993. The reading was held at Tapas Restaurant and accompanied by selected posters, books and broadsides by Jess. Blaser had contributed handsomely to an Albright-Knox Art Gallery display of Jesses in the summer of 1993.[14] For this leg of the tour, Blaser stayed in Gloucester with old friend Gerrit Lansing. Although they didn't meet often, Blaser always remembered Lansing with affection for his erudition, his poetry, and his defense of *Les Chimères* contra Duncan. In *The Astonishment Tapes*, Blaser says that Lansing knew that he (Blaser) "was doing something very special in the language and he catches that it's musical" (*AT*, 70).

At Providence, Blaser gave a reading and connected with poet and publisher Samuel Truitt, then a student at Brown University, who would later interview him in Washington, DC. The Truitt interview was held on 18 April 1994 at the Embassy Row Hotel where Robin and David were staying and revised in the summer of 1996 for publication in *Talisman*. In this important interview, Blaser talks about *The Holy Forest*, the serial poem, dictation, the sacred, and his "great companions." On the serial, for instance, he says:

> My own suspicion is that we [Spicer and Blaser] had also perhaps been listening a little bit to what was going on at the Tape Music Center in San Francisco. This would be the early 1960s. This was a place where wonderful composers like Pauline Oliveras were working. And there were other wonderful people. As a matter of fact David Tudor was in town.... And I've often wondered if we did not in some sense ... if we'd not become sensitive to the term out of music without ourselves really knowing much about the process of serial composition in music.... But it's a particular experience of the poem that you do not have the simple, direct plain lyric control. In some way you've given up lyric control. The "I" as subject who controls everything is not there. (Blaser 1996, 10–11)

Dictation is another topic of the Truitt interview. Blaser was reading Avital Ronell at the time, *Dictations: On Haunted Writing* and *Finitude's Score*. He relates her talk of haunted writing to Spicer's "low-ghosts" (a Spicerian pun on "logos"). However, Blaser says, "I do not use the word dictation to describe my own writing process. For me, dictation belongs to Jack, who earned it and undertook its dangers..." (Blaser 1996, 13). When Truitt turns him toward the sacred, Blaser says that the sacred is shifting (18) and this is where his difference lies with Duncan: "My quarrel with Duncan was about where the sacred was. And I am saying it is not behind us but here. Now. In the moment" (18). Nonetheless, Duncan remains a "great companion." Other "companions" named in the interview are Sappho, Lucretius, Virgil, Dante, Montaigne,

Olson, Creeley, and Spicer, although Blaser says he doesn't want to name them all because that would be to tempt "black magic" (21). There should be a poem for Spicer in addition to "The Practice of Outside," Blaser says, although "a lot of energy went off" with that essay (22). Questioned on his choices, Blaser says:

> The basic level is that these writers have written what I could not write. What I did not write. And that they are moments of … I choose the common … moments of intense consciousness for me. I find them and I read them. And I'm ravenous. I read everything as I read through them. And they become points at which that radiance … They are the process of that radiance and they are pointing toward modes of moving into the world that I find absolutely magical. (Blaser 1996, 21)

Blaser followed the Buffalo–Boston–Providence tour with more of the same. In March of 1994, poet Jeff Derksen invited Blaser and Creeley to participate on a panel titled "Nationalisms and Poetic Communities" as part of the Markin-Flanagan Distinguished Writers Program at the University of Calgary. After Calgary, in April of that spring, Blaser accepted an invitation from Rachel Blau DuPlessis to read at Temple University in Philadelphia in the "Poets and Writers Series." This Philadelphia trip, apart from the art galleries and restaurants, included a dinner with DuPlessis, Marjorie Perloff, and graduate students (Blaser to Thesen, 9 April 1994). Farwell accompanied Blaser this time, and they moved on to Washington after the Temple gig. Hosted by poet Tom Mandel, they combined an art crawl with a reading at the Cafe Riche—a "wonderfully funky place with books lining the bar," David writes of it—about 25 for dinner and 35 for the reading (Farwell 1994, notebook). Another notable gig was the Berkeley launch of *The Holy Forest* in June 1994. Blaser stayed at the Durant and read at Black Oak Books—his reading arranged by Ira Silverberg and introduced by Michael McClure. A "full, seated audience, plus drop-ins" he reports to Laura MacDonald at Coach House (13 June 1994)—"signed lots of The Holy Foret" [sic]. On this trip, he spent "over 5 hours" in "splendid conversation" with Jack Foley, interviewing for public radio, KPFA and *Poetry Flash* (Blaser to MacDonald, 13 June 1994). With Steve Dickison of Small Press Distribution in Berkeley, he took a "3 hour walking 'talk,'" promising a "'talk-style' essay" for Dickison's series *Dictation*. In San Francisco, Kevin Killian and Norma Cole arranged a reception for Blaser at Small Press Traffic— "jam packed … food, wine and the most intelligent audience possible" (Blaser to MacDonald, 13 June 1994).

In October 1994, Blaser traveled to SUNY, Albany. A write-up in the *Gazette Reporter* (24 October 1994) by Patrick Kurp introduces Blaser as "one of those misplaced artists whose work is ignored or misunderstood or, worse, ignored because it is misunderstood," a comment that would become less true as *The Holy Forest* circulated. On this trip, Blaser gave a round table discussion with Olson scholar Don Byrd and poet-scholar Pierre Joris titled "Toward a *Fin de Siecle* Poetics." In a note to Blaser after these events, Kurp thanks Blaser for the reading and compares *The Holy Forest* to the "wisdom books" of Montaigne (*Essais*), Burton (*Anatomy of Melancholy*), and Melville (*Moby-Dick*) (28 October 1994). About this trip, Blaser comments to Sharon Thesen, "Albany with Pierre Joris and Don Byrd—Nicole Peyrafitte and Marge Byrd equally pleasures—3 two hour 'talks' and a reading—everything seeming to me plots for a future in writing—a rich 'mental' community there—" (31 October 1994).

BIG POETRY AND THE RECOVERY OF THE PUBLIC WORLD

The Recovery of the Public World Conference of 1995, 1–4 June, was one such gathering of a "'mental' community." It was planned over the preceding year by a core committee of Blaser's Vancouver friends, most of them former students— Edward Byrne, Tom McGauley, Charles Watts, and I met at the house of Karen Tallman and Brian DeBeck—and timed to celebrate Blaser's 70th birthday. Toward the end of the process, many more from the Vancouver community came together in the form of dozens of volunteers and multiple institutional sponsors. Charles Watts worked wonders in getting out grant applications and invitations to the poetry world. Christos Dikeakos designed a poster that featured a back-of-the-head photo of Blaser sitting at his desk, surrounded by books flying through the air. Dikeakos, Karen Tallman, and Brian DeBeck handled the food for the Friday night banquet at Vancouver's Heritage Hall, 3102 Main Street. Somehow, they loaded an industrial-sized barbeque on a truck and fed the multitude. The hall was decorated in white and purple. Someone had decorated Blaser, too, with a large leafy laurel crown, before he was teased and roasted with stories from hosts Kevin Killian and Ellen Tallman (Fig. 8.2).

The "Recovery" conference was a big, four-day affair, with poets and scholars from the U.S., the U.K., Canada, and Australia. Scott Watson arranged for an art show at the Charles H. Scott Gallery, directly across the lane from the conference venue at the Emily Carr College of Art and Design on Granville Island. The show was titled "In Search of Orpheus: Some Bay Area Poets and

Fig. 8.2 Blaser at the opening dinner of the Recovery of the Public World Conference, Vancouver, B.C., 1995. Photo by David Farwell, reproduced courtesy of David Farwell

Painters 1945–65" with work by Helen Adam, Paul Alexander, Lyn Brockway, Tom Field, Fran Herndon, Harry Jacobus, Jess, John Butler, Duncan, Spicer, and Blaser himself. Writing of the show for the SUNY Buffalo poetics listserv[15] after, Kevin Killian notes that Fran's work really shone, and that she got a standing ovation at the opening. The four days were packed from morning to afternoon with panels; evenings were given to group poetry readings. In spite of the busyness, the feeling was festive. Granville Island was not only the site of Emily Carr then, but of a public market, a theater, the Scott Gallery, and numerous artisanal shops and eating places.

In his review of the conference, Killian remarks on the book table, organized by Black Sheep Books. It featured bargains such as a White Rabbit edition of Helen Adam's *The Queen o' Crow Castle* (1958), illustrated by Jess, for a mere $15: "Try and get one in San Francisco for less than $100.00," Killian writes. Otherwise, "Dodie is right about Susan Howe & that she stole the show during this one long reading with 22 poets"; "Steve McCaffery is a God"; and "Joanne Kyger read a piece about seeing Quan Yin-the-Buddhist goddess—or whatever—and Dodie interviewed her in the women's 'washroom' asking her if she really saw Quan Yin and JK said, 'Yes, but you have to be on the right substance'" (Killian 1995). Killian notes with wonder that Blaser attended everything (the stamina!) and had the last word with a reading of "Exody," "Even on Sunday," and "Nomad."

Beyond the grand party that it was, the conference was significant in a number of ways. It produced spin-off publications, for instance. In *Sulfur* 37, editor Clayton Eshleman published a number of conference papers, including Charles Watts's "Foreword," and Blaser's conference address, "Hello!" As Watts writes, the conference was the "first occasion to present diverse examination and celebration of Robin Blaser's life work in poetry" (Watts 1995, 82). In "Hello!" Blaser thanks "this extraordinary gathering" (Blaser 1995a, 85) and reiterates the main argument of his "Recovery" essay: that reality is "multidimensional and multi-logical" (89) and the reduction of it invites the perils of dogmatism. In this *Sulfur* issue, the conference papers of Jed Rasula and Peter Quartermain also appear along with Blaser's poem, "Nomad" (Blaser 1995c, 117). Another important publication commemorating the conference was Ralph Maud's special issue #8 of the *Minutes of the Charles Olson Society*. This issue included a conference schedule (2–3) and Blaser's memoire of his first meeting with Olson (Blaser 1995e, 4–14). Maud also published a number of Olson–Blaser letters. The major publication from the conference, though, was *The Recovery of the Public World*, edited by Watts and Byrne. This volume, with sections titled "Companions," "Translation," "Heterologies," and "The Outside," consists of edited versions of the conference papers. Some conference goers presented papers on Blaser, but many also presented in areas apposite to Blaser—essays on Spicer or Language poetry or theory. The occasion, after all, invited meditation on a "public world." *Even on Sunday*, a latecomer in the spin-off publications in 2002, was a collection of essays and archival materials on Blaser meant to sharpen the focus on exegesis and provide some archival context for Blaser's poems (Nichols 2002).

So what came of this event? Certainly it called together some strong movers in the poetry world. Not everyone, however, was sold on the idea of a *recovery* of the public world, nor did they agree that there had ever been a public world to recover. In retrospect, the conference papers catch a mood in the thinking and practice of poetry that reflects academic and poetry communities in the 1990s as well as the broader historical moment. Beneath the fun, the food, the compliments, and the schmoozing, were some undercurrents, like those at the Spicer conference, that could have made for contention. I have argued that Blaser's work is contrary to some of the trends that marked the theory decades. These trends shifted the terms of the conversation about poetry far away from Blaser's Dantean project of making a world image. What the conference left unspoken was a deep conversation about this project. Without that conversation, it simply slipped away with Blaser suitably fêted and rather better known than he had been before, but never taken on seriously. I have singled out three moments of the conference that I think capture important intellectual positions of the 1990s, all of them contrary to Blaser's project. I will sketch these out and then place Blaser's "big poetry"—Dantean poetry—in this context to see how it fares.

My first example is a paper given by Adorno scholar, Robert Hullot-Kentor. He begins an essay titled "Past Tense: Ethics, Aesthetics, and the Recovery of the Public World" this way:

> Those of you clinging to the sides of your chairs in dread anticipation of a discussion of ethics, aesthetics and the public world can relax. I don't intend to launch into these matters with any pretence that they are alive to us; as if the various debates implicit in the topic are just waiting for troops to join battle. Though not so long ago people did vigorously discuss such issues without too terrible a sense of putting themselves on, these concepts and their nexus now have a stale, remote, archaic quality. A team of archaeologists sent out on their behalf that somehow turned up their mummified remains in a cache of steel grey army trunks and unraveled the shrouds would—under their very eyes—see these concepts change to dust. (Hullot-Kentor 1999, 365)

In the essay that follows, Hullot-Kentor says that the public realm has always been "a façade for economic manipulation" (Hullot-Kentor 1999, 370). The ever-intensifying effects of transnational capitalism, however, mean that the individual can no longer even imagine a world because the social whole has disappeared into the everywhere and nowhere of the global market that, Hullot-Kentor says, delivers brutal inequality under the mask of formal rights (371). Dialectical opposition to an everywhere and nowhere is simply not thinkable and we are left with the "slack ideal of cultural multiplicity" in place of real change "that is sensed as beyond our powers" (372). The "recovery" of a public world is therefore doubly delusional: first, because there has never been a public world to begin with, and second, because the world as it is eludes the mechanisms of political control.

Hullot-Kentor's point that the social whole cannot be grasped experientially because of world changes that have exacerbated a democratic deficit is oddly complemented by philosophies that have undermined the credibility of a shared world image: which world? whose world? In a completely different kind of discourse, Steve McCaffery makes the point in his conference essay titled "Blaser's Deleuzean Folds." The essay shows how theory—perhaps inadvertently—contributes to the collapse of worldliness. McCaffery reads Blaser through the philosophy of Deleuze and with good reason: Blaser turned to the baroque explicitly in "Image-Nation 25 (Exody" where he collages in passages from Deleuze's *The Fold* (*HF*, 396). McCaffery's is a careful, nuanced reading of Blaser's "origami" (McCaffery 1999, 378) and a brief summary is unfair; however, I do want to lift out one crucial element. McCaffery points out that the concept of the real as a continuous fold is incompatible with the model of the fragment—the edged entity as exemplified in the imagery of Blaser's early serials. In "Aphrodite of the Leaves," for example, "in fragments / in some object / the city is loved, / glass // cut into light" (*HF*, 125). In contrast to the fragment, the fold would seem to preclude relationships between discrete entities such as self and other. There are unintended echoes here of Hullot-Kentor, although in a different lexical register and to a different end. There is no world in high-end theory because there are no hard-edged distinctions between entities.

As thematized in poststructuralism and Deleuze's philosophy, the decentering of the self was received by many literary critics in the 1970s and 1980s as a liberation not only from the naïve reality claims of an ego-centered consciousness (perception taken as unmediated truth), but also from the pretensions of traditionally privileged groups—male, white, middle class, let's say—which had inherited their authority unexamined from a metaphysical tradition that theory had placed under severe question. Blaser's version of decentering, McCaffery points out, is implicit in the serial poem: the self that is enfolded in the world is subject to its temporal processes and to othernesses unassimilated to consciousness ("the perfect fusion of the ant and the broccoli") (McCaffery 1999, 378). Yet because his focus is on lived experience, Blaser treats this enfoldment as a polarity of self and other; hence the fragment (discrete entity) and the fold (continuous entity) seemingly coexist in his work. McCaffery answers the apparent contradiction, rightly, I think, with the comment that Blaser gives theory an affective rather than a systematic reading, which allows him to place "the particulate alongside an open acceptance of the non-totalizable" (381). In other words, what seems discrete at the level of consciousness is continuous in ranges unavailable to perception; what seems to be distinctively a self is always already an other.

In the context of a conference on the possibility of a public world, however, the question that comes of a Deleuzean reading of Blaser is how psychological or ontological decentering might translate into practical agency. Without at least the possibility of agency, the idea of a public poetry of Dantean scale seems fantastic. Agency is the subject of Charles Altieri's essay, "Some Problems

About Agency in the Theories of Radical Poetics." Altieri focuses on Charles Bernstein, not Blaser, and particularly on the shift from writer to reader in the attentions of Language poets. If there can be no generalizable addressee for poetry, he says, then poetry will either be balkanized—its audience limited to coterie—or reduced to "uncomfortable states, from depressive alienation to infantile rage, that the gods offer the marginalized" (Altieri 1999, 412). The focus on the reader as a producer of meaning seems to undercut the possibility of poetry as the site of possible idealizations and exemplarities. Exemplarity, in Altieri's view, supposes that the reader identifies provisionally with the world of the text, the point being to expand his or her imaginative range. If, however, all idealizations are to be considered as ideologically suspect, then radical poetry is left with negation ("the negative work of resistance") or formalism ("a version of compositional dynamics in which the pleasures of the material text are asked to carry the axiological burdens" (Altieri 1999, 418)). As negation it will be limited to a critique of what is; as formalism, it will be stuck with exposing its own devices. In neither case, can the poet propose anything like a world view because as we know, there are many worlds, none of them whole and none disinterested or spontaneous. Hence the unspoken question: recovery of what public world?

To summarize: poetry cannot take on the kind of big Dantean project Blaser proposes because first, there is no possibility of grasping the social whole on a planet where the global economy and private interests dictate policy and make a sham of democratic public engagement.[16] Secondly, the stuff of experience—form and substance, self and other, the individual and society—has been superseded not only on the street but in philosophy (not to mention science), by processes that cannot be grasped as discrete. Hence there is no self to grasp a world that is not there anyway. Thirdly, the mediated nature of experience as it is shaped by various social determinants (language, the culture industry, social place) and the cultural manyness of any conceivable readership for anything undercuts the possibility of poetry as idealization. It would seem, then, that, as Hullot-Kentor says, concepts like ethics, aesthetics, and the public world do indeed turn to dust before our eyes, and with them, of course, big world-saying poems.

The title of "The Recovery of the Public World" conference comes from a book of essays on Hannah Arendt and from Blaser's own essay of the same title. I have noted that Blaser embraced Arendt's contested public–private distinction in "Particles" (see Chap. 6). In tying the public good to wealth, Hullot-Kentor is in accord with Arendt's critics on this point. Yet in "Particles," Blaser insists that the public realm is not exhausted by goods. If the only definition of "public" is what people share through physical need, or, for that matter, what they can *agree* on as "good," then there is no public space in the Arendtian sense and no link to the arts as Blaser understood them. However, when Blaser argues in that essay that what we share is our particularity he is speaking of singular articulations of a shareable world. The poet's agency lies in such articulations. The political realm, in the common sense meaning of the term "politics" as the administration of shared needs, is called upon to serve its constituents: it is not mandated to fabricate those constituents. Arendt's "space of appearance," and I think on this point Blaser's open space poem is analogous to the Arendtian concept, is a continual enactment of what is there to be considered.

Blaser's implicit response to the *political* challenge to the arts as exemplified in Hullot-Kentor's paper is thus the poem as open space. The open space poem not only indexes the absence of a public world on the other side of the page, but dramatizes what one might look like if it existed: genuinely diverse perspectives brought to bear on shared conditions of life. The early problem with which Blaser had had to wrestle back in 1945 Berkeley was that of hard right political authority and the authoritarian elements of modernist art. The point then was to deconstruct such authority. Fifty years later, the problem was not just state-sponsored repression, although hard authority had never gone away, especially for vulnerable minorities; rather it was the soft tyranny of an ubiquitous market that had been allowed to slip the control of the *demos*. In the memorable phrasing of John Lancaster, Reagan-era public policy, signposted by the fall of the Berlin Wall in 1989, marked an unhooking of the "jet engine of capitalism" from the "oxcart of social justice" (Lancaster 2010, 23). Blaser's open space brings the revolutionary aspirations of modernism into contact with the civic malaise characteristic of the historical postmodernity Hullot-Kentor references, in order to keep alive the thought of a political response to the ascendency of economic interests over democratic agency.

The *theoretical* challenge exemplified in McCaffery's essay Blaser answers with the "operational language" (see Chap. 6), introduced in "The Stadium of the Mirror." He never denies the *"pleats of matter, and the folds of the soul"* (*HF*, 396), nor, for that matter, the indeterminacy of language or the micro and macro infinities of science; in fact, he embraces this kind of language. He does suggest, though, that poetry is concerned with a world scaled to human perception, and that this human world requires an "operational language" capable of articulating lived experience as a significant dimension of the real. The infinities that undo form (and hence an image-nation) do not, in Blaser's view, discredit experience, but rather become the essential accompaniment to it—the polarized "unthought." And here I'll repeat that polarity, like death, is simply a descriptor of experience. In the depths of the atom or the structure of language, there is stable polarity and no death. As for the social determinisms that seem to undermine agency, Blaser suggests that it is a positivism to expect spontaneity of consciousness and then, because spontaneity has been exposed as mediated, give it all up.[17]

The question of agency in poetry and art, then, comes down to the rigor and sincerity with which the poet is able to articulate the real. In what seemed a curious miscommunication on the occasion of the "Recovery" conference, Blaser responded to Altieri's questioning of agency in poetry by insisting on the existential given: *there* was the agency, he said (Blaser 1999, 429). At the time, this comment seemed like a misapprehension of Altieri's position because the givenness of anything, after all, was what was up for debate. I suggest that Blaser was moving from a different set of assumptions. If we follow his distinction between the poem as open space rather than exemplary content—has this not been possible in poetry at least since Williams's "Red Wheelbarrow"?—and if we also allow Blaser an operational language, then the existential given is the necessary response. The poem brings to appearance *what is*. Blaser's *Syntax*, for instance, is a study in appearings—many of them, like that of Opal Whiteley, of persons little known or forgotten and not powerful who have nonetheless freshly brought to appearance something that renders the world alive in a way it would not have been, had there not been the saying. The route from there back to public matters is that what appears then becomes a solicitation: it is there to be counted and accounted for in public policy.

This defense of the poem as public still doesn't get at the Dantean scope of Blaser's project, however. The difference is between a world view that drew its authority from God and the much humbler view-from-here. In the absence of God, the problem is one of scale. Blaser's way of dealing with it is to build up a virtual community (critical mass) through collage. Despite the quarrel with Duncan over language and experience, there is a correspondence in Blaser's serials to Duncan's Poetry as a grand collage—the ongoing narrative of the human. What is proposed as an idealization is no one perspective and certainly not that of the poet, but rather the poem as meta-structure—as the space itself—that, through the accommodation of your view and mine, his view and hers, the living and the dead, offers measure and method, so we can see what everybody is doing and hence who we are.[18]

Blaser argues in his "Recovery of the Public World" essay (*Fire* 64–86), as he does in the poem "Fousang" from *Pell Mell* (*HF* 253–56), that contemporary culture dislikes memory. The poet's job in such a context is to bring it up from the dark. The "Recovery" essay ends this way:

> The *Mahābhārata* and *The Ṛgveda*, like *Gilgamesh* and the *Odyssey*, are events in human consciousness which accompany the teachings of the Biblical prophets, Zoroaster, Kung Fu-tse, Gautama Buddha, Christ, and Mohammed. These move us as events in the history of consciousness: of how it is that men and women became human. I mean by these to suggest the tradition, along with those historical processes which derive from them, that created a world or worlds. We need to know how old we are. We need to trace the consciousness of that ageing. In order to gain "an attitude that knows how to take care and preserve and admire the things of the world" (Arendt, *Between Past and Future* 225). Perhaps, then, we could turn with greater assurance and finer judgment to the modern project which is devoted to change. (*Fire*, 86)

This is perhaps to say that poetry performs its public office when it brings measure to bear on its times. The twentieth century was an epoch of forgetting: on the ground, forgetting took shape as the massive deracination of people and destruction of cultures through war, economic conquest, and the mesmerism of technology; in the intellectual stratosphere, it took the form of severe and prolonged critique of cultural histories as contaminated ideology, a critique that informs the bottom sense of many of the "Recovery" conference essays. Blaser's insistence that the postmodern was a corrective to modernism, not a wholly new moment, is relevant here. The corrective had to address the authoritarian strand in modernism by opening up the field to a more flexible form of measure, but it also had to hold onto the revolutionary hopes of the moderns and the cultural memory of the worlds they came from.

DEPARTURES

The major poetic and academic events of Blaser's first decade of retirement as I have sketched them above were counterpointed by a busy domestic schedule. There were holidays with David—a trip to Portland in October of 1990 to raid Powell's Books and look at some Goyas; a jaunt to Pender Island in June 1991which David remembers for the exquisite local fauna (eagles, herons, deer, otter, and seals) and for Blaser resolutely making notes on "Bach's Belief." There was a quick one to Seattle in 1992 to see the new Frank Gehry museum because the roof on Trafalgar Street had to be fixed and longer vacation plans were canceled that year. In 1993, Robin and David made a two-week road trip to Idaho via Montana to attend a 50-year high school reunion in Twin Falls. David took a nap while Robin went to the reception, but they both climbed on a school bus for the next day's rafting adventure. This was the planned entertainment for the reunion—rafting in two spots on the Snake River. Unfortunately, the bus went off the road between spots, and after having to push it out, they ended up rafting in the same spot twice. This trip ended with a side jaunt to Portland—more Powell's Books and a look at the Rodin and Degas sculptures at the Art Gallery. While they were gone, friend and neighbor Grant Wood undertook to paint the hall a deep mustard yellow. The new color turned out to be a stunning backdrop for the large Tom Field and Paul Alexander paintings (Fig. 8.3).

These years in the late 1980s and early 1990s, however, were fraught with deaths, and not only from AIDS. In 1992, Ina Mae died, after a decline into dementia in a nursing home. Robin and David had visited the family in Idaho in October 1989. It was a typical Blaser–Farwell jaunt that began with David stressed—three days of ironing before departure, he complains in his trip notes—then a road trip through Creston, B.C. and a north-south route to Coeur d'Alene and Boise. David remembers that after visiting his mother at the home, Blaser decided she needed a sweater: shopping malls duly ransacked. The best that Twin Falls could offer was an inexpensive pink knit, not what Blaser had in mind, but it would have to do. When he delivered the gift, Ina Mae looked at him and held it up to herself. She knew her son and understood the gesture. In a poem faxed to me four years later, Blaser returns to this visit.

Fig. 8.3   Robin Blaser and David Farwell in hotel room, on vacation in Victoria, B.C., 1996. Photo by David Farwell, reproduced courtesy of David Farwell

The poem is titled "the visit, sept. 17, 1989," but Blaser crossed it out and wrote "Home" at the top of the page:

> mother, I disappointed you because I was not
> what I was
> mother, you disappointed me because you were not
> what you were
> this defines love   and its losses   I could not
> come back
> you could not come back,   so
> blessed me   with laughter and questionary hands. (Blaser 2003a)

A death is worse when there is both love and alienation. In the letter to Schelling and Waldman cited above, Blaser writes of his "grief and stress":

> ...I flew to family concerns in Twin Falls, Idaho, to be tolerated by the priests of the Requiem Mass and to stand there reading from a lectern assigned passages from Ezekiel and Timothy, the first a poet, both of them selected by <u>Christianism</u> to read as supernaturally moral—that stressed me out— (21 August 1992)

After the death of Robert Blaser in 1978, Ina Mae had turned more openly to the Catholic Church, released from her husband's disapproval. So the Mass. But by then, stung by the loss of friends from AIDS, the anti-gay rhetoric of the Christian right, and the Colorado legislation then afoot, Blaser had truly become, as he says in "Image-Nation 24 ('oh, pshaw,'" "exodic" (*HF*, 388).

In addition to the death of Ina Mae and the AIDS deaths of Luis Posse, Rob Dunham, and Rory Ralston, the departure of Roy Kiyooka from Vancouver arts circles rocked the scene in 1994. A beloved poet, painter, photographer, sculptor, and teacher, Kiyooka died 8 January 1994, found slumped over his desk, a cup of tea at hand. Blaser admired Kiyooka and wrote a eulogy remembering Kiyooka's "visionary seriality" (Blaser 1994a, Eulogy for Kiyooka). In particular, he praised a triptych of 1978, a photomontage in which "the shadowy reflection of a leafy human figure" seems to be "Roy speaking to us."

Closer to Blaser and a larger presence in his world, Warren Tallman was found dead in his apartment in early summer of 1994, his trademark cigarette still in hand. Karen Tallman organized a major memorial event at the Western Front (Blaser to Thesen, 7 July 1994). It was her idea to move Warren's room to the Front, "hideous, brown couch, bucket of cigarette butts, and the pieces of his passion" (Blaser to Thesen, 8 July 1994). Of the memorial, Peter Quartermain writes to Blaser: "It was an astonishing moving festive and communal event" (25 July 1994). With 30 people delivering tributes, Quartermain's stands out for its concise capture of Warren's presence in the Vancouver community:

> Warren has now moved from the physical world into the world of the mind, into
> at last the arms of memory, Mother of the muses, Delilah of deceivers, Seducer.
> That is, finally, a move into definition, a definition in which he can't answer back;
> finally, perhaps, he will be what we want him to be, and tamed.
>   THAT is our loss. (25 July 1994)

Viscerally attached to the bottle despite family interventions that got him to the Betty Ford rehab center, Warren was troubling and troublesome, but he had also done much to bring the New American poetry to Vancouver and to support the local poetry and arts scene. His conferences and parties were legendary and he provided financial support for the community by backing publishing ventures and buying local art (he had some fine Bill Bissetts, for instance). At the time of his death, Warren was planning to pay Talonbooks for publishing Adeena Karasick, then a young poet who Warren wanted to support (Blaser to Thesen, 8 July 1994). Writing to Thesen, Blaser remarks that Karl Siegler of Talon refused, "saying something to the effect that he decided himself whatever 'manipulation' he accepted. Dear Karl!" (8 July 1994). Warren was also a very astute reader of the New American poetry, particularly the work of Robert Creeley. His essays in the collection *Godawful Streets of Man* on the New Americans were seminal.

Blaser's relationship with Warren had had its tensions over many years. Although to my knowledge the grievances were never fully articulated, they had something to do with radically different styles—Blaser was elegant, scholarly, high art; Warren unbuttoned and populist. As well, there seems to have been some jealousy over Ellen. This was not sexual jealousy but jealousy of Ellen's love and attention. When Ellen left Warren (he had managed to embrace the free love of the 1960s as well as the hard drinking of the 1950s) and came out as a lesbian, it was Blaser that she chose to partner with in buying the Trafalgar Street duplex and Blaser with whom she was best friends until her death in 2008. In conversation, Robin would say that Warren accused him of "stealing Ellen." Then there was the drive-me-crazy factor over the recording of the *Astonishments Tapes*. Warren's constant interruptions and efforts to steer the conversation away from the heady poetics that interested Blaser were an irritant, and Blaser complained that it was Warren's interference that had stopped the recordings. Of course, there would have been no recordings if Warren had not initiated them.

At the time of Warren's death, Blaser had his own health problems—a prostate exam had led to the discovery of a tumor that had to be removed, benign, Blaser said, but later he would develop a slow cancer. Peter Quartermain writes on 25 July 1994, "What is all this about surgery? T-E-L-L." This and more of the dental miseries that had plagued Blaser periodically for years. He insisted that his dental work preserve his Wife-of-Bath gap between the front teeth. Otherwise, he would not quite be he. The upshot was that Robin did not make the Western Front event, but he did write a poem for Warren called "of is the word love without the initial consonant." As usual, the poem brings an armful of flowers to a friend's death, "weigella,   soft   pink," and a distinctive memory (*HF*, 408). Warren had a mythology about his drinking; he was in love with the lady in the bottle who always seemed to call him back from periodic dryouts. "A nervous handshake between body and mind seals the covenant they call addiction," Ramsey Scott writes in *The Narco-Imaginary* (Scott 2016, 173).

> the old friend reads
> to a television camera,   thin at the throat,
> dry lips   of an 'alcohol of adoration'   and
> her   'glass skirt'   trails shimmering and brittle
> 'sufficient grief makes us free' (*HF*, 408)

The poem is dedicated to Warren and signed "Robin Blaser / with The Doors & WCW" (*HF*, 408), a salute to Warren's love of popular culture and the plain speech of William Carlos Williams. To Thesen, Blaser writes that "Ellen, Sarah, and Karen came up to talk—with an unfinished letter Warren was writing to Revenue Canada—marvelous, crazy, anarchistic—the very qualities I loved about Warren" (8 July 1994). In the same letter, he continues a conversation with Thesen on Heidegger and Celan: "my conscience that I did not recognize that Heidegger's Being, beginning in poetic thought and ending in poesis, also wrapped around and hid terrifying political practices of our tradition—that Being and origin spoil there." And then: "Warren would be so impatient with this—as he often was with me—." "Of," Blaser had written. To be prepositional is to be among things. "The ring of," Olson began, in a poem about the birth of Venus. So limping in, amid the triumphs and ravishments of the decade, there it was: (L)of.

Notes

1. The data on the rise of AIDS comes from "Thirty Years of HIV/AIDS: Snapshots of an Epidemic," published by amfAR: The Foundation for AIDS Research.
2. Renee S. Grozelle describes the bathhouse raids and the Zeller murder in "The Rise of Gay Liberation in Toronto: From Vilification to Validation."
3. In addition to collaborating on the posthumous publication of Posse's poems, Blaser and Dunham co-edited a collection of essays titled *Art and Reality: A Casebook of Concern*, first presented at a conference titled *Art and Reality*, 10–13 August 1982, and sponsored by the Centre for the Arts at SFU.
4. The Perkins anthology: David Perkins, *English Romantic Writers*.
5. The Fraser Valley is a region just east of Vancouver consisting of a number of towns and rural farming areas. It has a history of social conservatism. The ad ran on 4 November 1989 under the heading "Time is Running Out—Concerning Gay Games Vancouver—August 4–11, 1990" and was attributed to "Christian leaders who live in Greater Vancouver" (Davidson 2007, 158). For a full account of Gay Games III and homophobic resistance to the event, see Judy Davidson, "Homophobia, Fundamentalism, and Canadian Tolerance: Enabling Gay Games III in Vancouver."
6. For example, the Rev. Jerry Falwell, influential founder of the Moral Majority in 1979 and a political influence within the Republican Party, was vocal in his condemnation of homosexuality and worked to prevent AIDS research and relief. In a speech given to an "I Love America" rally in Cincinnati, Ohio, 4 July 1983, Falwell said: "Herpes, AIDS, venereal diseases … are a definite form of the judgment of God upon a society" (Falwell 1983, n.p.).
7. Blaser's essay "The 'Elf' of It" (reprinted in *The Fire*, 283–98) was first published in *Robert Duncan: Drawings and Decorated Books*, a catalog edited by Christopher Wagstaff for a two-part exhibition at the University Art Museum and Pacific Film Archive, 9 February–12 April 1992 and the Bancroft Library, 9 February–30 May 1992, University of California, Berkeley. Wagstaff curated the show.
8. Blaser wrote the "Preface to the Early Poems of Robert Duncan" (reprinted in *The Fire*, 299–304) for a first volume of Duncan's *Collected Works*, to be published by the University of California Press. Plans for the volume were revised, however, and Blaser's "Preface" was published as a chapbook by Michael Boughn of Toronto's Shuffaloff Books.
9. Before his death in 1970, Olson had conceived of a *Curriculum of the Soul* that would cover a range of projects to be carried out by various fellow poets. Blaser's task was to write something on "Bach's Belief." Blaser finally completed the essay in 1995, just in time for the "Recovery of the Public World" conference.

10. Nichol's major long poem, *The Martyrology*, consists of nine books, some published together, others separately. I have given the citation for the first two books below. Blaser followed the unrolling of this poem with interest and affection.

11. For a contrast with Blaser, see Duncan's poem, "Variations on TWO DICTA OF WILLIAM BLAKE" beginning with the line "The Authors are in eternity" (Duncan 1964, 48).

12. Blaser opens "The Practice of Outside" with a poem from a Spicer notebook: "...My heart / Is completely broken. Only an enemy / Could pick up the pieces. / 'Fragments of what,' the man asked, 'what?' / A disordered devotion towards the real / A death note" (Quoted in *Fire*, 113).

13. The extent to which Heidegger embraced the Nazi regime remains under prolonged scholarly investigation and it is a debate that involves not only his behavior as Rector of Freiburg University under the Third Reich but also his philosophy. I wish to acknowledge this complex argument which requires another occasion for comment.

14. A letter from Laura Catalano at the Albright-Knox Gallery, 2 July 1993, confirms receipt of four Jess canvases that Blaser had loaned the Gallery for this show, which was curated by Michael Auping: *The One Central Spot of Red* and the three Hawthorne ovals.

15. The Buffalo listserv is a digital poetry newsletter from SUNY, Buffalo, sent to subscribers. The circular has been ongoing since 1994 (Poetics List at listserv. buffalo.edu).

16. Historian Perry Anderson's *The Origins of Postmodernity* lists the social and economic changes in the 1970s and 1980s that brought about the demise of revolutionary utopianism and the modernist art practices aligned with it. These include the digital revolution in communications technologies, the internationalization of finance, the outsourcing of manufacturing jobs from wealthy to developing countries with a cheaper labor force, and the capacity of the global art market to absorb dissent. The consequent death of revolutionary energy Anderson says, found expression in postmodern irony or identity politics, the latter a weaker form of resistance than the demand for distributive justice and meaningful democracy. See in particular Anderson's commentary on Fredric Jameson's analysis of the postmodern in a section of the book called "Five Moves" (Anderson 1998, 54–66).

17. See Blaser's "Poetry and Positivisms" (especially *Fire* 41–43; 61–62).

18. Blaser never did tune in to the din of the internet, but his view of public space suggests that he would have considered social media to belong to the social— that is, to the personal and partisan, rather than the truly communal. This is an argument that requires a separate essay and it would be difficult to secure against counter examples or charges of elitism, but the difference between much that is to be found on the web and a space of appearance is that between self-expression and a distinctive articulation of the world that others can recognize, even across ideological differences.

CHAPTER 9

The Irreparable

Blaser's two big projects of the millennium were "Dante Alighiere: Great Companion," a poem that had been a lifetime in coming, and *The Last Supper*, the libretto he wrote in collaboration with British composer Sir Harrison Birtwistle. In and around these projects were many public talks on the Irreparable,[1] a concept that Blaser came upon in philosopher Giorgio Agamben's *The Coming Community* in about 1994 and which he worked and re-worked for more than a decade. In the Dante poem and the libretto, the Irreparable is a foundational concept. A letter to Sharon Thesen (18 March 1994) includes four pages of quotations from Agamben, carefully copied out, and a few months later, Blaser went to Berkeley to meet him. To Thesen he writes: "I left the day before, 13th, for Berkeley to hear and meet Giorgio Agamben—we lunched à deux—most useful &, for me, rich—stayed to hear him last night—and just returned—" (19 October 1994). In a 2005 note to Meredith Quartermain, Blaser says, "My! I struggled with my University philosophy courses—until I realized that all glorious thought was a passionate embrace of what the mind could travel ... to my mind Plato and Aristotle were passionate—now, I know I was right to think so—thus, I reread them for the passion of their language— the WHERE of where the mind can go ... step by step in the light of footsteps ... of thought which is love—thinking is love—Oh!" (3 January 2005). Thus, it was with the Agamben readings: rather than extrapolate philosophy from poetry, Blaser pressed philosophy into poetry's service. He liked Agamben's writings because he read them as congenial to his own, just as earlier he had read Whitehead and Merleau-Ponty as fellow travelers.

In *The Coming Community*, Agamben defines the Irreparable this way:

> The Irreparable is that things are just as they are, in this or that mode, consigned without remedy to their way of being. States of things are irreparable, whatever they may be: sad or happy, atrocious or blessed. How you are, how the world is—this is the Irreparable. (Agamben 1993a, 90)

© The Author(s) 2019
M. Nichols, *A Literary Biography of Robin Blaser*,
Modern and Contemporary Poetry and Poetics,
https://doi.org/10.1007/978-3-030-18327-1_9

One of a nexus of terms, each of them explaining and extending the others, the Irreparable is closely related to *whatever* and *being-such*, two more terms Agamben pirates from common usage for philosophical purposes. *Whatever* is the idea that particular entities (this person, this cow, this tree) can neither be subsumed under an abstract universal (a generic name) nor reduced to a list of their material qualities or predicates.

> In this conception, such-and-such being is reclaimed from its having this or that property, which identifies it as belonging to this or that set, to this or that class (the reds, the French, the Muslims)—and it is reclaimed not for another class nor for the simple generic absence of any belonging, but for its being-*such*, for belonging itself. Thus being-*such*, which remains constantly hidden in the condition of belonging ("there is an *x such that* it belongs to *y*") and which is in no way a real predicate, comes to light itself: The singularity exposed as such is whatever you *want*, that is, lovable. (Agamben 1993a, 1–2)

The idea that belonging is embedded in the singular, not the generic—that what can be held in common is the capacity of singular beings to belong together as singularities—is close to Blaser's argument in "Particles." This concept of community differs from the identity politics of the 1990s and the tendency therein to emphasize socially assigned, generic qualities as the most relevant criteria of social belonging, so that being red or French or Muslim would be exactly the point. Another point that Agamben makes in the above passage is that the world in its "suchness" is the world perceived through love (it is "whatever you *want*, that is, lovable"). This was an idea that Blaser had explored from another angle in his 1986 essay "Mind Canaries" on Christos Dikeakos's collages. In that piece, Blaser had found in Octavio Paz the thought that technology treats the world as an obstacle to be overcome—as lump or mass—while art treats the world as *form* (*Fire*, 237). In different language, this thought returns through Agamben's *whatever*. In "a bird in the house," from *Streams II*, Blaser had written "it's / the face one wants" (*HF*, 359). The role of Beatrice in Dante's venture through the *Commedia* might be remembered here: the face of the beloved is what draws the poet onward through the worlds—it is what makes him *want* to go to hell and back. When Blaser has his poet marry a tree in *Cups*, he commits that poet-self to the world in its phenomenality and what he called the suddenness of form (recall Jiménez jumping out from behind the bushes in "Great Companion: Robert Duncan"). "'It springs on you'" is the title of a poem in *Pell Mell*: "the sweetness crashed into / the mind incessantly out there" (*HF*, 305).

Another passage significant to Blaser in *The Coming Community* was Agamben's meditation on the relationship between words and things. Language is generic by its nature: "cat" is not identical to *this* animal. Beings and things are always more and less than their names: they are more because whatever they are called fails to fully account for their suchness (this cat here); they are less because the generic name refers to uncounted manifestations of similar entities (other cats). Between the thing and its name is a relationship of non-identity: there is, Agamben writes, "the name 'rose' insofar as it signifies the rose and the rose insofar as it is signified by the name 'rose'" (Agamben 1993a, 96–97). Blaser had thought about language in similar terms since "The Hunger of Sound." For example, in a beautifully concise little poem about language in *Pell Mell* called "The Ruler," he plays off a child's alphabet book—"A" is for alligator, "D" is for dog—to imagine these bookish beasts in the language boat, "rowing in three dimensions, / never to get there" (*HF*, 277). Here again is the thought of language as reach: words reach for things that they never finally grasp. By 2004, Blaser could condense his thinking about language into a single sentence: "language is love." This is the last line of the second edition of *The Holy Forest* (506) and the title of a 2004 lecture at Naropa.

I am suggesting that Blaser used the terms of Agamben's philosophy as a kind of shorthand for his poetics. The Irreparable features in a talk at the Kootenay School of Writing (KSW) in 1994; at Naropa in 1995, 2001, and 2003; at a Buffalo conference on Robert Duncan in 1996; at Temple University in 2002; and at Poets' House in New York in 2005. Peter and Meredith Quartermain produced *The Irreparable* as a chapbook through their Nomados Press (Blaser 2003b), and the essay was printed again in *The Fire: Collected Essays* (98–110) in 2006. While the basic argument remained the same, Blaser oriented these variants to the occasion. For example, when he was invited to give the 10th anniversary address at the KSW in 1994, Blaser addressed the leftist sympathies of the collective indirectly.[2] Marx was a great thinker of social justice, he says, but he did not have an adequate theory of language or of time, meaning that the narratives of Marxism allow for closures. Citing Agamben, he says that humanity cannot "take possession of [its] own historical nature" (Blaser 1994c, 15)—it cannot write the end of its story without lapsing into the thought of totality, and that circles us back to totalitarian thinking.

> Would it be too much or too cruel to ask for a world conversation on the possibility that fascism, communism's disappearance into totalitarian management, and nazism are epidemics of western metaphysics and religion?—answers in poesis—not aesthetics. Certainly racism, sexism, capitalism, consumerism, homophobia sit comfortably, having drinks of that metaphysics. (Blaser 1994c, 12)

The "isms" that Blaser lists rely on the generic naming of persons and things, a precondition for both privilege and repression. Poetry, from Blaser's perspective, resists the generic. The poet's task—as opposed to that of a political activist or social worker who must deal with exigencies on the ground—is to rethink the cultural unconscious, including the "Lockean notion of what is substantial," the Kantian idea that "'there is one domain of value, the domain of moral value that is altogether immune to assaults of luck,'" and the Hegelian account of "the forward march of universal spirit" (Blaser 1994c, 28). Poetic work of this kind would imply a re-imagination of the assumptions back of one's mode of life.

In the published version of "The Irreparable," imagination is an important theme, explored through an open space piece crowded with voices—John Berger, Hélène Cixous, David Levi Strauss, Jean-Paul, Nerval, Baudelaire, Mallarmé, Rimbaud, Jarry, Spicer, Flaubert, Oz Shelach, and Dante. In his conversation with Michael Smoler at Naropa in 1999 ("Sounding the Air"), Blaser says, "my head is full of voices ... it's not as though you're sitting there all by yourself in some kind of nineteenth century notion of genius ... you're there working and it is my belief that it's an absolutely open space" (Smoler 1999, 2–3). What changed over time with this strategy in Blaser's poems and essays was simply the intensity of it: the voices got louder and more numerous and Blaser more discreet at playing the host. Moving among them in "The Irreparable," drink in hand so to speak, Blaser tracks the imagination's exile from public discourse. Instead of functioning as the meeting ground of the receptive and projective faculties, imagination has become synonymous with the fantastic and unreal. So he writes:

> Given over to the "unreal," "real experience" here amounts to an irremediable shrinkage of human nature and a vulnerable, manipulated "reality" lacking in "truth value" of any kind. Such a "reality" in its overwhelming empowerment endangers democracy and junks us into the midst of "the destruction of experience." (*Fire*, 101)

This argument, adapted from Agamben's *Infancy and History*,[3] protests the banishment of the imagination as *merely* subjective. The "mere" is the flip side of a demand for an objective reality beyond the situated, historical kind of knowing that Blaser sees as the only kind possible. This is also the argument of Blaser's earlier essay, "Poetry and Positivism." British Prime Minister Margaret Thatcher's famous TINAism, or "there is no alternative," the slogan that ushered in the neo-conservative dismantling of the welfare state in the 1980s, is a political analogue of the scientific and philosophical positivism that Blaser challenges, a kind of shouting down of any reality other than the one of those in power. "So, I have tried to track *The Irreparable*," Blaser writes in this essay, "—the destruction of experience, the shattered transcendentals, the current enormity—in the recognition of these for what they are—as if by chance to discover an opening into our contemporary task: 'to redefine the concept of the transcendental in terms of its relation with language.' I call this the *poiesis* of thought—or more simply the honest work of language..." (*Fire*, 107).[4]

In addition to the Irreparable as a poetic–philosophical glyph—something to think with—there is another sense in which the word, lower case, may have resonated in Blaser's later work. The common sense meaning of the term is that of something that can't be repaired. Over the 1990s and 2000s, Blaser had to come to terms with the inevitables of aging. So, in a lyric from 2002:

> I've caught the unease
> of old age in my hands

and wrung it dry
in order to remain
within its kaleidoscope,
there to collide among all colours
of *kalos*—beauty
of *eidos*—form
of *skopos*—watcher of
lovers of
irreparables. (*HF*, 483)

The word "irreparables" here carries the philosophical meaning for the reader who wishes to seek it out, but it also has the more mundane sense of the unfixable (pun intended). Blaser renders it plural, rather than singular as does Agamben. One experiences many irreparables, not the least of them the passing of the world's beauties—*kalos, eidos*. The beloved face of things. "No love deserves the death it has," Spicer had written (Spicer 2008, 393). But Blaser would take a milder stance. In a poem called "'the sounding air'" in *Pell Mell*, he had written, "nothing repairs, but that is the / comfort, flowing in what system, / the sounding air of the mind" (*HF*, 288).

Blaser's long fascination with the Irreparable came from the fit of this concept to his major themes, particularly his revisionary thinking of the sacred and his meditation on language and community. In his method—the collage work and the historicizing of language—Blaser turns the poem into a view-from-here of the kind of public space—a community of singularities—that was (is) missing in the world of real politics. Blaser's embrace of the Irreparable also points to a visionary role for poetry. As he had said in "Even on Sunday" and would say again in *The Last Supper*, a scandal shared by both religion and politics as they were (are) practiced is the disenfranchisement and persecution of those who are as they are existentially and those, like the migrant or refugee, whose lives may be deemed worthless by this or that power, this or that popular opinion.[5] These are certainly issues for practical politics on the other side of the page, but Blaser claims the *whatever* community as a poet's job too because it is a mode of life that requires imagination. In a letter to Phyllis Webb, Blaser writes that community is

> …something more than the simply personal or private— … "deep poetry" has, I think, a larger readership than ever before—that neither that "deepness" nor its readership informs the <u>infantilism</u> of the public world (which is not simply its mercantilism) is precisely the problem of poetic practice and its honesty—that "community" also <u>enfolds</u> what we have read in a lifetime, as well as whatever we're inclusive about now—so the "community" I have in mind is large and aware—the guardians, the companions, the helpers of the mind's heart—. (6 January 1995)

And Olson: "So few need to, / to make the many / share (to have it, / too)" (Olson 1983, 33).

GREAT COMPANION: DANTE ALIGHIERE

The great poet of the mind's heart had always been Dante for Blaser, and by 1996 he was working on "Great Companion: Dante Alighiere," a poem that had been coming since his childhood reading of the Doré illustrated *Inferno*. Blaser takes an opening epigraph from *De Vulgari Eloquentia* I.1—"*the speech born-in-one's-house is that which we acquire without rule*"—to introduce this long, complex poem that situates Dante in a narrative of the modern condition and an argument for poetic speech. The first section gathers up Blaser's history in poetry. Here are the first three lines:

> entering the territory—*map is not territory*—the boy
> looked up from the book he held in his lap, startled
> that it seemed the size of half of himself... (*HF*, 437)

The phrase "*map is not territory*" comes from Alfred Korzybski's *General Semantics Seminar 1937*, a collection of lectures delivered at Olivet College in Michigan. Korzybski argues that changes in the world require new knowledge maps: "In every field, personal, human, national, etc., 'insanity' included, old orientations involved an *is* of 'identity'. It will take many hours to make it clear to you and remember that we as a group have *denied* flatly that *is* of identity: *Map is not the territory*. If it can be shown that the old is based on the 'is' of identity, we can see where the old stands" (Korzybski 2002, 29). Korzybski is oriented to psychology and neuroscience, but he moves through "every field." In 1937, Hitler was making plans to start an expansionist war for *Lebensraum* and there was a political urgency to the seminars. Korzybski's idea that a changing world requires a changing narrative resonates with the same thought among the poets of Blaser's generation.

Here, in the first line of the Dante poem, Korzybski's phrase does a great deal of work. First, it recalls the "map" of Blaser's childhood and the loss of it at Berkeley. The image of a small boy reading an outsized edition of the *Inferno* initiates the Dante companionship in "The Hunger of Sound." That poem was about a child entering the territory of language; this poem comes after the youth had lost the Catholicism that he had used to map his world. When the adult poet enters the mapless, the whole trajectory of his life in language begins to unfold—his wandering through *The Holy Forest*, trying to find a way to be at home.

"Map is not territory" also serves as a kind of shorthand for Blaser's contention that poetry is a particular kind of language use—that poetic language is a language of affect (affect, not sentiment). Dante's choice of Italian rather than Latin for the *Commedia* was not just a decision about which formal features might best suit his poem, but about the mode in which the story would be told—it would be a *journey* through the cosmos and an intense spiritual *experience*. A few lines on in his tribute to Dante, Blaser writes, "*the phenomena of consciousness are / the phenomena of religion*" (*HF*, 438), a clear declaration of the significance of religion as perceptual experience and of experience as the affective foundation of religion. From this perspective, the *Comedy* is a venture in religious *feeling*, much beyond whatever elements of dogma it may include.

Blaser is also able to gather up his interest in the Irreparable with Korzybski's economical phrase. Agamben's *whatever* is another way to think about relinquishing a fixed identity (red, French, Muslim)—the "is" Korzybski speaks of. The opening three lines of the poem thus establish a personal journey with Dante, a venture in language, a biography, and a poetics. Blaser's note on the poem zooms in on the word "territory":

> A Note
> on my use of the word 'territory'—*territorio, zona*—to indicate the largeness each of us enters upon, which in contemporary terms seems to me mapless. We enter a territory without totalities of God, without totalities of spirit, Hegelian or otherwise, and without totalities of materiality on the record of Marxist practice in the 20th century. We have, as Lyotard has argued, paid far too much in terror for our totalities. The contemporary resurgence of religion, at least in North and South America, is exceedingly corrupt, and in its own terms blasphemous. This aging Roman Catholic looks across at the three great religions of Abraham—the Christian, the Jewish and the Muslim—and fears they are dying into violence. It is as if we were repeating the second century ANNO DOMINI.
> Dante is our contemporary in the *Comedy* and our guide to a poetics of interrogation. The *Comedy* is our greatest poem of interrogation, and the language of the *Inferno*, the *Purgatorio* and the *Paradiso* is Ulyssean. Although Dante did not know the *Odyssey* except through Virgil, Odysseus haunts him even in his dreams. (*HF*, 457)

The Odyssean journey was also Pound's in the *Cantos* which pointedly begins with a retelling of Odysseus's descent to Hades to inquire of Tiresias how to get home. It was Olson's too in *The Maximus Poems*, in his insistence that a long poem with history in it—epic in the twentieth century—had to be a finding out for oneself. Spicer becomes Odyssean with the serial poem, always to be continued. Spicer knew Korzybski's work and liked the phrase enough to use it as a poem title—"The Territory Is Not The Map"—in *Heads of the Town Up To The Aether* (Spicer 2008, 254). So Blaser's closest models and contemporaries hover in back of this tribute to Dante and the claiming of him for present use.

The major push of "Dante Alighiere" is the situating of hell, purgatory, and paradise on earth. Hell is not just about the "brutalities of / God's judgment"; it is about the blockage of thought and the loss of the *"good of the intellect"* (*HF*, 442). In hell, the damned are forever fixed in their spiritual condition at death. Dante places Lucifer not in flames but in the ice of the ninth circle, where the futile flapping of his great wings simply deepens the freeze. Transported to earth, hell is the "fix" that comes from the demand for closure—a kind of "icehouse of language" (*HF*, 442). At the level of personhood, hell follows from self-interest: "Philippe Sollers, in his brilliant contemporary /

reading of Dante, notices that self-interest—the / closed self—is a fundamental characteristic of the / damned" (*HF*, 442). At the level of philosophy, hell follows from the demand for certitude; at that of practical politics, it takes shape through the imposition of rigid, ideologically narrow maps on vast fluid territories. Blaser gives an historical example of such an imposition in the Puritan venture in "unmapped America." They had, Blaser writes, "a ferocious / time with omniscience":

> ...who in this community
> should be allowed to receive the body and blood of
> Christ?—the answer: the successful—speaking in
> the voice of—the coherence of—capitalism— (*HF*, 447)

On the historical record, what came of the Puritan colonies was the decimation of Native America and the advance of capitalism—what Blaser elsewhere calls the "gobble" (*Fire*, 97). In this context, the poet's job is to unfreeze the words, loosen the ideologies, re-wild the wilderness.[6] In a comic scene taken from Rabelais's fantasy of frozen language in *Gargantua and Pantagruel*, Blaser imagines a great babble arising from the unthawing of words (*HF*, 442–43). In terms of his own genealogy as a poet, the babble would have been coming from Joyce, a fellow twentieth century Ulysses adrift in the melt down of Irish Catholicism.

Blaser gives two generous sections in "Dante Alighiere" to Shelley and Pound, poets who reached for paradise and wound up struggling through hell. A political radical, Shelley "took the initial steps into our uncovered / Hell" to run "wildly into a dark forest" (*HF*, 450). It is "The Triumph of Life" that Blaser has in mind, where Shelley envisions "'people ... hurrying / to and fro, / Numerous as gnats'" (Quoted in *HF*, 450), in an endless stream, devoid of meaning. Jean Jacques Rousseau was Shelley's hero, "emblematic of 'political and / metaphysical transition'—of originary language—of / revolutionary possibility—of human liberty through / oppositional writing—of the stake in desire of any / one of us—" (*HF*, 451). Yet in Shelley's poem, Rousseau takes his place as one of the "*deluded crew*" (HF, 450). "The Triumph of Life" seems to despair of the Enlightenment hope for a better world and it breaks off with the question, "'*Then, what is life?*'" (*HF*, 453). If Shelley had ever meant to answer that question, he died before he could do so, drowned in a storm in the Gulf of La Spezia on 8 July 1822. Blaser comments:

> Shelley and Rousseau—like many of us—were
> enamoured of an absolute—the universal from which
> human freedom might escape into a community of
> meaning— (*HF*, 453)

The history of the Enlightenment faith in social evolution, like the romantic quest for freedom and the Puritan lunge after righteousness, is full of disappointments. Yet in the twentieth century, no less a poet than Pound pinned his hopes on a regime that renewed the promise, however cynically, to replace religious tyranny and aristocratic privilege with the collective good. Unfortunately, Italian fascism was built on the old gesture of expulsion and sacrifice, practiced against racialized others and "enemies" of the state.[7] The Pound segment of the poem is about an interview at Rimini, conducted by the Italian reporter Luigi Pasquini. Pound was largely silent, but pressed by the reporter on a mundane question—"So where are you living now'"—Pound reportedly answered, "'I live in hell'" (*HF*, 455). The point, in Pound's words: "'Here is Hell. Here'" (*HF*, 456). "'Poor bastards,'" Spicer had written in *Heads of the Town*, "'trying to get through hell in a hurry'" (Spicer 2008, 300).

When hell moves to the surface of the earth, "Purgatory and Paradise / also shift to the imagination of the *irreparable*—" (*HF*, 447). Blaser saw the earthly paradise at the end of Purgatory as within the range of "moral and intellectual concern and thought" (*AT*, 106). In *The Astonishment Tapes*, he says that "It's a completely human effort to get to the terrestrial paradise" (106). The means are the pagan virtues: prudence, fortitude, temperance, and justice (*AT*, 115). The heavenly paradise, in contrast, opens only through grace and the Christian virtues: faith, hope, and charity (*AT*, 116)—that is, it requires a supernaturalism. "Dante Alighiere" pays a lyrical tribute to the *Paradiso* as a dance of the heart and imagination—"this / discourse with cosmos—*the glorious wheel*, the radiance / speaking, horizon brightening, a swift fire in a cloud, / the sun-struck rubies of conjugated souls—the ladder / of splendours" (*HF*, 448). The language of paradise, Blaser says, is "Odyssean, eager, and infinite" (*HF*, 449); it is "every artist at his or her limit— / living sparks, rubies, the river of topazes—the laugh- / ter of flowers—to find this rose in the farthest petals, / which Charles Olson calls the *longest lasting rose*—" (*HF*, 449). The languages of mysticism—the metaphysics of light in the *Commedia*, the *via negativa* that Spicer adapted to his poetic practice, the "*waves of the marvelous*" (*HF*, 448) in surrealism—express, by a circuitous route, the desire to be at home in the world, *finally*.[8] "Dante's *Paradiso* remains / in the arms of Beatrice," Blaser writes, "—for hers is the first name of the / love that moves his language among the stars" (*HF*, 449): *imago* of the ego dissolved in light, *imago* of the pacified mind.

Agamben analyzes this wish "'to be at home everywhere'" (Agamben 1991, 92) as a paradox: home is not a point of departure to which one returns, but a place that the journey produces: it is end, not origin. Blaser had come to this thought in "Image-Nation 25 (exody." The poem concludes with the image of an old rocking chair from the railcar in Orchard, Idaho. On the backrest of the chair was a picture of the Wandering Jew, a legendary figure condemned to wander the earth until the second coming. In some accounts, this was punishment for mocking Jesus on the way to Calvary. The story is blatantly anti-Semitic, a prejudice Blaser vehemently rejected, but in the poem, it becomes a metaphor of the human condition, funneled through Blaser's personal history. The rocking chair and the railcar are emblems of *his* homeplace, but right there at the center of it is the nomad. "I rock there," Blaser says (*HF*, 396)—at home and wandering, at home in wandering.[9] Without this loosening of the grip on the real, the human effort—metaphysical or literal—to name and claim a home for this or that regime, this or that ideology circles back to hell on earth: "'it is easy today to descend to Avernus'" the Sibyl says in the *Aeneid* (Quoted in *HF*, 442).

Purgatory, then, is the condition that Blaser claims for a habitude in this poem and that he says "renames the poetic condition—the experiment of / writing—the feel of writing" (*HF*, 449). In *The Astonishment Tapes*, purgatory is "the realm in which you are given the possibility of relearning love—any range of your life that has not known love, understood it, been able to act in it, since it is an action and nothing else but an action that will then finally return you to yourself. The purgatory is where you relearn love..." (*AT*, 106). And a little later, "the very human issue of the possibility of change, the turning of events ... [is] sacramental.... The sacramental is not so simple as simply meaning the disclosure of the sacred, but it is the whole recognition of love in its proper issue and of the mysterious and the unknown as you meet them, and then the imagery for them begins to fill" (*AT*, 121). Dante is a "great companion" because he is the poet who moved from "frozen / silence" to a new poetry (*HF*, 442). This phrase restates the plot of *The Holy Forest*. The poems do not remain in the dark wood of the *Inferno*, although Blaser certainly passed through it in his struggle out of silence in the Boston years. Rather "the story is of a man / who lost his way in the holy wood" (*HF*, 73)—a tale of wandering. The wandering is a poet's alternative to the positivisms, the self-interest, the detached mind, and the authoritarian thinking that signpost the road to hell on earth. Blaser's fondness for Korzybski's phrase, "*map is not territory*," and his treatment of the poem as open space is a response to the very human tendency to enact paradise as closure. In "Fousang," from *Pell Mell*, Blaser writes that "the birds of paradise grow / feet and claws" (*HF*, 254). The resistance to closure is poetic love. Practiced as a poetics of open space, and translated into a mode of life, this kind of love is contrary to the mental conditions that make hell possible. That's the politics of the thing.

In 1995, Peter Quartermain had introduced Blaser to Annalisa Goldoni, an Italian scholar who had come to Vancouver to work with George Bowering on a translation of his *Kerrisdale Elegies*. Blaser had lunched with Goldoni and liked her immediately. The connection led to an invitation to participate in a conference on "Dante in Contemporary North American Poetry" to be held in Pescara, 22–23 April 1997. Blaser was happy to accept and this is where he launched "Dante Alighiere." The first publication of the poem was in *Testo & Senso*, a journal of the conference proceedings edited by Goldoni and Andrea Mariana, released in 2000 (Blaser 2000a, 15–27). Agamben did not attend, but Allen Mandelbaum, a celebrated translator of the *Commedia* was there, as were old friends Meredith and Peter Quartermain and Kathleen Fraser. Blaser and Farwell took advantage of the occasion for an art tour of Rome, Florence, and Venice, returning to Vancouver on 9 May via London. Given the peripatetic nature of purgatory where Blaser had landed in "Dante Alighiere," it just seems right that this "Great Companion" would coincidentally help to launch the next big adventure.

THE LAST SUPPER

As important as the Dante project was to Blaser, the main event of his millennium was most certainly the collaboration with composer Sir Harrison Birtwistle on *The Last Supper*, an opera for which Blaser wrote the libretto. The story began when Peter Quartermain put Blaser in touch with Nicholas Johnson, formerly connected with the Ferry Press that had published *Image-Nations 1-12 and The Stadium of the Mirror* in 1974. In the spring of 1996, Johnson invited Blaser to read at the 6 Towns Poetry Festival at Stoke-on-Trent in November of that year. Blaser would read with Denise Riley and then go on to London, Preston, and Southampton. Blaser and Farwell planned the trip as a three-week holiday as well as a reading tour. After Stoke-on-Trent, they headed to London to mark their 21st anniversary on 4 November in high style at Rules, a restaurant in Covent Garden advertising itself as the oldest in London (established 1798) and serving traditional British fare, including game that came with a buckshot warning. In the usual fashion, they toured the city for its architecture—St. Paul's, Old Bailey, where David half expected Rumpole[10] to appear, and a Thames cruise to Greenwich. David photographed the pomp and ceremony of the Remembrance Day parade and the two of them took in the National Gallery; the Tate; the Athenaeum; Cambridge, where Blaser searched out Wittgenstein's grave; Oxford; and the British Museum to see the Elgin marbles again. They visited Blake's grave to pay respects and Highgate Cemetery to say hello to Marx. In Southampton, Blaser read with Wendy Mulford and Lee Harwood, hosted by Peter Middleton. A scholar of the New American poetry and a poet himself, Middleton had attended the "Recovery of the Public World" conference and would later publish the essay he wrote on Blaser for it in *Even on Sunday* (Middleton 2002, 179–206).

In London, Blaser read at the Three Cups Pub and there begins the tale of *The Last Supper* (Fig. 9.1). Among the audience members was Patrick Wright. Wright had studied with Blaser at Simon Fraser during the 1970s, doing graduate work on HD. He then returned to London in 1979 to become a writer and broadcaster.[11] With friend Peter Blegvad, a cartoonist and former protégé of Clayton Eshleman's, Wright came to the Three Cups reading and stayed to chat with Blaser afterwards. At that time, he was hosting a cultural program, *Night Waves*, on Radio 3 for the BBC. Wright suggested an interview with Blaser for the program and they taped it in London on that visit. The meeting, so soon after the publication of *The Holy Forest* in 1993 and the "Recovery of the Public World" in 1995, brought Wright and Blaser together again over mutual interests. Wright was still interested in poetry and he had included a chapter on Mary Butts in his book, *On Living in an Old Country*; Blaser's Butts essay was scheduled for publication in the Wagstaff collection (Blaser 1995b, 159–223).

Through the connection with Wright, Blaser would meet the composer Sir Harrison Birtwistle and begin the adventure of *The Last Supper*. Wright knew Birtwistle from decades prior when Birtwistle had been his music teacher at

Fig. 9.1 Blaser in London, en route to the Tate, 1996. Photo by David Farwell, reproduced courtesy of David Farwell

Port Regis School, a preparatory school in Dorset (Wright interview, 29 July 2017). After Blaser's London visit, he gave the composer a copy of *The Holy Forest*. He knew that Birtwistle wanted to set the last supper of Christ and needed a librettist. In March of 1997, Wright floated the idea to Blaser. At that time, Blaser was busy with the Dante poem, and gearing up for Rome, but he was interested and proposed a dinner in London on the way back from the Dante trip. He invited Wright and his wife, Claire Lawton, and Sheila and Harrison Birtwistle to join him and Farwell for dinner at Orso's, an Italian place in Covent Garden on that 8 May touch down. Blaser was particularly impressed by Claire's vintage, Kurt Geiger ankle boots—black patent with gold toes and heels. As both Farwell and Wright remember, Blaser insisted on paying for everyone and the bill was astronomical. At this first meeting, nothing much of substance was discussed, but there was a mutual sniffing out between poet and composer. The next day, Blaser and Farwell flew home to Vancouver. So Dante led Blaser circuitously to *The Last Supper*.

That summer, Wright began to act as a go-between; he wrote to Blaser that Birtwistle was interested in preliminary talks and he sketched out the composer's initial vision: "a musical dramatization of the Last Supper, more ritual than operatic, and not simply a statement of belief (which Birtwistle doesn't have)" (6 July 1997). Blaser responded to the project with great excitement. The topic was exactly right for him and he could draw on a lifetime of readings in religion, poetry, and philosophy. In November of 1997, he and Farwell rented a cottage on Salt Spring Island and Blaser wrote the entire script in two weeks (Farwell interview, 28 August 2016). But Blaser had never collaborated with a composer before. Birtwistle responded to the manuscript with a "this will not do" and then the real work began. In January of 1998, Birtwistle was to launch his orchestral work *Exody*, named after Blaser's serial poem, at a world premiere in Chicago. It had been commissioned by conductor Daniel Barenboim and the Chicago Symphony. Blaser and Farwell bought tickets and planned to attend. Wright would also be there as would Sheila and Harrison Birtwistle and Andrew Rosner, Birtwistle's agent at Allied Artists. As it happened, Barenboim was called to Israel at the last moment over the death of his father and the concert was postponed, but Blaser, Farwell, Wright, Birtwistle, and Rosner had already assembled. This Chicago meeting occasioned a first serious discussion of the collaboration.

The project unfolded over the next two years. The spring of 1998 through to that October was a period of intense labor. In a letter to Wright, Blaser says, "My head is so into the libretto, I barely peek out of its commotion to account for other matters" (20 April 1998). A week later, to Birtwistle, he writes that "this libretto is the adventure of my lifetime in writing" (28 April 1998). The premise of the opera is the return of Christ and the disciples in the year 2000. Birtwistle added a Chorus composed of nine women to the male cast of 13 (Christ and the disciples) and a character called Ghost. In the lecture notes he would later prepare to coincide with the premiere at the Staatsoper in Berlin, Blaser says that Ghost is "meant to conjure not only ghosts and Geists, but also Holy Ghost, lo spirito Santo, le Saint-Esprit, der Heilige [Geist] out of Western tradition, and ghosts of the past and present" (Blaser 2000, "Berlin lecture"). In this lecture, delivered 12 April 2000 at the American Academy in Berlin and on 17 April at the Staatsoper, he remembers discussing the problem of the all-male cast with Birtwistle. In response, he reports, Birtwistle offered a mezzo-soprano for the part of Ghost. A female Ghost gave Blaser another layer: not only did he have a character who could represent the haunted history of Christianity, the secularization of the sacred in the twentieth century (Ghost loses the "Holy"), his own querying voice and that of his audience, but he also had a return of the repressed in the voices of women—Ghost and the Chorus Mysticus, as it came to be called.

Written in Latin, Greek, and English, *The Last Supper* is structured as a series of tableaux accompanied by Visions projected behind the stage. Ghost enters first with the question "*Quis sit Deus? Quod est nomen eius?*" (*LS*, 5). These questions, lifted from Jean-Luc Nancy's *The Inoperative Community*, sound the keynote for the opera. Blaser's strategy when dealing with loaded words like "God" was always to break them down. So, at the beginning of the process, Blaser writes to Birtwistle: "I was, with those Latin phrases, playing around with a Mosaic problem—God is not a name—rather a word for the nameless that is outside us (though we have come—monotheistically—to think it is a name for the One and Only)" (29 April 1998). The "Mosaic problem" is the capture of God's name. When Moses asks God what he should say to the people when they ask who has sent them their prophet, God replies that his name is I AM. The opera begins, then, with the problematizing of the *who* and *what* of God. Ghost and the Chorus then invite the disciples to return. At the Berlin performance, the on-stage Chorus Mysticus was supplemented by a pre-recorded Chorus Resonans that sounded from off-stage at key points, adding to the layered, haunted quality of the soundscape. As the disciples enter, they identify themselves and begin to build a table for the Supper. This scene culminates in the appearance of Christ.

The next major moment, after the assembly of the disciples and the building of the table, is the foot washing. As Christ washes the feet of the disciples in a ritualized manner, he names the abuses of historical Christianity—the dust of centuries that clings to their feet. During this scene, an image of the Crucifixion ("Vision I, The Crucifixion") is projected behind the stage (*LS*, 23). Here's the paradigm:

Christ	Now, Andrew
Andrew	What's this?
Christ	The sacrifices to hate and hell,
	offering my cross to their lips on the stake.
All twelve	Out of the dust.
Chorus Mysticus	*de pulvere* (*LS*, 27)

When Judas enters, he carries a bolt of red cloth that is at once a carpet for Christ, a table cloth, and an emblem of the rivers of blood spilled in Christ's name. In the next scene, "The Stations of the Cross" ("Vision II"), Blaser collages in Canadian poet A.M. Klein's poem about the military Messiah. Ghost sings, "*Don't you hear Messiah coming in his tank, in his tank? / Coming in his armour-metalled tank?*" (*LS*, 35). When spiritual experience congeals into dogma, the tanks are not far behind.

The view of the divine that comes out of the libretto sharply contrasts with the dogma of organized religion and the crimes against life that have been committed in the name of it. "Vision II" begins with a discussion of betrayal that ends with Christ inviting the disciples to celebrate life (rather than their own self-righteousness) and join him in the Garden. This is a segue to the last, brief tableau. The opera ends with the betrayal of Christ in the Garden before the crucifixion ("Vision III, The Betrayal") marked by the crowing of a cock (*LS*, 39).[12] These tableaux reverse the order of biblical events (betrayal to resurrection becomes resurrection to betrayal), leaving the question of who betrays who or what open at the end of opera. The implication of this reversal of chronology is that the historical record of Christianity is behind us, but it remains to be seen whether we continue to betray Christ's "religion of love" (Blaser 2000, "Berlin lecture"). The Garden scene tosses the end of the story back to the audience with the implied question, what would *you* do with Christ now? In his lecture notes, Blaser writes that the libretto is "not concerned with theology. I think it is 'exhausted' [Nancy's term]. I have no interest here in atheism—the political and social practice of it has become an aspect of twentieth-century brutality. And I am not interested in the dualism of blasphemy" (Blaser 2000, "Berlin lecture"). Elsewhere in the lecture he says that the opera *is* concerned with "1.) the great historical event—Christ: invention of a religion of love; 2.) & these themes: I AM; shatters of the hearts & minds, who is the betrayer and what has been betrayed—." He goes on to remark in notes taken from Regina Schwartz's *The Curse of Cain: The Violent Legacy of Monotheism*, that "if we do not think about the Bible, it will think for us." Here is Blaser's argument that the modern secular state claims for itself powers that are religious at base—it appropriates and misuses the supposed authority of a hypostatized divinity for human ends. Over the ages, this has resulted in the persecution and domination of reviled others, as Blaser had written in "Even on Sunday."

The alternative offered in Blaser's *Last Supper* is a radical Christology. First, there is the deconstruction of the "I AM" with which the opera begins. The more serious the inquiry into the nature of God, the more difficult it is to pin Him down and claim the Absolute for dogma. Then there is the issue of anti-Semitism, an example of the Christian misappropriation of God's judgment. Judas is the last of the disciples to return and the other eleven immediately reject him as the betrayer of Christ. Just so, some medieval Christians blamed the Jews for the murder of Christ, thus turning their anti-Semitism into a "virtue."[13] In the opera, the self-righteousness of the eleven is set alongside Christ's gentle welcome of Judas. Blaser has Christ say to him, "you did what you had to do. / We both hoped to gather the people / around the Messiah" (*LS*, 30). In his apocryphal Gospel (*LS*, 21), Judas is cast as chosen for and cursed in the role of betrayer. Another important element of this Christology is the celebration of the body. In a song drawn from Thomas Traherne, Blaser's Christ gives thanks for the earth and sky, for living creatures, and the joys of the senses (*LS*, 25). This love of life is contrary to the moralizing elements of Christianity, which are those most likely to produce authoritarian behaviors.

The Last Supper draws together Blaser's thinking about the sacred over decades and the deceptively simple language of it pulls in a wealth of concentrated scholarship. From the philosophers, we hear Agamben on the *Irreparable*, Jean-Luc Nancy from *The Inoperative Community*,[14] and Hannah Arendt on the "subterranean stream"[15] of western tradition; from the poets, Richard Crashaw and Thomas Traherne,[16] a lyrical and luminous mysticism; from Swinburne the bitter failures of historical Christianity[17]; from Nerval and Jean-Paul the terrible death of God[18]; from Olson, the violets, those persons who spring up in dark times; from Spicer, the ghostly; and from A.M. Klein, the military Messiah.[19] All these voices sound alongside the Hebrew prophets of the Old Testament and the apostles of the New. Dante haunts the entire work through the *Vita Nuova* and the vision of the flaming heart.

Blaser was not used to the push-pull of collaboration or to imposed deadlines. The journey from the cottage on Salt Spring in November 1997 to the Berlin premiere of *The Last Supper* on 18 April 2000 was stressful and full of bumps and grinds. Meredith and Peter Quartermain were companions of the process, and in fact Peter wound up with the job of inputting many versions of the manuscript from 1999 onward until it finally came to rest in the Glyndebourne production and the Boosey and Hawkes publication; Blaser remained stubbornly luddite when it came to computers. Over the process of the composition, he was asked for numerous changes, some congenial to him and others not. He liked Birtwistle's sense of drama (the building of a table for the Supper and the bolt of red cloth that covered it), but he was attuned to the resonances of the language in ways that sometimes clashed with the composer's focus on the musical soundscape. By December of 1999, however, there was a complete script. Wright comments, "I have just read through the libretto and think it wholly magnificent. I notice all sorts of things have changed, and while I can imagine you had many moments of exasperation as Harry called you for this and that, I don't see anywhere, where this text doesn't appear to be working very precisely on its own terms" (18 December 1999).

Blaser and Farwell arrived in Berlin on 9 April 2000, tuxedos packed, for pre-opening talks and rehearsals. Met by Stan Persky and a representative of the Berlin Staatsoper, they were driven to Wannsee where they stayed at the American Academy. Blaser gave his lecture there before leaving for Berlin. The premiere was a grand affair. Flying in from Vancouver, Christos and Sophie Dikeakos, Abraham Rogatanick, Ellen and Sarah, and Scott Watson were there for the event, and Stan Persky, of course, who was already spending the greater part of his year in Berlin. The opera was widely reviewed in both German and British papers, most of them positive. J.J. Gordon, in *Die Welt*, for instance, thought it heir to the "greatest works of our century" (Gordon 2000). On the negative side, Andrew Clark, of the *Financial Times*, panned it as unsingable, politically correct "claptrap" (Clark 2000). Stan Persky, in a full-length review article for *The Vancouver Sun*, writes: "What perhaps doesn't become clear until a second reading—or a café interview with the author—are the underlying politically radical premises of Blaser's risky reinterpretation of the Biblical story.... Blaser argues that born-again Christian fundamentalism is 'a power-seeking movement, and should they take power, it would be a rebirth of fascism.'" Persky concludes his review with a description of his post-performance walk with Blaser:

> At the end of the evening, around midnight, under an Easter Week full moon, the elderly poet wanders across the cobblestone Bebel Platz, next door to the opera house. In the center of the broad, darkened public square is a glowing rectangle of light. You look down through a square of glass into a lighted basement room beneath your feet that contains only empty, white bookshelves. This is the site where the Nazis, in May 1933, conducted a public burning of books. (Persky 2000, A9)

This public artwork by Micha Ullman was installed in 1995, Persky tells us, just five years previously.

As usual, Robin and David availed themselves of the trip to Berlin to sight-see and visit museums. They also fit in a performance of *Mahogonny* at the Deutsche Oper. On the way home, Blaser tacked on a reading at Trinity College, Cambridge (28–30 April 2000), invited by Kevin Nolan, then direc-tor of the Cambridge Conference of Contemporary Poetry. He read with John James and Marjorie Welish, introduced by Patrick Wright. As Wright remem-bers, the reception of the reading was mixed. While the European contingent was interested and engaged, Cambridge was a Prynne stronghold and the old argument over poetics dating back to the Ferry Press publication of *Image-Nation 1-12 and the Stadium of the Mirror* had, perhaps, set the reception. Prynne did not attend. Wright introduced Blaser as a key figure in a west coast poetry community notable for its engagement with the city's art scene. It was an indirect remark on what Wright saw as the insularity of Cambridge, and Andrew Crozier, Blaser's editor at the Ferry Press in the 1970s, responded with displeasure. The gig, then, was less than satisfying, but Blaser wrote dip-lomatically to Nolan afterwards that "it was full of NEWS in poetry and poet-ics" (10 May 2000). He and Wright never discussed the down side (Wright interview, 29 July 2017).

Back in Vancouver, however, *The Last Supper* turned out to be a project that just would not end. First, there was the fête. The Western Front, one of Vancouver's oldest artist-run centers, launched its first Distinguished Speaker fundraiser and asked Blaser to give a talk on the opera. Then there were requests for more changes that leaned toward a flattening of the language. One of the funders of the opera, for instance, proposed that Blaser's list of the marginal-ized from the foot-washing scene—"Jews, Blacks, aborigines, women, / Gypsies, homosexuals" (*LS*, 29)—be replaced by the less controversial word, "downtrodden." Blaser replied with an angry fax to Andrew Rosner, refusing to attend the Glyndebourne rehearsals and performance:

> Sir Harrison [it was no longer Harry, at this point], as I suggested, may write in whatever he pleases—even "downtrodden."
> I shall require that Boozie [sic] and Hawkes designate the libretto as follows: Adapted from a libretto by Robin Blaser. (25 July 2000)

Responding the next day, Rosner was apologetic, but said that Birtwistle thought the changes minor. Blaser did not. Again Patrick Wright was called upon, this time to calm the waters. On 27 July, Quartermain sent three ver-sions of the manuscript to Wright: the Berlin version, a version with Birtwistle's revisions, and a version combining these two. In an accompanying note, Quartermain writes: "We neither of us believe that ANY of the versions … is 'unsingable,' and do not expect Sir H to reject them without reason" (27 July 2000). This note drew an elegant apology from Birtwistle (28 July 2000), and a mollified Blaser agreed to preside at Glyndebourne. Opening night was on the 21 October 2000. Wright prepared a graceful and succinct commentary for the program notes that presents the libretto as "an extraordinary work of cultural archaeology" (Wright 2000, 41), and Blaser stayed with the Birtwistles at Mere for a few days before moving on to Glyndebourne.

In an interview with me, Wright remarked that Blaser did not fully understand the culture of the professional music world, where the librettist is understood to be a minor functionary who can be expected to produce on demand and change the script as instructed (22 July 2017). Requests may come from major funders as well as the composer. One such objected to Christ's line, "The Holocaust broke my heart" on the ground that it was a cliché. Blaser changed the line to "The Holocaust shattered my heart" (*LS*, 30), but would not alter it further. Citing the Berlin *Tagesspiegel*, Wright notes that in this line, Blaser's Jesus makes a "political correction" against which "the *mea culpa* of the Pope [Jean Paul II] is little more than a cat licking itself clean" (Quoted in Wright 2000, 45). In the end, however, and after all the drama of the Glyndebourne preparations, everyone seemed pleased. Writing to Birtwistle after the performance, Blaser says, "I'm just sitting around marveling over The Last Supper at Glyndebourne. Extraordinary. Splendour has so many guises" (3 November 2000).

WANDERS

After the push of *The Last Supper*, Blaser turned to a series of short lyrics. With a title that picks up the Odyssean theme of "Dante Alighiere," *Wanders* (2001–2002) is full of domestic life on Trafalgar Street—neighborhood doings, birds in the yard, thoughts and memories that came to mind at the shiny white wooden kitchen table or on the porch in the smoking chair. *Wanders* eased its way into the world first as an ongoing conversation with Meredith Quartermain. Blaser had a lively fax correspondence with the Quartermains, sometimes up to four of them a day, and he sent the poems as he was writing them. Meredith responded with poems of her own that matched the rhythm and syllable counts of Blaser's lines. The result was a chapbook, published by the Quartermains under their Nomados imprint in 2002, which aligned Blaser's poems with Quartermain's on facing pages. As Meredith recalls, this was not precisely a collaboration. She and Blaser did not write their poems together; they *conversed*.

One element of this exchange that really stands out is the delight that both poets took in sound. Words became a topic in the email exchange—the more outrageous and fun to say the better. "Love 'layer ear'—'Furl we go'—I'm caught by these shapes of the unshaped," Blaser writes in a fax (Blaser to Meredith Quartermain, 25 April 2001). He had sent off this poem:

> "there, there, there,"
> Somewhere said, offering
> comfort that didn't comport, who is
> dressed to the nines, who is
> unaware of ten pins
> to hold our sweetness up.
> "there," I said, "is there, unshaped." (Blaser, Quartermain 2002, 12)

And Quartermain responded:

> layer more ear
> love-wire then, whistling
> immirth nomadic diverse, in that
> fledge over thralls, in that
> gallivant to thimbles
> of move with wakeful not.
> Furl, we go afar trans-fleet. (Blaser, Quartermain 2002, 13)

In the Blaser poem is the unmapped territory ("there, there, there") that is so crucial to "Dante Alighiere" and *The Last Supper*, resonating behind the language of platitude. Quartermain then picks up on the wandering of the language away from cliché, the layering in the ear that Blaser's poem and hers requires. Her poem vibrates with words bursting into vagrancy: "fledge over thralls"? "gallivant to thimbles / of move"? Some "nomadic diverse" here is "whistling / immirth." A little "more ear" and off we go "trans-fleet." In a 27 May 2003 post, Ron Silliman reviewed *Wanders* on his blog, describing the poems as written in "ping-pong fashion." "The nerve endings in my brain tingle at all the little connections made in pieces like these," he writes (Silliman, 27 May 2003).

After Peter and Meredith had both shuffled off the working world in 1999, there was more time for books and movies and music and art shows and dinners and Thursday lunches for Peter and Robin. One issuance of this important friendship was the printing of Blaser's chapbooks and broadsides. Peter had been running a small, fine handset edition press for years, and Slug, as it was called, metamorphosed into Nomados (digital) and then Keefer Street (another handset) under the joint efforts of both Quartermains. To mark the celebration of the "Recovery of the Public World" conference, the Quartermains brought out Blaser's "Nomad" in 1995 (reprinted in *The Holy Forest*, 429), and followed it with a number of postcards and broadsides over the years. When Robert Creeley came to town in 2003 and did a reading with Blaser at the Vancouver East Cultural Centre ("the Cultch"), the Quartermains published his "After School" and Blaser's "a song"[20] through Keefer Street and hosted a large, celebratory dinner party afterwards. The Nomados chapbook edition of *The Irreparable* (Blaser 2003b) came out with Meredith's cover collage, incorporating Odilon Redon's beautiful *The Heart Has Its Reasons* in the image. *Wanders* has an original watercolor of Peter's on the cover. In a memorial for Blaser printed in New York in the *Poetry Project Newsletter*, Meredith describes a conversation with Blaser. It is entirely accurate to the hundreds of faxes that passed between them.

"I'm furious," Robin wrote to me on January 5, 2002. "HOW DID YOU GET THAT BOOK BEFORE I DID—I ordered it last spring—when it was just announced." The book in question was Avital Ronell's *Stupidity*. I had sent him a page of tantalizing quotes as well as a copy of an ironic set of test questions from her essay "The Rhetoric of Testing." Our correspondence was all by fax (Robin had no use for email)—his letters handwritten and often decorated around the signature with elaborate, abstract line drawings. At 9:55 a.m. the next day he sent a long quotation from Fernando Pessoa beginning "The Great Sphinx of Egypt dreams into this paper." (Meredith Quartermain 2009, 6)

In 2012, three years after Blaser's death, the Quartermains brought out the last, uncollected poems through Keefer Street, *Never Let the World Go By*, so to water the flowers of friendship and keep the record straight.

GIGS AND PARTIES

As well as the short lyrics he was writing after the big events in Berlin and Glyndebourne, Blaser took on an ambitious schedule of gigs, often with extensive art tours tacked on. At 75, he was living intensely, more so than most people half his age. After the Glyndebourne launch of *The Last Supper* and Cambridge reading, he was off to the Poetry Center in San Francisco and the University of California at Davis to participate in Gary Snyder's "Places on Earth" series. Steve Dickison and Kevin Killian hosted in San Francisco, and Robin and David stayed at Fran Herndon's place in her absence—instructions on plant watering duly noted. On this occasion, Blaser visited with Don Allen, and Bob Gluck hosted a garden party in his honor. A note from Peter Gizzi, beloved poet and Spicer scholar to whom Blaser entrusted the executor's duties of Spicer's literary estate along with Kevin Killian, encloses a poem by Adrienne Rich on the occasion of the San Francisco reading, titled "Driving Home from Robin Blaser's Reading" and dedicated to Gizzi and Elizabeth Willis. Rich remembers "his courtliness / offering operatic mystery / in lighted face and gesture" (Gizzi to Blaser, 2000).[21]

The next year, Blaser was invited to participate in the 2001 International Meeting of Poets at Coimbra, Portugal and this became an occasion for another three-week European trip. He and Farwell started in Berlin on 5 May, visiting with Thomas, Ilonka, and Stan for a few days before moving on to Paris, where they revisited the Café Soufflot, Blaser's hang-out on his first trip there in 1959. Blaser and Farwell tramped around Paris for almost two weeks before moving on to Bilbao (Fig. 9.2). Blaser was eager to see the Frank Gehry museum, a sculpture in itself with its architectural shifts of perspective and the giant Jeff Koons flower-bedecked dog (*Puppy*, 1992) greeting visitors. He also had a chance to go shopping, another favorite thing to do after art touring and martini time, and he found a pink jacket that became a favorite. Finally, on 25 May, David and Robin climbed on Air Portugalia to Porto and took the train from there to Coimbra. The themes that year were "Traditions of Poetry" and "Poetry and the Other Arts." Harold Bloom gave the keynote and received an honorary doctorate. He seemed drunk, David recalls, but probably wasn't (Farwell 2001, Coimbra trip notes). Significantly for Blaser, John Ashbery was also on the program, arriving in a limo to give a reading in the crypt of the

Fig. 9.2 Blaser in pink jacket, Bilbao, Spain, 2001. Photo by David Farwell, reproduced courtesy of David Farwell

Museu nacional machado de Castro. He and Blaser went off into a corner to get acquainted again while Farwell and Ashbery's partner, David Kermani, cruised the buffet. José Saramago was another pleasure of the occasion. Although Blaser does not seem to have developed a correspondence with him, he composed "Ichnograph 1" with words from Saramago's *The Gospel According to Jesus Christ*. It begins like this:

> ...for thought, when all is said and done ... is
> like a great ball of thread coiled around itself,
> loose in places, taught in others, inside our head... (Undated, "Ichnograph 1")

Blaser charmed the organizers of the event and was invited back in 2007. By then, however, he had to decline for health reasons (Blaser to Ramalho de Sousa Santos, 9 February 2007).

In the meantime, Farwell kept the suitcases handy. In 2002, Rachel Blau DuPlessis invited Blaser to Temple University for a week-long residence, meetings with graduate students, and a lecture on the Irreparable. Ron Silliman attended the after party at DuPlessis's home and Blaser and Farwell brought the gin. This trip east included a stop at the University of Maine at Orono for a reading and talk alongside Robert Creeley, hosted by Steve Evans and Jennifer Moxley. Blaser was particularly impressed by Moxley's collection of poems, *The Sense Record*.

In the spring of 2003, the University of Idaho in Boise invited Blaser to the campus—a recognition, finally, from home. Blaser read some of the Idaho poems—"Mr. Dandelion," "Tumble Weed," and "Image-Nation 24 ('oh, pshaw,'"—and the family sat in the front row: Gus and Millie Blaser (brother and sister-in-law) with their daughter Debbie Blaser Hepworth and her husband, Clyde (Farwell 2003, photo album). The invitation occasioned a road trip, made in a rented SUV that David named "Lucky." So fitted out, they toured the homeplace: a stop to see sister Hope, a visit to the Twin Falls cemetery to pay respects to the relatives who had moved in there, a trip to Orchard to see the old schoolhouse—derelict, but still standing—and the water tank which figured so largely in *Cups*. On the way back, it was cherry pie and ice cream at the Oregon Trail restaurant in Baker City.

For Naropa in June 2004, Blaser gave his "Language is Love" lecture: "I am always pleased to be asked to Naropa—here to wander around in the ambiance of the Buddha, who did not become god," he began (Blaser 2004c, n.p.). The theme of the talk is the "foundational activity of language in our 'form-of-life,'" and it draws again on Agamben, this time from *The Open: Man and Animal* and *Means without End: Notes on Politics*. Blaser's notes for this lecture are sketchy, mostly consisting of quotations, but these suggest that he was drawn to Agamben's distinction between "forms-of-life" available to the citizen and "naked life" without legal status or visibility (Agamben 2000, 4–5). In *Means without End*, Agamben moves from this distinction, through Arendt's discussion of the World War II refugee, to consider the contemporary precariat. This line of thought might have drawn Blaser into consideration of what an Arendtian "space of appearance" might look like for such a population, had he been able to pursue it. His "language is love" epigram, worked out at the existential level in "Hunger of Sound," takes on new resonance in the context of the voicelessness and invisibility of disenfranchised persons.

In September and October of 2004, Blaser gave a reading at the Woodland Pattern Book Center in Milwaukee, before moving on to Tucson for an event hosted by Tenney Nathanson and Charles Alexander of POG, a collective of poets, literary critics, and artists they had founded in 1966. Alexander, Director of Chax Press, had this to say:

> The challenge of poetry is to find, in and through language, a way of "ceaselessly rending open" language, or as Foucault says, "an unfolding of a space in which it is once more possible to think." Robin Blaser's poetic "reopens words into action" as well as into the social, the community, by allowing poet and reader to be together in the poem, in the open, into such "image-nations" as Blaser makes,

where the contradictions and negations allow for something ELSE, a pathway of crossing boldness... (Alexander 2004, "Introduction")

Blaser and Farwell made an additional trip to Bisbee, at the invitation of Michael Gregory. Bisbee, as Gregory explains in a letter, is an old mining town that has become an artists' colony. Bill Brodecky Moore, from the Buzz Gallery days in San Francisco, was living in Bisbee and hosted a reception for Blaser and Farwell after the reading.

Between the gigs, Blaser and Farwell enjoyed holidays on B.C.'s Gulf Islands and cultural pleasure trips. Ellen and Sarah were both musicians and deeply involved in the music world. Ellen had studied music at Mills College before moving on to Berkeley where she and Blaser met in the 1940s. She played the flute and Sarah the cello. On occasion, Ellen, Sarah, Robin, and David would make opera runs. In 2002, they flew to Santa Fe to attend the American premiere of Finnish composer Kaija Saariaho's opera, *L'Amour de Loin* with a libretto by the Lebanese-born writer, Amin Maalouf. The opera was of particular interest to Blaser not only for the music, but because it was based on the story of Jaufré Rudel de Blaye, a troubadour of the twelfth century and early practitioner of "Amors"—the poetic love that was so close to Blaser through Dante. In *Language and Death*, a book that Blaser read carefully, Agamben comments on the troubadours that "Amors" meant to them "the advent of the poetic word" (Agamben 1991, 68).

For Blaser, "Amors" had simply become a way of life. Among the countless dinners, deck parties, and outings of the 2000s, Blaser's 80th birthday celebration, hosted by Karen Tallman and Brian DeBeck, was a standout. The Quartermains printed invitations on beautiful rag paper—canapés and hors d'oeuvres from 5 to 7 pm—but the party went on. The poets came and the therapy crowd and the visual artists. Kevin Killian and Steve McCaffery arrived from out of town. Brian DeBeck worked his magic on the barbeque and the cake was a thoroughly extravagant pyramid of 80 profiteroles, donated by Trafalgar's restaurant, a spot that Blaser had been using for years as a second kitchen. The Tallman–DeBeck home is a large, gracious place with generous porches front and back, fitted out with great cedar ledges that are perfect for setting drinks and plates of things. Blaser held court on the back porch.

Right after the birthday bash, in June of 2005, Blaser and Farwell headed out to Ottawa to accept the Order of Canada. Jerry Zaslove, loyal friend and colleague that he was, had been working behind the scenes to nominate and gather support for the honor. This was a particularly welcome award, given the long years of silence from the Canadian literary establishment. There had to be outfits, of course, one for the ceremony of Investiture at 1 Sussex Drive in the morning and another for dinner in the evening. Robin chose a dove-gray suit and patterned silver tie; David was in tan, with a gold tie (Farwell 2005, photo album). For the dinner, it was tuxedos (Fig. 9.3). What else? Farwell's photo-documentary of the event shows Blaser chatting with then Governor General Adrienne Clarkson and getting acquainted with other award recipients.

Fig. 9.3 Blaser dressed
for Order of Canada
ceremony, Ottawa, 2005.
Photo by David Farwell,
reproduced courtesy of
David Farwell

Over the last five years of his life, the official accolades that had hitherto eluded Blaser seemed to pour in. After the Order of Canada, it was the Griffin Lifetime Recognition award in the spring of 2006. In his feature-length write-up of the event for the *Globe and Mail*, George Bowering sketched Blaser's biography and then offered a few concise words on the achievement of the poetry: "For Blaser, the challenge has been to combine the lyrical, usually associated with the first-person poem, with the public world" (Bowering 2006). Precisely. When the award was announced, the University of California Press publication of the second edition of *The Holy Forest* and first edition of *The Fire* were in the final stages of production. Then press editor Laura Cerutti wanted a picture for the back cover of the essays. We had something lined up, but she had spotted a picture of Griffin trustee Robert Haas and Blaser on stage after the announcement had been made. Blaser's arms are lifted in joy and triumph and greeting. She wanted that one.

The California Press release of Blaser's collected poems and essays occasioned a packed Western Front launch in Vancouver, 8 December 2006. Peter Quartermain was the MC and the event was supported by the Press, Duthie

Books, Farwell, the Quartermains, Ellen and Sarah, Christos and Sophie Dikeakos, Brian DeBeck, and Karen Tallman. Christos, Sophie, Brian, and Karen made food magic; Ellen brought astonishing, boulder-sized hunks of cheese to the table; and I made cookies and squares until the cows came home, as David would say. Five friends did a warm-up reading, each of them choosing a poem they particularly liked from *The Holy Forest*—George Bowering, Michael Varty, Stan Persky, Daphne Marlatt, and Ellen. Michael Varty was a recent friend and fierce supporter of Blaser. He then worked at Duthie Books, Kitsilano branch, and he had gotten to know Blaser through the very frequent book orders. Blaser haunted the place, conveniently local to him, and because he wanted everything new that he found of interest, and could not always remember what he had ordered, Varty kept tabs, quietly canceling duplicate orders.

Two years later, the Griffin Trust honored Blaser again with the Poetry Prize for *The Holy Forest*. This award was more than honorary; it came with a cash prize of $50,000. So David packed the suitcases again and they were off to Toronto to receive it, hobnobbing with Adrienne Clarkson and old friend Michael Boughn. With the windfall, Farwell suggested that they go someplace and spend it, so in August they set off on a three-week tour of Montréal, St. John, Halifax, and New York (25 August to 18 September). In Central Park, they hired a bicycle cart, powered by a handsome Turkish lad that they both quite liked. Farwell remembers that Blaser was seemingly tireless that day and interested in everything. He found a wealth of things to look at and stop over in the park and when they were finally done, he asked their obliging pedaller to take them to the Met (Farwell interview, 15 July 2017).

These later years bear eloquent witness to the seamlessness of Blaser's life and work. In the poetry, Blaser made a case for a mode of life; in life he lived the poetry. The voices that crowd into a poem like "Dante Alighiere" or an essay like "The Irreparable" have a domestic analogue in the voices that crowded onto the upper deck during the August fireworks in Vancouver, or at receptions on Blaser–Farwell travels, or into the celebratory parties, or just coming through in the 'hood. In *Wanders*:

> everyday, the carpenter
> on the new house next door
> greeted me—'Morning Glory',
> white hair standing straight up,
> then, he found out
> I was a professor and
> said—'how are you, Sir'—
> I said—'let's get back
> to Morning Glory,
> that's better than emeritus'. (*HF*, 477–78)

THE LAST IMAGE-NATION

In the midst of all the fun, Blaser was planning another big project. After *The Last Supper*, Blaser had conceived of a major Image-Nation poem that would take him to al-Andalus, those regions of the Iberian Peninsula under Islamic rule from 711 to 1492. Tariq ibn Ziyad, leading an army of Berber and Arab Muslims, conquered the ruling Christian Visigoths in 711. What followed were centuries of Islamic leadership in the region, albeit with shifting boundaries. In 1492, King Ferdinand and Queen Isabella conquered Granada, the last city under Muslim control, and expelled the Sephardic Jews who had lived in relative peace under Islamic rule. What attracted Blaser to this history was the moderate government that had permitted Jews, Christians, and Muslims to abide in the same territory. Although non-Muslims had to pay extra taxes for "protection," they were allowed to practice their religions and resolve their own legal disputes. The result was a cross-fertilization of cultures and a flowering of the arts, still highly visible in the architecture of Spain. Maria Rosa Menocal in *The Ornament of the World* (2002), describes the Iberia of this period as "a complex culture of tolerance" (11), the golden age of Spain.

The long Arab and Jewish presence in medieval Spain has far reaching implications for the study of European cultures. Introducing his *After Jews and Arabs*, Ammiel Alcalay writes that an integration of Hebraic and Arabic sources into European scholarship "would certainly both enrich and change the way we think about standard authors such as Chaucer, Dante, Petrarch, Boccaccio, or Cervantes; books like *Sir Gawain and the Green Knight*, *The Pearl*, or *The Book of Good Love*; movements like the *dolce stil novo*, the English courtiers and metaphysicals, or forms like the romance lyric and the picaresque narrative, to mention only some" (Alcalay 1993, 7). This is a list that goes straight to the heart of Blaser's fascination with Dante. It also contrasts strongly with twenty-first century hostilities between Israelis and Palestinians, Islamic and Christian fundamentalists. The possibilities of a revisionary history of Arabic, Hebraic, and Christian cultures would have appealed strongly to Blaser as poet's work: what a poet can do about these political matters is break down the congealed rhetoric on both sides of the divide.

It is not a coincidence that Blaser took up this Image-Nation project about the time of the bombing of the World Trade Center in New York on 11 September 2001. It was an event that affected him deeply, as evidenced in faxes and letters he wrote to friends. To the Quartermains, 12 September 2001:

> Oh! This horror that will not leave any of us to ourselves—
>   Now, it seems "Arabs" did it—how much such terror belongs to the Western Tradition!!—composed of Hebrew, Christian, Muslim elements—all the history of one god—the Absolute of the philosophical tradition—sacrifice is implicit in it—only there is no god to come out of the air to save Isaac—fundamentalist Rightness, which is blasphemous in their own terms. Mix this with economic and political problems—and yesterday comes true—that is, down there where the truth—no capital—always is.

Blaser began the project with reading and note-taking. In his notes on Harold Bloom's introduction to Menocal's book, he writes: "RB—instruction to himself—put all this together—including Don Quixote, which I've already begun tracking before reading these useful remarks by Harold Bloom" (Undated, "Notes for the last Image-Nation"). Alcalay's book he read twice, plundering it for bibliography as well as copying out and starring passages on "[t]he excising of references to the Levant, with its common and uncommon, Semitic and non-Semitic past (Hebrew, Arabic, and African; Persian and Turkish; Zoroastrian and Manichean; Islamic and Judaic), from most if not all standardized versions of the European curriculum..." (Alcalay 1993, 3). Reading Hent DeVries's *Philosophy and the Turn to Religion*, he writes: "To be accounted for—'religion's central characteristics'" / "its exclusionist and destructive potential, and especially its intrinsic relationship to violence" (Undated, "Notes for the last Image-Nation"). These lines are circled.

Where Blaser would have taken this Image-Nation is not clear in his notes. These are mostly mnemonic—he copied out passages he liked and recorded the page numbers. *Why* he wanted to write the poem is not hard to guess. He had just completed *The Last Supper* in which he severely criticized the historical record of Christianity. He had spent his writing life repositioning the sacred in the secular, and in his later work this task took on urgency in the context of East-West conflict that had put on the face of religion. He was deeply invested in the European sources of the *dolce stil nova* and given the scholarship he was reading for the project, these sources would have to be rethought to incorporate Levantine history. So he read, sitting at the kitchen table, and got himself ready for a trip to Spain. Writing to the Quartermains, 17 January 2004, he says that he and David have just taken their first Spanish lesson.

On 20 March 2004, Blaser and Farwell left for Spain. Granada was the first stop, then Cordoba and Seville. They would move on to Berlin and finish with a tour of Florence, Siena, Assisi, and Rome, accompanied by Berlin friends, Thomas Marquard and Ilonka Opitz. In Granada, they rented a car and named it "Maria" "in the hope that divine intervention might save us from Spanish suicide drivers," David writes (Farwell 2004, photo album). Farwell's photo-documentary of the trip tracks the tour of fortresses, palaces, towers, gardens, cathedrals and monuments. The architecture of the three cities literally holds together the tangled history of the place, and this is what Blaser had come to see. In a letter to Don Allen, 2 May 2004, he writes, "I was tracking Jewish-Christian-Muslim architectural remains since the late eleventh and twelfth centuries—in an effort to think about a time when such could decently live and think together. I am eager to find the poem of it. And, of course, visited Garcia Lorca's execution spot and his likely grave."

What Blaser was able to take in on this trip and what he had been reading posed a myriad of dots to be connected, where the links had been severed or buried. The *topos* of the project was potentially vast, and the "poem of it" would have had to have been very artfully rendered, given the complexity of the history, the cultures, the languages, and the politics involved, historical and current. After the trip, Blaser went back to his reading, but it was no good. As Farwell remembers, he would sit at the kitchen table as was his wont and read the same paragraph over and over. A notebook, running from 2003 to 2008, tells the story of this last reach for a big poem. It is full of mnemonic notes on some heavy reading, including Žižek's *The Puppet and the Dwarf: The Perverse Core of Christianity*; Stefan Jonsson, *Subject Without Nation: Robert Musil and the History of Modern Identity*; Edward Said, *From Oslo to Iraq*; Henry Adams's *History of the United States of America During the Administrations of Thomas Jefferson* and *History of the United States of America during the Administrations of James Madison*; Steven Mithen's *The Singing Neanderthals*; Karl Jaspers's *The Axial Age*; Matthew Stewart's *The Courtier and the Heretic: Leibniz, Spinoza, and the Fate of God in the Modern World*; Richard Dawkins's *The God Delusion*; Chris Helger's *American Fascists: The Christian Right and the War on America*; Agamben's *Profanations*; Robert Irwin's *The Alhambra*. These notes, however, are minimal, more so than those that Blaser was making before the trip to Spain, and this suggests that he did not get far with them. Interspersed with the book titles are notes on many articles from *Harpers*, *Le Monde diplomatique*, *The Walrus*, *The New York Review of Books*, *The London Review of Books*, and *Scientific American*. Those that caught his eye were usually on current affairs or matters relating to the three cultures he was tracking, the Christian, the Judaic, and the Islamic, but these notes are not sustained either. A third layer in this notebook and the real astonishment of it, is a series of little poems, comments, and observations that point to where the mind wanted to go. All of the entries in this notebook are dated, uncharacteristically for Blaser. So on 31 August 2004,

> Year by year, the mind gets / grows closer
> To the heart—take it from me
> and keep watch for the signals
> it's once-upon-a-time and then
> again—say Hi! Hello!
> To where our secular task
> must go. (Blaser 2003–2008, notebook)

On 5 March 2006:

> If the phone rings, tell them
> I'm out on the porch / talking
> to the raindrops

On 20 May 2006:

> When you hit 81, you're glad it's not a home run

On 18 August 2006:

> Very, very
> quite contrary
> that's the way
> my mind goes

On 20 August 2006:

> The house laughs

On 22 August 2006:

> fagot / faggot – French <u>fagot</u> – a bundle of sticks
>   Ha! Ha! Ha!

On 22 December 2006:

> the way the rain on the steps picks up the porch light, so that you walk on
> sparkles

On 12 February 2007:

> <u>Birdie</u>
> The birds in the holy tree [perhaps a misspelling of "holly"]
> talk about me:
> "Would he like to be
> a bird on a branch
> with us?"
> I answer yes and
> the birds say, "Oh my"

On 19 March 2007:

> in the flaming heart of my mind

> Oh! Jack Spicer, Robert Duncan, Jess, Robert Creeley, Charles Olson, Oh! my
> loves—loves, loves—Oh!
> losses!! – oh!!! – losses
> Losses!!! Losses!!!
> Thank you   Oh! – I weep!
> OH!
> Oh! Thank you! God Bless!!

On 10 April 2007:

> <u>where have all the flowers gone</u>
> from my mind's content?

And finally, another strand in this notebook, is the words, usually with a little note on the definition or etymology: atonic (lack of tone, vital energy); Mozarabic (a would-be Arab); parashah (a lesson from the Torah); alkahest; inspissate; steatopygous; fissile; atavism; piebald; ummah. And so on.

I have quoted at length because it seems to me that this notebook is a kind of record of mind melting into heart. The body had begun its betrayals and the large conceptual structures that Blaser was after in this last Image-Nation had become too difficult to sustain. His sensoria, however, were wide open. The short lyrics continued right into spring of 2008. Tossed in with Blaser's working papers is a single sheet, dated 14 June 2003:

> When writing, all the vowels and
> consonants fly out of the ancient
> human body where they began
> and scramble in the air to free
> their destiny in your poem. Oh, Ariel help. (Blaser 2003c)

So as Blaser had said in "The Stadium of the Mirror," "The *Image-Nations* will have no formal end, no completion of what they feel or know. They are too adventurous for that. And too nearly overwhelmed by the *intentionless and non-communicative utterances of a world* (Arendt)" (*Fire*, 36).

BUTTERFLIES OF DARKNESS

In the 1990s, Blaser had begun to experience the losses of friends that come with age, some of them predictable but others not. Karen Tallman's teen-aged son, Jesse, died in a fire in 1996. In a note for the memorial tribute, dated 26 February 1996, Blaser writes, "Thursday morning when Ellen phoned to tell me this, I yelled angry words over and over again. Rage in the air, because I had nothing else to say. Sometimes you lose your heart in the way things go in the world" (Blaser 1996, "for Jess Dennis DeBeck"). In his memorial notes, he turned to "'the universe is part of ourselves,'" the elegy he had written for the poet bpNichol, which repeats the line "the larks of heaven perch and nothing" (*HF*, 269)—language circling absence. Former student and loyal friend Charles Watts died in 1998 of melanoma while Blaser was writing *The Last Supper*. Watts had been a regular interlocutor, often sitting with Blaser late into the night until the ashtray filled up and Farwell, unable to sleep through their racket, would emerge from the bedroom in a bathrobe to announce that it was time for Charles to go home. Blaser would talk him all the way to the door. Then there was Angela Bowering, of cancer the following year. Angela had been present through the "Astonishment" sessions in 1974 and she and Blaser kept up a conversation until the end. He loved her feisty intelligence. Jimmy, Blaser's youngest brother, died in April of 2001. They had not been particularly close. Robin was 12 years older and had left home before Jimmy came of age. They had also lived very different lives. But still....

Further afield, the poetry world was full of leave-takings. John Wieners died in 2002, old friend that he was—a dear piece of Boston falling out of the world. In January of 2004, Blaser got a call from Christopher Wagstaff that Jess Collins had gone. "He was found a day or so after and seemed to be asleep," Blaser wrote, "I am sad." And then a story:

> There has been some magic around this: Jess's self-portrait returned to me on the day he died. A long conversation last week with Fran Herndon who described Jess's attention to her new paintings—she'd taken them over to show him—and he was, as Fran says, absolutely THERE for her painting. Absolutely there in ART. (Blaser 2004b, "Jess Collins memorial notes")

On 29 August 2004, Don Allen died. Allen and Blaser had had a prolific correspondence right to end. Blaser had shared his own health problems with Allen, even when he didn't talk much about them to anyone else, and Allen had taken to sending little notes and clippings in later years, some of them gleefully pornographic. In his notes, Blaser writes:

> Dear Don, just now, memory sends me back—we're in New York listening to Oscar Pettiford's trio—when was that?—the Five Spot?—thanks to you Oscar came to our table—I said I'd never heard a solo bass—he got up and gave us the most beautiful depth of heart I've ever heard. (Blaser 2004a, Don Allen memorial)

In a poem he dated 21 September 2003, *before* Allen died, Blaser had found a poem for just that evening. In *The Holy Forest*, the poem is dedicated to "Stan Pettigrove," perhaps a misremembering of the bassist's name.

> how many infatuations
> how many charms
> of staccato two-tone phrases
> more or less than
> four to the bar
> jumping
>> how many beautiful
>> people smiled in
>> The Five Spot,
>> sat down, said
>> 'let's dance'
>> and the smile
>> goes on
>> bass
>> in the heart
>> years after. (*HF*, 491)

To Mike Boughn (9 September 2004), Blaser wrote that he had no companions in grief for Don, or none locally anyway,[22] who had had the same lifelong relationship with the friend and editor who had stitched together the New American poetry.

Around about this time, Blaser took to calling himself and Creeley the last of the Mohicans. When Creeley himself left the room on 30 March 2005, Blaser took it hard. In a note to the Quartermains (16 July 2005), he says that "The death of Creeley so haunts me that I wander and wonder in love with 'our' map." In October of 2006, Blaser trekked out to Buffalo to read at "On Words," a Creeley memorial conference organized by Steve McCaffery and Myung Mi Kim (12–14 October). The conference had a distinguished list of participants: Ben Friedlander, Alan Golding, Peter Gizzi, Peter Middleton, Rachel Blau DuPlessis, Stephen Fredman, Michael Davidson, Charles Altieri, Peter and Meredith Quartermain, Marjorie Perloff, Charles Bernstein, Susan Howe, John Ashbery, Rosmarie Waldrop, paying respects. Buffalo was "clobbered" as the headlines had it with a freak snow storm on the 13th, right in the middle of the conference. "The worst October storm in Buffalo's history," said *The Buffalo News*—two feet of snow, power blackouts, three fatalities.

There were more deaths in Blaser's world, non-stop it seemed. Landis Everson, the beauty that everybody had loved in Berkeley, committed suicide with his service revolver in 2007, cheating illness of its final indignities. And then the big one. Ellen Tallman, on 19 July 2008, died of post-surgery complications after years of struggle with diabetes, a loss that left a crater-sized hole in the arts and therapy communities and the same in the hearts of her family and friends. Farwell's photos of the wake at Trafalgar Street show Blaser in his black suit, with a face as naked as a human face can be. Ellen had a host of friends and they filled the house. The cover image of her on the program for the memorial was headed with a couple of lines from Creeley's "Old Song": "If I know still you're here, then I'm here too / and love you *and love you*" (Creeley 2006, 607). But it was as if an incoming tide had finally reached Blaser's feet.

At this point, Blaser was sick himself. There had been a litany of illnesses since the mid-1990s, ranging from the inconvenient to the serious. There were the old dental problems and a slow prostate cancer. To me in a fax, he wrote that he had to go for "roto-rooter surgery—afterward no sitting for a WHILE" (Blaser to author, 21 August 2000). Next, he reported to Don Allen, "I did not lose my prostate. I was reamed out—more—it is still a pleasure—" (29 October 2001). Then there was cataract surgery in 2002 (To Allen, 16 March 2002), and a number of serious viral infections that he had trouble fighting off. Years of smoking had left him with a compromised immune system. Too late to quit now, he would opine, and then, turning to me, for you there might be some point.

It was sometime in 2005, Farwell remembers, that Blaser woke up in the middle of the night with a strange tingling sensation (Farwell interview, 15 July 2017). It was a stroke. Blaser denied any impairment, but the CT scan showed otherwise and his short-term memory was impacted. In a notebook entry dated 6 May 2005, he reflects on this turn of events: "Thinking over my mild stroke of about 3 weeks ago—one day Ellen said: 'You're not handling "Life" very well'—that strikes me as unfortunately true—so, as Creeley would say,

'Onward!'" (Blaser 2003–2008, notebook). Onward it was. Blaser had been relying on Farwell to manage his trips for some time, but the dependence began to intensify. In fact, he could not travel at all without David, and yet the two of them kept going.

Given Blaser's health, his last active year, 2008, seems extraordinary. In the dead of a Montréal winter, snow piled on the sides of clogged roads, he read at the Atwater Library and Concordia, the trip organized by Oana Avasilichioaei who was directing the Atwater series. She and Erin Mouré were fans and Blaser returned the compliment. In October, it was Denver to read at the invitation of Eleni Sikelianos. Farwell tells this reading as an extraordinary one (Farwell interview, 15 July 2017). Blaser seemed to delight in the poems and wanted to read them two or three times. The reading went on, with students coming and going, and Blaser enjoying his own poetry. Then there was the gig at Berkeley— "magic" that it was Berkeley so late in the game, Blaser would have said. Robert Haas had invited him to read in the "Lunch Poems" series, and he gave a stunning hour-long performance, calling on his Berkeley companions to come and join at the beginning of the reading by opening with poems of Spicer's and Duncan's before moving on to his own. In the range of this reading, beginning with Spicer's "No one listens to poetry," then reaching back to Boston with "Quitting a Job" and all the way forward to lyrics too recent to have made it into the 2006 *Holy Forest*, Blaser was pitch perfect in tone and pacing, balancing the high seriousness of "Image-Nation 5 (erasure," the political engagement of "As If By Chance," and the humor of the shorter lyrics. Organizers had the event filmed and made available on YouTube. No one watching the performance would guess that Blaser's health had become an issue. As David had said in an email to Sikelianos a month before, both of them worrying a little about the Denver gig, "his memory is not so hot, [but] he can still talk poetry until the cows come home" (Farwell to Sikelianos, 13 June 2008). Blaser ended that Berkeley reading with a lyric that perfectly counterpointed the Spicer poem with which he began. It is titled "14 August 2005" and dedicated to David:

> and I have! I hope – said
> this is my silver day – now
> make it golden – a walk,
> a talk – a voice
> > and it does
> have a heart
> > a chime
> when gold sounds so dark,
> so deep in the heart
> of life – I hold you,
> I told you life wanders
> well-met – oh! I hope
> I have told you. (Blaser 2012, n.p.)

The reading took place on 6 November 2008; Blaser did one more that November, in the library at Simon Fraser where he read from "Dante Alighiere." Then it was his feet in the water.

On 30 January 2009, David took Robin to emergency at St. Paul's Hospital. He was not sleeping, he was unsteady and had fallen, and he seemed confused. After transfer to the Vancouver General, he was diagnosed quickly: brain tumor, biopsy scheduled for 3 February. It was inoperable. When he was released from the hospital, friends stepped forward to spell David off on the care. There was a schedule—some of us took lunch and others took dinner times. Blaser was not always happy about this invasion of his kitchen, but it had to be. David recorded some of his *bon mots*: "Has there been anything else said today that would make me feel fed up?" (Farwell 2009, "Notes on Blaser's health"). Somehow, the cancer had created a craving for sweets, and the cookies and cakes and bars and chocolates rolled into the kitchen as if on a human conveyor belt. No point in quitting now. There were some glorious moments. On Valentine's Day, still in the hospital, Blaser was given a day pass and we had lunch at Pastis—Soma Feldmar,[23] Scott Watson, Barbara Schumiatcher, David and I around the table. He looked wonderful and he was glad to be out. "You know what hospitals are—," he had said to David, "all blank walls and dead ends." And then, "I'm going home—Zapadoola!" (Farwell 2009, "Notes on Blaser's health").

One of the bittersweet events of those months was the Simon Fraser honorary degree. In a letter dated 29 January 2009, just a day before the hospital, Blaser received a confirmation letter from Michael Stevenson, President and Vice-Chancellor of SFU, that the university was delighted that Blaser would accept an honorary doctorate at spring convocation. Tom Grieve had been trying to make this happen for years. He succeeded only after Blaser had received the Order of Canada, the Griffin Lifetime, and the Griffin Poetry Prize. When it became clear that Blaser would likely not make it to the June ceremony, Simon Fraser came to him. On 12 March, university officials convened in Sarah's living room downstairs at Trafalgar Street, piped in by the SFU bagpipers in full kilt. It was another packed out event, full of friends and former colleagues and out-of-towners like Brian Fawcett who had come to say good-bye. David had worked hard to get Robin ready. There had to be a tux and it had to be adjusted to accommodate a rapidly changing body. The result was a suit that didn't quite fit. Blaser was pleased about the whole thing, but a little vague on what it was for. When it came time for him to stand up and accept the degree, he dropped his pants. David took a dive forward to arrest the descent, but everybody saw and giggled. It was perfect. Poet moons university. He had been wanting to do that for years. In a write-up of the event for *aq magazine*, Grieve said that "SFU consummately did the right thing" (Grieve 2009, 26), but it was late in the game.

Just shortly before Robin's death, when things were getting radical, David found a spot for him at the St. James Hospice in East Vancouver. It was a pretty place with spacious lawns and a kindly staff. It was a place of yes. No point in quitting now. Friends visited. Christos Dikeakos brought in a wonderful basil plant one day that scented the room when you touched it. One evening I got a phone call from David that the doctor thought it might be tonight. When I got there, the room was jammed. I had brought some martini glasses and we drank vodka out of them. But it wasn't that night. His heart wouldn't quit, the doctor said later, although just about everything else had. Locked in the arms of Sister Morphine, he would struggle up for a moment and the nurse would hit him up again. "Butterflies of darkness," he said on one of these surfacings.

EPILOGUE

At first, I was going to skip the details of Blaser's death. Poetry loves death, but it can only go as far as the lintel ("The larks of heaven perch and nothing"). When Robin's body began to fail him, however, something wonderful—"magical"—happened. The community that had grown up around him and the irrepressible laughter he could make bubble up through the hardness of life was suddenly made present to itself as people gathered to help or say good-bye. "The truth is laughter," he had written in poem after poem of *Syntax*. Those who came with lunches and dinners, who baked cookies, who got on planes to Vancouver, who sent messages, who wrote letters,[24] who held readings in far-away places, who packed the grand wake at Trafalgar Street that David held for him and that Christos and Sophie and Karen and Brian cooked for filled the open space he had made. The wake was a party and a half, as David would say—"a large crowded reception / in a private house" (*HF*, 265). Let them come and look, David said, and they did. People filled the garden and wandered through the house, gawking at the paintings and poking into Robin's study with its marvels of books, and pictures, and *objets*. Ralph Maud presided in the garden. At the burial a few days later in the New Westminster cemetery, David brought a case of Armagnac and a couple of flats of rented glasses. There was a coffin—no cremation for an old Catholic. People read poems and threw them in the grave so that Blaser would have something to read in the underworld. David tossed in a bottle of Armagnac for a snort along the way, and we drank the rest. Sophie Dikeakos smashed her glass on the coffin. When it was over, we walked back to the road outside the cemetery and stood there watching as they moved him under the earth.

NOTES

1. I have followed Agamben in capitalizing the term Irreparable and I have italicized the word "*whatever*" to distinguish his usage of it.
2. No generalization will adequately describe the KSW. For a fuller picture, see the anthology *Writing Class: The Kootenay School of Writing Anthology*, edited by Michael Barnholden and Andrew Klobucar, and the KSW's website (kswnet. org) for a record of texts, images, and audio files of events.

3. See particularly Chap. 2 of *Infancy and History* where Agamben discusses the ancient role of imagination as mediating between sense and intellect and contrasts this role with the expulsion of imagination in Cartesian philosophy and modern science (Agamben 1993b, 24–30).

4. The phrases in this passage—"the destruction of experience," "the shattered transcendentals," "as if by chance" are all unacknowledged references. The first refers to Agamben's discussion of experience in *Infancy and History* (13–63); the second sounds very much like a reference to Jean-Luc Nancy's essay title, "Shattered Love," in *The Inoperative Community* (82–109), especially the passage on love as "coming from the outside" (97): transcendence is a "practice of outside"—a form of poetic love, to rephrase Nancy in Blaser's terms. The last phrase, "as if by chance" is the repurposed title of Blaser's own poem (*HF*, 347–49).

5. I am referencing Agamben's analysis of "'life unworthy of being lived'" (Agamben 1998, 139) in the chapter "Life That Does Not Deserve to Live" from *Homo Sacer* (136–43).

6. Consider, in this context, the many works of Susan Howe which "re-wild" the wilderness, especially *The Birth-mark: Unsettling the Wilderness in American History*.

7. Alexander De Grand argues that Italian fascism evolved from national syndicalism (the idea that workers' unions could be the base for social emancipation, rather than an international working class). Following World War, I, "[t]he first program of the Fascist movement in March 1919 was an expression of the desire of these former socialists and syndicalists to combine some residual radicalism with nationalism" (De Grand 1982, 139). It was possible to believe in the early stages that the Fascist movement was socially progressive. As the party developed, however, it became more aggressively nationalist, elitist, authoritarian, and collectivist (142).

8. For a discussion of the metaphysics of light, see Blaser's commentary on Dante in "Dante and the Metaphysics of Light," *The Astonishment Tapes* (94–156). The *via negativa* is a term from Christian mysticism meaning a meditative discipline of not knowing—not presuming to know God. It is the mirror reverse (and therefore related to) the vision of light in Dante's *Paradiso*. In "'My Vocabulary Did This To Me,'" Blaser links Spicer's "practice of outside" to this discipline of the Christian mystics (*Fire*, 259). The "waves of the marvelous" is a phrase from Victor Hugo's *William Shakespeare* that Blaser takes from Gwendolyn Bays's citation in *The Orphic Vision: Seer Poets from Novalis to Rimbaud* (Bays 1964, 116–17) in "The Stadium of the Mirror" (*Fire*, 29). The phrase predates André Breton's use of it to describe the surrealist image; for Blaser it would have resonated both with Spicer's attachment to the "unknown" and to his and Spicer's early interest in surrealism.

   The mystical and surrealist traditions come out of a desire for a supreme relationship with the cosmos, whether through extraordinary illumination, self-negation, or a deep exploration of the depths in oneself. For this reason, I have said that they express the desire to be at home, *finally*—that is, they express the desire for an intimate and enduring connection with what the conscious mind must perceive as "not-me."

9. Agamben proposes that "home" is the habitude the mind makes of its homelessness in language. Citing the poetry of Giorgio Caproni (Agamben 1991, 98) in a fragment that Blaser repeatedly quotes in his Irreparable talks, Agamben says

it is as if one arrives at a home that has never been. The image of the Wandering Jew on the back of the Blaser family rocking chair (*HF*, 396)—a combination of homeliness and permanent vagrancy—catches this uncanny human condition that Agamben describes in *Language and Death* (Agamben 1991, 91–98).

10. *Rumpole* was the name of a serialized television drama. The titular character was an eccentric British barrister.

11. On his time at SFU, Wright says: "I consider all my books to be exercises in 'poetics', shaped by my five years in Vancouver (1974–1979) but of a more applied kind" (Wright to author, email 30 August 2017).

12. The relevant passages in the New Testament linking Peter's betrayal of Christ to the crowing of a cock are in Matthew 26.73–75; Mark 14:29–30; and John 18.27.

13. In *The Pursuit of the Millennium*, Norman Cohn tracks the killing of European Jews during the Crusades by impoverished crusaders. The murder of whole Jewish communities was motivated partly by the thought of booty and partly by religious fantasies, among which was the one that attributed blood guilt to the Jews for the death of Christ (Cohn 1970, 70).

14. Nancy's essay, "Divine Places" in *The Inoperative Community* is particularly important to *The Last Supper*. Nancy begins this essay with the question "What is God?"—"*Quid sit Deus*"—the question with which Blaser opens the opera. An important concept that Blaser takes from Nancy is the thought that "*God is the being we are not*" (Quoted in *LS*, 6). This is say that the gods prevent humanity from thinking itself as *all*. Later in this essay, Nancy moves to a commentary on the irreducible difference of gods and mortals; the gods expose mortals to their mortality. They assemble us, or once did; now, an assembly around their absence brings to presence exposure itself—the existential condition of being open to the world—of being finite and therefore always bound to the alterities of time and place and other beings (Nancy 1991, 143). A really radical Christology would then have to think Christ as the man-god who carries within him his own utmost exposure. He is that figure who assembles, without resolving, self and Other in the same place. From this perspective, Christ is truly the door, the way: as the god who is also the Son of Man, he is a limit concept of pure possibility—the open as such.

15. Blaser incorporates phrases from Hannah Arendt in these lines for Ghost:

> I watch with you
> the subterranean stream
> of our history
> come to the surface. (*LS*, 5)

The phrase "subterranean stream" comes from a passage in Arendt's "Preface" to the first edition of the *Origins of Totalitarianism* (Arendt [1951] 1973, ix) and Blaser quotes it frequently in his talks and essays as well as in *The Last Supper*.

16. Blaser takes lines from Richard Crashaw's "The Weeper" and "On the Bleeding Wounds of our Crucified Lord" (Crashaw 1970, 120–37; 110). The latter comes into a lyrical aria written for Judas: "I looked upon his silver face and wept" (*LS*, 21). From Thomas Traherne, he takes Christ's celebration of the

body and all living things: "Give thanks / As I give thanks for the Being thou givest—" (*LS*, 25). The Traherne source is titled "Thanksgivings for the Body," from *A serious and pathetical contemplation of the mercies of God in several most devout and sublime thanksgivings for the same* and reads "I give Thee thanks for the being Thou givest…" (Traherne 1991, 183). Both Crashaw and Traherne emphasize the love of God and the radiance of creation rather than God's judgment.

17. The foot-washing scene incorporates Algernon Charles Swinburne's "Before a Crucifix" (Swinburne 2015, 208–14). In this poem, Swinburne lists some of the many abuses of historical Christianity, imagining the crucified body of Christ as an emblem of the bodies persecuted in his name.

18. The German writer, Johann Paul Friedrich Richter (1763–1825)—pen name Jean-Paul—was a source for Gérard de Nerval. "Christ among the Olives," from *Les Chimères* is about the death of God. It opens with these lines from Jean-Paul: "Dieu est mort! le ciel est vide … / Pleurez! enfants, vous n'avez plus de père!" In Blaser's translation: "god is dead! The sky is empty … / weep, children, you no longer have a father" (*HF*, 103).

19. The A.M. Klein poem is titled "Ballad of the Days of the Messiah" (Klein 1997, 77–78).

20. The "song" of Blaser's that the Quartermains printed along with Creeley's "After School" begins "there's a bluebird / in your eye." It was reprinted in the second edition of *The Holy Forest* as the last poem of the serial *So* (*HF*, 493).

21. The Rich poem came to Blaser with a note from Peter Gizzi:

> I enclose a poem Adrienne Rich gave us after your reading. And the interview with B.C.—the show was amazing and I found Spicer everywhere—to my mind. I'll call.

"B.C." is the artist Bruce Conner. (Gizzi to Blaser, 2000)

22. Creeley certainly shared the loss of Don Allen with Blaser. In his memorial notes on Allen, Blaser quotes Creeley's notes on Allen's death (Blaser 2004a).

23. Soma Feldmar is a former student of Blaser's at Naropa and an exegete of his work. Her MFA and PhD theses investigate the "poethical" elements of Blaser's language along lines proposed by Joan Retallack, Emmanuel Levinas, and Julia Kristeva (Feldmar to author, email 29 September 2017).

24. Anne Waldman's letter to Blaser during the last stages of his illness is particularly moving:

> In Buddhism it is considered very auspicious to be aware of your own impending death. This way you can work with fear and attachment. Start to let go. And you are blessed with David at your side.
>
> …
>
> O dear Robin. You are the best! And I love you. And I think of you. And you are in my prayers. Bon courage. (10 February 2009)

ARCHIVAL REFERENCES

The materials listed below are housed in the following archives:

1. The Bancroft Library, University of California, Berkeley. Hereafter cited as Bancroft.
2. Charles Olson Research Collection, Thomas J. Dodd Research Center, Archives and Special Collections. University of Connecticut, Storrs, Connecticut. Hereafter cited as Dodd.
3. Contemporary Literature Collection, Special Collections and Rare Books Division. W.A.C. Bennett Library, Simon Fraser University. Burnaby, B.C. Blaser fonds. Hereafter cited as Blaser fonds.
4. The Letters of John Wieners. Edited by Michael Seth Stewart. Unpublished manuscript. Private collection of Michael Seth Stewart. Forthcoming from University of New Mexico Press. Hereafter cited as Stewart collection.
5. The private collection of David Farwell, Vancouver, B.C. Hereafter cited as Farwell collection.
6. The private collection of Miriam Nichols, Vancouver, B.C. Hereafter cited as Nichols collection.
7. The private collection of Mark Samac, Boise, Idaho. Hereafter cited as Samac collection.

CORRESPONDENCE

Adam, Helen. 29 January 1965. To Stan Persky. MsA1 Box 1, Folder 1. Blaser fonds.

"Alfreda." 8 December 1959. To Blaser. MsA1 Box 27, Folder 6. Blaser fonds.

© The Author(s) 2019
M. Nichols, *A Literary Biography of Robin Blaser*,
Modern and Contemporary Poetry and Poetics,
https://doi.org/10.1007/978-3-030-18327-1

Allen, Don. Letters to Blaser:
    22 September 1954. MsA1 Box 1, Folder 3. Blaser fonds.
    4 July 1956. MsA1 Box 1, Folder 3. Blaser fonds.
    10 June 1957. MsA1 Box 1, Folder 3. Blaser fonds.
    22 July [c.1957–1958]. MsA1 Box 1, Folder 3. Blaser fonds.
    11 October 1959. MsA1 Box 1, Folder 4. Blaser fonds.
    27 October 1959. MsA1 Box 1, Folder 4. Blaser fonds.
Ashbery, John. Letters to Blaser:
    10 June 1958. MsA1a Box 1, Folder 11. Blaser fonds.
    c August 1959. MsA1a Box 1, Folder 11. Blaser fonds.
    22 October 1959. MsA1a Box 1, Folder 11. Blaser fonds.
    10 May 1961. MsA1a Box 1, Folder 4. Blaser fonds.
Auer, Sophia Nichols. 31 July 1936. To Blaser. MsA1a Box 1, Folder 12. Blaser fonds.
———. 15 May 1938. To Blaser. MsA1a, Box 1, Folder 12. Blaser fonds.
Baird, Nini. 13 November 1975. Memo to Arts Steering Committee. MsA1 Box 46, Folder 3. Blaser fonds.
Birtwistle, Sir Harrison. 28 July 2000. To Blaser. MsA1 Box 3, Folder 1. Blaser fonds.
Blaser, Robin.
    To Don Allen:
        8 October 1959. MsA1 Box 2, Folder 2. Blaser fonds.
        24 November 1962. MsA1 Box 2, Folder 2. Blaser fonds.
        7 June 1997. MsA1 Box 2, Folder 2. Blaser fonds.
        29 October 2001. MsA1 Box 2, Folder 3. Blaser fonds.
        16 March 2002. MsA1 Box 2, Folder 3. Blaser fonds.
        2 May 2004. MsA1 Box 2, Folder 3. Blaser fonds.
    To Sir Harrison Birtwistle:
        28 April 1998. MsA1 Box 3, Folder 2. Blaser fonds.
        29 April 1998. MsA1 Box 3, Folder 2. Blaser fonds.
        3 November 2000. MsA1 Box 3, Folder 2. Blaser fonds.
    To Ina Mae Blaser:
        14 August 1940. MsA1a, Box 6, Folder 10. Blaser fonds.
    To Ina Mae Blaser and Sophia Nichols:
        16 April 1955. MsA1a Box 6, Folder 2. Blaser fonds.
        1 August 1955. MsA1a Box 6, Folder 11. Blaser fonds.
        2 October 1955. MsA1a Box 6, Folder 12. Blaser fonds.
        1 November 1955. MsA1a Box 6, Folder 12. Blaser fonds.
        10 May 1959. MsA1a Box 6, Folder 12. Blaser fonds.
        4 August 1959. MsA1a Box 6, Folder 12. Blaser fonds.
    To Blaser Family:
        19 June 1943. MsA1a, Box 6, Folder 10. Blaser fonds.
        22 June 1943. MsA1a, Box 6, Folder 10. Blaser fonds.

24 June 1943. Postcard from Museum of Science and Industry to family. MsA1a, Box 6, Folder 10. Blaser fonds.

25 June 1943. MsA1a, Box 6, Folder 10. Blaser fonds.

5 July 1943. MsA1a Box 6, Folder 10. Blaser fonds.

7 July 1943. MsA1a, Box 6, Folder 10. Blaser fonds.

10 July 1943. MsA1a, Box 6, Folder 10. Blaser fonds.

19 September 1943. MsA1a, Box 6, Folder 11. Blaser fonds.

28 September 1943. MsA1a, Box 6, Folder 11. Blaser fonds.

19 March 1944. MsA1a, Box 6, Folder 11. Blaser fonds.

17 July 1955. MsA1a Box 6, Folder 11. Blaser fonds.

8 August 1959. MsA1a Box 6, Folder 12. Blaser fonds.

15 August 1959. MsA1a Box 6, Folder 12. Blaser fonds.

3 September 1959. MsA1a Box 6, Folder 12. Blaser fonds.

2 October 1959. Postcard to family. MsA1a Box 6, Folder 12. Blaser fonds.

6 October 1959. MsA1a Box 6, Folder 12. Blaser fonds.

To Michael Boughn:

6 May 1999. MsA1 Box 3, Folder 10. Blaser fonds.

9 September 2004. MsA1 Box 3, Folder 12. Blaser fonds.

To John Button:

22 February 1965. MsA1 Box 4, Folder 16. Blaser fonds.

To Jess [Collins]:

14 March 1959. BANC MSS 79/68c. Folder 4, No. 3. Robin Blaser papers. Hereafter cited as Blaser papers, Bancroft.

7 May 1960. Folder 4, No. 11. Blaser papers, Bancroft.

10 October 1962. Folder 5, No 2. Blaser papers, Bancroft.

17 October 1962. Folder 5, No. 4. Blaser papers, Bancroft. Also in MsA1 Box 5, Folder 10. Blaser fonds.

To Robert Creeley:

3 May 1993. MsA1a Box 6, Folder 30. Blaser fonds.

23 July 1993. MsA1a Box 6, Folder 30. Blaser fonds.

To Andrew Crozier:

7 September 1973. MsA1 Box 5, Folder 17. Blaser fonds.

n.d. "This is absolutely the last." MsA1 Box 5, Folder 17. Blaser fonds.

To Robert Duncan:

16 March 1957. BANC MSS 79/68c. Folder 2, No. 1. Blaser papers, Bancroft.

1 June 1957. Folder 2, No. 2. Blaser papers, Bancroft.

15 June 1957. Folder 2, No. 4. Blaser papers, Bancroft.

16 June 1957. Folder 2, No. 5. Blaser papers, Bancroft.

10 February 1958. Folder 3, No. 3. Blaser papers, Bancroft.

18 February 1958. Folder 3, No. 5. Blaser papers, Bancroft.

8 April 1958. Folder 3, No. 9. Blaser papers, Bancroft.

29 May 1958. Folder 3, No. 12. Blaser papers, Bancroft.

23 June 1958. Folder 3, No. 13. Blaser papers, Bancroft.

30 June 1958. Folder 3, No. 14. Blaser papers, Bancroft.

23 August 1958. Folder 3, No. 15. Blaser papers, Bancroft.

30 August 1958. Folder 3, No. 16. Blaser papers, Bancroft.

11 April 1959. Folder 4, No. 4. Blaser papers, Bancroft.

27 June 1959. Folder 4, No. 5. Blaser papers, Bancroft.

17 August 1959. Folder 4, No. 8. Blaser papers, Bancroft.

15 March 1963. Telegram to Duncan with Duncan's added note. Folder 5, No. 7. Blaser papers, Bancroft.

14 May 1963. Telegram to Duncan with Duncan's added note. Folder 5, No. 9. Blaser papers, Bancroft.

16 November 1965. Folder 5, No. 21. Blaser papers, Bancroft.

To Robert Duncan and Jess Collins:

28 May 1956. Folder 1, No. 7. Blaser papers, Bancroft.

30 November 1956. Folder 1, No. 9. Blaser papers, Bancroft.

11 July 1957. Folder 2, No. 7. Blaser papers, Bancroft.

20 August 1957. Folder 2, No. 9. Blaser papers, Bancroft.

1 December 1958. Folder 3, No. 19. Blaser papers, Bancroft.

6 January 1959. Folder 4, No. 1. Blaser papers, Bancroft.

15 August 1959. Folder 4, No. 7. Blaser papers, Bancroft.

29 September 1959. Folder 4, No. 9. Blaser papers, Bancroft.

30 August 1965. Folder 5, No. 20. Blaser papers, Bancroft.

To Brian Fawcett:

11 June 1976. MsA1 Box 8, Folder 1. Blaser fonds.

To Jim Felts:

30 July 1952. MsA1 Box 32, Folder 1. Blaser fonds.

To Parker Hodges:

2 October 1962. MsA1 Box 65, Folder 23. Blaser fonds.

To Ralph Maud:

2 April 1972. MsC 172. Contemporary Literature Collection. Bennett Library. Simon Fraser University. Ralph Maud fonds. Hereafter cited as Maud fonds.

5 June 1973. MsC 172. Maud fonds.

11 July 1973. MsC 172. Maud fonds.

To Laura MacDonald:

13 June 1994. MsA1a Box 6, Folder 46. Blaser fonds.

To Margaret McClintock:

6 November 1993. MsA1a Box 3, Folder 53. Blaser fonds.

To Paul Monette:

14 March 1990. MsA1 Box 11, Folder 27. Blaser fonds.

To Miriam Nichols:

21 August 2000. Fax. Nichols collection.

To Kevin Nolan:

10 May 2000. MsA1 Box 76, Folder 10. Blaser fonds.

To Charles Olson:

29 April 1957. Charles Olson Research Collection, Dodd. Hereafter cited as Olson papers, Dodd.

18 May 1957. MsA1 Box 12, Folder 6. Blaser fonds.

27 February 1958. Olson papers, Dodd.

28 February 1958. Olson papers, Dodd.

29 May 1958. Olson papers, Dodd.

29 March 1959. Olson papers, Dodd.

12 July 1959. Telegram. Olson papers, Dodd.

5 August 1959. Olson papers, Dodd.

16 May 1966. *Minutes of the Charles Olson Society.* No. 49 (March 2003): 14.

14 July 1966. *Minutes of the Charles Olson Society.* No. 49 (March 2003): 16.

To Stan Persky:

16 April 1963. MsA1 Box 13, Folder 3. Blaser fonds.

17 April 1963. MsA1 Box 13, Folder 3. Blaser fonds.

To Jeremy Prynne:

21 September 1973. MsA1 Box 27, Folder 5. Blaser fonds.

To Meredith Quartermain:

25 April 2001. MsA1 Box 15, Folder 1. Blaser fonds.

3 January 2005. MsA1 Box 15, Folder 1. Blaser fonds.

To Meredith and Peter Quartermain:

12 September 2001. MsA1 Box 13, Folder 9. Blaser fonds.

17 January 2004. MsA1 Box 14, Folder 1. Blaser fonds.

16 July 2005. MsA1, Box 15, Folder 1. Blaser fonds.

To Andrew Rosner:

25 July 2000. MsA1 Box 42, Folder 11. Blaser fonds.

To Ramalho de Sousa Santos:

9 February 2007. MsA1 Box 76, Folder 11. Blaser fonds.

To Andrew Schelling:

18 March 1993. MsA1a Box 4, Folder 46. Blaser fonds.

To Andrew Schelling and Anne Waldman:

21 August 1992. MsA1 Box 17, Folder 18. Blaser fonds.

To Jack Spicer:

23 October 1950. Box 1, Folder 6. BANC 2004/209. Jack Spicer 1939–1982. Bancroft. Hereafter cited as Spicer papers, Bancroft.

30 November 1951. Box 1, Folder 6. Spicer papers, Bancroft.

19 February 1957. Blaser fonds.*

13 April 1957. Blaser fonds.*

19 August 1957. MsA1 Box 16, Folder 22. Blaser fonds.

29 May 1958. Blaser fonds.*

30 October 1962. MsA1 Box 16, Folder 22. Blaser fonds.

To Spicer, Undated:

"you've no idea." Box 1, Folder 6. Spicer papers, Bancroft.

"Dearest Jack – well, the sound has come." [Draft of letter]. In Harvard notebook.

MsA1 Box 33, Folder 5. Blaser fonds.

To Sharon Thesen:

9 April 1994. MsA1a Box 7, Folder 22. Blaser fonds.

7 July 1994. MsA1a Box 7, Folder 22. Blaser fonds.

   8 July 1994. MsA1a Box 7, Folder 22. Blaser fonds.
   31 October 1994. MsA1a Box 7, Folder 22. Blaser fonds.
   18 March 1994. MsA1a Box 7, Folder 22. Blaser fonds.
   19 October 1994. MsA1a Box 7, Folder 22. Blaser fonds.
To Phyllis Webb:
   6 January 1995. MsA1 Box 38, Folder 5. Blaser fonds.
To Widener friends:
   29 August 1959. MsA1 Box 27, Folder 1. Blaser fonds.
To Patrick Wright:
   20 April 1998. MsA1 Box 18, Folder 15. Blaser fonds.
To Jerry Zaslove:
   12 July 1984. MsA1 Box 18, Folder 19. Blaser fonds.
Brodecky Moore, Alvin W. [Bill]. 28 December 1963. Letter to *Art Forum*. MsA1 Box 77, Folder 11. Blaser fonds.
———. 17 September 1975. To Blaser. MsA1 Box 3, Folder 20. Blaser fonds.
Broughton, James. 18 August 1957. To Blaser. MsA1 Box 19, Folder 9. Blaser fonds.
Buck, Paul. 23 April 1959. To Blaser. MsA1 Box 27, Folder 6. Blaser fonds.
Catalano, Laura. 2 July 1993. To Blaser. 2 July 1993. MsA1a Box 1, Folder 55. Blaser fonds.
Chardon, Lola. 2 September 1960. To Blaser. MsA1 Box 19, Folder 12. Blaser fonds.
Clarke, Jack. 4 December 1971. To Colin Stuart. MsA1 Box 17, Folder 1. Blaser fonds.
Coleman, Victor. 9 November 1969. Letter to Blaser. MsA1 Box 5, Folder 8. Blaser fonds.
Collins, Jess [Jess]. To Blaser:
   28 August 1962. MsA1a Box 2, Folder 6. Blaser fonds.
   [?] October 1962. MsA1a Box 2, Folder 6. Blaser fonds.
   19 October 1962. MsA1a Box 2, Folder 6. Blaser fonds.
Corso, Gregory. 26 September 1958. Postcard to Blaser. MsA1a Box 2, Folder 11. Blaser fonds.
Creeley, Robert. 5 September 1955. To Spicer. Box 1, Folder 19. Spicer papers, Bancroft.
Duncan, Robert. 22 May 1962. To Spicer. MsA1 Box 35, Folder 2. Blaser fonds.
———. 8 June 1963. To Blaser. Folder 5, No. 11. Blaser papers, Bancroft.
Easley, Eleanor Beamer. 16 July 1961. To Ina Mae Blaser and family. MsA1 Box 59, Folder 3. Blaser fonds.
Everson, Landis. To Blaser. 3 December 1951. MsA1 Box 7, Folder 7. Blaser fonds.
Farwell, David. 13 June 2008. Email to Eleni Sikelianos. MsA1a Box 16, Folder 9. Blaser fonds.
Fawcett, Brian. 9 May 2014. Email to author. Nichols collection.

Feldmar, Soma. 29 September 2017. Email to author. Nichols collection.

Felts, James. Letters to Blaser:
    12 July 1952. MsA1 Box 8, Folder 6. Blaser fonds.
    16 July 1952. MsA1 Box 19, Folder 4. Blaser fonds.
    5 July 1959. MsA1 Box 8, Folder 6. Blaser fonds.
    3 August 1959. MsA1 Box 8, Folder 6. Blaser fonds.
    6 October 1959. MsA1 Box 8, Folder 6. Blaser fonds.

Gizzi, Peter. 2000. To Blaser. MsA1 Box 26, Folder 1. Blaser fonds.

Grissom, Dr. R.M. 26 August 1966. To Stan Persky. MsA1 Box 13, Folder 1. Blaser fonds.

Haselwood, David [Dave]. 22 October 1962. To Board of Directors, Auerhahn Society. MsA1 Box 16, Folder 21.

Haskins, Sue. 13 July 1958. To Blaser. MsA1 Box 27, Folder 6. Robin Blaser fonds.

Hearst, Tracey. 14 February 1967. Thank you card to Blaser. MsA1 Box 20, Folder 4. Blaser fonds.

Jantzen, Blanche. 12 March 1964. To Blaser. MsA1 Box 10, Folder 2. Blaser fonds.

———. n.d. To Blaser. "It would be better." MsA1 Box 10, Folder 2. Blaser fonds.

"Joe." 6 March 1961. Postcard to Blaser. MsA1 Box 19, Folder 13. Blaser fonds.

Jonas, Steve. 5 February 1961. To Blaser. MsA1a, Box 3, Folder 15. Blaser fonds.

Jones, Leroi (Amiri Baraka). 30 September 1958. To Blaser. MsA1a Box 3, Folder 16. Blaser fonds.

Kennedy, Gerta. 24 November 1957. To Blaser. MsA1 Box 19, Folder 9. Blaser fonds.

Kloth, Arthur. 2 September 1956. MsA1 Box 10, Folder 18. Blaser fonds.

———. 15 January 1956. MsA1, Box 10, Folder 18. Blaser fonds.

Kurp, Patrick. 28 October 1994. To Blaser. MsA1 Box 24, Folder 10. Blaser fonds.

Levertov, Denise. Letters to Blaser:
    15 September 1958. MsA1a Box 3, Folder 35. Blaser fonds.
    21 July 1962. MsA1 Box 19, Folder 14. Blaser fonds.
    16 October 1964. MsA1a Box 3, Folder 35. Blaser fonds.
    15 December 1964. MsA1a Box 3, Folder 35. Blaser fonds.
    "Tuesday." MsA1a Box 3, Folder 35. Blaser fonds.

Maud, Ralph. 12 June 1966. To Blaser. MsA1 Box 11, Folder 13. Blaser fonds.

McClure, Michael. 15 September 1957. To Blaser. MsA1a Box 3, Folder 54. Blaser fonds.

Newman, G[erald] M. 3 September 1969. Memo to Blaser. MsA1 Box 45, Folder 14. Blaser fonds.

Nichols, Sophia. See Auer, Sophia Nichols.

Olson, Charles. 16 July 1959. To Don Allen. Olson papers, Dodd.
———. To Blaser:
   3 May 1957. Olson papers, Dodd.
   13 May 1958. Olson papers, Dodd.
   8 December 1958. *Minutes of the Charles Olson Society.* No. 8. (June 1995): 29.
   15 April 1959. *Minutes of the Charles Olson Society.* No. 8 (June 1995): 32.
   21 June 1966. *Minutes of the Charles Olson Society.* No. 49 (March 2003): 15–16.
O'Neill, Hugh. 15 November 1948. To Spicer. Box 3, Folder 17. Spicer papers. Bancroft.
Persky, Stan. Letters to Blaser:
   14 March 1961. MsA1 Box 12, Folder 20. Blaser fonds.
   11 April 1963. MsA1 Box 13, Folder 2. Blaser fonds.
   9 May 1963. MsA1 Box 13, Folder 2. Blaser fonds.
   5 August 1966. MsA1 Box 13, Folder 1. Blaser fonds.
Prynne, Jeremy. 15 November 1971. MsA1 Box 13, Folder 6. Blaser fonds.
———. 21 August 1972. To Ralph Maud. MsA1 Box 53, Folder 5. Blaser fonds.
Quartermain, Peter. 14 December 1986. Guggenheim reference letter. MsA1a Box 15, Folder 11. Blaser fonds.
———. 25 July 1994. Fax to Blaser. MsA1a Box 4, Folder 27. Blaser fonds.
———. 27 July 2000. To Patrick Wright. MsA1 Box 42, Folder 6. Blaser fonds.
Schelling, Andrew. 30 November 1992. To Blaser. MsA1a Box 4, Folder 46. Blaser fonds.
Sherburne, Donald. 12 May 1982. To Blaser. MsA1 Box 23, Folder 8. Blaser fonds.
Smith, F. 21 October 1959. To Blaser. MsA1 Box 19, Folder 11. Blaser fonds.
Spicer, Jack. [21 February 1957]. To Blaser. Box 1, Folder 7. Spicer papers, Bancroft.
———. Undated Letters to Blaser:
   "Berkeley seems to be having." Box 1, Folder 7. Spicer papers, Bancroft.
   "Except for the impropriety." Box 1, Folder 7. Spicer papers, Bancroft.
   "I don't see correcting poems." Box 1, Folder 7. Spicer papers, Bancroft.
   "It is hard to be sure about anything." Box 1, Folder 7. Spicer papers, Bancroft.
   "The sequence of your letters." Box 1, Folder 7. Spicer papers, Bancroft.
   "Thanks for your letter." Box 1, Folder 7. Spicer papers, Bancroft.
———. 6 October 1962. To Jim Herndon. MsA1a Box 8, Folder 3. Blaser fonds.
Stanley, George. To Blaser:
   23 May 1960. MsA1a Box 5, Folder 11. Blaser fonds.
   15 August 1961. MsA1a Box 5, Folder 11. Blaser fonds.
   7 December 1961. MsA1a Box 70, Folder 21. Blaser fonds.
Stevenson, Michael. 29 January 2009. To Blaser. MsA1a Box 22, Folder 2. Blaser fonds.

Stuart, Colin. n.d. Note to Blaser. MsA1 Box 17, Folder 1. Blaser fonds.

Tallman, Warren. 9 December 1965. To Blaser. MsA1 Box 17, Folder 5. Blaser fonds.

Tarn, Nathaniel. To Blaser:

   1 July 1967. MsA1a Box 17, Folder 7. Blaser fonds.

   31 December 1967. MsA1a Box 17, Folder 7. Blaser fonds.

Waldman, Anne. 10 February 2009. To Blaser. MsA1a Box 5, Folder 31. Blaser fonds.

Wieners, John. n.d. The Letters of John Wieners. Edited by Michael Seth Stewart. Unpublished manuscript. Forthcoming from the University of New Mexico Press. Stewart collection.

———. To Blaser:

   26 September 1957. MsA1a Box 5, Folder 38. Blaser fonds.

   27 September 1957. MsA1a Box 5, Folder 38. Blaser fonds.

   12 April 1958. MsA1a Box 5, Folder 38. Blaser fonds.

Wixman, Myrsam. 23 October 1955. To Spicer. Box 4, Folder 18. Spicer papers. Bancroft.

Wright, Patrick. To Blaser:

   6 July 1997. MsA1 Box 18, Folder 16. Blaser fonds.

   18 December 1999. MsA1 Box 18, Folder 16. Blaser fonds.

———. 30 August 2017. Email to author. Nichols collection.

*The starred letters from Blaser to Spicer are in the Blaser fonds at SFU. However, it seems that they have been misfiled during the process of re-archiving the Blaser collection. The box and call numbers are not currently available.

Miscellaneous Documents

Alexander, Charles. 2004. "Introduction to Robin Blaser." Tucson reading. MsA1 Box 40, Folder 17. Blaser fonds.

Blaser, Robin. 1932. Report card. Samac collection.

———. 1951a. "It seems wise." 28 September. Notebook. MsA1 Box 33, Folder 2. Blaser fonds.

———. 1951b. "A little later." 29 September. Notebook. MsA1 Box 33, Folder 2. Blaser fonds.

———. 1951c. "I literally tear." 8 October. Notebook. MsA1 Box 33, Folder 2. Blaser fonds.

———. 1953. "The Pacific Spectator." MsA1, Box 31, Folder 4. Blaser fonds.

———. 1956. "Boston: The Arrival." MsA1 Box 35, Folder 2. Blaser fonds.

———. 1958. "A Preface of Works to Come." Ms. MsA1 Box 34, Folder 1. Blaser fonds.

———. 1959a. "European trip notes." MsA1 Box 43, Folder 5. Blaser fonds.

———. 1959b. "Out of America." July. MsA1 Box 43, Folder 5. Blaser fonds.

————. 1959c. "Application for employment." 11 November. Box 1, Folder 6. Spicer papers. Bancroft.

————. 1963a. "La Richesse Necessaire." MsA1 Box 77, Folder 11. Blaser fonds.

————. 1963b. *Peacock Gallery Exhibition*. Brochure. 12 October. MsA1 Box 76, Folder 18. Blaser fonds.

————. 1965a. Guggenheim application. MsA1 Box 36, Folder 9. Blaser fonds.

————. 1965b. "Kenkyusha." Notebook. 4 August. MsA1 Box 35, Folder 1. Blaser fonds.

————. 1970. "English 810: Classical Sources and Mythology for the Study of Contemporary American Poetry." MsC 172. Sean Somers file. Maud fonds, SFU.

————. 1972. *Curriculum Vitae*. 1 May. MsA1 Box 45, Folder 14. Blaser fonds.

————. 1975. "The Arts in Context: Outline of a Course in the Renaissance Context." 26 May. MsA1 Box 46, Folder 3. Blaser fonds.

————. 1985. "New Poetics Colloquium notes." MsA1 Box 37, Folder 7. Blaser fonds.

————. 1986. "Guggenheim application." September. MsA1a Box 15, Folder 11. Blaser fonds.

————. 1992. "Belief, Doubt, and Politics." Naropa lecture. MsA1a Box 20, Folder 3. Blaser fonds.

————. 1993a. *The Holy Forest*. 1st Edition. See References.

————. 1993b. Notes for KGNU Radio Interview with Seth Hunter Eisen. MsA1a Box 20, Folder 6. Blaser Fonds.

————. 1994a. Eulogy for Roy Kiyooka. MsA1 Box 38, Folder 6. Blaser fonds.

————. 1994b. Eulogy for Rory Ralston. MsA1 Box 15, Folder 5. Blaser fonds.

————. 1994c. "Image-Nation 24." See References.

————. 1994d. ["Thinking about Irreparables, a talk"] Ms. combining a transcript from the tape recording of the Kooteney School of Writing talk and a handwritten ms. MsA1 Box 39, Folder 6. Blaser fonds.

————. 1996. "for Jess Dennis DeBeck 'Dusty.' October 20, 1977–February 22, 1996." Memorial notes. MsA1 Box 38, Folder 11. Blaser fonds.

————. 1999. Angela Bowering memorial notes. MsA1 Box 3, Folder 16. Blaser fonds.

————. 2000. "Berlin lecture on *The Last Supper*." MsA1a Box 20, Folder 1. Blaser fonds.

————. 2002. "The Irreparable." Temple University talk. Ms. MsA1 38.14. Blaser fonds.

————. 2003a. "Home." 5 August. Unpublished poem. Fax to author. Nichols collection.

————. 2003b. *The Irreparable*. See References, chapter 9.

————. 2003c. "When writing." MsA1 Box 38, Folder 7. Blaser fonds.

————. 2003–2008. Notes for the last Image-Nation. MsA1a Box 15, Folder 2. Blaser fonds.

————. 2004a. Don Allen memorial notes. MsA1a Box 15, Folder 12. Blaser fonds.

————. 2004b. Jess Collins memorial notes. 6 January. MsA1a Box 15, Folder 12. Blaser fonds.

————. 2004c. "Language is Love." Naropa lecture. Ms. MsA1a 20, Folder 3. Blaser fonds.

————. 2007. Ellen Tallman, birthday tribute. 11 November. MsA1a Box 15, Folder 12. Blaser fonds.

Blaser, Robin. Undated:

"A myth for Cleo." Notebook. MsA1 Box 34, Folder 6. Blaser fonds.

"And linguists teach." Notebook. MsA1 Box 35, Folder 2. Blaser fonds.

"Aphrodite." Lecture notes. Ms. MsA1 Box 44, Folder 11. Blaser fonds.

Blaser to Duncan, draft letter. Notebook. MsA1 Box 33, Folder 5. Blaser fonds.

"Constant awareness." Notebook. MsA1 Box 34, Folder 9. Blaser fonds.

"The Desert." Ms. MsA1a Box 10, Folder 1. Blaser fonds.

"Dear Jack, now you're dead." Notebook. MsA1 Box 33, Folder 6. Blaser fonds.

"Find you the path." Ms. MsA1a, Box 10, Folder 1. Blaser fonds.

"His philosophy." Notebook. MsA1 Box 33, Folder 4. Blaser fonds.

"Ichnograph 1." Ms. MsA1 Box 38, Folder 7. Blaser fonds.

"In the meantime." Note. MsA1 Box 27, Folder 4. Blaser fonds.

"Jennifer." Notes. MsA1 Box 33, Folder 8. Blaser fonds.

"Problems." Notebook, brown ringed. MsA1 Box 36, Folder 2. Blaser fonds.

"This moment." Black notebook. MsA1 Box 34, Folder 5. Blaser fonds.

"Notes for the last Image-Nation." MsA1 Box 44, Folder 1. Blaser fonds.

"The Wife of Bath." Ms. MsA1a, Box 10, Folder 1. Blaser fonds.

Blaser, Robin and Friends. [1974] 2015. "The Astonishment Tapes." Transcript by Miriam Nichols of 1974 audio recording. Blaser fonds.

Bowering, George. 2006. "A Berkeley Renaissance Man." *Globe and Mail.* Clipping. MsA1a Box 19, Folder 6. Blaser fonds.

Civil Service Commission of San Francisco. 1960. Librarian's examination. MsA1 Box 27, Folder 7. Blaser fonds.

Cold Mountain Institute. 1975. Brochure. MsA1 Box 28, Folder 2. Blaser fonds.

Cope, Patricia. n.d. A History of Augustus F. and Minnie Catherine John Blaser and Some Members of the Blaser and John Family. Ms. MsA1a Box 31, Folder 3. Blaser fonds.

Coyote. 1941. Twin Falls High School Year Book. MsA1a, Box 39, Folder 1. Blaser fonds.

Coyote. 1942. Twin Falls High School Year Book. MsA1a, Box 39, Folder 2. Blaser fonds.

Creeley, Robert. 2004. Don Allen memorial notes. (Quoted in Blaser 2004a, Don Allen memorial notes.) MsA1 Box 15, Folder 11. Blaser fonds.

Douglas, Margret, Ace Hollibaugh, Yetta Lees, Sandy Lockhart, David Potter, Prudence Wheeldon. 1969. "Who Has Broken Contract With Whom? The

Case of the Political Science, Sociology and Anthropology Department Against the Administration of Simon Fraser University." Memo. 30 September. MsA1 Box 46, Folder 2. Blaser fonds.

Everson, Landis. n.d. "The Laments of Alcibiades." Ms. MsA1 Box 7, Folder 8. Blaser fonds.

Farwell, David. 2001. Coimbra trip notes. Farwell collection.

———. 2002. Photo album, trip to Santa Fe. Farwell collection.

———. 2003. Photo album, trip to Idaho. Farwell collection.

———. 2004. Photo album, trip to Spain. Farwell collection.

———. 2005. Photo album, Order of Canada award. Farwell collection.

———. 2007. Photo album, trip to Seattle. Farwell collection.

———. 2008a. Photo album. Farwell collection.

———. 2008b. Photo album, trip to New York. Farwell collection.

———. 2009. Notes on Blaser's health. MsA1a Box 22, Folder 5. Blaser fonds.

Gordon, J.J. 2000. "A First for the Last Supper." *Die Welt.* 13 April. www.berlineworldwide.com/daten/2000/04/13/0413b21c162280.htx. Clipping in MsA1 Box 42, Folder 10. Blaser fonds.

Hulcoop, John. 1982. "November 6th, 1982." MsA1 Box 23, Folder 8. Blaser fonds.

Killian, Kevin. 7 June 1995. "My Report." UB [University of Buffalo] Discussion Group.poetics@ubvm.cc.buffalo.edu. MsA1 Box 75, Folder 36. Blaser fonds.

Kurp, Patrick. 1994. "Poet Robin Blaser to Visit Albany." *Gazette Reporter.* 24 October. Clipping in MsA1 Box 43, Folder 11. Blaser fonds.

Marion the Naughty Librarian. n.d. [Untitled Poem]. MsA1 Box 27, Folder 6. Blaser fonds.

Quartermain, Peter. 3 December 1993. Introduction to launch of *The Holy Forest,* 1st edition, at the Western Front. Ms. Forwarded in email to author. February 2016. Nichols collection.

———. 25 July 1994. Warren Tallman memorial tribute. MsA1a Box 4, Folder 27. Blaser fonds.

———. 2000. Introduction to *The Last Supper.* Western Front. 6 June. MsA1a Box 4, Folder 27. Blaser fonds.

———. 2006. Introduction to launch of *The Holy Forest,* 2nd edition. Western Front. 8 December. MsA1 Box 40, Folder 2. Blaser fonds.

School Memories. 1937. Autograph book. Samac collection.

Smoler, Michael and Robin Blaser. 17 June 1999. "Sounding the Air with Robin Blaser." Ms. MsA1 Box 70, Folder 18. Blaser fonds.

Wagstaff, Christopher. 1986. Interview with Robin Blaser at Cartright Hotel, San Francisco. 19 June. Ms. MsA1a Box 16, Folder 1. Blaser fonds.

Wheeler, Dennis. 1976. DEATH-WORK. Notes. 3 February. MsA1 Box 37, Folder 1. Blaser fonds.

INTERVIEWS

The following is a list of interviews conducted by the author and digitally recorded. Not all of them are cited in the text, but they have informed this biography.

Baker, Ron. 23 February 2015, New Westminster, B.C.
Bernstein, Charles. 4 December 2014, New York.
Birtwistle, Sir Harrison. 25 November 2013, London, U.K.
Blaser, Millie. 19 August 2014, Boise, Idaho.
Bowering, George. 26 April 2014, Vancouver, B.C.
Brown, Lewis. 21 June 2014, San Francisco.
Browne, Colin. 17 May 2014, Vancouver.
Burton, Hilde. 30 December 2008, San Francisco.
Cole, Norma. 18 June 2014, San Francisco.
Dikeakos, Christos. 24 May 2014, Vancouver.
Ellingham, Lewis. 4 June 2014, San Francisco.
Farwell, David. 11 November 2014, Vancouver.
———. 31 January 2016, Vancouver.
———. 12 February 2016, Vancouver.
———. 28 August 2016, Vancouver.
———. 15 July 2017, Vancouver.
Grieve, Thomas. 11 April 2014, Vancouver.
Hindmarch, Maria (Gladys). 23 March 2014, Vancouver.
Lister, Ardele. 3 December 2015, New York.
Kelley, Paul. 9 August 2015, Vancouver.
Killian, Kevin. 15 June 2014, San Francisco.
Knutson, Susan, 12 April 2014, Vancouver.
Kyger, Joanne. 23 June 2014, Bolinas, California.
Mandel, Tom. 22 March 2016, Facetime.
Maud, Ralph. 7 April 2014, Vancouver.
———. 14 May 2014, Vancouver.
McGauley, Tom. 21 December 2015, Vancouver.
McNaughton, Duncan. 29 June 2014, San Francisco.
Morris, Michael. 21 March 2014, Vancouver.
Palmer, Michael. 11 June 2014, San Francisco.
Stan Persky. 19 October 2013, Vancouver.
———. 11 November 2013, Vancouver.
———. 16 November 2013, Vancouver.
———. 14 December 2013, Vancouver.
Peter and Meredith Quartermain, 15 April 2014, Vancouver.
Meredith Quartermain. 21 July 2017, Vancouver.
———. 27 August 2016, Vancouver.
Peter Quartermain. 27 August 2016, Vancouver.
Samac, Mark. 2 July 2013, Telephone, Vancouver to Boise, Idaho.

———. 21 August 2014, Boise.

Stanley, George. 8 March 2014, Vancouver.

Stouck, David. 30 April 2014, Vancouver.

Tallman, Karen. 3 May 2014, Vancouver.

Truitt, Sam. 25 March 2016, Facetime.

Ulrych, Miriam. 23 April 2014, Vancouver.

Wagstaff, Christopher. 18 June 2014, San Francisco.

Waldman, Anne. 13 February 2015, New York.

Watson, Scott. 1 March 2014, Vancouver.

Wright, Patrick 22 July 2017, Facetime.

Zaslove, Jerry. 28 February 2015, Vancouver.

REFERENCES

Abbott, Steve and Kevin Killian. 1986. "The White Rabbit Symposium and Jack Spicer Conference." In *Poetry Flash* No. 161 (August): 12–16.

Agamben, Giorgio. 1991. *Language and Death*. Translated by Karen E. Pinkus with Michael Hardt. Minneapolis, Oxford: University of Minneapolis Press.

———. 1993a. *The Coming Community*. Translated by Michael Hardt. Minneapolis, London: University of Minnesota Press.

———. 1993b. *Infancy and History: Essays on the Destruction of Experience*. Translated by Liz Heron. London: Verso.

———. 1998. *Homo Sacer: Sovereign Power and Bare Life*. Translated by Daniel Heller-Roazen. Stanford: Stanford University Press.

———. 2000. *Means Without End: Notes on Politics*. Translated by Vincenzo Binetti and Cesare Casarino. Minneapolis, London: University of Minnesota Press.

———. 2004. *The Open: Man and Animal*. Translated by Kevin Attell. Stanford: Stanford University Press.

Alcalay, Ammiel. 1993. *After Jews and Arabs*. Minneapolis and London: University of Minnesota Press.

Alighieri, Dante. 1973. *Vita Nuova*. Translated by Mark Musa. Bloomington & London: Indiana University Press.

Allen, Donald, ed. 1960. *The New American Poetry*. New York: Grove Press.

Altieri, Charles. 1981. *Act & Quality: A Theory of Literary Meaning and Humanistic Understanding*. Amherst: University of Massachusetts Press.

———. 1999. "Some Problems About Agency in the Theories of Radical Poetries." The *Recovery of the Public World: Essays on Poetics in Honour of Robin Blaser*. Edited by Charles Watts and Edward Byrne. Vancouver: Talonbooks. 411–27.

Altieri, Charles and Robin Blaser. 1999. "An Exchange Between Charles Altieri and Robin Blaser." *The Recovery of the Public World: Essays on Poetics in Honour of Robin Blaser*. Edited by Charles Watts and Edward Byrne. Vancouver: Talonbooks. 428–31.

Anderson, Perry. 1998. *The Origins of Postmodernity*. London, New York: Verso.

© The Author(s) 2019
M. Nichols, *A Literary Biography of Robin Blaser*,
Modern and Contemporary Poetry and Poetics,
https://doi.org/10.1007/978-3-030-18327-1

Andrews, Bruce and Charles Bernstein. 1984. "Repossessing the Word." In *The L=A=N=G=U=A=G=E Book*. Carbondale and Edwardsville. Southern Illinois University Press. ix–xi.

Arendt, Hannah. (1951) 1973. *Origins of Totalitarianism*. San Diego, New York, London: Harcourt Brace & Company.

———. (1958) 1959. *The Human Condition*. Garden City, NY: Doubleday & Co., Inc.

Artaud, Antonin. 1965. "Van Gogh: The Man Suicided by Society." Translated by Mary Beach and Lawrence Ferlinghetti. *Antonin Artaud Anthology*. 2nd Rev. Edition by Jack Hirschman. San Francisco: City Lights Books. 135–63.

Atwood, Margaret. 1972. *Survival: A Thematic Guide to Canadian Literature*. Toronto: House of Anansi.

Bancroft, Marian Penner. n.d. "UBC in the Sixties: A Conversation with Audrey Capel Doray, Gathie Falk, Donald Gutstein, Karen Jamieson, Glenn Lewis, Jamie Reid, and Abraham Rogatnick." *Vancouver Art in the Sixties: Ruins in Process*. Accessed 6 January 2019. www.vancouverinthesixties.com/essays/ubc-in-the-sixties.

Barnholden, Michael and Andrew Klobucar, eds. 1999. *Writing Class: The Kootenay School of Writing Anthology*. Vancouver: New Star Books.

Barthes, Roland. (1968) 1980. *Writing Degree Zero*. Translated by Annette Lavers and Colin Smith. New York: Hill and Wang.

Bataille, Georges. 1992. *Theory of Religion*. Trans. Robert Hurley. New York: Zone Books.

Bays, Gwendolyn. 1964. *The Orphic Vision: Seer Poets from Novalis to Rimbaud*. Lincoln: University of Nebraska Press.

Benjamin, Walter. 2015. "Surrealism: Last Snapshot of the European Intelligentsia." In *The Challenge of Surrealism: The Correspondence of Theodor W. Adorno and Elisabeth Lenk*. Edited and translated by Susan H. Gillespie. Minneapolis, London: University of Minnesota Press. 17–29.

Bernstein, Charles, Susan Bee and Andrea Actis. 2010. "'But Sometimes a Sign's All You Need': A Conversation with Susan Bee & Charles Bernstein." *The Capilano Review* 3.12 (Fall): 8–21.

Bett, Stephen. 2017. *So Got Schooled: In the Tower, On the Field*. Victoria, B.C.: Ekstasis Editions.

Blake, William. 2008. *Milton: A Poem. Blake's Poetry and Designs*. Edited by Mary Lynn Johnson and John E. Grant. Norton Critical Ed. 2nd Ed. New York: W.W. Norton & Company. 144–203.

Blaser, Robin. 1958. "Quitting a Job." *Yugen* 3 (1958): 22–23.

———. 1960. "Out to Dinner." *Yugen* 6 (1960): 17.

———. 1967. "Preface." In *Pacific Nation* 1 (June): 3.

———. 1969. "Particles." In *Pacific Nation* 2. 27–42.

———. 1970. "The Holy Forest" section of the "THE HOLY FOREST." *Caterpillar* 12. 24–47.

———. 1974. "Blaser on Burnham." *Criteria* 1.2 (November): 3–5.

———. 1975. Letter to Stephen Vincent. In *Shocks* 5 (February): n.p.

———. 1983. "The Violets: A Cosmological Reading of a Cosmology." *Process Studies* 13.1 (Spring): 8–37.

———. 1986. "No Matter." Introduction to *Freeing the Shadows*. By Luis Posse. Vancouver: Talonbooks. 3–9.

———. 1987. "'My Vocabulary Did This to Me.'" *A Book of Correspondences for Jack Spicer*. Edited by David Levi Strauss and Benjamin Hollander. *Acts 6*. 98–105.

——. 1990. "Rose." *The Sodomite Invasion Review* No. 1 (Summer): 5.

——. 1991a. "Check Out Your Lintels: Poetry and Doors." SUNY Buffalo Lecture. 24 April. PennSound. writing.upenn.edu.

——. 1991b. "Even on Sunday." *The Sodomite Invasion Review.* (Summer): 24–26.

——. 1991c. "Homotextualism." SUNY Buffalo Lecture. 25 April. PennSound. writing.upenn.edu.

——. 1992a. "Belief, Doubt, and Politics." Naropa Lecture. See Archival References.

——. 1992b. "The 'Elf' of It." *Robert Duncan: Drawings and Decorated Books.* Edited by Christopher Wagstaff. Berkeley: Rose Books. 21–28; 44–53.

——. 1993a. *The Holy Forest.* Edited by Stan Persky and Michael Ondaatje. Toronto: Coach House Press.

——. 1993b. Notes for KGNU Radio Interview. See Archival References.

——. 1993c. Poetry Reading and Discussion at SUNY, Buffalo. 15 September. PennSound. writing.upenn.edu.

——. 1994a. Eulogy for Roy Kiyooka. See Archival References.

——. 1994b. Eulogy for Rory Ralston. See Archival References.

——. 1994c. "Image-Nation 24 ('oh, pshaw'." *The Sodomite Invasion Review.* No. 6 (Summer): 24–25.

——. 1995a. "Hello!" *Sulfur* 37 (Fall): 84–94.

——. 1995b. "'Here Lies the Woodpecker Who Was Zeus.'" *A Sacred Quest: The Life and Writing of Mary Butts.* Ed. Christopher Wagstaff. Kingston, New York: McPherson & Company. 159–223.

——. 1995c. "Nomad." *Sulfur* 37 (Fall): 117.

——. 1995d. *Preface to the Early Poems of Robert Duncan.* Toronto: Shuffaloff Books.

——. 1995e. "Quicks and Strings." *Minutes of the Charles Olson Society* #8 (June): 4–14.

——. 1999. "out of the velvet—the denim—the straw of my mind." *99 Poets/1999: An International Poetics Symposium.* Ed. Charles Bernstein. *boundary 2* 26.1 (Spring): 52–53.

——. 2000a. "Great Companion: Dante Alighiere." *Testo & Senso.* Eds. Annalisa Goldoni and Andrea Mariani. Rome: Euroma. 13–27.

——. 2000b. *The Last Supper.* London: Boosey and Hawkes.

——. 2002. Interview with author. In *Even on Sunday: Essays, Readings, and Archival Materials on the Poetry and Poetics of Robin Blaser.* Edited by Miriam Nichols. Orono: National Poetry Foundation. 349–92.

——. 2003a. "Home." 5 August. See Archival References.

——. 2003b. *The Irreparable.* Vancouver: Nomados Press.

——. 2006a. *The Fire: Collected Essays.* Edited by Miriam Nichols. Berkeley: University of California Press.

——. 2006b. *The Holy Forest: Collected Poems.* Edited by Miriam Nichols. Berkeley: University of California Press.

——. 2012. *Never Let the World Go By.* Vancouver: Keefer Street Press.

Blaser, Robin and Charles Altieri. 1999. "An Exchange Between Charles Altieri and Robin Blaser." *The Recovery of the Public World: Essays on Poetics in Honour of Robin Blaser.* Eds. Charles Watts and Edward Byrne. Vancouver: Talonbooks. 428–31.

Blaser, Robin and Rob Dunham, eds. 1986. *Art and Reality: A Casebook of Concern.* Vancouver: Talonbooks.

Blaser, Robin and Friends. (1974) 2015. "The Astonishment Tapes." Ms. Transcript by Miriam Nichols. Contemporary Literature Collection. Special Collections and Rare Books Division. W.A.C. Bennett Library, Simon Fraser University. Burnaby, B.C.

———. 2015. *The Astonishment Tapes.* Ed. Miriam Nichols. Tuscaloosa: University of Alabama.

Blaser, Robin and Meredith Quartermain. 2002. *Wanders.* Vancouver: Nomados Press.

Blaser, Robin and Samuel R. Truitt. 1996. "An Interview with Robin Blaser." *Talisman* No. 16 (Fall): 5–25.

Bowering, George. 1980. *Particular Accidents: Selected Poems.* Edited by Robin Blaser. Vancouver: Talonbooks.

———. 1981. "Introduction to Blaser Reading." On *Robin Blaser Reading at* The Coast Is Only a Line. Videotape. Contemporary Literature Collection, Bennett Library, Simon Fraser University.

———. 2006. "A Berkeley Renaissance Man." *Globe and Mail.* Clipping. See Archival References.

Brodecky Moore, Bill. 2003. "Buzz Gallery." *Big Bridge.* July. Accessed 17 February 2014. bigbridge.org/issue9/bgpage2.htm.

Buffalo News, The. 2006. "Surprise Storm Leaves WNY: [Western New York] Reeling." Saturday, 14 October. A1.

Butts, Mary. 1928. *Armed with Madness.* Drawings by Jean Cocteau. London: Wishart & Co.

———. 1979. *Imaginary Letters.* Edited by Robin Blaser. Vancouver: Talonbooks.

———. 1992. *The Taverner Novels: Armed with Madness and Death of Felicity Taverner.* New York: McPherson & Company.

Canovan, Margaret. 1997. "Hannah Arendt as a Conservative Thinker." In *Hannah Arendt Twenty Years Later.* Edited by Larry May and Jerome Kohn. Cambridge, MA and London, U.K.: MIT Press. 11–32.

Carson, Anne. 2002. *If Not, Winter: Fragments of Sappho.* Toronto, New York: Random House/Vintage Canada.

Cassirer, Ernst. (1946) 1953. *Language and Myth.* Translated by Susanne K. Langer. New York: Dover Publications Inc.

Clark, Andrew. 2000. "THE ARTS: Birtwistle Dishes Up a Sad Turkey OPERA 'THE LAST SUPPER' in Berlin." *The Financial Times.* 20 April.

Cohn, Norman. 1970. *The Pursuit of the Millennium.* Revised Edition. New York: Oxford University Press.

Corso, Gregory and Walter Höllerer, Editors. 1961. *Junge Amerikanische Lyrik.* München: Hansen.

Crashaw, Richard. 1970. *The Complete Poetry of Richard Crashaw.* Edited by George Walton Williams. Garden City, NY: Doubleday & Company.

Creeley, Robert. 1993. Introduction to Poetry Reading and Discussion at SUNY Buffalo, Robin Blaser. 15 September. PennSound. writing.upenn.edu.

———. 2006. *The Collected Poems of Robert Creeley, 1975–2000.* Berkeley, Los Angeles, London: University of California Press.

Dart, Ron. 2002. *Robin Mathews: Crown Prince of Canadian Political Poets.* Dewdney, B.C.: Syntaxis Press.

Davey, Frank. 1975. "Introduction." *TISH No. 1–19.* Edited by Frank Davey. Vancouver: Talonbooks. 7–11.

———. n.d. "The Conference that Never Was: The 'Landmark' 1963 Vancouver Poetry Conference." Accessed 12 July 2016. publish.uwo.ca.

Davidson, Judy. 2007. "Homophobia, Fundamentalism, and Canadian Tolerance: Enabling Gay Games III in Vancouver." *International Journal of Canadian Studies/ Revue international d'études canadiennes* 35: 151–75.

Davidson, Michael. 1989. *The San Francisco Renaissance: Poetics and Community at Mid-Century.* Cambridge, New York: Cambridge University Press.

De Certeau, Michel. 1986. *Heterologies: Discourse on the Other.* Translated by Brian Massumi. Foreword by Wlad Godzich. Minneapolis: University of Minnesota Press.

De Grand, Alexander. 1982. *Italian Fascism: Its Origins & Development.* Lincoln and London: University of Nebraska Press.

DeVries, Hent. 1999. *Philosophy and the Turn to Religion.* Baltimore, London: Johns Hopkins University Press.

Dewhurst, Robert. 2013. "Measure: A Quarterly to the Poem, 1957–1962." *Let the Bucket Down: A Magazine of Boston Area Writing* 1 (2013): 7–22.

Dudek, Louis. 1988. *Infinite Worlds: The Poetry of Louis Dudek.* Edited by Robin Blaser. Montréal: Véhicule Press.

Duncan, Michael. 2013. "An Opening of the Field: Jess, Robert Duncan, and Their Circle." In *An Opening of the Field: Jess, Robert Duncan, and Their Circle.* Edited by Michael Duncan and Christopher Wagstaff. Portland, OR: Pomegranate Communications, Inc. 9–49.

Duncan, Robert. (1944) 1968. "The Homosexual in Society." *Politics* Vol. 1. Introduction by Hannah Arendt. Preface by Dwight MacDonald. New York: Greenwood Reprint Corporation. 209–11.

———. 1950. *Medieval Scenes.* San Francisco: Centaur Press.

———. 1955. *Caesar's Gate.* Mallorca: Divers Press; Rpt. 1972. Berkeley: Sand Dollar.

———. 1958a. "LETTER (1st of a Series." In *Measure* 2 (Winter): 62–63.

———. 1958b. *Letters.* Highlands, N.C.: J. Williams.

———. 1960. *Faust Foutu: An Entertainment in Four Parts.* Stinson Beach: Enkidu sur Rogate.

———. 1964a. *Roots and Branches.* New York: New Directions.

———. 1964b. *Writing Writing.* Albuquerque, N.M.: Sumbooks.

———. 1966a. *A Book of Resemblances.* New York: Henry Wenning.

———. 1966b. *The Years as Catches.* Berkeley: Oyez.

———. 1967. "Returning to Les Chimères of Gérard de Nerval." In *Poetry/Audit* IV, No. 3. 42–61.

———. 1968. *Bending the Bow.* New York: New Direction.

———. 1975. *The Venice Poem.* Sydney, Australia: Prism.

———. (1975) 1980. "Dear Jack." In *The Collected Books of Jack Spicer.* Edited by Robin Blaser. Santa Barbara: Black Sparrow Press. 362–63.

———. 1978. *Medieval Scenes.* Kent, Ohio: Kent State University Libraries.

———. 1984. *Ground Work: Before the War.* New York: New Directions.

———. 1985. "The Truth and Life of Myth." *Fictive Certainties.* New York: New Directions. 1–59.

———. 1987. *Ground Work II: In the Dark.* New York: New Directions.

———. 2011. *The HD Book.* Edited by Michael Boughn and Victor Coleman. Berkeley: University of California Press.

———. 2012. "*Beat Scene* Interview (with Colin Sanders, 1980)." In *A Poet's Mind: Collected Interviews with Robert Duncan, 1960–1985.* Edited by Christopher Wagstaff. Berkeley: North Atlantic Books. 63–80.

Duncan, Robert and Denise Levertov. 2004. *The Letters of Robert Duncan and Denise Levertov.* Edited by Robert J. Bertholf and Albert Gelpi. Stanford: Stanford University Press.

Dunham, Rob. 1986. "Finisterre." Afterword to *Freeing the Shadows*. By Luis Posse. Vancouver: Talonbooks. 169–89.

Ellingham, Lewis. 1983. "Blaser's Trail: Robin Blaser in San Francisco." *Poetry Flash* No. 126 (September): 1, 8.

Ellingham, Lewis and Kevin Killian. 1998. *Poet, Be Like God*. Hanover and London: Wesleyan University Press.

Emerson, Ralph Waldo. 1982. *Selected Essays*. Edited by Larzer Ziff. Harmondsworth, England, New York: Penguin Books.

Enomoto, Randy. 1967. "A Recovery of Intelligence (Ezra Pound and Fascism)." In *Pacific Nation* 1. 83–91.

Everson, Landis. 2004. "Landis Everson in Conversation with Kevin Killian." *Jacket* 26 (October). Accessed 18 February 2018. jacketmagazine.com.

Faas, Ekbert. 1983. *Young Robert Duncan: Portrait of the Poet as a Homosexual in Society*. Santa Barbara: Black Sparrow.

Falwell, Jerry. 1983. In "Rev. Jerry Falwell Gives Speech Saying AIDS Is the Gay Plague." *Today in History: 4 July*. Accessed 29 December 2017. skepticism.org/timeline/july-history/7606-rev-jerry-falwell.

Fawcett, Brian. 2010. "Robin and Me; The New American Poetry and Us." *Robin Blaser*. By Stan Persky and Brian Fawcett. Vancouver: New Star Press. 63–120.

Foucault, Michel. 1970. *The Order of Things*. New York: Random House/Vintage.

Froshaug, Arnt. 1949. "Loyalty Oath Opposition Grows with Two Meets Scheduled Today." *Daily Californian* No. 3 (15 September). Accessed 18 February 2018. oac.cdlib.org.

Frye, Northrop. (1971) 1995. *The Bush Garden: Essays on the Canadian Imagination*. Toronto: House of Anansi.

Gordon, J.J. 2000. "A First for the Last Supper." *Die Welt*. 13 April. www.berlinworld-wide.com/daten/2000/04/13/0413b21c162280.htx.

Grant, George. 1969. *Technology and Empire*. Toronto: House of Anansi.

Greenberg, Clement. 1993. "Modernist Painting." In *Clement Greenberg: The Collected Essays and Criticism*. Vol. 4. Edited by John O'Brian. Chicago and London: University of Chicago Press. 85–93.

Grieve, Tom. 2009. "Robin Blaser 1925–2009." *aq magazine* (November): 26–27.

Grozelle, Renee S. 2017. "The Rise of Gay Liberation in Toronto: From Vilification to Validation." *Inquiries* 9 (01). http://www.inquiriesjournal.com/a?id=1510.

Gundolf, Friedrich. n.d. *The Mantle of Caesar*. Translated by Jacob Wittmer Hartmann. London: G. Richards and H. Toulmin at the Cayne Press.

Guthrie, W.K.C. 1966. *Orpheus and Greek Religion*. New York: W.W. Norton and Co., Inc.

Hamalian, Linda. 1991. *A Life of Kenneth Rexroth*. New York: Norton.

History of Sodomy Laws in the United States, The. n.d. California. Accessed 18 February 2018. glapn.org.

Harold Times. 1990. "Journalism Professor Floyd Arpan Dies at 79." 2 January. Accessed 17 November 2016. haroldtimesonline.com.

Hart, Lawrence. 1945. "Some Elements of Active Poetry." *Circle* 6: 2–12.

Hawthorne, Nathaniel. 1987. *Nathaniel Hawthorne's Tales*. New York, London: W.W. Norton & Company.

Heidegger, Martin. 1971. *Poetry, Language, Thought*. Translated by Albert Hofstadter. New York, Hagerstown, San Francisco, London: Harper & Row, Publishers.

Herndon, James [Jim]. (1975) 1980. "Robin." Letter to Blaser. In *The Collected Books of Jack Spicer*. Edited by Robin Blaser. Santa Barbara: Black Sparrow. 375–78.

Hillman, James. 1997. *The Thought of the Heart and The Soul of the World*. Woodstock, Connecticut: Spring Publications, Inc. 1–88.

Howe, Susan. 1993. *The Birth-Mark: Unsettling the Wilderness in American Literary History*. Middletown, CT: Wesleyan University Press.

Hullot-Kentor, Robert. 1999. "Past Tense: Ethics, Aesthetics and the Recovery of the Public World. In *The Recovery of the Public World: Essays on Poetics in Honour of Robin Blaser*. Edited by Charles Watts and Edward Byrne. Vancouver: Talonbooks. 365–72.

Huyssen, Andreas. 1986. *After the Great Divide*. Bloomington and Indiana: Indiana University Press.

Jarnot, Lisa. 2012. *Robert Duncan: Ambassador from Venus*. Berkeley: University of California Press.

Johnston, Hugh. 2005. *Radical Campus: Making Simon Fraser University*. Vancouver, Toronto: Douglas & McIntyre.

Joyce, James. 1975. *Finnegans Wake*. London: Faber and Faber.

Kaiser, Ernst. 1946. "The Development from Surrealism." *Circle* 9: 74–81.

Kafka, Franz. 1942. "In the Penal Colony." Translated by Eugene Jolas. *Horizon* Vol. 5, No. 27 (March): 158–83.

Kantorowicz Ernst. 1957. *The King's Two Bodies*. Princeton, New Jersey: Princeton University Press.

Killian, Kevin. 1995. "My Report." UB [University of Buffalo] Discussion Group. 7 June. poetics@ubvm.cc.buffalo.edu. Transcript in MsAl Box 75, Folder 36. Blaser fonds.

———. 2002. "Dialogue of Eastern and Western Poetry, Boston, 1956." In *Even on Sunday: Essays, Readings, and Archival Materials on the Poetry and Poetics of Robin Blaser*. Edited by Miriam Nichols. Orono, ME: National Poetry Foundation. 255–73.

Kingsley, Charles. 1916. *The Water-Babies*. New York: Dodd, Mead & Co.

Klein, A.M. 1997. "Ballad of the Days of the Messiah." *Selected Poems*. Edited by Zailig Pollock, Seymour Mayne, Usher Caplan. Toronto, Buffalo, London: University of Toronto Press. 77–78.

Kootenay School of Writing. *New Poetics Colloquium*. Accessed 20 October 2017. kswnet.org.

Korzybski, Alfred. (1937) 2002. *General Semantics Seminar 1937*. 3rd Edition. Brooklyn, NY: Institute of General Semantics.

Kosik, Karel. 1976. *Dialectics of the Concrete*. Translated by Karel Kovanda with James Schmidt. Dordrecht, Holland: D. Reidel Publishing Company.

Kurp, Patrick. 1994. "Poet Robin Blaser to Visit Albany." *Gazette Reporter*. 24 October.

Lacan, Jacques. 1977. "Subversion of the Subject and Dialectic of Desire." In *Écrits*. Translated by Alan Sheridan. New York, London: W.W. Norton and Company. 292–325.

Lancaster, John. 2010. *I.O.U.: Why Everyone Owes Everyone and No One Can Pay*. New York, London, Toronto, Sydney: Simon & Schuster.

Larventz, Don. 1990. "What Do Men's Bodies Mean?" *The Sodomite Invasion Review* No. 1 (August): 1.

Lauder, Adam. 2015. "Robert Smithson's Vancouver Sojourn: Glue Pour, 1970." *Canadian Art* (Summer). Accessed 21 October 2017. Canadianart.ca/features/Robert-smithsons-vancouver-sojourn-glue-pour-1970.

Lefort, Claude. 1968. "Editor's Foreword." *The Visible and the Invisible*. By Merleau Ponty. Translated by Alphonso Lingis. Evanston: Northwestern University Press. xi–xxxiii.

Leider, Philip. 1967. "Vancouver: Scene with No Scene." *artscanada*, Vol. XXIV, Nos. 109/110. (June/July): 1–8.

Levertov, Denise. 1983. *Poems 1960–1967*. New York: New Directions.

Lindsay, Vachel. 1919. *The Chinese Nightingale and Other Poems*. New York: Macmillan.

Lingis, Alphonso. 1968. "Translator's Preface." *The Visible and the Invisible*. By Merleau Ponty. Edited by Claude Lefort. Evanston: Northwestern University Press. xl–lvi.

Lowndes, Joan. 1983. "The Spirit of the Sixties by a Witness." *Vancouver: Art and Artists 1931–1983*. Vancouver: The Vancouver Art Gallery. 142–51.

Lyotard, Jean-François. (1984) 1985. *The Postmodern Condition: A Report on Knowledge*. Translated by Geoff Bennington and Brian Massumi. Minneapolis: University of Minnesota Press.

MacDonald, George. 1905. *Phantastes: A Faerie Romance for Men and Women*. Ed. Greville MacDonald. London: Arthur C. Fifield.

———. 1919. *At the Back of the North Wind*. Philadelphia: D. McKay.

Maud, Ralph. 1991. *Robin Blaser in Vancouver*. Filmed by Kit Lucas. Instructional Media Centre, Simon Fraser University.

Mayer, Hans. 1982. *Outsiders: A Study of Life and Letters*. Translated by Denis M. Sweet. London, Cambridge: The MIT Press.

Maynard, James. 2018. *Robert Duncan and the Pragmatist Sublime*. Albuquerque: University of New Mexico Press.

McCaffery, Steve. 1999. "Blaser's Deleuzean Folds." *The Recovery of the Public World: Essays on Poetics in Honour of Robin Blaser*. Edited by Charles Watts and Edward Byrne. Vancouver: Talonbooks. 373–92.

McCaslin, Susan. 2015. "Trailblazing with Blaser." 28 July. Accessed 14 April 2017. www.cascadiapoetryfestival.org.

McDevitt, Tom. 2002. *Lava: A History*. Pocatello, Idaho: Little Red Hen.

McLuhan, Marshall. 1964. *Understanding Media: The Extensions of Man*. New York: Mentor.

McTavish, Robert. 2013. *The Line Has Shattered: Vancouver's Landmark 1963 Poetry Conference*. Delta B.C.: Non-Inferno Media.

Merleau-Ponty, Maurice. 1968. *The Visible and the Invisible*. Translated by Alphonso Lingis. Edited by Claude LeFort. Evanston: Northwestern University Press.

Menocal, Maria Rosa. 2002. *The Ornament of the World*. Boston: Little, Brown.

Middleton, Peter. 2002. "An Elegy for Theory: Robin Blaser's Essay 'The Practice of Outside.'" *Even on Sunday: Essays, Readings and Archival Materials on the Poetry and Poetics of Robin Blaser*. Edited by Miriam Nichols. Orono, ME: The National Poetry Foundation. 179–206.

Nancy, Jean-Luc. 1991. *The Inoperative Community*. Translated by Peter Connor, Lisa Garbus, Michael Holland, Simona Sawhney. Minneapolis, London: University of Minnesota Press.

Nichol, bp. 1994. *Martyrology Books 1 & 2*. Toronto: Coach House Press.

Nichols, Miriam, ed. 2002. *Even on Sunday: Essays, Readings and Archival Materials on the Poetry and Poetics of Robin Blaser*. Orono: National Poetry Foundation.

Northwestern University Bulletin. 1942. Vol. 43, no. 9 (December): 65–69.

O'Hara, Frank. 1957. *Meditations in an Emergency*. New York: Grove Press.

Olson, Charles. 1970. *The Special View of History*. Edited by Ann Charters. Berkeley: Oyez.

————. 1983. *The Maximus Poems*. Edited by George Butterick. Berkeley: University of California Press.

————. 1997. *Collected Prose*. Edited by Donald Allen and Benjamin Friedlander. Berkeley: University of California Press.

O'Neil, Paul. 1959. "The Only Rebellion Around." *Life* (30 November): 114–30.

People History, The, 1936. n.d. Accessed 16 February 2018. peoplehistory.com.

People History, The. n.d. "Cost of Living 1955." Accessed 30 January 2017. thepeople-history.com/1955.html#cost_of_living.

Perkins, David, ed. 1967. *English Romantic Writers*. New York: Harcourt, Brace & World.

Persky, Stanley [Stan]. 1963. "Peacock." *Open Space 0: A Prospectus*. n.p.

————. 1964. "A CHANGE." In *Open Space 7*, n.p.

————. 1967a. "California Sociology." In *Pacific Nation* 1. 98–100.

————. 1967b. "Orpheus Editor." In *Pacific Nation* 1. 108–13.

————. 1969. "Program Notes." In *Pacific Nation* 2. 107.

————. 2000. "The Last Supper on Stage." Europa Column. *The Vancouver Sun*. 25 April. A9.

————. 2010. "Reading Robin Blaser." In *Robin Blaser*. By Stan Persky and Brian Fawcett. Vancouver: New Star Books. 3–45.

Petro, Pamela. 2003. "The Hipster of Joy Street: An Introduction to the Life and Work of John Wieners." *Jacket* 21 (February). jacketmagazine.com.

Poets' Theater, The. Accessed 31 January 2017. poetstheatre.org/history.

————. Accessed 31 January 2017. oasis.lib.harvard.edu.

Posse, Luis. 1986. *Freeing the Shadows*. Vancouver: Talonbooks.

Pound, Ezra. 1963. *Translations*. New York: New Directions.

————. 1968. *The Spirit of Romance*. New York: New Directions.

————. 1993. *The Cantos*. New York: New Directions Press.

Quartermain, Meredith. 2002. "Preface." *Wanders*. By Meredith Quartermain and Robin Blaser. Vancouver: Nomados Press. 1.

————. 2009. "With Respect: Remembering Robin Blaser (1925–2009)." *The Poetry Project Newsletter* #220. (October/November): 6. www.poetryproject.org.

Quartermain, Peter. 1995. "The Mind as Frying Pan: Robin Blaser's Humor." *Sulfur* 37 (Fall): 108–16.

Rabelais, François. n.d. *Gargantua and Pantagruel*. New York: Dodd, Mead & Company.

Rasula, Jed. 1995. "Taking Out the Tracks: Robin Blaser's Syncopation." *Sulfur* 37 (Fall): 95–107.

Rilke, Rainer Maria. 1948. *Letters of Rainer Maria Rilke*. Vol. 2, 1910–1926. Trans. Jane Bannard Greene and M.D. Herter Norton. New York: Norton.

Rogatnick, Abraham. 2006. "A Passion for the Contemporary." *B.C. Binning*. Edited by Abraham Rogatnick, Ian M. Thom, Adele Weder. Vancouver, Toronto: Douglas & McIntyre. 1–40.

"Romer, Governor of Colorado, et al. v. Evans et al., 517 U.S. 620 (1996)." Legal Information Institute. Cornell University Law. Accessed 29 December 2017. http://www.law.cornell.edu/supct/html/94-1039.ZO.html.

Ronell, Avital. 1986. *Dictations: On Haunted Writing*. Bloomington, Indiana: Indiana University Press.

———. 1994. *Finitude's Score: Essays for the End of the Millennium.* Lincoln: University of Nebraska Press.

Rumaker, Michael. 2013. *Robert Duncan in San Francisco.* San Francisco: City Lights.

Ruthven, K.K. 1969. *A Guide to Pound's Personae (1926).* Berkeley and Los Angeles: University of California Press.

Schneiderman, Josh, ed. 2009. *The Correspondence of Kenneth Koch & Frank O'Hara.* Part II. Lost and Found: The CUNY Poetics Document Initiative. Series 1, No. 2 (Winter): 1–30.

Scott, Ramsey. 2016. *The Narco-Imaginary.* Brooklyn: Ugly Ducking Press.

Shaw, Nancy. n.d. "Siting the Banal: The Expanded Landscapes of the N.E. Thing Co." *Vancouver Art in the Sixties: Ruins in Process.* Accessed 10 April 2017. vancouverartinthesixties.com.

Shelley, Percy Bysshe. 1951. "The Triumph of Life." In *The Selected Poetry and Prose of Percy Bysshe Shelley.* Edited by Carlos Baker. New York: The Modern Library. 343–59.

Silliman, Ron. 1987. "'My Vocabulary Did This to Me.'" In *Acts 6: A Book of Correspondences for Jack Spicer.* Edited by David Levi Strauss and Benjamin Hollander. 67–71.

———. 2003. "Wanders." http://ronsillimanblogspot.com. 27 May. [Downloaded copy in MsA1 Box 15, Folder 1. Blaser fonds.]

Sophocles. 1954. *Oedipus at Colonus.* Translated by Robert Fitzgerald. In *Sophocles I.* Edited by David Grene and Richmond Lattimore. Chicago & London: The University of Chicago Press. 77–155.

Spicer, Jack. 1964. "PROTESTANT LETTER." In *Open Space* 7, n.p.

———. (1975) 1980. *The Collected Books of Jack Spicer.* Edited by Robin Blaser. Santa Barbara: Black Sparrow Press.

———. 1980. *One Night Stand & Other Poems.* San Francisco: Grey Fox Press.

———. 1998. *The House that Jack Built: The Collected Lectures of Jack Spicer.* Edited by Peter Gizzi. Hanover and London: Wesleyan University Press.

———. 2008. *My Vocabulary Did This to Me: The Collected Poetry of Jack Spicer.* Edited by Peter Gizzi and Kevin Killian. Middletown: Wesleyan University Press.

Stanley, George. 1967a. "On Strangers." In *Pacific Nation* 1. 101–105.

———. 1967b. "You." In *Pacific Nation* 1. 47–53.

———. 2011. "'This Is the Place': A Conversation with George Stanley." *The Capilano Review* 3.4 (Spring): 5–25.

Stockwood, Mervyn. 1942. "The Case for Reconstruction." *Horizon* Vol. 5, No. 27 (March).

Stouck, David. 2013. *Arthur Erickson: An Architect's Life.* Vancouver, Toronto: Douglas & McIntyre.

Strauss, David Levi. 1987. "Introductions." In *Acts 6: A Book of Correspondences for Jack Spicer.* Edited by David Levi Strauss and Benjamin Hollander. 1–2.

Swinburne, Algernon Charles. 2015. *Selected Verse.* Edited by Alex Wong. Manchester, U.K.: Carcanet Press.

Tallman, Warren. 1976–77. "Wonder Merchants: Modernist Poetry in Vancouver During the 1960's." *Godawful Streets of Man: Essays by Warren Tallman. Open Letter* 3.6 (Winter): 175–207.

"Thirty Years of HIV/AIDS: Snapshots of an Epidemic." amfAR: The Foundation for AIDS Research. Accessed 28 December 2017. www.amfar.org/thirty-years-of-hiv/aids-snapshots-of-an-epidemic.

Twin Falls Evening Times. 1939. "An' Daisy Mae—She Gits Her Man." Monday, 27 March. P5.

Torra, Joseph. 1994. "Introduction." In *Stephen Jonas: Selected Poems.* Edited by Joseph Torra. Hoboken, N.J.: Talisman House Publishers. 1–13.

Traherne, Thomas. (1699) 1991. "Thanksgivings for the Body." *From a Serious and Pathetical Contemplation of the Mercies of God.* In *Selected Poems and Prose.* Edited by Alan Bradford. London, New York: Penguin Books. 169–83.

Truitt, Samuel R. and Robin Blaser. 1996. "An Interview with Robin Blaser." *Talisman* No. 16 (Fall): 5–25.

Vidaver, Aaron, ed. 1999. *Minutes of the Charles Olson Society Newsletter. A Vancouver 1963 Issue.* No. 30 (April).

Vincent, Stephen. 1975. Letter to Blaser. In *Shocks 5* (February): n.p.

Wagstaff, Christopher. 1986. Interview with Robin Blaser. See Archival References.

———, ed. 1995. *A Sacred Quest: The Life and Writing of Mary Butts.* Kingston, New York: McPherson & Company.

———. 2013. "'This Here Other World': The Art of Robert Duncan and Jess." In *An Opening of the Field: Jess, Robert Duncan, and Their Circle.* Eds. Michael Duncan and Christopher Wagstaff. Portland, OR: Pomegranate Communications, Inc. 51–88.

Wall, Jeff. 2014. "Foreword." *Christos Dikeakos: Nature Morte.* Kelowna: Kelowna Art Gallery.

Watson, Scott. 1983. "Art in the Fifties: Design, Leisure, and Painting in the Age of Anxiety." *Vancouver: Art and Artists 1931–1983.* Vancouver: The Vancouver Art Gallery. 72–101.

———. n.d. "Transmission Difficulties: Vancouver Painting in the 1960s." Accessed 10 April 2017. http://transmissiondifficulties.vancouverartinthesixties.com/pages/24.

Watts, Charles. 1995. "Foreword." *Sulfur* 37 (Fall): 81–83.

Watts, Charles and Edward Byrne, eds. 1999. The *Recovery of the Public World: Essays on Poetics in Honour of Robin Blaser.* Vancouver: Talonbooks.

Whalley, George. 1953. *Poetic Process.* London: Routledge and K. Paul.

Wheeler, Dennis and Ardele Lister. 1977. "'Some People Will Do Anything to Avoid Criticism': A Conversation with Dennis Wheeler." *Criteria* 3.1 (February): 13–17.

Whitehead, Alfred North. (1929) 1978. *Process and Reality: An Essay in Cosmology.* Edited by David Ray Griffin and Donald W. Sherburne. New York, London: The Free Press/Collier Macmillan Publishers.

Whitman, Walt. 1977. "Preface to Leaves of Grass, 1855." *The Portable Walt Whitman.* Edited by Mark Van Doren. New York: Penguin. 5–27.

Wieners, John. 1986. *Selected Poems 1934–2002.* Santa Barbara: Black Sparrow Press.

Wolf, Leonard. 1946. *Hamadryad Hunted.* Berkeley: Bern Porter Books.

Wolin, Sheldon. 1994. "Hannah Arendt: Democracy and the Political." In *Hannah Arendt: Critical Essays.* Edited by Lewis P. Hinchman and Sandra K. Hinchman. Albany, NY: State University of New York Press. 289–306.

Wright, Patrick. 1985. *On Living in an Old Country: The National Past in Contemporary Britain.* London: Verso.

———. 2000. "Facing up to the Subterranean Stream: The Challenge of Robin Blaser's Libretto." *Glyndebourne Touring Opera Programme.* Edenbridge, Kent, U.K.: Westerham Press Ltd. 41–46.

Yeats, William Butler. (1962) 1971. *Selected Poems.* Edited by Norman Jeffares. London and Basingstoke: Macmillan London Ltd.

———. 1978. *Mythologies.* New York: Collier Books.

INDEX

A

Ackerman, Gerald, 44
Act & Quality (Altieri), 9n6
Active poetry/activists, 38
Activism, 138, 140, 157
   See also Civil rights
Adam, Helen, 98, 108, 116, 123, 209
Adams, Cleo, 19, 36, 122
Adams, Henry, 248
Adam's Way (Duncan), 102, 129
"African Elegy, An" (Duncan), 48
After Jews and Arabs (Alcalay), 246
After Lorca (Spicer), 75
After the Great Divide (Huyssen), 190n5
"After the Pleasure Party" (Melville), 73
"Against Wisdom as Such" (Olson), 108
Agamben, Giorgio
   on the Irreparable, 195, 221–223,
      227, 235, 255n1
   philosophy of, 224, 225, 229,
      242, 243, 248, 256n3,
      256n4, 256n5, 256n9
AIDS, 157, 192–198, 215, 217, 219n1,
   219n6
   See also Anti-gay legislation;
      Homophobia; Sexuality
Alcalay, Ammiel, 246, 247
Alcibiades, 44, 54
Alexander, Charles, 243

Alexander, James, 98, 108, 130n2
Alexander, Paul, 96, 97, 112, 113, 115,
   209, 215
Alhambra, The (Irwin), 248
Alice in Wonderland (Carroll), 75
Allen, Donald (Don)
   correspondence with RB, 53–54, 61,
      68, 70, 90, 99, 106, 247, 252
   editor of *Evergreen Review*, 69, 70, 81,
      84, 85
   editor of *The New American Poetry*, 1,
      3, 54, 68, 70, 104, 217
   friendship with RB, 69–72, 84, 90,
      106, 110, 240, 251, 258n22
Allen, Steve, 96, 130n1
Altieri, Charles, 9n6, 211, 213, 252
Ambassador from Venus (Jarnot), 41, 102
"American Express" (Corso), 104
*American Fascists: The Christian Right and
   the War in America* (Helger), 248
"Among My Friends, Love is a Great
   Sorrow" (Duncan), 42, 202
"Among School Children" (Yeats), 79
Amory, Hugh, 63
Anarchism, 37–39, 42, 48, 62, 146, 218
Anatomy of Melancholy (Burton), 208
*Ancient Near East, The: An Anthology of
   Texts and Pictures* (Pritchard), 162n11
Anderson, Perry, 220n16

© The Author(s) 2019
M. Nichols, *A Literary Biography of Robin Blaser*,
Modern and Contemporary Poetry and Poetics,
https://doi.org/10.1007/978-3-030-18327-1

Andrews, Bruce, 142, 162n16
"And when I pay death's duty", 62, 65
Anthropocentrism, rejection of, 17, 151
    See also Nature
Anti-gay legislation, 37, 192, 193,
    198, 217
    See also Homophobia; Sexuality
"Aphrodite of the Leaves," 211
"Apocalypse for Three Voices" (Spicer),
    49, 50
Arendt, Hannah
    politics of, 148, 149, 195, 214, 235,
        242, 257n15
    on public vs. private space, 198, 212
Aristotle, 47, 221
Armed with Madness (Butts), 118, 175,
    176, 203
Arpan, Eleanore Holferty, 31–32, 40
Arpan, Floyd G., 31
Art and Reality: A Casebook of Concern
    (essays), 219n3
Artaud, Antonin, 78
"Artist of the Beautiful, The"
    (Hawthorne), 114, 122, 130n10
Ashbery, John, 1, 60, 69, 73, 89, 90,
    104, 150, 240, 252
Aste, Tony, 107
Auden, W.H., 39
Auer, Simon (RB's step-grandfather),
    14, 15, 23
Auer, Sophia Nichols (RB's grandmother)
    death, 102
    financial support of RB, 29, 33, 35,
        36, 55
    influence on RB, 14–17, 21, 33, 186,
        190n8
    personality, 14–17, 21, 22, 25
Auerhahn Press, 102, 110, 111, 129
Avison, Margaret, 135
Axial Age, The (Jaspers), 248

B
"Bach's Belief" (essay), 197, 215,
    219n9
Back of the North Wind, At the
    (MacDonald), 203
Baert, David, 165

Baggs, Camilla, 176
Baker, Ron, 127, 129, 140
Balas, Lars, 81
Balas, Tom, 65, 67, 81
Baldwin, James, 104
Balkind, Alvin, 135, 136
"Ballad of the Days of the Messiah"
    (Klein), 234, 258n19
Barbarism with a Human Face
    (Lévy), 187
Barenboim, Daniel, 233
Barthes, Roland, 6, 138, 188, 190n9
Bataille, Georges, 83, 180
Baudelaire, Charles, 224
Bays, Gwendolyn, 256n8
Beatniks (Beats), 96, 97, 99, 103, 104,
    130n1
Beckett, Samuel, 69
"Beckoning Fair One, The"
    (Onion), 35
"Before a Crucifix" (Swinburne), 258n17
Berger, John, 224
Berkeley, see University of California,
    Berkeley
Bernstein, Charles, 142, 162n16, 179,
    189n2, 196, 212, 252
Bett, Stephen, 162n7
Beyond Formalism (Hartman), 187
Billy the Kid (Spicer), 98, 126
Birth Mark, The: Unsettling the
    Wilderness in American History
    (Howe), 256n6
Birtwistle, Sir Harrison, 221, 231–233,
    236–238
Bissett, Bill, 134, 217
Black Mountain College, 34, 34n8,
    60–62, 64, 97, 98, 100, 169, 170
Black Mountain Review (magazine),
    62, 70, 134
Blake, William, 16, 65, 100, 187,
    194, 231
Blaser, Augustus Fredrick (Gus; RB's
    grandfather), 12, 22, 34n2, 55
Blaser, Fredrick Augustus (RB's great
    grandfather), 11–12
Blaser, Harold James (Jimmy; RB's
    brother), 20, 24, 250
Blaser, Hope (RB's sister), 15, 20, 242

Blaser, Ina Mae McCready (RB's mother)
  death, 197, 215–217
  relationship with RB, 11, 20–21, 24,
    34, 55, 57–59, 69, 121
  at Sacred Heart Academy, 11, 14, 25,
    34, 34n7, 121
Blaser, Irvin (Gus; RB's brother),
  15, 20, 24
Blaser, Robert Augustus (RB's father)
  illness and death, 168, 169
  personal history, 34
  relationship with RB, 13, 14, 17, 19,
    22–24, 28, 29, 32–33, 58, 59,
    168, 169
Blaser, Robert Francis
  attitudes and perspectives; appearance
    and personality, 16, 17, 20, 22–28,
    32, 95, 129, 143, 160, 181;
    Catholicism of, 24–25, 29, 40,
    42, 43, 47, 109, 195, 217;
    empathy with social outcasts, 27,
    68, 237, 242; landscape of the
    imagination, 17–20, 32, 43, 83,
    117, 120, 121, 176, 229; lifestyle,
    58, 67, 68, 95, 104, 182, 184,
    232, 243; love of art, 84, 89, 95,
    112–115, 137, 138, 184, 185;
    pursuit of the sacred, 4–6, 18,
    23–25, 49, 86, 115, 145, 146,
    151, 153, 155, 173–176, 180,
    187, 198, 206, 225, 230, 233,
    235; rich interior life, 25, 27, 52,
    145; sense of "otherness," 17, 24,
    27, 53, 196, 229
  conferences lectures, and reading
    tours; at Atwater Library and
    Concordia (2008), 253; at
    Berkeley (2008), 253; Berkeley
    Poetry Conference (1965), 124,
    127; at Co-operative Christian
    Campus Ministry at UBC (1980),
    174; The Holy Forest reading tours
    (1993–94), 205–208;
    International Meeting of Poets at
    Coimbra, Portugal (2001), 240;
    "Language is Love" lecture at
    Naropa (2004), 242; Mary Butts,
    Conference at University of

California, Davis (1984), 176; at
  Naropa University in Denver
  (1992), 196; Nationalisms and
  Poetic Communities at University
  of Calgary (1994), 207; at New
  College of California (1983), 174,
  175; New Poetics Colloquium
  (1985), 179; "On Words"
  (Creeley memorial conference;
  2006), 252; "Places on Earth"
  series (2000), 240; The Recovery
  of the Public World Conference
  (1995), 208–215; at SUNY,
  Buffalo (1991), 194, 196; at
  Temple University (2002), 207,
  223, 241; 6 Towns Poetry Festival
  at Stoke-on-Trent (1996), 231; at
  University of Idaho, Boise (2003),
  242; White Rabbit Symposium
  (1986), 179–182
education; childhood and adolescence,
  17–18, 20; at Berkeley, 45–48,
  50–52, 54–55
European cultural trips; Berlin (2000),
  236, 237; Coimbra, Portugal
  (2001), 240; Glyndebourne, U.K.
  (2000), 237; grand tour (1959),
  83–91; Greece (1972), 145, 146;
  London (1996), 231; Pescara,
  Italy (1997), 230; photographs of,
  15, 21, 26, 166, 192, 208, 216,
  232, 241, 244; Spanish tour
  (2004), 247
personal history; awards and
  accolades, 243, 245, 254; at
  Berkeley, 33–56; birth, 11, 34; in
  Boston, 57–86; childhood and
  youth, 13–34; early forays into
  the creative arts, 17–18, 23–25,
  27–28; emerging homosexuality,
  19, 24, 27, 30, 36, 40; illness
  and death, 218, 252–255; as
  librarian, 59, 84, 91n1, 96, 100,
  109; as teacher/professor, 54,
  100, 138–146, 173–182,
  197–198; photographs of, 104,
  105; in San Francisco, 64, 84,
  90, 91, 95–129

Blaser, Robert Francis (*cont.*)
poetry and prose of; autobiographical
elements, 117, 119, 121, 123,
199–203, 238; childhood memories,
82, 119–122, 226, 229; collage
elements, 5, 123, 185–187, 196,
211, 214, 225, 234; as collective/
communal, 6, 149, 151, 187, 207,
208, 214, 220n18, 222, 225, 255;
elegiac, 193, 198–205, 218, 250;
homoeros, 117, 119–122, 175, 195;
influence of Dante, 4, 82, 83, 118,
119, 121, 202, 226–230; irreparable
(concept), 195, 221–225, 227, 229,
235, 239, 241, 245; landscape of the
imagination, 18, 81, 82, 117, 120,
121, 176, 229; language, philosophy
of, 49–50, 117, 152–154, 222–224;
myth, 28, 115, 119–122, 124, 142,
143, 146, 152, 174, 176, 178, 199,
200, 203; open space, poetics of, 5,
23, 65, 109, 145, 146, 187, 191,
213, 214, 224; the Other, 77, 79,
80, 153, 196; politics in, 148, 149,
212, 225, 228, 246; productive
periods, 85, 86, 100;
psychoanalytical elements, 75, 118,
153; the "real," 4, 78, 80, 85, 176,
204, 211, 213, 229; relationship
with nature, 118, 119, 122, 151,
178, 185; religious imagery, 49–50,
118, 119, 228–230; religious
influence on, 28, 49–50, 119, 143,
195, 235; structuralist and
deconstructive theory, 5, 81, 83,
153, 181, 235; struggles with
writing, 31, 51–52, 72, 84, 85, 123;
surrealism, 75–77, 79, 100, 114,
119, 151; tree imagery, 82, 83, 117,
120–122, 191, 200, 222, 249 (*See
also* Blaser, Robin Francis, attitudes
and perspectives, pursuit of the
sacred)
poetry and prose of, criticism of RB's
poetry; Marshall and Wieners, 80;
Mrs. Arpan, 31–32; Olson,
71–73; Prynne, 155
relationship with Robert Duncan; at
Berkeley, 1, 2, 35, 42–45, 48–50,
62, 118, 175, 176; friendship and
correspondence with, 6, 33, 36,
42–45, 55, 60, 61, 63, 64, 66–70,

72, 74–78, 83–85, 87, 90, 96,
106, 114, 198–205, 249, 253;
poetry and poetics, companionship
with, 5, 41, 42, 47–50, 52–53, 55,
60, 68, 75, 76, 78, 82, 100, 117,
118, 151, 175, 186, 187,
197–205, 214, 219n7; quarrels
with, 99–102, 105–107, 114,
123–126, 129, 204, 206; in San
Francisco, 1, 96, 98–116, 176,
179; in Vancouver, 133, 135, 208
relationship with David Farwell, 1,
161, 185, 192–194; final year,
253–255; romance with, 167,
168; travels with, 207, 215, 216,
231–232, 237, 240–245, 247,
253; Turner Tour, 182–185
relationship with father, 2, 11–14, 17,
19, 28, 33, 58, 120, 124, 168, 169
relationship with Jim Felts, 1, 36–37,
41, 52, 60, 87, 91, 95, 105, 182
relationship with Stan Persky;
companion in poetry, 123, 126,
146, 147, 150, 157, 191, 192, 195,
198, 236, 245; life with, 133, 135,
157, 158; romance with, 102–108
relationship with Jack Spicer; at Berkeley,
1, 33, 40–56, 107, 175, 176; death
of, 1, 126–129; friendship and
correspondence with, 1, 6, 33,
41–45, 48–51, 53–55, 60, 62, 63,
70, 73, 75, 98–102, 104, 105, 249,
253; poetry and poetics,
companionship with, 3, 5, 43–45,
48–51, 54, 55, 60, 78, 79, 81, 100,
102, 108, 110, 116–118, 123, 125,
149, 151, 156–157, 179–181, 187,
195, 197, 201, 204, 206, 207,
220n12, 223, 225, 229, 235,
256n8; quarrels with, 78, 101, 102,
106, 108, 110, 111, 131n12; in San
Francisco, 1, 96–129; in Vancouver,
135, 137, 140, 146, 147, 208
relationship with Colin Stuart, 158–160
relationship with Scott Watson, 159,
176, 208, 236, 254
works; "And when I pay death's duty,"
62, 65; "Aphrodite of the Leaves,"
211; *Astonishment Tapes, The*, 7, 12,
16, 37, 41, 56n1, 126, 130n8,
130n9, 159, 199, 206, 229, 230,
256n8; "Bach's Belief" (essay), 197,

215, 219n9; *Boston Poems, The*, 74–83, 100, 129, 151; *Charms*, 8, 148, 151; *Chimères, Les*, 100, 116, 124–126, 199, 200, 203, 206, 258n18; *Cups*, 18, 34n5, 96, 100, 104, 114, 116–122, 130n10, 148, 153, 175, 202, 222, 242; *Cups* (painting), 116; "Curriculum Vitae," 24, 27, 96; "Dante and the Metaphysics of Light," 256n8; "Desert, The," 17–18, 32; "Diary, April 11, 1981," 185, 187, 188; "Even on Sunday", 195–198, 209, 225, 231; *Exody*, 191, 229; *Faerie Queene, The*, 89, 100, 116, 122; "Find you the path," 28; "Fire, The" (essay), 4, 7, 31, 49, 55, 63, 116, 117, 148, 151, 200, 203; *Fire, The: Collected Essays of Robin Blaser*, 148, 149, 170, 174, 191, 223, 244; "For years I've heard," 85, 86; "Fousang," 214, 230; "George Bowering's Plain Song" (essay), 170, 171; "Great Companion: Dante Alighieri," 4, 226–230; Great Companion: Robert Duncan," 199–205; "Here Lies the Woodpecker Who Was Zeus" (essay), 176; *Holy Forest, The*, 5, 8, 49, 74, 75, 82, 83, 85, 90, 99, 101, 108, 115, 121, 122, 129, 151, 191, 204–208, 223, 226, 230, 231, 239, 244, 245, 251, 253, 258n20; "Hunger of Sound, The," 5, 69–71, 75, 80, 81, 83, 223, 226, 242; "Ichnograph 1," 241; "Image-Nation 1 (the fold," 8; "Image-Nation 4 (old gold," 18–20; "Image-Nation 5 (erasure," 152, 200, 253; "Image-Nation 6 (epithalamium," 120, 148, 152; "Image-Nation 7 (l'air," 151, 155; "Image-Nation 8 (morphe," 152; "Image-Nation 9 (half and half," 47, 152; "Image-Nation 10 (marriage clothes," 154; "Image-Nation 11 (the poesis," 120; "Image-Nation 12 (Actus," 153; "Image-Nation 24 ('oh, pshaw,'" 195, 217, 242; "Image-Nation 25 (exody," 209, 211, 229; *Image-Nations*, 101, 108, 151–155, 186, 231; Last Image-

Nation, 246–250; *Infinite Worlds: The Poetry of Louis Dudek*, 171–173; "Irreparable, The" (essay and chapbook), 223–224, 239, 245; "Lake of Souls," 49, 187; *Last Supper, The* (libretto), 221, 225, 231–240, 246, 247, 250, 257n14, 257n15; "Letter(s) to Freud," 65, 75, 77, 92n12; "Lives of the Poets," 43, 52, 53; "Medium, The," 123; "Mind Canaries" (essay), 176–179, 222; *Moth Poem, The*, 31, 100, 107, 108, 116, 122, 123, 127; "My Vocabulary Did This To Me" (essay), 179–182; *Never Let the World Go By*, 240; "Ode for Museums, All of Them!," 90; "Of is the word love without the initial consonant," 218; "Out of America," 87; "Out of the Window," 148; "Out to Dinner," 73; "Pacific Spectator, The," 53, 56; "Paradise Quotations," 123; *Park, The*, 13–14, 16, 18, 22–23, 34n4, 100, 114, 116, 122, 127; "Particles" (essay), 146, 148, 149, 151, 196, 198, 212, 222; *Pell Mell*, 23, 185, 191, 193, 196, 198, 214, 222, 223, 225, 230; "Poem by the Charles River", 62, 65, 81; "Poetry and Positivisms" (essay), 191, 224; "Practice of Outside, The" (essay), 9n5, 42, 77, 128, 151, 156–157, 159, 207, 220n12; "Preface to the Early Poems of Robert Duncan" (essay), 219n8; "Preface to Works to Come, A," 75, 78, 119, 120; "Quitting a Job," 73, 75, 86, 253; "Recovery of the Public World, The" (essay), 191, 209, 212, 214, 231; "Song in Four Parts for Christ the Son," 49–50; "Sophia Nichols," 16, 108; "Stadium of the Mirror, The" (essay), 9n5, 50, 151–155, 213, 250, 256n8; *Syntax*, 5, 72, 185–188, 214, 255; "Ten Songs for Love," 72; *Truth is Laughter, The*, 186; "Tumble-Weed," 33, 169; "Two Astronomers with Notebooks," 99; "Violets, The" (essay), 9n3, 174; *Wanders*, 238–240, 245; "Wife of Bath," 27–28

Boccaccio, Giovanni, 246
Bonnard, Pierre, 114, 183
Book of Resemblances, A (Duncan), 52
Boone, Bruce, 179, 181
Boorman, John, 187
Borderers, The (Wordsworth), 55
Borregaard, Ebbe, 97, 100, 108, 124, 128
Boston, RB's time in, 57–86
Boston Newsletter, The, 62, 65, 75
Boston Poems, The, 74–83
Botto, Ken, 115
Boughn, Michael, 219n8, 245, 251
Bowering, Angela, 7, 250
Bowering, George, 6, 7, 134, 135, 145,
    159, 169–172, 189n3, 190n4, 194,
    230, 244, 245
Bowles, Paul, 39
Boyce, Jack, 115
Braun, Erika, 49
Brautigan, Richard, 116, 147
Brockway, Lyn, 96, 112, 113, 209
Brodecky Moore, William (Bill), 101,
    102, 112, 115, 156, 243
Bromige, David, 108, 135
Bronzino (Agnolo di Cosimo), 86
Broughton, James, 98, 130n2
Bruin (school newspaper), 25
Buck, Paul, 59
Burroughs, William, 67, 104, 110
Burton, Hilde, 38, 95
Burton, Richard Francis, 54–55
Burton, Robert, 208
Bush, George Herbert Walker, 192
Bush Garden, The (Frye), 170, 190n4
Butler, John, 209
Butterick, George, 71, 158
Button, John, 60, 65, 127, 147
Butts, Mary, 2, 118, 175, 176, 203
Buzz Gallery, 115, 243
Byrd, Don, 207
Byrne, Edward, 208, 209

C
Caesar's Gate (Duncan), 52, 201
"California Sociology" (Persky), 147
Canada
    vs. America, 193
    indigenous art, 137, 171
    modernism, 171, 172

nationalism, 137, 138, 169, 170,
    189n2, 190n4
poetry scene/CanLit, 159, 169–173,
    190n4
RB's connection with, 6, 169–173,
    184, 243–244
Cantos, The (Pound), 3, 4, 42, 43,
    204, 227
Carroll, Lewis, *see Alice in Wonderland*
Carson, Anne, 175, 198
Catholicism
    and Dante, 4, 5, 47
    and politics, 195–197, 246–247
    in RB's poetry, 2, 4, 5, 14, 23, 49,
        117, 120, 121, 153, 226–230,
        233–236
    RB's relationship with, 24–25, 29, 40,
        42–43, 109, 195, 198, 217
    See also Religion
Causal Mythology (Olson), 162n11
Cavafy, Constantine, 187
Certeau, Michel de, 180, 181
Cerutti, Laura, 244
Cervantes, Lorna Dee, 197
Cervantes, Miguel de, 246
Chamberlain, Lori, 179
Charms, 8, 148, 151
Chaucer, Geoffrey, 27, 34n7, 86, 246
"Chess Game, The" (Spicer), 75
Chimères, Les, 100, 116, 124–126, 199,
    203, 206, 258n18
"Church and Reconstruction, The"
    (Stockwood), 39–40
Circle (magazine), 3, 38–40, 48
Civil rights, 3, 5, 24, 157
    See also Activism
Cixous, Hélène, 224
Clark, John, 51
Clarkson, Adrienne, 243, 245
Cobb, Edith, 7
Cocteau, Jean, 63, 79, 81, 100, 147,
    151, 152
Cohn, Norman, 257n13
Cold Mountain (personal growth
    institute), 34n3, 158, 160, 165, 167
Coleridge, Samuel Taylor, 123, 145
Collage
    in poetry of Duncan, 3, 42, 47, 125, 214
    in poetry of RB, 5, 123, 124, 185,
        186, 210, 214, 225, 234

in visual arts, 113, 114, 137, 176, 177,
    222, 239
  See also Open space
Collected Books of Jack Spicer, The, 42, 45,
    50, 98, 129, 151, 156–157
Collective humanity (concept), 38–39,
    42, 47–48, 149
College of Idaho, 31, 33, 34n1, 35
Collins, Jess
  art of, 3, 53, 84, 98, 108, 113–115
  relationship with RB, 84, 100, 102,
      105–107, 111, 124, 128, 202,
      220n14, 251
Coming Community, The (Agamben),
    221–223
Communal, poetry as, 6, 42, 149, 225
Composition by field, 46, 113, 187
Comroe, Julius, 91
"Conference that Never Was, The: The
    'Landmark' 1963 Vancouver Poetry
    Conference" (Davey), 161n1
Connolly, Cyril, 39
Conselman, Bill, 19
Coolidge, Clark, 135
Coomer, Mike, 108
Cope, Patricia, 11, 12
Copithorne, Judith, 134, 135
Corbin, Henry, 187
Corman, Cid, 64
Corso, Gregory, 73, 84, 97, 104
Cosmology
  Olson's views on, 71, 72, 174
  as poetic element, 5, 28, 119, 121, 142,
      151, 180, 181, 193, 197, 226
*Courtier and the Heretic, The: Leibniz,
    Spinoza, and the Fate of God in the
    Modern World* (Stewart), 248
Crashaw, Richard, 235, 257–258n16
Creeley, Robert, 60, 66, 109, 135, 150,
    173, 205–207, 217, 239, 242, 249,
    252, 258n20, 258n22
Crivelli, Carlo, 86
Crozier, Andrew, 154, 155, 237
Cultural memory (concept), 141,
    172–174, 215
Cups, 18, 34n5, 96, 100, 104, 114,
    116–123, 130n9, 148, 153, 175,
    202, 222, 242
Cups (painting), 116
"Curriculum Vitae," 24, 27, 91n1, 96

D
da Vinci, Leonardo, 86
Dahlberg, Edward, 62
Dante
  in *Cups*, 118, 119, 121
  Dantean poetry of RB, 210, 212, 214
  "Great Companion: Dante Alighiere,"
      226–230, 245, 254
  influence on RB, 3–5, 48, 70, 71, 82,
      83, 141, 143, 174, 206, 221,
      222, 224, 232, 235, 238, 239,
      243, 246, 256n8
  philosophies of, 45, 47, 202
  works; *Divine Comedy*, 47, 71, 105,
      118, 121, 202, 222, 226, 229,
      230; *Inferno*, 4, 47, 82, 121, 226,
      227, 230; *Paradiso*, 71, 118, 119,
      227, 229, 256n8; *Purgatorio*,
      118, 121, 227, 229, 230; *Vita
      Nuova*, 118, 119, 121, 148, 235
"Dante and the Lobster" (Beckett), 69
"Dante and the Metaphysics of Light,"
    256n8
"Dante Études" (Duncan), 202
Davey, Frank, 7, 134
Davidson, Judy, 219n5
Davidson, Michael, 41, 179, 252
Dawkins, Richard, 248
Dawson, David, 134, 135
Dawson, Fielding, 65
DeBeck, Brian, 208, 243, 245
De Chirico, Giorgio, 53
De Grand, Alexander, 256n7
Deleuze, Gilles, 6, 211–212
DeMolays, 24–25, 29
Depression (Great), impact on RB's
    family, 14–15, 20–21
Derksen, Jeff, 207
Derrida, Jacques, 6, 179
"Desert, The," 17–18, 32
"Development from Surrealism, The"
    (Kaiser), 38
DeVries, Hent, 247
Dewhurst, Robert, 65
"Dialogue of Self and Soul, A" (Yeats), 79
"Diary, April 11, 1981," 185, 187, 188
Dickinson, Emily, 6, 100, 142
Dickison, Steve, 207, 240
Dictations: On Haunted Writing
    (Ronell), 206

Dikeakos, Christos, 137, 138, 165, 176–178, 208, 222, 236, 245, 255
Dikeakos, Sophie, 138, 165, 222, 236, 245, 255
Di Prima, Diane, 101, 110
Divine Comedy (Dante), 47, 71, 105, 118, 121, 202, 222, 226, 229, 230
Domestic Scenes (Duncan), 68
Donahue, Billy, 66
Doolittle, Hilda (H.D.), 2, 47
Doray, Audrey Capel, 135
Doray, Victor, 135
Doré, Gustave, 4, 47, 70, 105, 226
Dorn, Edward (Ed), 65, 66, 155
Drug use
  by beatniks, 96
  by Boston poets, 62, 66–68, 98
Duchamp, Marcel, 136, 137, 177, 178, 183
Dudek, Louis, 6, 171–173, 177
Dull, Dora, 99, 104, 108, 111
Dull, Harold, 99, 102, 104, 108, 130n2, 147
Duncan, Michael, 114
Duncan, Robert
  at Berkeley, 1, 2, 35, 41–45, 48–50, 62
  and grand collage, 3, 42, 47, 125, 214
  illness and death, 199–200
  poetry of, 52, 68, 75, 76, 108, 114, 130n8, 185–187, 201–205
  relationship with Jack Spicer, 1, 42–45, 48–50, 55, 63, 64, 75, 80, 97, 99–102, 105–107, 116, 118, 123, 128
  relationship with RB (*see* Blaser, Robin Francis, relationship with Robert Duncan)
  in San Francisco, 96, 98–100
  in Vancouver, 133, 135
  thoughts on poetry, 65, 77, 125, 200, 204
  works; *Adam's Way*, 102, 129; "African Elegy, An," 48; "Among My Friends, Love is a Great Sorrow," 42, 202; *Book of Resemblances, A*, 52; *Caesar's Gate*, 52, 201; *Les Chimères*, 124–126; *Domestic Scenes*, 68;

"Elegiac Fragment, An," 42; *Faust Foutu*, 52, 63, 98; *Ground Work II*, 202, 204; "Heavenly City, Earthly City," 42; "I am a Most Fleshly Man," 42; "King Haydn of Miami Beach," 48; *Letters*, 52; *Medieval Scenes*, 43–44, 117, 130n8, 202; "My Mother Would be a Falconress," 108; "Night Scenes," 101; *Passages*, 108, 151; *Poet's Masque*, 48–49; *Structure of Rime*, 101, 108, 151; "Toward the Shaman," 75; "Variations on TWO DICTA OF WILLIAM BLAKE," 220n11; *Venice Poem, The*, 43–44, 49, 50, 126; "WHOSE," 202, 203; "Woman's Drunken Lament, A," 42; *Writing Writing*, 52; *Years as Catches, The*, 42
Dunham, Rob, 142, 145, 193–194, 217, 219n3
Dunkiad (Spicer), 49
Dunn, Carolyn, 62, 64, 130n2
Dunn, Joe, 61, 62, 64, 84, 98, 100, 130n2, 179
DuPlessis, Rachel Blau, 197, 207, 242, 252
Durkee, Dana, 61, 66
Dynasts, The (Hardy), 55

E
Early Spanish Main, The (Sauer), 146
Easley, Eleanor (RB's cousin), 95
Edwards, Ernie, 115
"Ego Dominus Tuus" (Yeats), 79
Eigner, Larry, 65
Einstein, Albert, 92n6
"Elegiac Fragment, An" (Duncan), 42
Elegiac poetry, 193, 198–205, 218, 250
Elephant in the Room, The (Di Prima and Spellman), 101
Eliot, Mary, 145
Eliot, T.S., 2, 3, 39, 54, 100
Ellingham, Lewis
  on Berkeley poets, 42, 48
  on RB, 89, 99, 100, 123, 175

on Spicer, 60, 61, 63, 97, 102, 110, 126, 127
"Elves, The" (Levertov), 74
Emerson, Ralph Waldo, 4, 9n4, 57, 91n2, 100
Empson, William, 39
English Romantic Writers (Perkins), 219n4
Enomoto, Randy, 148
Erickson, Arthur, 139
Eshleman, Clayton, 197, 209, 231
Essais (Montaigne), 208
Euripides, 35
Evans, Steve, 242
"Even on Sunday", 195, 197, 198, 209, 225, 235
Evergreen Review (magazine), 54, 68–70, 81, 84, 85, 96
Everson, Landis, 37, 44–45, 48–49, 51–52, 54, 60, 69, 99–100, 108, 182, 252
Everson, William, 37
Exody (Birtwistle), 233
Exody (Blaser), 191, 229
Experimental Review (magazine), 75

F
Faas, Ekbert, 41
Faerie Queene, The, 89, 100, 116, 122
Falwell, Jerry, 219n6
Farwell, David
    personal history and family, 166, 167, 184
Faust Foutu (Duncan), 52, 63, 98
Fawcett, Brian, 6, 141, 142, 157, 159, 168, 192, 254
Feldmar, Soma, 254, 258n23
Felts, Jim
    personal history, 36–37
    See also Blaser, Robin Francis, relationship with Jim Felts
Feves, Angene, 144
Field, Tom, 62, 96, 97, 112, 113, 115, 209, 215
"Find you the path," 28
Finitude's Score (Ronell), 206
Finnegans Wake (Joyce), 2, 4, 42, 119
Fire: Collected Essays of Robin Blaser, The, 148, 149, 170, 174, 191, 223, 244

"Fire, The" (essay), 4, 7, 31, 49, 55, 63, 116, 148, 151, 200, 203
Fischer, Ernst, 149
Fitzgibbon, Brian, 144
Flaubert, Gustave, 224
Fleming, Ian, 39
Floating Bear, The (Di Prima and Jones), 101, 134
Fold, The (Deleuze), 211
"For years I've heard," 85, 86
Foucault, Michel, 5, 9n5, 138, 153, 156, 242
Found poems, see Collage
Four Quartets (Eliot), 3
"Fousang," 214, 230
Frankfort, Henry, 162n11
Franco, Michael, 206
Fredman, Stephen, 252
Freeing the Shadows (Posse), 193
Freud, Sigmund, 75, 76, 119, 159
Friedlander, Ben, 252
From Oslo to Iraq (Said), 248
Frost, Nemi, 97, 115
Frye, Northrop, 170–172

G
Gadd, Maxine, 134
Gardiner, Dwight, 7
Gargantua and Pantagruel (Rabelais), 228
Gay rights, *see* Civil rights
General Semantics Seminar 1937 (Korzybski), 9n1, 226
George, Stefan, 45, 143
"George Bowering's Plain Song," 170
Gilbert, Gerry, 134, 148, 166
Ginsberg, Allen, 65, 70, 84, 96, 101, 104, 109, 135, 170, 181, 198
Girard, René, 174, 187
Gizzi, Peter, 240, 252, 258n21
Gleason, Madeline, 98
Gluck, Bob, 240
Go (Holmes), 96
God Delusion, The (Dawkins), 248
Goldberg, Darryl, 165, 167
Golding, Alan, 252
Goldoni, Annalisa, 230
Goodwin, Helen, 135
Göring, Hermann, 45

Grahn, Judy, 174, 190n6
Grant, George, 172
Graves, Robert, 199
"Great Companion: Dante Alighiere,"
    4, 226–230
"Great Companion: Robert Duncan,"
    199–205
Greenberg, Clement, 6, 112–114,
    130n7, 136
Greene, Graham, 39
Gregory, Michael, 243
Grieve, Tom, 141, 159, 254
Ground Work II (Duncan), 202, 204
Grozelle, Renee, 219n2
Gundolf, Friedrich, 45, 46
Gysin, Brion, 104

H
Haas, Robert, 244, 253
Haimsohn, George, 48
Halley, Bill, 22
Halprin, Anna, 135
Hamadryad Hunted (Wolf), 43
Hamalian, Linda, 41
Harden, Ed, 145
Hardy, Thomas, 55
Harrison, Jane, 176
Hart, Lawrence, 38
Hartman, Geoffrey, 6, 187
Harvard University, 1, 55, 59, 60,
    84, 86
    See also Boston, RB's time in
Haselwood, David, 110
Haskins, Sue, 59, 86
"Haunted Mind, The" (Hawthorne), 117
Hawkins, Bobbie Louise, 135, 197
Hawthorne, Nathaniel, 6, 34, 57, 105,
    114, 117, 118, 122
Heads of the Town Up to the Aether
    (Spicer), 63, 97, 101, 104, 110,
    126, 227, 229
"Heavenly City, Earthly City"
    (Duncan), 42
Heidegger, Martin, 204, 218, 220n13
Helger, Chris, 248
Heraclitus, 187
"Here Lies the Woodpecker Who Was
    Zeus" (essay), 176

Herndon, Fran, 96–98, 110, 112–115,
    147, 209, 240, 251
Herndon, Jim, 97, 99, 111
Hesiod, 146
Heterologies (Certeau), 180
Hillman, James, 202
Hindmarch, Maria, 127, 134, 135, 143,
    148, 158
Hippie culture, 133, 138
*History of the United States of America
    During the Administrations of James
    Madison* (Adams), 248
*History of the United States of America
    During the Administrations of
    Thomas Jefferson* (Adams), 248
Hodes, Ida, 98
Hodges, Parker, 130n4
Hogan, Linda, 197
Hogg, Robert, 135
Hollander, Benjamin, 179
Hollo, Anselm, 197
Hollyhock Retreat Centre, *see* Cold
    Mountain (personal growth
    institute)
Holmes, John Clellon, 96
Holy Forest, The, 5, 8, 49, 74, 75, 82, 83,
    85, 90, 92n12, 99, 101, 115, 116,
    121, 122, 191, 204–208, 223, 226,
    230–232, 239, 244, 245, 251, 253,
    258n20
"Holy Forest, The," 8, 108, 129, 151
Holy Grail, The (Spicer), 180
Homer, 141, 151
Homo Sacer, 256n5
Homophobia
    and AIDS crisis, 192–198, 217,
        219n1, 219n6
    anti-gay legislation, 37, 192, 193,
        198, 217
    faced by RB and friends, 31, 64, 74,
        166, 184
    See also Anti-gay legislation; Sexuality
Homosexuality, *see* AIDS; Anti-gay
    legislation; Sexuality
Horizon (magazine), 3, 38–40
Horwitz, Roger, 193
Hotel Wentley Poems (Weiners), 66, 67, 110
Howe, Mary Manning, 63
Howe, Susan, 209, 252, 256n6

Howl (Ginsberg), 70, 96, 97
Hoyem, Andrew, 110
Hugo, Victor, 256n8
Hulcoop, John, 168, 169
Hullot-Kentor, Robert, 210–213
Human Condition, The (Arendt), 162n13
Huncke, Herbert, 67
"Hunger of Sound, The," 5, 69, 71, 75,
    80, 81, 83, 153, 154, 223, 226, 242
Huyssen, Andreas, 190n5

I

"I am a Most Fleshly Man" (Duncan), 42
Ibsen, Henrik, 42
"Ichnograph 1," 241
Image-Nation, last (unpublished), 246–250
"Image-Nation 1 (the fold," 8
"Image-Nation 4 (old gold," 18–20
"Image-Nation 5 (erasure," 152, 200, 253
"Image-Nation 6 (epithalamium," 120,
    148, 152
"Image-Nation 7 (l'air," 151, 155
"Image-Nation 8 (morphe," 152
Image-Nation 9 (half and half," 47, 152
"Image-Nation 10 (marriage clothes,"
    152, 154
"Image-Nation 11 (the poesis," 120
"Image-Nation 12 (Actus," 153
"Image-Nation 24 ('oh, pshaw,'" 16,
    195, 217, 242
"Image-Nation 25 (exody," 209, 211, 229
Image-Nations, 101, 108, 151–155,
    186, 250
Imagery
    natural, 17–20, 82, 83, 118–122, 222
    religious, 117, 118, 120, 122,
        228–230, 233–236
    surreal, 76–79, 100
    and syntax, 72
Imaginary Elegies (Spicer), 48, 52, 75
Imaginary Letters (Butts), 118, 175
Infancy and History (Agamben), 224,
    256n3, 256n4
Inferno, 4, 47, 82, 121, 226, 227, 230
*Infinite Worlds: The Poetry of Louis
    Dudek*, 171–173
Inoperative Community, The (Nancy),
    233, 235, 256n4, 257n14

Irby, Ken, 176
Irreparable (concept), 195, 221,
    222, 224, 225, 227, 241, 245,
    255n1, 256n9
"Irreparable, The" (essay and chapbook),
    223–224, 239, 245
Irwin, Robert, 248
Isherwood, Christopher, 39

J

J (magazine), 98, 105
Jacobus, Harry, 53, 96, 112, 113,
    115, 209
James, John, 237
Jantzen, Blanche, 102, 109–112, 129,
    130n6
Jarnot, Lisa, 41, 102
Jarrell, Randall, 39
Jaspers, Karl, 248
Jeffers, Robinson, 37, 39
Jepson, Wayne, 23
Jess, *see* Collins, Jess
Jiménez, Rosario, 35, 43,
    199–200, 222
John, Charles (RB's great grandfather), 12
John, Elizabeth (RB's great
    grandmother), 12
John, Minnie (RB's grandmother), 12
Johnson, Aaron (RB's great great
    grandfather), 13
Johnson, Ina (RB's great grandmother),
    13–15, 34n6
Johnson, John (RB's ancestor), 13
Johnson, Judith, 197
Johnson, Mary Ann (RB's great great
    grandmother), 13
Johnston, Hugh, 138, 139
Jonas, Steve, 1, 60, 61, 64, 65, 67, 68
Jones, LeRoi (Amiri Baraka), 66, 73,
    101, 116
Jones, Tom, 25, 33, 35
Jonson, Ben, 86
Jonsson, Stefan, 248
Jordan, Larry, 115
Joris, Pierre, 197, 207
Joyce, James, 2, 42–43, 78, 119, 122,
    175, 228
Junge Amerikanische Lyrik (Corso), 73

K

Kaiser, Ernst, 38–39
Kantorowicz, Ernst, 41, 45–48, 51, 55, 97, 118, 125, 141, 143, 148
Kearns, Lionel, 134
Keats, John, 4, 149
Kelly, Robert, 197
Kennedy, Gerta, 63
Kerényi, Károly, 162n11
Kerouac, Jack, 66, 96, 97, 130n1
Killian, Kevin
    on Berkeley poets, ix, 41, 42, 48, 62
    and RB, 100, 181, 207–209, 240
    on Spicer, 60, 61, 63, 97, 100, 101, 110, 111, 127
"King Haydn of Miami Beach" (Duncan), 48
Kingship and the Gods (Frankfort), 162n11
King's Two Bodies, The (Kantorowicz), 47, 125
Kingsley, Charles, 18–19, 203
Kiyooka, Roy, 134, 217
Klee, Paul, 39
Klein, Abraham Moses (A.M.), 234, 235, 258n19
Kloth, Arthur, 60, 96
Knutson, Susan, 158, 159
Koch, Kenneth, 63
Koestler, Arthur, 39
Kolokithas, Dawn, 179
Kootenay School of Writing (KSW), 178, 223, 255n2
Korzybski, Alfred, 9n1, 226–227, 230
Kosik, Karel, 4
Krikorian, Leo, 97
Kristeva, Julia, 258n23
Kuharic, Martina, 7
Kurp, Patrick, 207
Kyger, Joanne, 66, 97, 101, 108, 130n2, 179, 209

L

Lacan, Jacques, 6, 138, 153
"Lake of Souls," 49, 187
Lamantia, Philip, 38, 96, 110
"Laments of Alcibiades, The" (Everson), 54

Landers, Dale, 101
Landscapes of the imagination
    Berkeley as landscape, 43, 176
    Idaho as landscape, 18–20, 32, 83, 119–121, 142, 229
    Pacific Nation, 146–150
    See also Nature
Language
    as communal and transhistorical, 44, 50, 81, 82, 117, 153, 180, 181, 224–225
    etymology, 5, 154, 204, 214, 250
    operational, 153, 213
    structuralist and deconstructive philosophies of, 5, 81, 83, 181
Language and Death (Agamben), 243, 257n9
Language poetry, 142, 148, 153, 162n16, 178, 180, 181, 212
Lansing, Gerrit, 62, 206
Larventz, Don, 195
Last Supper, The (libretto), 221, 225, 231–240, 246, 247, 250, 257n14, 257n15
Lawton, Claire, 232
Lawyer, Lori, 115
Layton, Irving, 171
"Leave the Word Alone" (Marshall), 62
Lectures, *see* Blaser, Robin, conferences, lectures, and reading tours
Lee-Nova, Gary, 136
Lefort, Claude, 153, 163n18
Leider, Philip, 113, 137
Leite, George, 38
Lerch, Elizabeth (RB's great grandmother), 11–12
Letters (Duncan), 52
"Letter(s) to Freud," 65, 75, 76, 78
Levertov, Denise, 1, 60, 73, 74, 109, 110, 126, 131n11, 135
Levinas, Emmanuel, 180, 258n23
Lévy, Bernard-Henri, 187
Life of Kenneth Rexroth, A (Hamalian), 41
Lindsay, Vachel, 2, 9n2
Lingis, Alphonso, 153, 163n18
Lippard, Lucy, 137
Lister, Ardele, 165, 166, 168, 183
Literary Behavior (magazine), 48

Lives of French Symbolist Poets, The (Persky), 127
"Lives of the Poets," 43, 52, 53
London, RB's time in, 86, 87, 230–232
Longfellow, Henry Wadsworth, 57
Lorca, Federico García, 2, 35, 42–43, 61, 99, 125, 199, 247
Loyalty Oath, 50, 56n4

M
M (magazine), 101
MacDonald, George, 123, 203
Mackintosh, Graham, 98, 108, 124, 146
Magick (magazine), 101
Mallarmé, Stéphane, 1, 224
Malory, Thomas, 187
Mandelbaum, Allen, 230
Manhattan Project, 3, 38
Man of Light in Iranian Sufism, The (Corbin), 187
Mantle of Caesar (Gundolf), 46
Marlatt, Daphne, 7, 134, 135, 245
Marquard, Thomas, 247
Marshall, Edward (Ed), 1, 60–62, 65, 70, 73, 80
"Martian" (Spicer), 45
Martin, John, 156
Martyrology, The (Nichol), 220n10
Marx, Karl, 38, 138, 149, 223, 227, 231
Masson, André, 39
Maud, Ralph, 70, 130n6, 141, 143, 145, 154, 162n10, 209, 255
Maximus Poems, The (Olson), 70–72, 155, 186, 227
Mayer, Hans, 196
Maynard, James, 75
McCaffery, Steve, 6, 179, 209, 211, 213, 243, 252
McCaslin, Susan, 142
McClure, Michael, 60, 65, 73, 96, 97, 110, 148, 179, 207
McCready, Cassius Dewitt (RB's grandfather), 14
McCready, Ina Mae (RB's mother), *see* Blaser, Ina Mae McCready (RB's mother)
McCready, Sophia, *see* Auer, Sophia Nichols (RB's grandmother)

McGauley, Tom, 208
McLaren, Juliet, 183
McLeod, Dan, 135
McLuhan, Marshall, 6, 9n7, 136–138, 172
McNeill, Bill, 108, 115
McTavish, Robert, 135
Mead, Margaret, 7
Means without End: Notes on Politics (Agamben), 242
Measure (magazine), 64–66, 68, 69, 73, 81, 84
Medea, 63
Medieval Scenes (Duncan), 43–44, 117, 130n8
Meditations in an Emergency (O'Hara), 91n5
"Medium, The," 123
Meltzer, David, 110, 130n2
Melville, Herman, 60, 73, 86, 208
Menocal, María Rosa, 246, 247
Merleau-Ponty, Maurice, 6, 77, 93n15, 138, 153, 156, 221
Metamorphosis, as poetic element, 18, 20, 114
Mezei, Kathy, 189n3
"Michael Robartes and the Dancer" (Yeats), 79
Middleton, Peter, 231, 252
Midsummer Night's Dream (Shakespeare), 123
Miki, Roy, 145
Miles, Josephine, 38, 45, 48
Miller, Arthur, 84
Miller, Henry, 37–39
Mills, John, 148
Milton (Blake), 194
"Mind Canaries," 176, 178, 222
Minutes of the Charles Olson Society (Maud), 70, 209
Mithen, Steven, 248
Moby-Dick (Melville), 208
Modernism
  Canadian, 171, 172
  postmodernism as reaction to, 2–3, 47–48, 171, 173, 213, 215, 220n16
  RB on, 38, 42–43, 47, 213
"Modernist Painting" (Greenberg), 112, 113

Monette, Paul, 193
Monroe, Marilyn, 84
Montaigne, Michel de, 206, 208
Montgomery, George, 65
Moore, Henry, 39
Moore, Marianne, 84
Moore, Richard, 48
Moore, William (Bill) Brodecky, *see*
    Brodecky Moore, William (Bill)
Moreau, Gustave, 114, 115, 122
Mormonism
    and RB's family, 2, 11–13
    rejection of by RB, 33
Morris, Michael, 135–138, 195
Mort d'Arthur (Malory), 187
Moth Poem, The, 31, 100, 107, 108, 116,
    122, 123
Mouré, Erin, 6, 253
Moxley, Jennifer, 242
"My Mother Would be a Falconress"
    (Duncan), 108
Myth
    Berkeley myth, 43–45, 50, 52, 54
    in RB's poetry, 28, 114, 119–122,
        124, 152, 200, 203
    reimagining of, 114, 122, 142, 152,
        176, 178, 199, 200
Mythopoiesis, 4–6, 45, 187
"My Vocabulary Did This To Me"
    (Blaser), 179–182, 256n8
"My Vocabulary Did This To Me"
    (Silliman), 179–181

N
Nancy, Jean-Luc, 233–235, 256n4,
    257n14
Narco-Imaginary, The (Scott), 218
Naropa University (Colorado), 150,
    196–198, 223, 224, 242, 258n23
Nation, The (Levertov), 101
Nature
    as poetic element, 17–20, 32, 82, 83,
        118–122, 222
    RB's regard for the creaturely, 16–18,
        119, 120
    RB's rejection of anthropocentrism,
        17, 151, 172, 178
    See also Anthropocentrism, rejection
        of; Landscapes of the imagination

Necessity of Art, The, A Marxist Approach
    (Fischer), 149
Nerval, Gérard de, 124–126, 224, 235,
    258n18
Never Let the World Go By, 240
New American poetry
    in Canada, 134, 141, 145, 170,
        201, 251
    RB's contribution to, 4–6
New American Poetry, The (Allen), 1, 54,
    64, 68–70, 72, 84, 90, 95, 101,
    104, 137, 147, 166, 171
New York, 51, 60, 69, 70, 182, 183
Newlove, John, 134
Nichol, bp, 6, 198, 220n10, 250
"Night Scenes" (Duncan), 101
Northwestern University, 28–32
Nurse, Ray, 144

O
Occult, as poetic inspiration, 36, 62, 75,
    78–80
"Ode for Museums, All of Them!," 90
"Ode to Walt Whitman" (Spicer), 61
Odyssey (Homer), 16, 214, 227
Oedipus at Colonus (Sophocles), 200
"Of is the word love without the initial
    consonant," 218
O'Hara, Frank, 1, 60, 65, 69, 72
Olson, Charles
    death of, 150
    poetics of, 3, 9n3, 46–47, 71, 77, 91n2,
        91n6, 113, 149, 151, 157, 170,
        174, 185, 187, 225, 227, 229
    relationship and correspondence with
        RB, 1, 34, 46–47, 60–62, 64, 65,
        67, 70–74, 84–86, 108–110,
        146, 173, 174, 183, 186, 187,
        191, 197, 207, 209, 219, 219n9,
        235, 249
    See also Maximus Poems, The (Olson);
        "Projective Verse" (Olson)
Ondaatje, Michael, 74, 191, 198
O'Neil, Paul, 130n1
O'Neill, Hugh, 43, 50, 202
O'Neill, Janie, 43, 202
Onion, Oliver, 35
On Living in an Old Country
    (Wright), 231

"Only Rebellion Around, The" (O'Neil), 130n1

"On Strangers" (Stanley), 147

"On the Bleeding Wounds of our Crucified Lord" (Crashaw), 257n16

On the Road (Kerouac), 130n1

Open, The: Man and Animal (Agamben), 242

Opening of the Field, The (Duncan), 100

Open space
  as communal/public, 5–6, 213, 214, 255
  in RB's poetry, 5–6, 23, 65, 145, 146, 187, 191, 213, 214, 224, 230
  See also Collage

Open Space (magazine), 5, 65, 108, 109, 112, 115, 123, 124, 146, 151, 157, 162n16, 187

Opitz, Ilonka, 247

Oppenheim, Meret, 79

Order of Canada, 243, 244

Order of Things, The (Foucault), 9n5, 156

Origins of Postmodernity, The (Anderson), 220n16

Origins of Totalitarianism, The (Arendt), 257n15

Orlovsky, Peter, 84, 104

Orphée (Cocteau), 63, 79, 81, 152

"Orpheus Editor" (Persky), 147

Orphic Vision, The: Seer Poets from Novalis to Rimbaud (Bays), 256n8

Othello (Shakespeare), 44

Other (concept)
  as poetic element, 180, 181, 196
  in RB's work, 77, 79, 153, 196

O'Toole (Monsignor), 24–25

"Out of America," 87

"Out of the Window," 148

Outsiders (Mayer), 196

"Out to Dinner," 73

P

Pacific Nation (magazine), 146–150, 187

Pacific Nation
  myth of, 147

"Pacific Spectator, The," 53, 56

Pacifism, 30, 38, 40

Pagels, Elaine, 159, 160

Painting
  artworks of RB, 115, 116, 209
  Canadian art, 136, 137
  formalism in, 112, 113

Palmer, Michael, 135, 179

Panipakuttuk, Joe, 185–187

"Paradise Quotations," 123

Paradisco, 118, 119, 227, 229, 256n8

Paris
  friends in, 69, 73, 104
  RB's trips to, 87, 89, 90, 99, 104, 240

Park, The, 13–14, 16, 18, 22–23, 34n4, 100, 114, 116, 122, 127

Parkinson, Ariel, 55

Parkinson, Tom, 43, 45, 48, 55

"Particles" (essay), 146, 148, 149, 151, 196, 198, 212, 222

Particular Accidents: Selected Poems [of] George Bowering, 169–171

Passages (Duncan), 101, 108, 151

Patchen, Kenneth, 171

Paul, Mercedes, 28

Paz, Octavio, 177, 178, 222

Peacock Gallery, 112–116

Pearson, Ted, 197

Pell Mell, 23, 185, 191, 193, 196, 198, 214, 222, 223, 225, 230

Penberthy, Jenny, 130n2

Perkins, David, 194, 219n4

Perloff, Marjorie, 207, 252

Perry, Sam, 135

Persky, Stan
  Open Space and other work, 5, 65, 74, 99, 107–109, 112, 135, 146, 157, 195, 198, 236
  personal history, 97, 103–109, 130n2
  See also Blaser, Robin Francis, relationship with Stan Persky

Perverse Core of Christianity, The (Žižek), 248

Petrarca, Francesco (Petrarch), 246

Phantastes (MacDonald), 123, 203

Philosophy and the Turn to Religion (DeVries), 247

Plato, 4, 44, 117, 172, 221

Plumb, Charles, 19

Poe, Edgar Allan, 6

"Poem by the Charles River," 62, 65, 81

"Poem to the Reader of the Poem, A"
(Spicer), 78, 147
Poet, Be Like God (Ellingham and
Killian), 41
Poetics (Aristotle), 47
"Poetry and Positivisms" (essay), 191, 224
Poetry/Audit (Duncan), 124–126
Poet's Masque, A (Duncan), 48–49
Politics
    of RB and companions, 42, 126,
        147–149, 157
    in RB's works, 213, 225, 238, 246
Porter, Bern, 3, 38, 43
Posse, Luis, 194, 198
Postmodernism, 3, 5, 6, 47–48, 134,
    137, 157, 170–173, 187, 190n5,
    213, 215, 220n16
Pound, Ezra, influence on RB's poetry, 2,
    3, 42, 43, 46, 47, 54, 61, 71, 74, 76,
    82, 100, 118–120, 138, 141, 143,
    148, 151, 158, 171, 204, 227, 228
"Practice of Outside, The," 9n5, 42, 77,
    128, 151, 156–157, 159, 220n12
"Preface to Leaves of Grass" (Whitman),
    162n8
"Preface to the Early Poems of Robert
    Duncan," 201, 219n8
"Preface to Works to Come, A," 75, 78
Primack, Ron, 102, 130n2
Pritchard, James, 162n11
Process and Reality (Whitehead),
    9n3, 72, 77, 173–174
Profanations (Agamben), 248
"Projective Verse" (Olson), 3, 70, 72,
    113, 170
Prometheus (Kerényi), 162n11
Prometheus Unbound (Shelley), 195
Proust, Marcel, 54
"Proverbs of Hell" (Blake), 65
Prynne, Jeremy, 154, 155, 237
Psychoanalysis
    and poetry, 3, 75, 118, 119, 138, 151,
        153, 211
    as response to World Wars, 38–39
    and surrealism, 75–79
Public world (concept), 5–6, 46,
    209–214, 225, 244
Puppet and the Dwarf, The (Žižek), 248
Purgatorio, 71, 118, 121, 227, 229, 230
Pursuit of the Millennium, The (Cohn),
    257n13

Q
Quartermain, Meredith, ix, 223, 236,
    238–240, 243, 245–247, 252,
    258n20
Quartermain, Peter, ix, x, 191, 209,
    217, 218, 223, 230, 236, 237,
    239, 243, 244, 246, 247, 252,
    258n20
Queen o' Crow Castle, The (Adam), 209
"Quitting a Job," 73, 75, 86, 253

R
Rabelais, François, 228
Ralston, Rory, 194, 195
Rand, Sally, 47
Rasula, Jed, 179, 209
Reagan, Ronald, 192, 213
Real (concept)
    and human experience, 46–47, 81,
        93n16, 153, 154, 213, 220n12
    in RB's works, 4, 80, 85, 176, 204,
        211, 213, 229
Recovery of the Public World, The (Byrne
    and Watts), 210
"Recovery of the Public World, The"
    (essay), 191, 214–215
Recovery of the Public World
    Conference, The (1995), 208–215,
    219n9, 231, 239
Redburn (Melville), 86
Redon, Odilon, 114, 183, 239
Reed, Ishmael, 197
Reid, James (Jamie), 134, 135
Religion
    fundamentalist, 195, 197, 219n5, 228,
        236, 246, 247, 258n17
    See also Blaser, Robin Francis, attitudes
        and perspectives, pursuit of the
        sacred; Catholicism
Retallack, Joan, 258n23
Rexroth, Kenneth, 37, 39–42, 48, 96,
    97, 171
Rexroth, Marie, 38
Rice, John A., 34n8
Rich, Adrienne, 240, 258n21
Richter, Johann Paul Friedrich (Jean-
    Paul), 224, 235, 258n18
Riley, Denise, 231
Rilke, Rainer Maria, 80, 142
Rimbaud, Arthur, 82, 224

Robert Duncan and the Pragmatist Sublime (Maynard), 75

Robert Duncan: Drawings and Decorated Books (catalogue), 219n7

Robert Duncan in San Francisco (Rumaker), 56n3

Roditi, Edouard, 39

Rogatnick, Abraham, 135, 138, 236

Ronell, Avital, 206, 239

Roosevelt, Franklin D., 27

"Rosa Alchemica" (Yeats), 79

Rosner, Andrew, 233, 237

Rosset, Barney, 69

Rothenberg, Diane, 197

Rothenberg, Jerome, 137, 197

Rousseau, Jean Jacques, 228

Rule, Jane, 135

Rumaker, Michael, 56n3, 65, 66, 84, 130n2

Russell, Bertrand, 39

S

Sacred Heart Academy, 11, 14, 25, 34n1, 34n7, 121

Said, Edward, 248

"Sailing to Byzantium" (Yeats), 79

Saint Mary's College, 29, 34n7

Samac, Mark (RB's nephew), 7, 13, 20–21, 23

San Francisco

Evergreen Review, San Francisco special issue, 69, 81, 84, 96

poetry scene, 95–129, 187

RB's time in, 1, 7, 36, 54, 56n2, 90, 91, 145, 146, 175, 176, 179–183, 206, 207, 240

See also Peacock Gallery; White Rabbit Symposium (1986)

San Francisco Renaissance, The (Davidson), 41

Sanders, Colin, 43

Sapir, Edward, 5

Sappho, 174, 175, 196, 198, 206

"Sappho, The Contemporary, and the Sacred: The Reappearance of Process" (talks), 174, 175

Sartre, Jean-Paul, 69

Sauer, Carl, 146

Schelling, Andrew, 197, 198, 216

Schorer, Mark, 48, 49, 55

Schumiatcher, Barbara, 254

Schuyler, James, 65

Schweickhardt, Frances, 25, 33, 35

Scott, Ramsey, 218

Sense Record, The (Moxley), 242

Serial poems

Charms, 8, 148, 151

Chimères, Les, 100, 116, 124–126, 199, 200, 203, 206, 258n18

Cups, 18, 34n5, 96, 100, 104, 114, 117–124, 127, 130n9, 148, 153, 175, 202, 222, 242

Exody, 191

Faerie Queene, The, 89

Image-Nations, 101, 108, 151–155, 186, 250 (*See also Image-Nations*)

Moth Poem, The, 31, 100, 107, 108, 116, 122, 123

Notes 1994–2000, 90

Park, The, 13–14, 16, 18, 22–23, 34n4, 114, 116, 122, 127

Pell Mell, 23, 185, 191, 193, 196, 198, 214, 222, 223, 225, 230

RB's thoughts on, 28, 44, 100, 111, 116–123, 130n8, 153, 206, 211, 214, 227

Syntax, 5, 72, 185, 214, 255

Serres, Michel, 6

Sexuality

AIDS crisis, 192–198, 217, 219n1, 219n6

homophobia, 31, 33, 64, 74, 120, 166, 167, 184, 192

poetry and writings on, 37, 196, 203

in RB's work, 195–196

See also Anti-gay legislation; Homophobia

Shadbolt, Doris, 137

Shakespeare, William, 44, 123

Shaw, Nancy, 161n3

Shelach, Oz, 224

Shelley, Percy Bysshe, 74, 187, 195, 228

Sherburne, Donald, 174

Short Sad Book, A (Bowering), 170, 171

Siegler, Karl, 142, 217

Sikelianos, Eleni, 253

Silliman, Ron, 179–181, 239, 241

Simon Fraser University (SFU)
 creation of and programming at,
  127, 138, 139, 143
 RB as professor, and scholarly works,
  16, 141, 146, 162n7, 162n12,
  173–182, 188, 189, 254
 student activism at, 140
Singing Neanderthals, The (Mithen), 248
Smithson, Robert, 136
Smoler, Michael, 150, 224
Snyder, Gary, 96, 108, 240
Sodomite Invasion Review, The
 (magazine), 195
"Song for Bird and Myself" (Spicer), 64
"Song in Four Parts for Christ the Son,"
 49–50
Sonthoff, Helen, 135
"Sophia Nichols," 16
Sophocles, 200
Spain, history of, and "Image-Nation,"
 246–250
Spellman, Andrew, 101
Spender, Stephen, 39
Spicer, Jack
 alcoholism and death, 110, 124,
  127–129, 140
 appearance and personality, 35, 41–42,
  60, 61, 106, 108–110, 116, 201
 at Berkeley, 1, 36, 38, 43, 48, 51, 55
 in Boston, 60–64
 poetics and language studies of, 3, 5,
  44, 45, 50, 75, 78, 83, 125, 146,
  179–182, 196, 204, 206, 225,
  227, 229, 256n8
 poetry of, 49, 52, 75, 76, 78,
  108–110, 156, 180, 220n12, 229
 in San Francisco, 96–100, 104, 130n2
 in Vancouver, 135–137, 140, 146
 works; *After Lorca*, 75; "Apocalypse
  for Three Voices," 49, 50; *Billy the
  Kid*, 98, 127; "Chess Game,
  The," 75; *Collected Books of Jack
  Spicer, The*, 42, 45, 50, 129, 151;
  Dunkiad, 49; *Heads of the Town
  Up to the Aether*, 63, 97, 102,
  110, 111, 127, 227, 229; *Holy
  Grail, The*, 180; *Imaginary
  Elegies*, 48, 52, 75; "Ode to Walt
  Whitman," 109, 61; "Poem to the
  Reader of the Poem, A," 78, 147;

"Song for Bird and Myself," 64;
  Troilus, 63
Spinoza, Baruch, 41, 118
Spirit of Romance, The (Pound), 118
"Stadium of the Mirror, The" (essay),
 9n5, 50, 151, 153–155, 213, 250
Stanley, George, 97, 99, 101–103, 108,
 115, 130n2, 147, 159, 195
Stein, Gertrude, 42, 52, 53, 170, 175, 182
Stevens, Wallace, 39, 43
Stevenson, Michael, 254
Stewart, Matthew, 248
Stewart, Michael Seth, ix, 8, 61–63
Stiles, Knute, 97, 115
Stockwood, Mervyn, 39
Story of Opal, The (Whiteley), 186
Strauss, David Levi, 179, 181, 197, 224
Structuralism
 as philosophy of language, 5, 81,
  83, 181
Structure of Rime (Duncan), 101, 108, 151
Stuart, Colin, 148, 158
*Subject Without Nation: Robert Musil and
 the History of Modern Identity*
 (Jonsson), 248
Surrealism
 surrealist movement, 3, 38–40, 100,
  114, 119, 229
 in the works of Duncan and Spicer,
  75, 256n8
 in the works of RB, 75–79, 151
Survival (Atwood), 170
Sutherland, John, 171
Sweeley, Marlin, 25, 33
Sweeney, Jack, 60, 69
Swift, Harriet, 64
Swinburne, Algernon Charles, 102, 235,
 258n17
Sylin, Svetlana, 165
Symonds, John Addington, 55
Symposium, The (Plato), 117
Syntax, 5, 72, 185–188, 214, 255

T
"Tables of the Law" (Yeats), 79
Tallman, Ellen, 126, 127, 133, 166, 167,
 208, 218, 252
Tallman, Karen, 126, 127, 145, 148,
 160, 208, 243, 245, 250

Tallman, Warren, 7, 127, 129, 133–137, 141, 190n4, 217–219
Talonbooks, 118, 134, 142, 165, 170, 175, 185, 217
Tanglewood Tales (Hawthorne), 105
Tarn, Nathaniel, 156, 197
Technology, RB's thoughts on, 137, 138, 172, 177, 178, 222
"Ten Songs for Love," 72
Thatcher, Margaret, 224
Themis (Harrison), 176
Theogony (Hesiod), 162n11
Thesen, Sharon, 6, 142
    correspondance with RB, 208, 217, 218, 221
Thomas, Dylan, 39, 141
Thoreau, Henry David, 100
Thought of the Heart, The (Hillman), 202
Tish (magazine), 134, 170, 171
Torra, Joseph, 61, 62
"Toward the Shaman" (Duncan), 75
Trail Coyote (college newspaper), 32
Traps for Unbelievers (Butts), 176
Triem, Eve, 98
Triptych (Blaser), 114, 115
"Triumph of Life, The" (Shelley), 187
Troilus (Spicer), 63
Trojan Women (Euripides), 35
"Trout Fishing in America" (Brautigan), 147
Trudeau, Pierre, 184, 193
Truitt, Samuel, 201, 206
Truth is Laughter, The, 186
"Tumble-Weed," 33, 169
Twain, Mark, 25
"Two Astronomers with Notebooks," 99

U
Ullman, Micha, 236
Ulrych, Miriam, 159, 160, 165, 167, 168
Ulrych, Tad, 160, 161
Ulysses (Joyce), 2, 78, 228
Understanding Media: The Extensions of Man (McLuhan), 9n7
University of British Colombia (UBC)
    arts festivals at, 135, 137
    conferences at, 174
    Hulcoop, John, faculty member, 168
    Persky, Stan, student at, 157
    relation to SFU, 139
    Robert Smithson's *Glue Pour* at, 137
    Tallmans at, 129
    Tish, 134
    Vancouver Poetry Festival at, 135
University of California, Berkeley
    Berkeley myth, 43–45, 50, 52, 54
    Berkeley Renaissance, 1, 41, 42, 54, 176
    literary scene, 2–3, 37–40
    RB's time at, 35–56
    the Writers' Conference, 48–50

V
Vancouver
    arts community in, 133–138, 165, 169, 208–210
    Gay Games III (1990), 195, 219n5
    RB's time in, 127, 129, 165–167
    See also Simon Fraser University (SFU)
Vander Zalm, Bill, 195
"Variations on TWO DICTA OF WILLIAM BLAKE" (Duncan), 220n11
Varty, Michael, 245
Venice Poem, The (Duncan), 43–44, 49, 50
Vietnam, anti-war poetry, 126, 147, 148, 150, 203
Vincent, Stephen, 156
Violence and the Sacred (Girard), 187
"Violets, The" (essay), 9n3, 174
Virgil, 206, 227
Visible and the Invisible, The (Merleau-Ponty), 77, 153
Vita Nuova (Dante), 118, 119, 121, 148, 235

W
Wagner, Linda, 135
Wagstaff, Barbara, 176
Wagstaff, Christopher, 112, 114, 176, 219n7, 231, 251
Wah, Fred, 134, 135, 158
Wahl, Gene, 35–37, 41, 56n1
Waiting for the Barbarians (Cavafy), 187
Waldman, Anne, 197, 198, 216, 258n24
Waldrop, Rosmarie, 252
Wall, Jeff, 137
Wanders, 238–240, 245

Waste Land, The (T.S. Eliot), 4
Water-Babies, The (Kingsley), 18, 19, 203
Watermelon Sugar (Brautigan), 116
Watson, Peter, 39
Watson, Scott, 136, 159, 176, 195, 208, 236, 254
Watts, Charles, 143, 208, 209, 250
Webb, Phyllis, 225
"Weeper, The" (Crashaw), 257n16
Welish, Marjorie, 237
Welty, Eudora, 39
West, Benjamin, 13
West, Tina (RB's great aunt), 14, 25
Whalen, Philip, 96, 110, 135
Whalley, George, 172, 173
Wheeler, Bill, 115
Wheeler, Dennis, 137, 168
Whitehead, Alfred North, 3, 9n3, 59, 72, 77, 146, 174, 175, 221
Whiteley, Opal, 186, 187
White Rabbit Press, 84, 98, 100
White Rabbit Symposium (1986), 179–182
Whitman, Walt, 31, 40, 100, 145, 150
Whorf, Benjamin Lee, 5
"WHOSE" (Duncan), 202–204
Wieners, John, 1, 8, 60–62, 64–68, 70, 71, 73, 80, 84, 97, 103, 110, 150, 251
"Wife of Bath, The" (Blaser), 27–28
Williams, Jonathan, 65, 70
Williams, William Carlos, 65, 71, 76, 170, 171, 175, 214, 218
William Shakespeare (Hugo), 256n8
Wilson, Peter Lamborn, 197
Winkler, Jack, 175

Winters, Yvor, 38
Witt-Diamant, Ruth, 98
Wittgenstein, Ludwig, 9n6, 231
Wixman, Myrsam, 96
Wolf, Leonard, 42, 43, 48, 51
Wolff, Sister Mary Madeleva, 29, 34n7
Wolin, Sheldon, 162n14
"Woman's Drunken Lament, A" (Duncan), 42
Wood, Grant, 194, 215
Woolf, Virginia, 39
Works and Days (Hesiod), 162n11
Wordsworth, William, 55
World War II, 37–39
Wright, Patrick, 231, 232, 237, 238
Writers' Conference (Berkeley), 48–50
Writing Class: The Kootenay School of Writing Anthology (Barnholden and Klobucar), 255n2
Writing Writing (Duncan), 52

Y

Years as Catches, The (Duncan), 42
Yeats, William Butler, 2, 43, 54, 63, 75, 78–80
"You" (Stanley), 147
Young Robert Duncan, The (Faas), 41
Yugen (magazine), 66, 73, 90

Z

Zaslove, Jerry, 145, 188, 243
Zeller, Kenneth, 193, 219n2
Žižek, Slavoj, 248